# INSIGHT

I

*Analyses of American Literature*

by

John V. Hagopian and Martin Dolch

with the assistance of

W. Gordon Cunliffe and Arvin R. Wells

HIRSCHGRABEN-VERLAG · FRANKFURT AM MAIN

ISBN 3-454-12700-9

Other volumes in this series:
**Insight II,** Analyses of Modern British Literature (Nr. 1271)
**Insight III,** Analyses of English and American Poetry (Nr. 1273)
**Insight IV,** Analyses of Modern British and American Drama (Nr. 1274)

Fünfte, ergänzte Auflage 1975

Das Urheberrecht (URG) gestattet die Vervielfältigung oder Übertragung urheberrechtlich geschützter Werke, also auch der Texte dieses Buches, nur, wenn sie mit dem Verlag vorher vereinbart wurde. Davon werden die in den §§ 53, 54 URG ausdrücklich genannten Sonderfälle nicht berührt.

Einbandentwurf: Nierhaus + Estenfelder, Frankfurt am Main

Satz, Druck, Bindearbeit: Fränkische Gesellschaftsdruckerei GmbH, Würzburg

TO THE SPIRIT OF COOPERATION
IN WHICH THIS BOOK WAS WRITTEN

# PREFACE

The purpose of this book is to encourage and improve the study of American literature in the German schools. As matters now stand, the German schools generally persist in ignoring the wide range, and artistic quality, of a major literature by offering in six to nine years of English study perhaps only one American novel or drama and three or four short stories. And all too often such minor authors as O. Henry, Erskine Caldwell, and Jack London are taught at the expense of Herman Melville, or Katherine Anne Porter, or William Faulkner.

American literature offers rich and valuable material for classroom treatment. This book deals with fifty works by thirty-one authors, spanning the entire history of American literature from Washington Irving to James Baldwin. We have tried to include something from every undisputed major figure and important selections from significant minor figures. On the whole, we were influenced by the list of works now available in German textbook editions, but we have also added stories and plays which we believe ought to be edited for schools. In fact, suitability for classroom use in terms of linguistic difficulty and appropriateness of subject matter has been a major consideration in the selection. That is why the majority of items are short stories and why only the more easily comprehensible rather than the more famous and important works by such difficult writers as Henry James and William Faulkner are included. We do not claim that these stories, novels, and plays represent the cream of American literature, but we do believe that with a few exceptions each has genuine literary merit and offers the student more than simply an opportunity to exercise and extend his command of the English language.

By American literature we mean simply a body of writings that happen to come from the United States and not a medium for gaining insight into American history, politics, social life, customs, and manners. Literature is neither an efficient nor a proper medium for the communication of that kind of information, although, of course, a certain amount of knowledge about the setting of fiction and drama is often necessary for the comprehension of their strictly literary content. That means that *Amerikakunde* is a necessary and appropriate subject for inclusion in other parts of the curriculum, e. g. in history and geography. The teacher of language and literature already has too much to do — and the subject has its own unique problems, without his assuming the burden of gratuitously added disciplines. Hence, in the critical analyses of this book, historical, sociological, and similar non-literary problems are discussed only where the literary work clearly invokes them. Our principal objective has been *explication de texte* along the lines of the American New Criticism, but the treatment varies according to the temperament of the critic. We have not all managed to become identical analysis-producing machines.

In general we have asked ourselves such questions as these:

*Can the story be divided into parts? How tightly or loosely are the parts related to each other? Is the exposition (i. e. background and setting) embodied in the dramatic action or presented as a separable element?*

*What is the point of view of the narrator? Is he inside the story (as a major or minor character) or outside (as an omniscient or limited observer)?*

*When and where does the action take place? How much time elapses? Which characters are central?*

*Is there a symbolic significance to names, places, actions, or thoughts?*

*How poetic is the rendering, and to what extent are the metaphors, images, and similes functional or merely decorative?*

*How many lines of force does the story have? When are they introduced and at what point do they converge?*

*What mood, tone, and pace does the story have?*

*Is the central meaning of the story explicitly stated, or is it implicit?*

It has not always been possible for us to answer each of these questions specifically, especially for the longer works; but these questions and the analyses in the text should provide a basis for lively and fruitful class discussion. One further point: we have tried to follow the law of literary criticism that says, "Given two or more possible interpretations of a literary work, the one which integrates the maximum number of details at their maximum limit of meaning into a single, unified whole is the best."

The contents of this book are arranged alphabetically by author, and each discussion consists of (1) a list of available German school editions with notations of their completeness, or a citation of the least expensive American or British edition, (2) a biographical sketch of the author, (3) a capsule plot summary of the work, (4) a critical analysis, (5) suggested questions and answers for class discussion, and (6) a selected bibliography of criticisms of the individual story, novel, or play. Also, at the end of the book is appended a selected general bibliography. Dr. Martin Dolch is responsible for the over-all planning and general integration of the book and for the biographies, capsule plot summaries, and bibliographies; Professor John V. Hagopian is responsible for most of the critical analyses. They have been assisted by two friends and colleagues, Mr. W. Gordon Cunliffe and Prof. Arvin R. Wells, who prepared additional critical analyses. The identity of each contributor is indicated by his initials at the end of the discussion for which he is responsible.

There remains the pleasant task of thanking all the others who have in one way or another assisted in the preparation of this book: our publishers, with whom the whole project originated, for liberally granting us any desired freedom in its realization; Thomas J. Mulvehill, director, and the colloquium at the Amerika Haus, Kaiserslautern, for stimulating discussions of some of the works; Frl. Stud. Ass. Rosemarie Mannheim, for much hard work in helping prepare the manuscript for publication; to Dr. David Smith and Dr. Georg

Eckert, for inviting Profs. Hagopian and Wells and Dr. Dolch to participate in the International Schulbuch Conference in Braunschweig, 28 June to 1 July, 1961, where the need for such a text was dramatically illuminated; and finally to our wives for their patient understanding during the stresses and strains of preparing this book.

John V. Hagopian, Ph. D.  
a. o. Professor für Amerikastudien  
Universität des Saarlandes

Martin Dolch, Dr. phil.  
Oberstudienrat  
Staatl. Math.-Naturwiss.  
Gymnasium Kaiserslautern

W. Gordon Cunliffe, B. A. (hons)  
Dolmetscher-Institut  
Universität des Saarlandes

Arvin R. Wells, Ph. D.  
Assistant Professor of English  
Ohio University  
Athens, Ohio, U.S.A

Spring, 1962

## PREFACE TO THE SECOND EDITION

The editors are gratified that the response to INSIGHT I both in Germany and abroad has warranted a second edition as well as a companion volume on modern British literature. We have brought up to date the biographical and bibliographical entries in an attempt to keep the book as useful as possible to scholars and university students. Cooperation on this project continues to be a source of great personal satisfaction to the editors.

Binghamton, New York  
Spring, 1964

John V. Hagopian  
Martin Dolch

## CONTENTS

Anderson, Sherwood . . . . . . . . . . . . . . . . . . . . . . . . 11
   The Egg . . . . . . . . . . . . . . . . . . . . . . . Hagopian 12
Baldwin, James . . . . . . . . . . . . . . . . . . . . . . . . . . 14
   This Morning, This Evening, So Soon . . . . . . . . . Hagopian 15
Benét, Stephen Vincent . . . . . . . . . . . . . . . . . . . . . . 22
   The Devil and Daniel Webster . . . . . . . . . . . . . Cunliffe 23
Bierce, Ambrose . . . . . . . . . . . . . . . . . . . . . . . . . 25
   An Occurrence at Owl Creek Bridge . . . . . . . . . . . Cunliffe 26
Cather, Willa . . . . . . . . . . . . . . . . . . . . . . . . . . 29
   Neighbour Rosicky . . . . . . . . . . . Cunliffe/Dolch/Hagopian 29
Crane, Stephen . . . . . . . . . . . . . . . . . . . . . . . . . . 35
   The Open Boat . . . . . . . . . . . . . . . . . . . . . . Dolch 36
Faulkner, William . . . . . . . . . . . . . . . . . . . . . . . . 41
   A Rose for Emily . . . . . . . . . . . . Hagopian/Cunliffe/Dolch 42
   That Evening Sun . . . . . . . . . . . . . . . . . . . Hagopian 50
   Death Drag . . . . . . . . . . . . . . . . . . . . . . Hagopian 55
Fitzgerald, F. Scott . . . . . . . . . . . . . . . . . . . . . . . 59
   Babylon Revisited . . . . . . . . . . . . . . . . . . Hagopian 60
Harte, Bret . . . . . . . . . . . . . . . . . . . . . . . . . . . 64
   The Luck of Roaring Camp . . . . . . . . . . . . . . . Cunliffe 64
Hawthorne, Nathaniel . . . . . . . . . . . . . . . . . . . . . . . 67
   My Kinsman, Major Molineux . . . . . . . . . . . . . . Hagopian 69
   Young Goodman Brown . . . . . . . . . . . . . . . . . Hagopian 73
   The Minister's Black Veil . . . . . . . . . . Cunliffe/Hagopian 78
   The Scarlet Letter . . . . . . . . . . . . . . . . . . . . Wells 82
Hemingway, Ernest . . . . . . . . . . . . . . . . . . . . . . . . 91
   Cat in the Rain . . . . . . . . . . . . . . . . Hagopian/Dolch 93
   A Canary for One . . . . . . . . . . . Dolch/Hagopian/Cunliffe 96
   The Killers . . . . . . . . . . . . . . . . . . Dolch/Hagopian 99
   A Day's Wait . . . . . . . . . . . . . . . . . . . . . . Dolch 103
   A Clean, Well-Lighted Place . . . . . . . . . . . . . . . Dolch 105
   The Old Man and the Sea . . . . . . . . . . . . . . . . . Wells 111
Irving, Washington . . . . . . . . . . . . . . . . . . . . . . . . 122
   Rip Van Winkle . . . . . . . . . . . . Cunliffe/Dolch/Hagopian 123
Jackson, Shirley . . . . . . . . . . . . . . . . . . . . . . . . . 128
   The Lottery . . . . . . . . . . . . . . . . . . . . . Hagopian 129
James, Henry . . . . . . . . . . . . . . . . . . . . . . . . . . . 132
   Daisy Miller . . . . . . . . . . . . . . . . . . . . . Hagopian 133

Lardner, Ring . . . . . . . . . . . . . . . . . . . . . . . . . . 139
   Haircut . . . . . . . . . . . . . . . . . . . . . . Hagopian 140
Melville, Herman . . . . . . . . . . . . . . . . . . . . . . . 144
   Bartleby the Scrivener . . . . . . . . . . . . . . Hagopian 145
   Benito Cereno . . . . . . . . . . . . . . . . . . Hagopian 150
   Billy Budd . . . . . . . . . . . . . . . . . Hagopian/Dolch 155
Miller, Arthur . . . . . . . . . . . . . . . . . . . . . . . . 165
   All My Sons . . . . . . . . . . . . . . . . . . . . . Wells 166
   Death of a Salesman . . . . . . . . . . . . . . . Hagopian 174
O'Neill, Eugene . . . . . . . . . . . . . . . . . . . . . . . 186
   Beyond the Horizon . . . . . . . . . . . . . . . . . . Wells 187
Parker, Dorothy . . . . . . . . . . . . . . . . . . . . . . . 194
   You were Perfectly Fine . . . . . . . . . . . . . Hagopian 194
Poe, Edgar Allan . . . . . . . . . . . . . . . . . . . . . . . 196
   The Gold-Bug . . . . . . . . . . . . . . . . . . . Cunliffe 197
   The Tell-Tale Heart . . . . . . . . . . . . . . . . Cunliffe 200
   The Cask of Amontillado . . . . . . . . . . Hagopian/Cunliffe 203
Porter, Katherine Anne . . . . . . . . . . . . . . . . . . . . 207
   The Jilting of Granny Weatherall . . . . . . . . . Hagopian 208
   The Old Order . . . . . . . . . . . . . . . . . . Hagopian 212
   Holiday . . . . . . . . . . . . . . . . . . . . . Hagopian 216
Powers, James F. . . . . . . . . . . . . . . . . . . . . . . . 220
   The Forks . . . . . . . . . . . . . . . . . . . . Hagopian 220
Salinger, Jerome David . . . . . . . . . . . . . . . . . . . . 225
   Down at the Dinghy . . . . . . . . . . . . . Hagopian/Dolch 225
Steinbeck, John . . . . . . . . . . . . . . . . . . . . . . . 230
   The Leader of the People . . . . . . . . . . . Dolch/Cunliffe 231
Thurber, James . . . . . . . . . . . . . . . . . . . . . . . 236
   The Secret Life of Walter Mitty . . . . . . . . . Hagopian 236
   The Macbeth Murder Mystery . . . . . . . . . . . Hagopian 240
Trilling, Lionel . . . . . . . . . . . . . . . . . . . . . . . 242
   The Other Margaret . . . . . . . . . . . . . . . Hagopian 243
Twain, Mark . . . . . . . . . . . . . . . . . . . . . . . . 248
   The Celebrated Jumping Frog of Calaveras County . . . . . Cunliffe 249
   Traveling with a Reformer . . . . . . . . . . . . Cunliffe 252
Warren, Robert Penn . . . . . . . . . . . . . . . . . . . . . 253
   Blackberry Winter . . . . . . . . . . . . . . . . Hagopian 254
Wharton, Edith . . . . . . . . . . . . . . . . . . . . . . . 260
   Mrs. Manstey's View . . . . . . . . . . . . Hagopian/Cunliffe 260
Wilder, Thornton . . . . . . . . . . . . . . . . . . . . . . 263
   Our Town . . . . . . . . . . . . . . . . . . Wells/Hagopian 264
Williams, Tennessee . . . . . . . . . . . . . . . . . . . . . 271
   The Glass Menagerie . . . . . . . . . . . . . . . . . Wells 272

Biography and General Criticism . . . . . . . . . . . . . . . . 281

# SHERWOOD ANDERSON

Sherwood Anderson was born on September 3, 1876, at Camden, Ohio. Since his father earned a poor living as an unsuccessful craftsman, Anderson had to leave school at the age of 11 to help support the family. He often felt irritated at his father's irresponsibility, and after the death of his mother, Anderson, aged 20, left his family and went to Chicago. After volunteering in the Spanish-American War in 1898/99, he spent a year at Wittenberg College to improve his education. During the following years he worked successfully for advertising agencies and as a businessman, but then began to write fiction. In 1912 business worries, his inability to choose a consistent course of life and difficulties in his marriage caused a breakdown. Anderson decided to make his living as an artist and abruptly left his wife and children. He found encouragement and stimulation in the literary circles of the Chicago Bohemia.

In 1916 he published his earliest novel but his first great success was *Winesburg, Ohio* (1919), containing grotesque sketches of frustrated, desperate people who are "condemned to go through life without friends." In his style Anderson identified himself with the plebeian tradition that had its sources in Lincoln, Whitman and Twain. His interest in Gertrude Stein's experiments turned into friendship when he visited Paris in 1921 where he helped and befriended Ernest Hemingway. During the following years his life was unsettled; he published several more novels and collections of short stories which contained some of his best work. After several years in New Orleans, where he launched William Faulkner on his writing career, he bought a farm near Marion, Virginia, in 1925 and became editor of two newspapers. The economic depression of the 1930's together with a decline of his creative powers, led him to social radicalism and, for some time, Communism. Up to his death in 1941, he continued to feel the urge to write: "I am pretty sure that writing may be a way of life in itself... I think the whole glory of writing lies in the fact that it forces us out of ourselves and into the lives of others. In the end the real writer becomes a lover." Of Sherwood Anderson's importance as an American artist Irving Howe says, "Anderson seemed the archetype of all those writers who were trying to raise themselves to art by sheer emotion and sheer will, who suspected intellect as a cosmopolitan snare that would destroy their gift for divining America's mystic essence, and who abominated the society which had formed them but knew no counterpoise of value by which to escape its moral dominion."

# The Egg

Text: *American Short Stories* IV pp. 91—94. Schöningh

*A man recalls his boyhood and the unsuccessful attempts of his father "to get up in the world." The father is a simple farm hand in an Ohio village, but his wife, a country school teacher, persuades him to start a chicken farm of his own. When the enterprise fails after 10 years, they open a restaurant. As his greatest treasure the father keeps a number of glass bottles containing grotesque malformations of chickens — with four legs, two pairs of wings or two heads — preserved in alcohol. He displays these behind the counter, and, as an additional attraction for customers, designs ways of entertaining them as a kind of showman. He practices several tricks with eggs, but his first performance is, like everything in his life, a complete failure. The final "triumph of the egg" leaves the boy wondering for the rest of his life why eggs have to be.*

The story was published in 1921 in a collection of short stories to which it gave the title "The Triumph of the Egg." It is an old-fashioned story in two ways: like the stories of Maupassant, it first introduces characters and setting in an elaborate exposition and then describes a dramatic event heavily charged with a moral. But it is a "modern" story in employing the limited point of view and in dramatizing a pessimistic existentialism. The limitations in the point of view would have been narrower and more restrictive had Anderson presented it through the eyes of a boy; but in having his narrator tell us of these events in retrospect after he has become a man, Anderson makes him something of a home-spun philosopher, a small-town Schopenhauer with the implication that his own life has fully confirmed the meaning of the events he witnessed in his boyhood. Thus, the point of view is exactly like that of Robert Penn Warren's "Blackberry Winter" and William Faulkner's "That Evening Sun."

The climax in the father's desperate attempt to entertain his customer, Joe Kane, is made not only comic but grotesquely comic — even cosmically comic — by being prefaced with a long development in which the egg, the source of life, is shown to be uncontrollable, a producer of grotesques, not the basis of a secure livelihood despite the propaganda of advertisers who would have us believe that life on a chicken-farm can be beautiful. Though the narrator writes as "a gloomy man inclined to see the darker side of life," there is a bizarre thread of comedy woven through the story.

"The Egg" is essentially a parable, and parable is one of the lesser forms of literary art: it states a general "truth" and then illustrates it with a little tale. Unless the reader already agrees with the moral, he cannot fully accept the story. As Irving Howe has said in his full-length study of Anderson, "Read for moral explication as a guide to life, his work must seem unsatisfactory; it simply does not tell us enough." "Tell" is perhaps the wrong word — it doesn't "show" us enough, for certainly Anderson "tells" us everything he wants us to believe. He fails because he does not *embed* his meaning in action, characterization, and dialogue, but merely attaches it to a story which without his editorial comment simply would not mean what he wants it to mean. In other words, the strategy of having a narrator within the story is not dramatically relevant to the story; it is a device for hanging a meaning on to it.

1. *With what inflection should the opening sentence be read?*

   Stress on "nature" would imply he *was* cheerful; stress on "cheerful, kindly" means he *was not* cheerful. The stress problem reveals two important points about the story: a) that scanning and rescanning is necessary before one can be sure of the meanings of many passages; b) that it is, after all, a "told" and not a "written" story.

2. *What in terms of the story are the largest possible philosophical implications of the title? When in the end the egg has its "complete and final triumph," what is it exactly that triumphs? In other words, what does the egg symbolize?*

   That the egg symbolizes not just Life, but the inevitable evil and misery of life, is made explicitly clear as soon as the narrator describes the first venture of his parents. He attributes his gloomy view of life to the fact that he was raised on a chicken farm and feels sure that most philosophers must have been raised that way, too. As the family travels to their second venture, the narrator hopes that their new life will be "a happy, eggless affair." Thus the father's efforts to become a success by his manipulation of an egg is doomed.

3. *The description of the parents' first venture is said to be a "digression." Why is it in the story? What does it tell us about the narrator? What dimension of meaning is achieved by having the narrator tell us of these events many years after they have occurred and he has become an adult?*

   The first venture into chicken-farming provides the pessimistic frame for the ensuing experience, which, without such a frame, might be taken as merely grotesque comedy. The last few sentences of the story complete the frame by extending it to the following generation and the present time. The bitter pessimism of the son as he tells the tale years later implies that nothing he has experienced since he was a boy contradicts the bleak view of life he had then learned.

4. *What are the implications of the place-names Butterworth, Bidwell, Pickleville? Why are the members of the family nameless?*

   Butterworth and Bidwell both involve dairy terms (a "biddy" is a chicken) in names with optimistic connotations ("worth" and "well"). But notice that the family really doesn't go to Bidwell, but to Pickleville; that is, like the father's grotesques, they are about to become "pickled" as hideous manifestations of misshapen life. The fact that the members of the family are not named keeps them from being specific people, tends to "universalize" their experience.

5. *In describing the journey to Pickleville, the narrator ironically uses the phrase "upward journey through life." What other ironical phrases can be found? Are they generally used to undercut a possible sentimental effect?*

13

"... rose from poverty to greatness" 92; "tiny fluffy things ... on Easter cards" 93; "his greatest treasure" 95; "to rise in the world" 97; "the jolly innkeeper effect" 98; and many others.

6. *Since the story is an autobiographical reminiscence, its point of view is that of the boy. What weakness is therefore involved in the central dramatic event?*

The one event to which the narrator was *not* a personal witness is the one most fully dramatized. It is therefore reduced to an act of his imagination and its credibility is weakened.

7. *Is the story a parable? If so, what is the meaning of the parable?*

The story is a parable in that, like the parables of Christ in the New Testament, it is used to illustrate a moral truth. It differs, however, in that it is not only completely secular in its frame of reference but also utterly negativistic in meaning. It seems to say: No matter how hard you try and no matter how good your intentions are, your own limitations and the basic laws of life doom you to failure and misery.

J. V. H.

Carter, Albert H., *Reading Recent American Literature*, Frankfurt 1967, pp. 24—33 — Joseph, Gerhard, The American Triumph of the Egg: Anderson's "The Egg" and Fitzgerald's "The Great Gatsby", *Criticism*, VII (1965), pp. 131—140 — West, Michael D., Sherwood Anderson's Triumph: "The Egg," *American Quarterly*, XX (1968), pp. 675—693.

# JAMES BALDWIN

James Baldwin was born on August 2, 1924, in New York City, the eldest of nine children of a Negro clergyman. As a child he experienced poverty and discrimination and, after leaving high school, helped to support his family. A fellowship he received in 1945 enabled him to devote himself to literary work. His first book was *Go Tell It on the Mountain (1953)*, a realistic yet poetic story of religious experience in Harlem; it was one of 350 books chosen by the Carnegie Corporation to represent the United States in Britain. In 1955 a collection of essays *Notes of a Native Son* followed, which mostly deal with the peculiar dilemma of Northern Negro intellectuals who can legitimately claim neither Western nor African heritage as their own. "Baldwin," a critic wrote, "has been enraged into a style; the harshness of his lot, his racial sensitivity, and the sense of alienation and displacement ... [have] moved him to ... lyrical, passionate, sometimes violent prose." Since then he has published three more novels (*Giovanni's Room*, 1956, *Another Country*, 1962, and *Tell Me How Long the Train's been Gone*, 1969) and two collections of essays (*Nobody Knows My Name*, 1961, and *The Fire Next Time*, 1963) and has become the most articulate voice of the American Negroes. A play, *Blues for Mister Charley*, ran on Broadway in 1964.

Baldwin has traveled in England and on the Continent; he lived for a long while in Paris. He is now a resident of Greenwich Village, New York.

He received several literary awards for the stories, novels and plays he has written. Speaking for himself, Baldwin says: "Some people feel that I make too much of being a Negro and others that I do not make enough. My effort is to make real that rare common ground where the differences between human beings do not matter. Sometimes this can only be done by describing the differences..."

## This Morning, This Evening, So Soon

Text:   James Baldwin, *This Morning, This Evening, So Soon*. Diesterweg

*The scene of the story is Paris, about 1958. After having lived there for twelve years, a colored singer from Alabama, who has recently made his way from great poverty to international fame as a filmstar, prepares to return to the USA. He is married to a Swedish girl named Harriet and has a seven-year-old son Paul. His elder sister Louisa is with them on a holiday before accompanying them on their voyage home; she tries to prepare Harriet for the problems facing the white wife of a Negro in the USA.*

*On the last evening but one before the departure the artist recollects the happy years he has spent in Paris where he met his wife; and the unpleasant experiences on his last visit to the USA eight years earlier. To him, life in the USA has been full of nightmares, and he wonders what it will be like for his son.*

*He talks to his French film director, Jean Luc Vidal, who made him a famous man. Together they spend the evening in the company of two young American negro couples and an Arab from Tunisia. The latter steals money from one of the American girls, but is treated with great tact and understanding. This experience plants a feeling of cheerfulness in the mind of the American singer who now begins to look forward to returning to the USA more confidently.*

James Baldwin's "This Morning, This Evening, So Soon," first published in 1960, appears to be a relatively simple story, but it is full of subtle and surprising complexities. A young American Negro, who has for 12 years been living in exile in Paris, where he has established a family (a Swedish wife and a 7-year-old son) and has found fame as a singer and actor, has decided to return to America. He is full of fear and anxiety, especially for his son who may suffer the spiritually crippling effects of American anti-Negro prejudice. But the experiences and reminiscences of his last 24 hours in Paris change his mood — they make him feel "very cheerful, I do not know why" and he finds himself smiling at the prospect of taking his son "all the way to the new world." This story is an honest, articulate, even eloquent exploration of the inner thoughts and feelings of a sensitive Negro American about his own country — probably the finest piece of literature yet written on this powerfully charged subject.

The story is divided into three sections which might have been subtitled (I) Family, (II) Friend, (III) Strangers; hence, it moves from the intimate center of the unnamed narrator's experiences outward into public life and society. Simultaneously, the narrator — and the reader — gains more and more understanding and insight into the complexities and changes in the current of his emotions, even though much happens that he does not fully understand. The "I" narrator tells us (in the present tense) about the events as they happen and (in the past tense) about his reminiscences, together with his own interpretations which are often much too explicit and preachy: "Everyone's life begins on a level where races, armies, and churches stop. And yet everyone's life is always shaped by races, churches, and armies; races, churches, and armies menace, and have taken, many lives."

Such comments give the reader the false notion that he is getting the meaning as well as the action from the narrator. As the narrator is intelligent and trained to be wary and critical, his observations are always appropriate to his character and are often apt and to the point. But he has had prejudices of his own ("I had always thought of Sweden as being populated entirely by blondes"), is super-sensitive to every act and gesture by a white man that might conceivably be interpreted as anti-Negro ("Was it my imagination or was it true that they seemed to avoid my eyes?"), and often speaks ("she is only an American like me") and feels ("I feel very cheerful, I do not know why") in ways that he does not fully understand. Hence the narrator does not, however much he may seem to, do all the reader's interpretive work for him. In fact, the fundamental meaning of the story remains implicit.

In the opening lines of the story, the narrator introduces the members of the intimate family circle: his wife Harriet; his sister Louisa, who has come to Paris for a brief holiday before accompanying him and his family back to America; his son Paul, to whom America is "only a glamorous word;" and "the director of the film" who remains unnamed at this point because he is not important until we reach the second section of the story. The strangers of the third section are, of course, not mentioned because the narrator is speculating on events *as they occur* and does not know who is going to appear or what is going to happen. Many of the undercurrents of the opening section will not have much impact on first reading because Baldwin holds back the vital information that the narrator and his sister are Negroes until after he has established his characters as a family unit. Only on second reading can we realize the immense tactfulness of Harriet when she explains to their son that his father's crankiness at breakfast "is because he is afraid they will not like his songs in New York. Your father is an *artiste, mon chou*, and they are very mysterious people, *les artistes*." The Negro question is avoided because "Harriet does not so much believe in protecting children as she does in helping them to build a foundation [of love] on which they can build and build again, each time life's high-flying steel ball knocks down everything they have built." And only on second reading can we understand why Louisa must seem to Paul "peculiarly uncertain of herself, peculiarly hostile and embattled," or the sinister significance of her insistence to Harriet that "We have *got* some expressions, believe me. Don't let anybody ever tell you America hasn't got a culture. Our culture is as thick as clabber milk."

It is in an atmosphere of family love that the narrator's fears emerge: "Paul has never been called any names before." Well aware of the fact that in America he and Harriet would never have been able to love each other, he broods over "all the threats it holds for me and mine." And he shrewdly observes that "Harriet is really trying to learn from Louisa how best to protect her husband and her son." The largest image of this first section is that of a family group full of love and good will facing a threatening experience in which each is eager to help and protect the other.

After Harriet and Louisa leave to spend an evening in Paris and after Paul has been delivered to the safe-keeping of the concierge, the narrator returns to his apartment to await the visit of Vidal, the director of the film which has made him famous. On the balcony he smokes, looks at Paris where he has "always felt at home" (but see *Notes of a Native Son*, where Baldwin describes the horrible experience of incarceration in a Paris jail), meditates and reminisces: "I love Paris, I will always love it, it is the city which has saved my life ... by allowing me to find out who I am." It was in Paris eight years before that he fell in love with Harriet just before returning to America for the funeral of his mother — "I felt ... for the first time that the woman was not, in her own eyes or in the eyes of the world, degraded by my presence." He was afraid of America and eager to return to Harriet. New York seemed like "some enormous, cunning and murderous beast, ready to devour, impossible to escape," and he was especially vulnerable because he "had forgotten all the tricks [of appearing subservient to the whites] on which my life had once depended." There are few subtleties in this transitional part of the story. The narrator is ambivalent about America, fears it but is attracted to it. There is a fine little sketch of the noise and power of New York, capped with the observation that "the human voices distinguished themselves from the roar by their note of strain and hostility." When his sister Louisa, who had met him at the ship, directed the cab driver to the New Yorker Hotel, the narrator was surprised, for Negroes had formerly been discriminated against there. Obviously the country was changing, but Louisa's optimism is tempered with humorous caution: "this place really hasn't changed very much. You still can't hear yourself talk."

The second section of the story begins with the arrival of Jean Luc Vidal, a "tough, cynical, crafty old Frenchman," a former Gaullist whose wife and son were lost in the war and who had spent time in a Nazi prison. This man is very fond of the young Negro whom he has made into an international star in a film significantly entitled *Les Fauves Nous Attendent*. But Vidal has done more for him than that; he had taught him to express in his art, and thus to relieve, his deep-felt hatred, and he had exposed the narrator's self-pitying anti-white prejudice. Such reverse prejudice had prevented him from responding to any individual white man just as effectively as anti-Negro prejudice blinds white people to the individuality of Negroes: "I am a French director and I have never been in your country and I have never done you any harm — but ... you are not talking to Jean Luc Vidal, but to some other white man, whom you remember, who has nothing to do with me." To Vidal the narrator can speak openly of his fears at returning to a country where "I always feel that I don't exist, except in someone else's — usually dirty — mind ... I don't want to put Harriet through that and I don't want to raise Paul there." Vidal reassures him that his return needn't be permanent, that his new status and the prospects of great wealth are worth the risk.

Section three opens at a discothèque where the narrator and Vidal encounter a group of touring American Negro students, two girls and two young men. The most beautiful of the girls approaches them, astonished at her luck "because it's in all the papers that you're coming home." These Negroes, like the narrator, obviously regard America as "home" despite the conditions of their life there. Their dialogue reveals their fear and hatred of the whites, but also their belligerent determination to fight back. One says, "I fear you are in for some surprises, my friend. There have been some changes made." Then, "Are you afraid?"

"A little."

"We all are," says another, "that's why I was so glad to get away *for a little while.*"

As the group goes bar-hopping, they are joined by an Arab named Boona, an erstwhile prize-fighter from Tunis and an acquaintance of the narrator. Though Boona is a disreputable fellow and obviously does not fit with the group, the narrator is trapped by his fear of expressing anti-Arab prejudice and cannot send him away. During the course of the night, Boona steals money from the purse of one of the girls; he is confronted and denies it — "Why she blame me? Because I come from Africa?" In this section of the story the narrator makes no commentaries on the action, and when the girl decides not to press the point ("I'm sure I lost it ... It isn't worth hurting your feelings") we can only assume that she has observed the Arab's desperation and is therefore willing to endure the loss of the money. The party breaks up at dawn, and the narrator goes home, stopping at the concierge's apartment to pick up his son: "I feel very cheerful, I do not know why." The concierge, referring to their trip to America, says, "What a journey! *Jusqu'au nouveau monde!*"

> I open the cage [of the elevator] and we step inside. "Yes," I say, "all the way to the new world." I press the button and the cage, holding my son and me, goes up.

The symbolism of the ending is clear. Although this Negro and his son are in the cage of their Negro skins, they are rising in the world. But what, exactly, has happened to explain or justify this optimism? The answer is that as the story moves in wider and wider orbits around the private individuality of this Negro, we see that his original feeling that everything was divided into his oppressed self and the hostile world was false, that he is part of a history and a humanity that is far more complex than that. The narrator cannot identify himself simply as an oppressed person, for much of the world does *not* oppress him. He finds love not only from his Negro sister, but from a Swedish woman who marries him and gives him a son and from a French film director who teaches him some hard truths about life. In the film he had been obliged to portray a mulatto boy who hated "all dark women and all white men" and he had not been throwing himself fully and honestly into the role. Vidal had goaded him:

"Have you never, yourself, been in a similar position?"

I hated him for asking the question because I knew he had the answer to it. "I would have had to be a very lucky black man not to have been in such a position."

"You would have had to be a very lucky *man*."

"Oh, God," I said, "please don't give me any of this equality- in-anguish business."

"It is perfectly possible," he said sharply, "that there is not another kind."

Vidal then gave him a stern lecture on history, pointing out that the white men — especially the French — are paying for their history of abuse of the colored peoples and that if revenge is what the Negro wants he will certainly have it. He then strikes home with a telling blow: "How will you raise your son? Will you teach him never to tell the truth to anyone?" The narrator then recalls how he had held his own father in pity and contempt for not being able to prevent or even to prepare for the humiliation and the anguish of Negro life in Alabama. "But for Paul . . . I swore I would make it impossible for the world to treat Paul as it had treated my father and me." But since the story does not end at that point, this must be taken as a temporary and transient stage in the narrator's development. And Vidal's wisdom, too, is by no means the last word.

The last word apparently has to do with Boona, i. e., with the contrast between the Arab from Tunis and the Negro from America, neither of whom wishes to go home. One of the Negro girls asks Boona, "Wouldn't you like to go back [to Tunis]?" and he replies, "That is not so easy." But their situations are not quite the same, as the narrator comes to realize; there is a profound difference in their racial histories. The Arabs do not identify themselves as Frenchmen, but the Negroes feel that they are Americans. In his balcony meditation the narrator had mused on the plight of the Arabs in Paris and how their treatment had caused such a degeneration among them. "I once thought of the North Africans as my brothers" and responded to "their rage, the only note in all their music which I could not fail to recognize." Yet because "they were perfectly prepared to drive all Frenchmen into the sea and to level the city of Paris" he could not identify with them, — partly because he owed his spiritual life to France and partly because his own rage against America is the anger one feels against the wrongs of a country one loves ("waiting for the first glimpse of America, my apprehension began to give way to a secret joy, a checked anticipation"). Furthermore, he had discovered aboard ship during his first voyage home that the white Americans "who had never treated me with any respect, had no respect for each other." True, they quickly came to call each other by their first names, but their friendliness "did not suggest and was not intended to suggest any possibility of friendship." And earlier in the story he had observed that the whites "could not afford to hear a truth which would shatter, irrevocably, their image of themselves." This is a condition which the Negro can and must help to correct. He shares with his sister Louisa the conviction that if the whites could be brought to confront the Negro honestly and to accept him for what he was — not only a fellow human being but a permanent and unshakable part of American culture — the entire culture could be made whole and healthy. Louisa had said that even Negroes must be brought to realize this truth:

"That's what I keep trying to tell those dicty bastards down South. They get their own experience into the language, we'll have a great language. But, no, they all want to talk like white folks ... I tell them, honey, white folks ain't saying *nothing*. Not a thing are they saying — and *some* of them know it — they *need* what you got, the world needs it."

It is this kind of racial pride that the Arabs in France do not share with the Negroes in America, that has been buttressed by the narrator's observation of the understanding and kindness displayed by the Negro tourists toward Boona. That is what makes him cheerful at the end. It is an achievement that he can face with pride the prospect of being a Negro in America.

1. *The story is told with little use of poetic metaphors ("life's high-flying steel ball" is a kind of language rarely used here). How would you describe the language of the story?*

    Apart from the juxtaposition of narrative and commentary (though the commentary trickles away as we approach the final portion) two elements seem to dominate the language: a) the high frequency of adjectives and adverbs — especially in pairs: "incredible and troubling riches," "orderly and progressive Sweden," "steadily and beautifully old-fashioned," "weirdest and most delightful surprises," etc; b) out of the flat, declarative style of the narrative, there is an enormous range of inflections in the dialogue: Paul's passionate vehemence of the child — "You are the greatest singer in France"; the compassionate reassurance of a loving wife, "Please try not to worry"; the affectionate sophistication of Vidal, "Well? Your nightmares, please"; the boisterous and hearty vitality of Louisa, "You know, some of them folks are *ashamed* of Mahalia Jackson?"; the insolence and insincerity of Boona, "He is the director of many films, many of them made me cry," etc. It is curious that the most monotoned of the principal characters is the wife Harriet; the others have a wide range of expression extending from their dominant type.

2. *What element of the story might be called a leitmotif?*

    The recurrence of Negro singing: the narrator sings aboard ship and in the film; Mahalia Jackson's singing on records forms the background to the important dialogue with Vidal; Pete, of the tourist group, strums a guitar and sings. It might be said that one of the historical characteristics of the American Negro is that he has always sung his way through trouble — hence, the development of the indigenous American art form, the spiritual. The title itself is taken from a Negro folk-song:

> "I got a gal an a sugarbabe too, my honey, my baby,
> I got a gal an a sugarbabe too, my honey, my sweet thing,
> I got a gal an a sugarbabe too, my honey,
> Gal don't love me, but my sugarbabe do
> > This mornin,
> > This evenin,
> > So soon.
> When they kill a chicken, she saves me the wing, . . .
> Think I'm aworkin ain't adoin a thing
> > This mornin,
> > This evenin,
> > So soon.
> Every night about a half past eight, . . .
> Ya find me awaitin at the white folks' gate
> > This mornin,
> > This evenin,
> > So soon."

3. *Baldwin avoids attempting to write in dialect, possibly because dialect has long been associated with anti-Negro literature and jokes, invoking stereotyped characters and situations. Nevertheless, he manages to convey differences between the speech of his Negro characters and that of others. How?*

By characteristic turns of speech, slang, violations of standard grammar and usage. For example, Louisa says, "I tell them, *honey*, white folks ain't saying nothing." "Honey", "ain't", and the double negative are all involved, despite the fact that she is a schoolteacher. But it is clear that she deliberately speaks so — uses the language of Southern Negroes when talking to or about them; otherwise her English is perfectly good. The narrator himself has cast off Negro speech after 12 years in France: "I had once known how to pitch my voice precisely between curtness and servility, and known what razor's edge of a pickaninny's smile would turn away wrath. But I had forgotten all the tricks on which my life had once depended"; the touring college students speak a very correct English until the polite formalities of first encounter are over and they can be themselves: "I don't want to bug you, man, but I fear your boy has goofed," "Talent I've got, but character, man, I'm lacking."

4. *The foreign reader can gain a great many insights not only into American Negro life in particular, but into American life in general. What are some that occur to you?*

American fathers never kiss American sons. Americans drop titles and use first names almost at once. Anti-Negro persons holding positions of authority generally address a Negro man as "boy"; other Americans tend to be friendly, "let's

21

hope they like you over here." The foreign reader can find dozens of such details, but the dominant trait about the Negro is his constant preoccupation with the assumed superiority of the whites.

J. V. H.

# STEPHEN VINCENT BENET

Stephen Vincent Benét was born on July 22, 1898, at Bethlehem, Pennsylvania, and spent his youth mostly in California and Georgia. His great-grandfather, grandfather and father were army-officers, the latter a widely read and cultivated man with a distinct interest in poetry. Stephen's elder brother and sister became writers. Heredity and environment thus destined his life: he always wanted to be an army-man and exercised great self-discipline. But scarlet-fever having weakened his eyes so that he could not join the army, he began to write early and published his first poetry at the age of 17, the year he went to Yale College, where he was a fellow-student with Archibald MacLeish and Thornton Wilder. He won early fame as a poet but also tried his hand at short stories. After taking the Master of Arts degree in 1920, he went to Paris and finished his first novel there. He married an American journalist with whom he was to lead a very happy life up to his death in 1943.

In order to make a living from writing he produced numerous short stories which were published in magazines, but he once confessed, "The short story was never exactly my forte." He was an instinctive poet, knowing and possessing the form since childhood, and writing a short story meant rigid discipline. In 1922 he wrote the famous "Ballad of William Sycamore" (Learning English Gedichtsammlung, 3. Aufl., S. 72), "the incarnation of the pioneer spirit set to perfect American transposition of the old ballad music." Benét's dissatisfaction with the current national scene drove him back to the more appealing heritage of earlier America and the American myth. In 1926/27, again in Paris as the recipient of a Guggenheim fellowship, he wrote a narrative poem of 367 pages celebrating the Civil War and the solidarity of the Union: "John Brown's Body", which became Benét's greatest popular and financial success. Sinclair Lewis cited it in his Nobel Prize speech in 1930 as evidence of the American literary renaissance, and Benét was awarded the Pulitzer Prize for Poetry for it. In 1936 the short story "The Devil and Daniel Webster" consolidated the national role which had been slowly materializing for Benét ever since the publication of his early ballads. During the Second World War Stephen Vincent Benét considered it his duty and not below his dignity to volunteer his talent for radio propaganda work. Again he achieved an immense popularity. He died while working at another long narrative poem "Western Star" dealing with the frontier spirit and the settlement of the West.

In his prose Benét's language and technique are conservative. At his best his style is fluent, natural and combines dignity and a delicate humor. He once advised a young writer, "Don't use four adjectives when one will do... Write of the simple things simply." Serious critics have ignored his work, but much of it has remained popular.

## The Devil and Daniel Webster

Text: *American Short Stories* V pp. 76—92. Schöningh
*Modern American Short Stories* pp. 15—27. Diesterweg
(The latter edition gives the text in a slightly condensed form.)

*Hard luck induces a New Hampshire farmer named Jabez Stone to sell his soul to the devil in exchange for seven years of prosperity. When the time comes for the price to be paid, Stone turns for help to his old neighbor, the famous lawyer and orator Daniel Webster. Webster argues with the devil but for the first time seems to have met his match. Finally they agree to put the case before a jury of 12 men (who turn out to be the worst traitors in American history) under the notorious Judge Hathorne. Although the evidence is not quite convincing the jury is so moved by Mr. Webster's eloquence that they find in Jabez Stone's favor. His contract is torn up, and the devil even has to promise never to bother any New Hampshire man again.*

"The Devil and Daniel Webster" combines elements of the tall tale and of the Kunstmärchen ("synthetic fairy-tale", as it is sometimes rather unhappily translated). The opening sentence sets the tone of regionalism that numerous collectors of folk-lore have taught us to look for in the fairy-tale[1]. In this pleasant old-fashioned atmosphere of attachment to the soil of New England Daniel Webster dominates the scene, as does, say, Rübezahl in the Riesengebirge. The two elements, the earthy (concerned with the details of country life before the days of mechanized farming) and the supernatural are employed throughout and help to create the authentic folk-tale atmosphere. The language correspondingly varies from the (perhaps rather self-conscious) naïveté of "he was the biggest man," "the Union's stay and New Hampshire's pride" to calculated supernatural effect: "his rolling voice in the hollows of the sky," "he could turn on the harps of the blessed and the shaking of the earth underground." The familiar Faust theme of the pact with the devil heightens to mythic dimensions the historical figure of Daniel Webster (1782—1852), who had predicted the Civil War and had pleaded for a preservation of the Union with passionate eloquence.

It is not the author's sole aim, however, to tell us a fairy-tale in an American setting. The chauvinistic element is very strong from the very outset, and the

---

[1] The comment on "border country" in the Diesterweg edition p. 48 is not only superfluous but wrong; in the context it has nothing to do with the "frontier," as the editor seems to believe.

"message" of the story turns out to be a patriotic one, a suitable memorial to Daniel Webster, who once said "in the mountains of New Hampshire, God Almighty has hung out a sign to show that there he makes men." Since the collectors of folk-tales are notoriously moved often by patriotic motives and national pride, the reader is prepared to meet with an element of this kind. Although the fantastic background and the hyperbole tends to soften any effect of militant, flag-wagging patriotism, the chauvinistic element dominates the story. Note that the regionalism of the beginning has by the third paragraph become "when he stood up to speak, stars and stripes came right out in the sky." But this is immediately followed by a series of rollicking exaggerations concerning the livestock on Daniel Webster's farm and the hero himself: "a man with a mouth like a mastiff, a brow like a mountain and eyes like burning anthracite." The exaggerations reinforce the patriotism by suggesting the virility of a young nation, with a shy, grinning pride that exceeds the bounds of logic but nevertheless asserts itself with humor. The sinister element marking the arrival of the devil is similarly mixed with a considerable amount of humor (e. g. the incident of the devil's notebook[1]). This element reaches its climax in the entrance of the devil's jury, the members of which are sketched in a few brief strokes. The figures, representing the villains of American history, are relevant to the moral of the story which emerges, when Daniel Webster realizes that it is really himself, an American patriot, that he is defending: "For it was him they'd come for, not only Jabez Stone." But Daniel Webster's oratorical powers were, we are assured, so irresistible that even the devil's jury is impressed. "For his voice could search the heart, and that was his gift and strength." The jury acquits Jabez Stone, and the devil receives his traditional drubbing; the carping critic would probably receive the same treatment. As we may consider that the devil has been too easily defeated, the story ends on a note of foreboding. Daniel Webster's final kick is not as effective as he intended. The last paragraph finishes with the local patriotism of the opening.

1. *Why doesn't the story begin with paragraph four, "There was a man named Jabez Stone..."?*

   Because the central figure and the hero is Daniel Webster; Jabez Stone is merely a tool by which the legend of his patriotism and eloquence is enhanced.

2. *Was there any legal flaw in Jabez Stone's contract with the devil?*

   None at all. The devil had not only fulfilled his end of the bargain to the letter, but had even extended — with surprising generosity — the prosperous life of Jabez Stone for an additional three years.

---

[1] Here one significant sentence is missing in the Schöningh edition p. 81 line 2: "... astonish you. He'd certainly be a prize; I wish we could see our way clear to him. But,..."

3. *Why then did the jury find for the defendant, Jabez Stone?*

Because Webster had appealed not only to their humanity (which divided them from the devil) but their status as American citizens (and certainly the devil is not an American). "... he showed how, out of the wrong and the right, the suffering and the starvations, something new had come [in America]. And everybody had played a part in it, even the traitors." It was a strictly emotional appeal but then patriotic speeches generally are.

4. *How does Benét gain the effect of a folk-tale in this story?*

The story is attached to a local tradition ("that's what I was told when I was a youngster"), country life is described with a wealth of familiar farming expressions ("If he planted corn, he got borers," i. e. vermin,...) and much homely detail "'There were two children down with the measles, his wife was ailing and he had a whitlow on his thumb'"); this is mixed with the supernatural world and the popular conception of the devil, who can be fooled.

5. *How are the humorous elements of this story employed?*

They serve to persuade the reader to accept the patriotic and sinister elements. These latter elements appear first mixed with humor and then by themselves. After the climax of Daniel Webster's speech there is a return to humor in the devil's abject behavior. It is to be noted that the humor does not nullify the patriotism — the exaggerations concerning, for example, Daniel Webster's farm give an effect of virility and rude plenty in a flourishing country.

6. *This story is often described as a contribution to "the epic of America" or as an "American Legend." Discuss.*

The regionalism of the genuine folk-story is here, and Daniel Webster's support of the cause of the Union provides a link with the history of the nation as a whole. But it is inevitable that a story concerned with a region of New England and with the traditional figures of New England history (the devil's jury) should lack relevance to the modern USA with its mixture of races and climates.

W. G. C.

# AMBROSE BIERCE

Ambrose Bierce was born on June 24, 1842, in the settlement of Horse Cave, Ohio, the tenth child of a poverty-stricken Calvinistic farmer. To escape his boyhood misery, he enlisted in the Union Army shortly after the outbreak of the Civil War, was severely wounded but continued to serve and gradually rose to the rank of Lieutenant. After the war, he remained with the army on a map-making expedition to the West until he was threatened with a peacetime reduction in rank and resigned to join his brother as an employee of the U. S. Mint in San Francisco. Ironically, he was promoted to brevet major by a mistake in the discharge orders, but by then was married and writing for newspapers. His first short story was printed in 1871. Soon afterwards he deserted his wife and three children to go to England and establish himself as a writer. He returned to San Francisco in 1876 and continued to write stories and satirical sketches while earning his living as a journalist. In 1896 he was sent to Washington on a muckraking assignment to expose the railroad lobby and remained in the East, though he gave up journalism in 1909 to devote his time to editing his *Collected Works* (12 vols., 1909—1912). After that task was completed, he went in 1913 to Mexico where he mysteriously disappeared; it is presumed that he died there in 1914.

He owes his place in American literature chiefly to two short stories — "An Occurrence at Owl Creek Bridge" and "A Horseman in the Sky" (both 1891) — and his famous cynical *The Devil's Dictionary* (1906). His other work consists largely of anecdotes and journalism, some of it of low quality.

## An Occurrence at Owl Creek Bridge

Text: Stockton, *The Lady or the Tiger?* / Bierce, *An Occurrence at Owl Creek Bridge* pp. 11—22. Hueber
*American Short Stories* III pp. 81—92. Schöningh
*Great American Short Stories* pp. 25—33. Klett
*Seven Anglo-American Short Stories* pp. 3—12. Diesterweg

*Peyton Farquhar, an Alabama planter devoted to the Southern cause in the Civil War, tries to destroy by fire the Owl Creek railroad bridge, which is in the hands of the Northern troops. Betrayed by a Federal scout, he his caught and condemned to be hanged from a cross-tie of the bridge. In the moment of execution he experiences his escape in a weird hallucination.*

The "old fashioned" short story often insists on a surprise ending, which is sometimes unconvincing, or mechanical, or both (as in O. Henry's "The Furnished Room"). The modern short story is usually a fragment of life that is in some way striking, perhaps for its psychological accuracy, and the surprise ending is generally scorned. "An Occurrence at Owl Creek Bridge" combines the best features of both types. The surprise ending occurs in the form of an ironical variation on that stalest of endings "... and then I woke up." But it is only a surprise ending to the very unsophisticated reader. The pattern of the whiplash reversal in the last sentence occurs in each of the three parts: "The sergeant stepped aside;" "He was a Federal scout;" "Peyton Farquhar was dead ..." They are signs of a careful craftsman putting details together and placing them in exactly the right place. The final effect is that events which would seem merely melodramatic in the hands of a lesser artist are so restrained and controlled that we observe rather than participate in the action. Bierce is a creator of tapestries: action is slowed down to scene, and structure is the juxtaposition of tableaux. There are no excessive details, and those given powerfully build up an atmosphere which is far more important to the story than the action. "An Occurrence at Owl Creek Bridge" meets an important test of literary art; namely, a summary of the plot boils away precisely those elements that make the story important. The morbid and pessimistic content of the story, which led Mencken to coin the epithet "Bitter Bierce" and van Wyck Brooks to refer to the author as "a dandified Strindberg", is far less important than the method.

The first section of the story, with its dreadful matter-of-factness in the description of the preparations for the hanging, represents, like the last sentence, the world of harsh reality. The doomed man's wishful thinking is, of course, psychologically true and prepares the reader for the cruelly disappointed dream of the third section.

The second section employs a familiar device of the story-teller and returns to the circumstances leading to the deception and capture of Peyton Farquhar. The sympathy evoked by the description of the main figure is here confirmed. The name, Peyton Farquhar, suggests the aristocrat, and the subsequent description shows him to be a man prepared to make sacrifices for an ideal. His capture by means of a trick and the powerful self-delusion of his imagined escape are thus the more poignant. This story is thus lent a deeper significance in the contrast implied between the North and the South, between hard reality and impractical ideals.

The third section of the story from the time when Farquhar falls from the bridge is marked by a dream-like unreality, beginning with the strange detachment with which Farquhar watches his hands freeing themselves and removing the noose from his neck and rising to a climax at the point where the man in the water sees the eye of the man on the bridge aiming at him through the sights of the rifle. The illusion that Farquhar has really escaped is sustained by the convincing practical detail of the swimmer encountering the hot bullets as he dives up (which was possible with the weapons of the period of the American Civil War) and by the "martinet's error" of the officer in ordering a volley instead of staggered shots. But the awareness that the escape is an illusion is gradually heightened by the fantastic paradisiacal scenery of the stones and trees on the river bank. The scenery becomes increasingly unreal, and the touching effect of wish-fulfillment fantasy reaches a climax in Farquhar's "meeting" with his wife. The last sentence is a return to hard reality, and a confirmation of the reader's worst expectations.

1. *What would be the sophisticated and the unsophisticated ways of reading this story?*

   To the unsophisticated reader, the ending comes as a simple surprise. For the reader who demands something more than a surprise ending, there is psychological truth in the wishful thinking of the man about to be executed, a common element of dreams and fantasies. There is irony in the variation on the most hackneyed of surprise endings. At the same time Bierce contrasts two ways of life and modes of thought which can be roughly summed up under the headings "idealism" and "realism." The story thus has a wide appeal.

2. *Discuss the structure of the story.*

The story goes in medias res, so that the reader's interest is immediately captured by the chief catastrophe. When, in section II, we learn of the events that had led up to the execution, our sympathies are aroused, to give the events in section III their full effect. A great deal would be lost if part II came first. Hemingway is known to have admired this story for its unusual and effective structure; his short story "The Snows of Kilimanjaro" is constructed on exactly the same line: "Both stories open with the situation of impending death, then flash back to explain how the situation came about, and then flash "forward" with the imaginary escape, only to conclude with the objective information that the death has indeed occurred" (Philip Young, *Ernest Hemingway*, Minneapolis 1959, pp. 30/31). Cf. also *Studies in Short Fiction* VI, 1969, pp. 361 ff.

3. *Do Bierce's views of life appear in the story?*

Bierce's attitude was deeply pessimistic, and in his other writings this pessimism is apt to appear in the form of a raw cynicism. Here the pessimism is more effective because it is implicit in the story. The ardent patriot (who is, however, also a slave-owner) misuses his idealism for purposes of war and is caught and hanged. His wife is "only too happy to serve ... with her own white hands" the soldier at the gate, who has come to lay a trap for her husband. Farquhar, smiling, calls himself a "student of hanging" and indeed meets with an arrangement that "commended itself to his judgment as simple and effective." He clings to the possibility of escape up to the last moment, but he is ruthlessly aroused from his rosy dreams. The cruelty and pointlessness of war is also illustrated in the story. The distressing event described here is merely "An Incident at Owl Creek Bridge," i. e. a very minor happening at an obscure place. In "A Horseman in the Sky" the same element of obscure sacrifice and suffering is emphasized — the hero's shooting of his own father passes almost unnoticed.

4. *How is the prisoner's state of mind indicated?*

We are told of "the swirling water of the stream racing madly beneath his feet." Then the prisoner's attention is caught by a piece of driftwood, and his thoughts are given as "How slowly it appeared to move! What a sluggish stream!" As in a slow-motion picture time almost comes to a standstill when he listens to the ticking of his watch during his last seconds: "He awaited each stroke with impatience and ... apprehension. The intervals of silence grew progressively longer; the delays became maddening." In this way the reader is prepared to accept the dream of escape that the prisoner experiences while falling. The loud noise "like the stroke of a blacksmith's hammer" made by the prisoner's watch moreover shows how preternaturally sensitive he has become. These small incidents indicate that the prisoner's relation to reality is disturbed; that he is capable of being deluded in the way revealed in the last section of the story.

W. G. C.

Bodden-Kaußen, *Model Interpretations of Great American Short Stories*, Stuttgart 1970, pp. 82—92 — Brooks and Warren, *Understanding Fiction*, New York ²1959, pp. 122—123 — Kopetzki, Robert, *Weltfreude und Todesnähe*, Frankfurt 1967, pp. 39—47 — Schöwerling, Rainer, Bierce, "An Occurrence...", *Die amerikanische Kurzgeschichte*, eds. Göller/Hoffmann, Düsseldorf 1972, pp. 149—158.

# WILLA CATHER

Willa Cather was born on December 7, 1873, in a farm-house near Winchester, Virginia, where the Cathers had tilled the soil for nearly a century. In 1883 her family moved to the frontier village of Red Cloud, Nebraska. She was taught at home and in high school to read extensively in the English and Latin classics; she also practised German and French and received musical instruction. In 1891 she entered the University of Nebraska and studied journalism. After her graduation in 1895 she became drama critic for the *Pittsburgh Leader* and began to publish poetry and stories. Then, for a few years she was head of the English Dept. at Allegheny High School, but in 1906 she went to New York and became managing editor of a magazine. A first collection of short stories appeared in 1905, a first novel in 1912. Like some of the short stories, the novels *O Pioneers!* (1913), *The Song of the Lark* (1915), and *My Ántonia* (1918) drew from her girlhood experiences in the Nebraska country. The best known and most popular of her novels, *Death Comes for the Archbishop* (1927), gives a picture of the history of the Spanish Southwest; and her next book, *Shadows on the Rock* (1931), deals with the French-Catholic colonial Quebec of 1697. Though not a Catholic herself, Willa Cather had a sympathetic understanding of the historic faith of the early French settlers.

All her writing was assisted by extensive traveling and careful studies of the cultural background of the settings. In 1922 she won the Pulitzer Prize for fiction, in 1933 she received the Prix Femina Américaine, and in 1938 she was elected to the American Academy of Arts and Letters. At various times she was awarded honorary degrees by five universities. Her novels were widely translated. When she died in 1947, "she had already come to appear as the survivor of some distant generation, remote from the talents and the problems of the past two anxious decades" (M. D. Zabel).

## Neighbour Rosicky

Text: Willa Cather, *Neighbour Rosicky*, Velhagen

*At the age of sixty-five Anton Rosicky is told by Doctor Ed Burleigh that he has a weak heart and cannot do heavy work any more. During the following winter months, he rests and reminisces over his life: he was born in Bohemia and still prefers to talk in Czech to his family. As a boy of eighteen he went to London where he spent two years of extreme poverty before he was helped on to New York. There he worked in a tailor shop for fifteen years, at first quite satisfied at having regular work and a happy "home life" with the family of a young Czech cabinet-maker. But as the years passed, he began to get restless, and turned to drinking until he realized that it was the unnatural world of a big city which worried him, and he made up his mind to live in the country. He bought some land in Nebraska and married a farm girl of Czech origin fifteen years younger than himself. They had a hard life but they were never discontented, because they had the same ideas about what was important in life.*

*His oldest son Rudolph has married an American girl from the town, and Anton Rosicky in his understanding way helps to overcome the problems of their inter-cultural marriage and to make sure his son will not leave the country and go to work in town. One day, ignoring the doctor's warning, he goes to his son's place and rakes up thistles in a field. He has a bad heart attack, and only his daughter-in-law's efforts keep him alive. A bond of affectionate understanding is established between them before he dies the following day.*

Willa Cather's "Neighbour Rosicky" was written in New York in 1928. The story deals with the last few months in the life of an elderly man whom the author admires greatly. Minor details of his appearance and behavior are dwelt on lovingly, and his life is obviously considered in some ways exemplary. The story has an autobiographical base, since the author's father was, like Rosicky, a victim of angina pectoris, was informed of his illness in late winter and died the following spring. Nevertheless, the author's attitude to the old man's death is in every way conventional. The modern reader has been taught to suspect "the proper feelings," especially concerning a death-bed, and to suspect insincerity — 'faking' as Hemingway called it. Willa Cather, however, is not disturbed by doubts of this kind:

"He wished it had been telling tales about some other man's heart, some old man who didn't look the Doctor in the eye so knowingly, or hold out such a warm brown hand when he said good-bye."

In keeping with this old-fashioned style is the author's manner of inserting comments on her characters:

"With Mary, to feed creatures was the natural expression of affection..."

or

"Embarrassment was the most disagreeable feeling Rosicky knew. He didn't often have it — only with certain people whom he didn't understand at all."

The voice of the teacher is unmistakably audible here, drawing the reader's attention to certain points in simple language and underlining the moral. Nothing is implicitly communicated, though there are many qualities that invite such communication. For example, when Rosicky recalls the bitter hunger he had observed in the past, he gives his work horses a little extra oats. The meaning of the extra oats is explicitly underlined ("It was his way of expressing what he felt..."), where a more sensitive writer (K. A. Porter, for example) would have let the incident speak for itself. Or, when Polly informs her husband of her father-in-law's heart attack, she says, "I was terribly scared" — and then makes quite clear why: "because, you know, I'm so fond of your father."

Rosicky and his family are, like the similar family in *My Ántonia*, intended to represent an ideal of sane and healthy living, and this ideal is conveyed by means of direct comment, as already shown, and, more dramatically, by means of anecdote. Sometimes comment and anecdote reinforce each other, as they do at the end of the second section, where the incident of the creamery agent underlines, as in a sermon, the author's direct statement concerning the open-handed way of life of the family that did not want "to be always skimping and saving." Even before, in Doctor Burleigh's reflections at the end of section I, their attitude had been justified with an Epicurean choice of values: "Maybe... people as generous and warm-hearted and affectionate as the Rosickys never got ahead much; maybe you couldn't enjoy your life and put it in the bank, too."

There is a further lesson for the reader in this exemplary family; the contrast between healthy rural life and the corruption and harshness of the big city. This lesson is again made quite plain. Rosicky looks back on the period of his life spent in New York, and his thoughts are reported as follows:

"It struck young Rosicky that this was the trouble with big cities; they built you in from the earth itself, cemented you away from any contact with the ground. You lived in an unnatural world..."

Nor is the author's missionary zeal exhausted here. The cities of the Old World are, it is implied, even worse than those of the New. Rosicky looks back on a happy time in New York, but his life in London was undiluted misery. As always, suffering can be better communicated by dramatic means than happiness, and Rosicky's account of his life in London stands without comment from the author. A sentimental strain becomes especially prominent in the interruption of "little Josephine" saying, "Poor little Papa, I don't want him to be hungry." It is as if the mention of London reminded the author of certain passages from Dickens. The London incident is made to yield its moral later in the story in Rosicky's reflection: "To this day he could recall certain terrible faces in the London streets." The author does not, however, want to simplify matters too much. The ideal character represented by Rosicky is not a simple product of healthy country life. The civilization of cities has played a part in his making — a fact that is conveyed when Polly observes the dying man's hands, or through the wife's remark "city-bred."

The didactic element in the story is so strong that the reader is apt to overlook the structure. The impression of Rosicky and his household is built up by a subtle interweaving of time and place. The opening visit to the Doctor introduces the two main themes: Rosicky's impending death and the problem of the oldest son's intercultural marriage with an American girl. The scene in the consulting-room also gives the author a chance to demonstrate Rosicky's stoicism and to reveal background particulars (e. g. that the hero is a Bohemian). The Doctor's reported reflections when his patient has left enables the author to take us back in time and reveal other aspects of Rosicky's character (hospitality, generosity etc.). The author's omniscient moralizing by which she presses the point home are unnecessary and somewhat intrusive, here and elsewhere.

The second section returns to the present with Rosicky's response to the Doctor's announcement, and ends with another exemplary incident, that of the creamery agent, again reinforced by the author's comments. The third section introduces the new element of Rosicky's musing on his youth. The story is not allowed to stick fast here, however; in the fourth section we return to the present, and the second theme is developed — the marriage of Rudolph to the American girl. Rosicky's handling of this situation is kind and tactful. Section five returns again to the past, in the old man's reflections and the long story of his Christmas experience in London which is meant to (and indeed does) reconcile the young wife to the hardships of country life; and in Mother Rosicky's cheerful description of her husband's calmness and equanimity in a period of drought, answering to her eldest son's apprehensions of hard times to come, though not quite convincing him. The last section describes his attitude more clearly; "he never worried about what had to be ... they would always pull through somehow." Then the two themes are merged; in spite of the Doctor's warnings he clears thistles from the alfalfa field, whose color wakes childhood memories in him; the ensuing heart attack brings about an affectionate confidence between him and his daughter-in-law. The fact that Polly is pregnant provides the death scene with a balancing prospect of rebirth. The story finishes, as it had begun, with the Doctor's reflections on Rosicky's life and death.

With this manipulation of time and the linking of two plots (the old man's past and the present and future of Rudolph and Polly), the story is more than the 'sketch' it is sometimes represented as being, although it lacks the rich development of a story like "Old Mrs. Harris."

Willa Cather's narrative style is neither poetic (since it lacks rich imagery and metaphor) nor dramatic. It is ruminative, more "summary" than "scene" and depends on the appeal of the characters and their values rather than upon the technique by which these are revealed. "There are certain things her style cannot do. It cannot register wit or amusement or even humor, save rarely; it never rises to passionate indignation; it lacks earthiness ... Dialogue is seldom more than adequate. But within its boundaries it is beautiful writing, liquid to the ear, lucent to the eye ... There are few to whom the adjective "classic" can be more truly applied, for beneath the quick sympathy there is a Roman gravity, a sense of the dignity of life which contemporary fiction has mainly lost." (Howard M. Jones in *Saturday Review*, August 6, 1938.)

1. *In what way does the story resemble and differ from a sermon?*

> Like a sermon the story is meant to convey a moral, which is indicated at the end of section I and experienced as a "message" by Polly in the middle of the last section, VI. There is a tendency to use anecdotes to underline a lesson; in the incident of the creamery agent (end of section II) we even see the text to be illustrated followed immediately by the supporting tale. But there is nothing of a "moralizing" style here, and the story is always kept moving, backwards and forwards in time, and it is dramatized through the interweaving of the two plots — Rosicky's past and the present and future of the newly-married couple.

2. *Compare this story with Hemingway's short stories, e. g. "A Clean, Well-Lighted Place".*

Hemingway's old men lose everything in life except their dignity because they cannot love (Santiago in *The Old Man and the Sea* is of a different kind); they have reached a state of emptiness which does not allow of any development. The prevailing impression is that of "conscious, accepted indifference to everything" (D. H. Lawrence). In their world violence is a natural state of affairs. Compassion is implied and not stated. In this story the opposite is true in each case. With the Rosicky's, "Life had gone well ... because ... they had the same ideas about life," i. e. they had loved life, so life had loved them. Anton Rosicky was "awful fond of his place," he "was so fond of his boys," and Polly observes that he "had a special gift for loving people." He doesn't "like to see nobody lookin' sad." Dishonest and cruel people are "the only things in his experience he had found terrifying and horrible." They had been forced upon him in the big cities, and so he is grateful for the "escape he had had" and is sure "if he could think of [his children] as staying here on the land, he wouldn't have to fear any great unkindness for them." What Rosicky really hoped for his boys was that they could get through the world without ever knowing much about the cruelty of human beings. "'Their mother and me ain't prepared them for that.'"

Both writers adopt a simple style — Cather's simplicity tends to be that of the nursery (she is fond of the word "little"), while Hemingway's tends to be that of the semi-literate adult.

3. *In what various ways does the "frame" of the Doctor function?*

The Doctor's function can be seen in several ways:
a) His warning introduces the perspective of death, accounts for the frequent recollections and sets the time limit for the story from the announcement to the death of Rosicky;
b) He adds his own recollections to those of the Rosicky family, thus lending a wider social perspective to the narrative;
c) He combines country and town on a higher level than Rosicky and Polly do. He is also "a man who had helped to do the work of great cities and had always longed for the open country and had got to it at last."
d) He is the "chorus" figure — he observes from a distance and comments in terms that represent the author's values — cf. esp. the last sentence, "Rosicky's life seemed to him complete and beautiful."

4. *How is Polly "brought ... to herself"?*

At the beginning she is "sensitive about having married a foreigner," as she is generally "afraid of being unusual or conspicuous in any way." She is "stiff and on her guard" with her mother-in-law, easily "irritated" and feeling "a certain suspicion." At first she addresses her father-in-law as "Mr. Rosicky," but when he sends her to the picture show in his kind, reassuring way (section IV), she feels the desire "to drop her head on his shoulder for a second." After he has told her about his life in London, as she had asked him to, Polly suggests that Rudolph's parents be invited for supper on New Year's Eve (section V). And with his heart attack at her home (section VI) the barrier between them finally breaks down, she calls him "Father" and is "awful good to him." She is perplexed by the "sudden feeling that nobody in the world, not her mother, not Rudolph, or anyone, really loved her as much as old Rosicky did." Since she has "that sweetness at her heart" that makes a fine woman, she is able to receive "some direct and untranslatable message" from looking at his hand, which seems to convey all his humanity. "She had never learned so much about life from anything" else, "it brought her to herself."

## 5. *How is death seen in this story?*

To old Rosicky the snow is nice, fine, falling quietly and graciously, covering everything in a light, delicate, mysterious way. "It meant rest for vegetation and men and beasts ..."[1] And to him the graveyard is nice as well, sort of snug and homelike, "and they were all old neighbours in the graveyard, most of them friends; there was nothing to feel awkward or embarrassing about."
In section II it says, "He was awful fond of his place" and "wasn't anxious to leave it." But by section IV he feels, "That kitchen with the shining windows was dear to him; but the sleeping fields and bright stars and the noble darkness were dearer still." He feels part of nature's eternal life and dies happily when Polly affirms that "she's got a baby comin'."

## 6. *Why is section III included?*

It seems to have little relevance to the story since it adds merely to the exposition of the background. But it serves to contrast the cities of London and of New York: "The only part of his youth he didn't like to remember was the two years he had spent in London," whereas about New York "he looked upon that part of his life as very happy." Both were big cities and as such "an unnatural world." But while London merely sustained a hopeless, dreary existence, New York offered opportunities. Here the idea of an immigrant coming to terms with American life is involved. There were two ways open in America to Rosicky: the continuation of his life in London by working as a tailor in New York — or the seizing of the opportunity for an entirely new way of life ("to see the sun rise and set and to plant things and watch them grow."

W. G. C./M. D./J. V. H.

Orvis, Mary, *The Art of Writing Fiction*, New York 1948, pp. 223—224. — Randall, John H., *The Landscape and the Looking Glass*, Boston 1960, pp. 240—246.

---

[1] cf. Robert Frost, "Stopping by Woods on a Snowy Evening," and its interpretations: Combecher, *Deutung englischer Gedichte* II, Frankfurt 1965, pp. 161—164; Haas, *Praxis des neusprachlichen Unterrichts*, 1964, pp. 295—302.

# STEPHEN CRANE

Stephen Crane was born on November 1, 1871, at Newark, New Jersey, the fourteenth and youngest child of a Methodist minister. Though the family had been prominent in New England since colonial days, it slowly declined into poverty after the death of the father in 1880. Unable to afford more than one year of university life, Crane turned to journalism at which he was not very successful because he devoted more space to sense impressions than to factual details. But harsh reality surrounded him in the slums of New York and New Jersey, and he embodied it in the first modern American naturalistic novel, *Maggie: A Girl of the Streets*, which he published at his own expense in 1893. It was a financial failure, but it attracted the attention of Hamlin Garland (who helped Crane to find markets for his sketches) and William Dean Howells (who arranged for the serial publication of his masterpiece, *The Red Badge of Courage*, 1895). This second novel, a pioneer work of American impressionism, was a great success and Crane's financial worries were over, for he came to be in great demand as a special correspondent of various newspapers. *The Red Badge of Courage* is the story of the psychological struggle — the bewilderment, fear, and desperation — of a young Northern soldier during the two-day battle of Chancellorsville in the Civil War. Though Crane had himself never experienced war, his imagination so vividly captured the feelings of a neophyte in battle that *The Red Badge of Courage* remains one of the great war novels in world literature.

As a reporter he traveled to the West and South of the USA, and at the beginning of 1897 left for Cuba to report on the war of independence from Spain. His ship sank, but Crane survived and transformed his experience into a brilliant short story "The Open Boat". Soon afterwards he sailed to Europe to experience the reality of war in Greece, and then settled in England, where he made friends with Joseph Conrad and Henry James. In 1898 he went as a war correspondent to Cuba, but returned to England in the following year. Having ruined his health by the vigor and intensity of his life, he died of tuberculosis at Badenweiler, Germany, in 1900 and was buried in New Jersey.

"Modern American literature," Carl van Doren has declared, "may be said, accurately enough, to have begun with Stephen Crane." He saw life as an "endless battle between man and nature... Man is in the implacable grasp of nature. It has only to tighten slightly, and he is crushed like a bug. His loudest shriek of agony would be as impotent as his final moan to bring help from that fair land that lies, like Heaven, over his head." He can but be brave, but then this is all he is required to do.

# The Open Boat

**Text:** Stephen Crane, *The Open Boat.* Westermann
Stephen Crane, *The Open Boat.* Hueber (not quite complete)
*American Short Stories* II pp. 64—91. Schöningh
*Modern English Short Stories* II pp. 19—32. Hueber (Gottschalk)
(gives the story in a shortened and simplified form)

*The captain, the cook, an oiler and a newspaper correspondent from the wrecked steamer "Commodore" try to reach the Florida coast in a small dinghy. Unnoticed from the shore they have to fight the sea for thirty hours until the boat founders in the surf and they have to employ their last strength to swim ashore. All are saved except the oiler, who dies on the beach.*

The success of *The Red Badge of Courage* had predestined Stephen Crane to become a war correspondent. In November 1896 the *New York Press* sent him to Florida to try to get to the insurrection on Cuba. He joined the crew of a small ship that was to take partisans and arms to Cuba. On the morning of January 2, 1897, the ship sprang a leak and sank. Having reached the Florida shore, Crane wrote a report on the shipwreck which was given nearly the whole front page of the *New York Press* on January 7 (it is reprinted in *American Short Stories* II [Schöningh] pp. 92—103). During the following five weeks he then wrote the short story "The Open Boat", the idea of which had already been conceived at the end of his report.

The subtitle "A tale intended to be after the fact: being the experience of four men from the sunken steamer 'Commodore'" refers to the actual event and seems to exclude any artistic interpretation; but the end of the story, "... they felt that they could then be interpreters" (of the great sea's voice) indicates what it is meant to be. Crane stresses the commonness of the experience, and accordingly avoids the first person narrator. Although it is not the correspondent who tells the story (he is even least prominent in the first two-thirds of the story), his reflections voice the subtleties of their common experience: "No one said that it was so. No one mentioned it." Even the correspondent's reflections on the long-forgotten verse about the dying soldier of the Legion is related to what all four feel: "The men in the dingey had not discussed these matters, but each had, *no doubt*, reflected upon them in silence and according to his mind. There was seldom any expression on their faces save the general one of complete weariness. Speech was devoted to the business of the boat."

From the very first line their situation is characterized by striking observations that mark the first use of the impressionistic technique in American fiction: "None of them knew the color of the sky ... all of the men knew the colors of the sea"; "they knew it was broad day because the color of the sea changed." Their gaze is fixed on the waves, and we see the waves with their eyes; they are not described but experienced, seen from the level of the men in the boat. The enormity of the waves ("slatey wall of water") is contrasted with the small size of the boat ("...a bathtub larger than the boat"; "just a wee thing wallowing, miraculously top-up, at the mercy of five oceans"). But the men experience them as living beings: "The craft pranced and reared, and plunged like an animal... she seemed like a horse making at a fence outrageously high"; "this wild colt of a dingey," "struggled woundily." The waves are "nervously anxious to do something effective in the way of swamping boats;" the seamen hear "the growl" or "the snarling of the crests" and "the roar of the surf."

The struggle, however, is not between boat and waves, but between man and nature. Their lives depend on the oiler's "thin little oar... ready to snap." They fight heroically but are bitterly disappointed within sight of the beach: they only feel "the serenity of nature amid the struggles of the individual," "the unconcern of the universe"; nature is indifferent, the shore is indifferent. In a poem, published a year after the story, Crane expressed the same view:

> A man said to the universe:
> "Sir, I exist!"
> "However," replied the universe,
> "The fact has not created in me
> A sense of obligation."

"When it occurs to a man that nature does not regard him as important... he at first wishes to throw bricks at the temple, and he hates deeply the fact that there are no bricks and no temples." With rage in him he jeers at nature and swears, "Why, in the name of the seven mad gods who rule the sea, was I allowed to come thus far...? If this old ninny-woman, Fate, cannot do better than this, she should be deprived of the management of men's fortunes... The whole affair is absurd." To drown a man who had worked so hard would be "an abominable injustice," "a crime most unnatural," "a shame." This feeling of injustice is expressed from the beginning when the waves are described as "most wrongfully and barbarously abrupt and tall" and "outrageously high." The men feel hostility all around them ("the wrath of the sea"), in the gulls ("uncanny, sinister, gruesome, ominous; ugly brute"), the shark ("the thing"), even in the tourists on the shore ("nature in the vision of men," i. e. they see the boat but remain indifferent).

Swearing is the answer the men find. It is no use to "indulge in pleas, bowed to one knee, and with hands supplicant" — "a high cold star on a winter's night" would be the only answer. Man has to resign and "consider his own death to be the final phenomenon of nature." The absurdity, however, combines "humor, contempt, tragedy, all in one." There is a grim humor in their conversation, particularly that of the narrator, the correspondent: "A singular disadvantage of the sea lies in the fact that after successfully surmounting one wave you discover that there is another behind it just as important..."; "The human back can become the seat of more aches and pains than are registered in books for the composite anatomy of a regiment"; "his teeth played all the popular airs"; "it struck him even then as an event in gymnastics"; and, at the climax of the rescue, "The correspondent, schooled in the minor formulae, said: 'Thanks, old man'." Contempt is repeatedly expressed (s. a.) and is also to be felt in a strange passage in part VII (omitted in the Hueber edition p. 30, following line 3): "It is, perhaps, plausible that a man in this situation, impressed with the unconcern of the universe, should see the innumerable flaws of his life, and have them taste wickedly in his mind, and wish for another chance. A distinction between right and wrong seems absurdly clear to him, then, in this new ignorance of the grave-edge, and he understands that if he were given another opportunity he would mend his conduct and his words, and be better and brighter during an introduction or at a tea." This is a grotesque answer to the absurdity of life, a scornful laughter at the childish conception of right and wrong and parental admonitions. He cannot distinguish between right and wrong, and understands nothing — "in this new ignorance."

It is not only humor and contempt that a man can summon up in the face of the absurdity of life. There is "the ethics of their condition" which determines his bearing and forbids any emotional display. And there is "the subtle brotherhood of men that was here established on the seas." They had become friends, there was a comradeship between them "that the correspondent, who had been taught to be cynical of men, knew even at the time was the best experience of his life." The captain is once "soothing his children," who feel "devotion to the commander" and are the most "ready and swiftly obedient crew." To the correspondent the cook and the oiler huddled together in their sleep "were the babes of the sea, a grotesque rendering of the old babes in the wood." There is tenderness in the way one asks the other to take over the rowing, "with the notes of every reluctance in his voice." When a man finally pulls them out of the water the correspondent sees that "a halo was about his head, and he shone like a saint." In his own calamity the correspondent suddenly feels sorry for the dying soldier of the Legion, and he realizes with compassion the pathos of man's situation.

The correspondent owes the experience of the brotherhood of men to the presence of death. Together they fight for their lives, they cling to life: "Was I brought here merely to have my nose dragged away as I was about to nibble the sacred cheese of life?" But death also takes a new form: "The main thing in his mind for some months[1] had been horror of the temporary agony. He did not wish to be hurt." Now he reflects "that when one gets properly wearied, drowning must really be a comfortable arrangement, a cessation of hostilities accompanied by a large degree of relief." So the "tale intended to be after the fact" leads to a new relation to life and death and the brotherhood of men. Dying to him "was no longer merely a picture of a few throes in the breast of a poet, meanwhile drinking tea and warming his feet at the grate; it was an actuality — stern, mournful, and fine."

---

[1] The Schöningh edition wrongly puts "moments" instead of "months."

Stylistically, the greatness of the story lies in its technique of offering a strong illusion of reality, a direct impression of life, and, at the same time, using the naturalistic detail in a symbolic way (the dinghy, the oar, the abandoned life-saving station, the gulls and sharks) and projecting the whole experience on the background of human existence. "The correspondent, face to face with death, attains heroic stature ... He can speak for more than himself; he can speak for all men ... in a way he has experienced death in the death of his brother and comrade, the oiler; and he can speak for death, too, having become brother to its servant, the sea" (Gordon/Tate).

1. *Who is the narrator and what is his relationship to the characters?*

   Although the story is told in the third person, the subtitle ("A Tale Intended to be after the Fact") suggests that it is the retrospective narration of the correspondent. He has, however, so completely identified himself with the brotherhood of the four who endured the harrowing experience of thirty hours in a small dinghy tossed and battered by a stormy sea that a narrowly autobiographical approach would have the effect of isolating him from the others. Hence, the community of the four men is stressed throughout.

2. *How much "distance" from the events is maintained?*

   The "camera" remains mostly within the boat, occasionally moving slightly off, frequently focusing on a specific detail. The narrative "camera" is maintained fairly steadily at the eye level of the correspondent. The vision of the others is narrated indirectly ("The captain ... *said* that he had seen the lighthouse at Mosquito Inlet"), but that of the correspondent is told directly ("... his eyes chanced on a small still thing on the edge of the swaying horizon"). The feelings and reflections of the others are given in general terms or in dialogue, but those of the correspondent, which dominate the narrative, are again directly told: "he reflected immediately that it was colder than he had expected to find it off the coast of Florida" ... "The correspondent knew that it was a long journey," etc. Occasionally there are details which the correspondent could not have directly observed during the action: "there was not a life-saving station within twenty miles in either direction; but the men did not know this fact" and "neither [the oiler nor the correspondent] knew they had bequeathed to the cook the company of another shark, or perhaps the same shark." But since the tale is told "after the fact," credibility is not violated.

3. *Crane has been called an "impressionist"; what impressionistic elements can be found in "The Open Boat"?*

   The first paragraph refers to the colors of sky and sea, and the story concludes with the white waves in the moonlight. The course of time is reflected on the water in the change of color "from slate to emerald-green streaked with amber lights"; "carmine and gold was painted upon the waters"; "the sunlight flamed on the tips of the waves."
   The color of the sky along the horizon is noticed: "the grays of dawn"; "a squall, marked by dingy clouds, and clouds brick-red, appeared from the south-east";

"a faint yellow tone came into the sky over the low land"; "the streaked saffron in the west passed before the all-merging darkness."

The lighthouse is "the point of a pin" at first, then assumes color as a "little gray shadow on the sky" until it rears high and lifts "its little gray length." The coast is seen as a "long black shadow" first, thinner than paper, then "from a black line it became a line of black and a line of white — trees and sand." Gray faces, slatey water with foam "like tumbling snow" or "white flames," and now and then a patch of brown seaweed, create an atmosphere of bleakness with a few contrasting splashes in it. Occasional absurd details reinforce the philosophical significance of the story: "following them went the water jar, bouncing gaily over the seas."

4. *Are there any significant differences among the four men in their attitude toward their plight? Is one any more optimistic or pessimistic than the other?*

The injured captain is first introduced as in a state of "profound dejection and indifference"; but his first words are, "Keep'er a little more south, Billie," and throughout the story he keeps his head and maintains the respect of the men whom he commands. It is he who initiates the exchange of addresses so that if anyone should not survive word can be sent to the proper place. Of the four, he maintains the steadiest calm, never becomes excited, never swears, never says a word more than is necessary to a given situation.

The cook is the most talkative, tending to be optimistic. It is the cook who is sure that there is a "house of refuge just north of the Mosquito Inlet Light, and as soon as they see us they'll come off in their boat and pick us up," and he who observes that "Bully good thing it's an on-shore wind."

The oiler is the most laconic, merely echoing commands, responding to requests, and occasionally making factual comments on their situation: "she won't live three minutes more, and we're too far out to swim." His death is foreshadowed when it is said that his oar was so thin that "it seemed often ready to snap."

The correspondent meditates the most and is the philosophical spokesman for the group.

But these differences tend to be blurred and lost by the fact that much of the dialogue and even some of the speculations are anonymous, reflecting the attitudes of the group as a single entity. They are all one unit, prisoners of the same absurd fate. This point is further reinforced by the fact that only the oiler "Billy" is referred to by name; they are the captain, the cook, the oiler, the correspondent — hence, they tend to lose their individuality, as if a n y captain, cook, etc. would serve.

Notice, too, that the isolation of these four in a constrained situation does not result in the uniqueness and separateness of each asserting itself, as in many modern works (e. g. Sartre's *Huis-clos*). Nor do we observe the heroism of a single man asserting himself against the sea, as in Hemingway's parable. The fate endured by Crane's characters is the collective fate of all men involved in Nature.

5. *How is Nature seen in this story?*

It is totally indifferent to the struggles of the individual, therefore without any justice. Its indifference is experienced as hostility, most viciously embodied in the shark, which is simply "the thing". The "glowing trail" und "bluish light" give it an ominousness far surpassing the "black bead-like eyes" of the gulls. To the oiler, the gulls look as if they "were made with a jack-knife"; the image of the knife is taken up again in connection with the shark: the threatening trail furrowed on the black waters "might have been made by a monstrous knife" — which is pointed at them. The "desire to confront a personification" induces the idea of Fate, but she is seen as an "old ninny-woman," "an old hen who knows not her intention"; god is only mentioned in swearing, the full absurdity of the whole affair is attributed to "the seven mad gods who rule the sea." The experience of nature is reduced to the all-important experience of the sea, and the experience of the sea means the experience of death; thus nature and fate and gods who rule the sea are used synonymously.

6. *How can man react to this experience of nature?*

Praying and promising amendment is senseless. He can stick to the ethics of his condition, i. e. be too proud to betray any emotion; he can use understatement, and can swear, and can laugh and jeer. The correspondent, in the presence of the shark, "did not wish to be alone. He wished one of his companions to awaken by chance and keep him company with it." So this is what is left to him: to establish "the subtle brotherhood of men," to make friends, to be a good comrade — offering him "the best experience of his life."

M. D.

Adams, Richard P., Naturalistic Fiction: The Open Boat, *Tulane Studies in English* IV, 1954, pp. 137—146 — Buitenhuis, Peter, The Essentials of Life: "The Open Boat" as Existentialist Fiction, *Modern Fiction Studies* V, 1959, pp. 243—250 — Day, Cyrus, Stephen Crane and the Ten-foot Dinghy, *Boston University Studies in English* III, 1957, pp. 193—213 — Gordon and Tate, *The House of Fiction*, New York 1954, pp. 308—312 — Marcus, Mordecai, The Three-fold View of Nature in "The Open Boat", *Philological Quarterly*, XLI, 1962, pp. 511—515 — Metzger, Charles, Realistic Devices in Stephen Crane's "The Open Boat", *Midwest Quarterly*, IV, 1962, pp. 47—54 — Oppel, Horst, Crane, "The Open Boat", in Göller/Hoffmann, *Die amerikanische Kurzgeschichte*, Düsseldorf 1972, pp. 191—204.

# WILLIAM FAULKNER

William Faulkner was born on September 25, 1897, at New Albany, Mississippi, to a family with deep roots in the American South. He was a poor student and a swaggering dandy, known to the community as "Count No-Count". During World War I, after being rejected for service in the American forces, he enlisted in the Royal Canadian Air Force, but was severely injured in a plane crash before he could see action. A restless veteran, he failed his courses at the University of Mississippi, tried a variety of menial jobs, and went on a walking tour of Italy, France and Germany. His first novel, *Soldier's Pay* (1926), inspired by the example of Sherwood Anderson and published with his help, received mixed reviews. It was just another "lost generation" novel. After another failure, *Mosquitoes* (1927), a treatment of Bohemian life in New Orleans, he took the advice of his life-long friend, Phil Stone, and wrote from the heart, producing *Sartoris* (1929), the beginning of the great Yoknapatawpha saga of the South. Except for brief sojourns to Hollywood and New York to produce scripts (which he did not regard as his own work), trips to Japan and Italy on behalf of the U. S. State Department, and to Stockholm to receive the Nobel Prize in 1950, he remained at home in an ancient plantation house in Oxford, Mississippi. He referred to himself as a farmer who writes "on the side", but he was in fact one of the most prolific of American writers, producing 31 volumes after the publication of his juvenilia, *The Marble Faun* (poems, 1924). Among the great tragedies are *The Sound and the Fury* (1929), *As I Lay Dying* (1930), *Light in August* (1932), and *Absalom! Absalom!* (1936), which show "the human heart in conflict with itself," — the only subject, as he said in his Nobel Prize address, worth "the agony and sweat" of the artist. He died in 1963.

R. P. Warren once wrote about Faulkner's books that "for range of effects, philosophical weight, originality of style, variety of characterization, humor, and tragic intensity," they "are without equal in our time and country." But he also found grave defects in Faulkner's work. "Sometimes the tragic intensity becomes mere emotionalism, the technical virtuosity mere complication, the philosophical weight mere confusion of mind." But "the unevenness is, in a way, an index to his vitality, his willingness to take risks, to try for new effects, to make new explorations of material and method." Another critic has said of Faulkner's style that it resembles that of the last quartets of Beethoven in the way in which "qualifying clauses are in turn qualified by further qualifying clauses... his style is an attempt to impose just the minimum form necessary to hold the chaos and flux of life" (cf. *Jahrbuch für Amerikastudien* IV [1959] pp. 170—179). Faulkner felt that "the writer's got to be demon-ridden to have the demon drive to express the breadth, beauty, injustice, and compassion of life," and consequently his style is one which, no doubt, baffles the untrained reader but is a source of brilliant insights and cognitive joy for those who learn how to read it.

## A Rose for Emily

Text: *American Short Stories* IV pp. 104—115. Schöningh

*At the occasion of Miss Emily Grierson's death the narrator reviews her life in Jefferson. Her father was an aristocratic man with a great sense of dignity, who did not approve of any young suitor for his daughter. When he died he left his daughter alone in an old house, with only a negro man to attend to her. In the following summer she had an affair with the foreman of a construction company, but the expected marriage never took place. From then on she never left the house, refused to take any part in local affairs and, after a few years of giving lessons in china painting, did not even admit any visitors. She became something like a monument, "like the carven torso of an idol in a niche" to the village people. Then, at the age of 74, she died. People entered her house full of curiosity and in a closed room they found the corpse of the young foreman, whom Miss Emily had poisoned with arsenic forty years earlier.*

Although "A Rose for Emily" was the first of some 75 short stories that Faulkner has published (it appeared in *The Forum,* April 1930, before being collected in *These Thirteen,* 1931) critics still refer to it as "the most famous of them all" (Millgate, p. 62) and as "among the very greatest written in our time" (Waggoner, l. c., p. 194). Like most of Faulkner's fiction, it is based on real-life events which occurred in Lafayette County — especially on the much-discussed marriage of Miss Mary Louise Neilson, a Southern aristocratic lady, with a Captain Jack Hume, the Yankee foreman of a construction company that paved the streets of Oxford in the 1920's; and on the grotesque episode of a crazy woman, Mag Hellrod, who drove public officials off her property at the point of a gun and allowed the dead body of her son to lie in bed for more than a week until it stank so badly that the untertaker had to drink a pint of whiskey before he could bring himself to bury it (see John B. Cullen, *Old Times in the Faulkner Country*). The latter episode also serves as a basis for *As I Lay Dying,* a novel published in the same year as "A Rose for Emily." However, sources do not explain fiction, — even if they do serve to acquit the author from the charge of having a diseased imagination, and the critical history of this story provides ample evidence that "A Rose for Emily" does need explanation.

Perhaps we can achieve the clearest understanding by funding the interpretations of previous critics, confirming accurate observations whenever they are supported by the text, discarding others that are not supported by textual evidence, and modifying others which may be accurate but not very important in the over-all structure or pattern of the work. When *These Thirteen* was first published, it was reviewed by the eminent critic, Lionel Trilling, who described it as "the story of a woman who has killed her lover and lain for years beside his decaying corpse." (*Nation,* Nov. 4, 1931, p. 492.) Such was Faulkner's reputation as a writer of horrifying, sadistic, and morbid shockers that this interpretation went unchallenged for many years. It was most ably refuted by Ray B. West, Jr. (l. c.), who says that "the final violence does not appear too shocking or horrible" because it culminates a gradually developing mood of mystery, foreboding, and decay and because it is ultimately subservient to the larger philosophical issue of the passage of time:

> There are, we are told, two views of time: (1) the world of the present, viewing time as a mechanical progression in which the past is a diminishing road, never to be encountered again; (2) the world of tradition, viewing the past as a huge meadow which no winter ever quite touches, divided from (us) now by the narrow bottleneck of the most recent decade of years. The

first is the view of Homer Barron and the modern generation in Jefferson. The second is the view of the older members of the Board of Aldermen and of the confederate soldiers. Emily holds the second view, except that for her there is no bottleneck dividing her from the past. (p. 243)

West further observes that both views are essentially wrong because the whole man comes to terms with both the past and the present, but those that adhere to the past are especially doomed to tragedy. He finds Emily Grierson to be a heroic, tragic figure with the conventional flaw of hybris in undertaking to regulate the natural time-universe. So preoccupied is Professor West with this large, abstract theme that he never even faces the question of Emily Grierson's possible necrophilia; for him Emily is a fallen monument of the past more than she is a madwoman.

William van O'Connor (l. c., pp. 68—69) sternly protests against this view, insisting that "the Old South and the new order are... *not* the poles of conflict. The theme is that a denial of normal emotions invites retreat into a marginal world, into fantasy. The severity of Miss Emily's father was the cause of her frustrations and her retreat... The story is simple enough when read as an account of Miss Emily's becoming mad."

Not so, say Cleanth Brooks and Robert Penn Warren (l. c.); "it is very easy to misread the story as merely a horrible case history (of abnormal psychology), presented in order to titillate the reader... Her madness is simply a development of her pride and her refusal to submit to ordinary standards of behavior." And though they do not take up West's theme of the past versus the present, Brooks and Warren do restore the reading of the story as a tragedy of a woman who "carried her own values to their ultimate conclusion."

But Floyd C. Watkins (l. c.), in the neatest structural analysis of the story to appear thus far, buttresses the theme of the past versus the present. He observes that the central event in each of the five sections of the story is an intrusion of the present into Miss Emily's isolation: I, the Aldermen enter in a futile effort to collect the taxes; II, the townsmen furtively break in to sprinkle lime against a terrible odor; and earlier to insist on the burial of Miss Emily's father, whose death she refuses to acknowledge; III, no outsiders enter Miss Emily's home — "her triumph in this part is when she buys the arsenic without telling what she plans to use it for"; IV, the Baptist minister and the relatives from Alabama come to interfere with her affair with Homer Barron; and V, the entire town comes to Miss Emily's funeral and later break into the upstairs room. This symmetrical pattern, according to Professor Watkins, reveals that "at the center of the story is the indomitableness of the decadent Southern aristocrat, and the enclosing parts reveal the invasion of the aristocracy by the changing order." The madness motif is not cited.

In a very significant comment on the story, Elmo Howell (*Explicator*, XIX [Jan., 1961], item 26) restores the dignity of tragedy as the essential characteristic of Emily Grierson's experience by eliminating the grotesque horror of necrophilia: "... there is no evidence in the story that she lay in the bed with Homer Barron after the night she murdered him." He offers four arguments in support of this reading: (1) the text specifically says that no one had seen the upstairs room in forty years, (2) when it is broken open the room is filled with pervading dust, (3) the strand of gray hair on the pillow may be explained by the assumption that her hair was already graying during the affair with Homer Barron, and (4) such a reading conflicts with the spirit of Faulkner's own comments on the story. The first three of these arguments can easily be refuted: (1) since the story is told from the point of view of a resident of the town who is no intimate of Miss Emily, the remark that no one had seen the upstairs room in forty years must mean that no *outsider* had seen it. The narrator is not privy to the secrets within the house; (2) dust in the Grierson house is by no means limited to the upstairs room — when the deputation called upon Miss Emily to collect the taxes, the entire house "smelled of dust and disuse... when they sat down, a faint dust rose sluggishly;" (3) the text is quite specific about the fact that Emily's hair turned gray only *after* the affair with Homer Barron was over. After the death of her father two years before she met Homer Barron, "she was sick for a long time," says the narrator — and then immediately tells, "When we saw her again, her hair was cut short, making her look like a girl..." However, the first appearance of Emily, six months after the disappearance of Homer Barron, reveals that "she had grown fat and her hair was turning gray." Of course, none of this necessarily means that Emily actually slept with a corpse, but it does mean that the long strand of iron-gray hair which was found on the pillow next to the corpse was placed there quite some time after Homer Barron's death. A satisfactory interpretation of this mysterious detail, which Faulkner placed in such an effective position, must be based on the assumption that Emily consciously placed the strand of hair on the pillow where her head had lain, presumably on the day when she locked the room for good. Though to some readers "a strand of hair" conveys the idea of "a single hair," the context makes it necessary that we read "a lock of hair." A single hair could never be discerned under a 30 years' layer of dust.

The act of cutting off one's hair (or locks of it) was a familiar gesture of grief and farewell or remembrance at the corpse or grave of a beloved person among the ancient Greeks: when Achilles mourns his dead friend Patroclus (*Iliad* XXIII), he and the other Greek warriors cover the corpse with locks of hair; in *Odyssey* IV Peisistratus mentions the custom of cutting one's hair in honor of a dead relative; in Euripides' tragedy *Electra* Orestes mourns his father by placing a lock of hair on his grave; Medea leaves a lock for her mother when she elopes with Jason; many similar passages could be found. Faulkner never affirmed his reference to a Greek custom in this story, but he did so in other places; e. g. in discussing Sam Father's death in *The Bear*, Faulkner himself has referred to the Greek conception of the master ordering his servant to kill him when he feels his life is finished (cf. Gwynn-Blotner, *Faulkner in the University*, Charlottesville 1959, under March 11, 1957). Emily Grierson, as a member of a Southern aristocratic family, can be expected to have read Homer and other classics, so her gesture can be seen as a conscious demonstration of grief and farewell. Is it merely coincidence that her lover is called Homer? Her name, too, is of classic origin (Latin Aemilius). Seen in this way, the conclusive detail of the strand of hair on the pillow beside the corpse becomes, whether consciously intended by Emily or not, a powerful symbol of Emily's rootedness in tradition.

The narrative moves relentlessly toward a shocking revelation in a magnificently structured shuttling back and forth in time. The shock does not negate the moral; Emily has assumed the proportions of a tragic figure strangely pathetic in her desperate passion and refusal to face reality.

The tragedy that Faulkner describes does, of course, involve the passing of time and the concomitant changing of customs. Thus, time in "A Rose for Emily" is significant as (1) cultural history, (2) personal experience, and (3) aesthetic technique.

Some amplification of Professor Watkin's analysis of the five-part structure of the story is also in order. Not only does each section, except the center, show some intrusion of the present upon the privacy of Miss Emily, but also, each section except the center ends with some reference to death — the first two as denials of its force and the second two as undeniable, implacable facts. Part I ends with Miss Emily refusing to pay her taxes because Colonel Sartoris had remitted her taxes "into perpetuity." "'See Colonel Sartoris,'" says Miss Emily, and the narrator adds in parenthesis, "Colonel Sartoris had been dead almost ten years." Part II ends with Emily refusing to acknowledge the death of her father, but submitting to his burial when the townspeople are about to resort to law and force. ". . . we knew that with nothing left, she would have to cling to that which had robbed her, as people will." This not only foreshadows her clinging to Homer Barron, who had robbed her of her dignity and had refused to marry her, but the last phrase indicates that in the view of the narrator what Miss Emily does is what "people will" do — though there may be an element of the grotesque in the way that she does it. Part III ends not with a direct reference to death, but to the purchase of arsenic "for rats." In its structural position as well as in its logical implication, the phrase is obviously an indirect reference to death. Part IV ends with Miss Emily's death, and Part V with the discovery of the death of Homer Barron. Since each section of the story moves toward a climax in death, the structural pattern obviously does not control the focus of our attention simply to the intrusions of the present upon the privacy of the past. Rather, it heightens the element of horror that is undeniable at the heart of the story.

But, of course, neither horror nor a conflict between old and new codes is incompatible with tragedy. The ending of "A Rose for Emily" clearly out-does the Jacobean dramatists and Poe in its Gothicism and its Liebestod melodrama. What could be more morbid than the description of the corpse of Homer Barron, "rotted beneath what was left of the nightshirt?" And the single-sentence paragraph, no matter how skillfully it has been foreshadowed, is obviously intended to come as a shock: "The man himself lay in the bed." But it is only the penultimate shock. The story might have ended there, but it doesn't. The final shock of the discovery of the strand of iron-gray hair reveals the motive for the crime; Emily Grierson, a lady of the old Southern aristocracy and at heart a sentimentalist, profoundly insulted by a man who had betrayed her, living no longer in a community in which a gentleman of the old code would revenge her honor for her, is compelled to do the deed herself. Yet she would gladly have abandoned the old code, with the approval of the rest of the town who have also abandoned it: "we said, 'They are married.' We were glad because the two female cousins [who came to prevent the marriage] were even more Grierson than Miss Emily had ever been."

But the crude Homer Barron, "with his hat cocked and a cigar in his teeth, reins and whip in a yellow glove," was not a sufficient source of vitality to make the transition to a new life possible. Nor was the old way of life, with its sterile courtesy and gentility, a sufficient source of vitality. Its most significant symbol is neither Colonel Sartoris nor Judge Stevens, who make their practical adjustments to necessity, but old Mr. Grierson himself:

> "We had long thought of them as a tableau, Miss Emily a slender figure in white in the background, her father a spraddled silhouette in the foreground, his back to her and clutching a horsewhip, the two of them framed by the back-flung front door."

> "People in our town . . . believed that the Griersons held themselves a little too high for what they really were. None of the young men were quite good enough for Miss Emily . . ."

Thus neither the past (her father) nor the present (Homer Barron) offered any genuine possibility for a full, rich life; under the stress of her powerful urge for that life so completely thwarted, she succumbed to the strain of madness that apparently ran in her family ("old lady Wyatt, her great-aunt, had gone completely crazy at last"). Whether or not that madness resulted in necrophilia as well as murder is difficult to determine exactly. Helen Nebeker has observed that the disappearance of the smell "after a week or two" cannot be ascribed to the townsmen sprinkling lime, as they never came near the rotting corpse, the source of the smell. She suggests "that almost immediately after the smell was reported and before gossip could really arise . . . somebody . . . had sealed that upstairs room," which "was somewhat customary practice in cases of contagious disease where death had occurred." This, of course, still leaves several days for Emily to cling to the corpse as she had done to her father's body "for three days". In any case, the woman who in the public eye remained upright as a community monument, "an idol in a niche," but who, in private, collapsed into a macabre ghoul, is a tragic figure. Faulkner said of her:

> I feel sorry for Emily's tragedy; her tragedy was, she was an only child, an only daughter. At first when she could have found a husband, could have had a life of her own, there was probably some one, her father, who said, "No, you must stay here and take care of me." And then when she found a man, she had had no experience in people. She picked out probably a bad

one, who was about to desert her. And when she lost him she could see that for her that was the end of life, there was nothing left, except to grow older, alone, solitary; she had had something and she wanted to keep it, which is bad — to go to any length to keep something; but I pity Emily. I don't know whether I would have liked her or not, I might have been afraid of her. Not of her, but of anyone who had suffered, had been warped, as her life had been probably warped by a selfish father...

[The title] was an allegorical title; the meaning was, here was a woman who had had a tragedy, an irrevocable tragedy and nothing could be done about it, and I pitied her and this was a salute ... to a woman you would hand a rose. (*Faulkner at Nagano*, ed. Rob. Jelliffe, Tokyo 1956, pp. 70—71.)

1. *Discuss the title of this story.*

On the one hand the title can be construed as a tribute to the main character, for whom Faulkner (and, to a certain extent, the other inhabitants of Jefferson) is able to show sympathy and psychological understanding. On the other hand the "rose" may be an ironical reference to the corpse that for a time was the source of the smell observed by the townsfolk. Notice the reference to "rose" curtains and "rose-shaded" lights in the room where the corpse is finally discovered.

2. *Faulkner has been described as a "Gothic" writer. What does this mean?*

The original "Gothic" writers produced novels of horror and mystery at the beginning of the 19th century. The doom-laden atmosphere that they clumsily created was developed in the nightmare stories of Poe and Hawthorne. Faulkner belongs to the same tradition, but is far more subtle in that he relates the doom of atmosphere to the psychological state of his characters (as here Miss Emily's actions can be partly accounted for by her father's treatment of her).

3. *What is the importance of the view-point of the narrator in this story?*

The author writes as if he himself were a townsman of his own Jefferson, thus achieving an effect of intimate knowledge that convinces the reader and, at the same time, adding a gossipy, humorous strain that, in contrast to the dreadfulness of the happenings, enhances the grotesque effect he is aiming at. As one somewhat removed from the main happenings, however, the narrator can show understanding for Emily's difficult circumstances and can analyse with detachment the psychological and other forces driving her.

4. *How does Faulkner manipulate time in this story?*

The story moves with deceptive casualness from one incident to another. It starts with the funeral, moves abruptly back to 1894, then forward again to "the next generation," back thirty years again to the incident of the smell, back another two years to the father's death, forward again one year to the beginning of the affair with Homer Barron and so on back to the starting point of the funeral. With this apparently haphazard arrangement Faulkner is able, first to give an impression of Miss Emily's background and then to allow the story to progress into gradually increasing horror.

5. *Faulkner has been praised for his psychological insight. Does he show this quality in the short story under review?*

The incident where Emily refuses at first to give up her father's dead body that is lying in the house is followed by a sympathetic explanation for Emily's strange behavior in her relationship for her father, previously summed up in the form of a melodramatic tableau. The horrors of the story are thus related to the darkness of the sub-conscious mind. Miss Emily acts under the compulsion of dark forces that are uncontrollable, hence the tolerance and understanding displayed by the author when she buys poison. The author speaks, in fact, in two voices; sometimes like a spectator from among the townspeople ("We were a little disappointed that there was not a public blowing-off") and sometimes with keen penetration, using more formal language ("as if it had wanted that touch of earthiness to reaffirm her imperviousness").

6. *What do we learn about the Southern States of the USA from this story?*

It is evident that Miss Emily is, in Faulkner's view, a manifestation of the old Southern form of society. The character of Colonel Sartoris, and of his time and place, is summed up in the fact that he grants Miss Emily, as a member of the aristocracy, exemption from taxation and in the brief aside "he who fathered the edict that no Negro woman should appear on the streets without an apron" — evidence of the Southern aristocratic high-handed treatment of the Negroes, who, after the Civil War, were, nominally at least, no longer slaves. The North American ("Yankee"), Emily's lover, with the vulgar-sounding name, distinguishes himself from his surroundings by his energy and noise. But the new age is not without its effect on the South. The generation that is in authority after Colonel Sartoris wish to collect their taxes — though it is true that they have not sufficient modern ruthlessness and drive to succeed here. At the beginning of the story, Miss Emily's house is pictured "lifting its stubborn and coquettish decay" among "gasoline pumps" of a new age.

7. *Does Faulkner see Miss Emily's life on a definite historical background?*

Yes. Like most of Faulkner's novels and stories it is part of the Yoknapatawpha saga, in which Colonel Sartoris is one of the major figures. Although only one date is given in this story, we can reconstruct the course of Miss Emily's life approximately. In 1894 Colonel Sartoris remitted her taxes (p. 105, Schöningh ed.). This date is later (p. 113) connected with Miss Emily's china-painting lessons: "Meanwhile her taxes had been remitted." As "she was about forty" then, she must have been born about 1854. The death of her father occurred after she had "got to be thirty and was still single" (p. 108), that is about 1885. The episode with the smell "was two years after her father's death and a short time after her sweetheart ... had deserted her." (p. 106), which places these events in 1887. Thirty years later the deputation of Aldermen came to her house, that is in 1917, an appropriate year for regaining tax revenues, for the U. S. entered World War I in 1917. — She died "at seventy-four," in 1928. — The story was published in 1930.

Tabulation of chronology:
| | |
|---|---|
| 1854 | birth of Emily |
| 1870's | building of the Grierson house |
| 1885 | death of Emily's father |
| 1887 | complaint about the smell = death of Homer |
| 1894 | remission of taxes by Colonel Sartoris |
| 1895—1902 | china-painting lessons given by Emily |
| 1907 | death of Colonel Sartoris |
| 1917 | visit of the deputation of aldermen |
| 1928 | death of Emily |

The only time reference not fitting into this tabulation is on page 105, "she ceased giving china-painting lessons eight or ten years earlier," i. e. before the deputation of aldermen came; but there is a difference of fifteen years between these events.

J. V. H./W. G. C./M. D.

Happel, Nikolaus, William Faulkner's "A Rose for Emily", *Die Neueren Sprachen*, 1962, pp. 396—404 — Inge, M. Thomas, *William Faulkner, A Rose for Emily* (Reprints of all criticism up to 1969), Columbus, Ohio, 1970 — Nebeker, Helen, Chronology Revised, *Studies in Short Fiction* VIII, 1971, pp. 471—473.

## That Evening Sun

Text: Faulkner, *Four Stories* pp. 69—89. Schöningh

*At the age of 24, Quentin Compson remembers a childhood episode in Jefferson, when he was nine, his sister Caddy (Candace) seven, and his brother Jason five. When his family's negro cook Dilsey falls ill, their negro laundress Nancy is called to help out. Since she is pregnant with the child of a white man, her negro husband Jesus threatens and then deserts her. Nancy is afraid he will come back and kill her, and clings to the Compson family for protection; but Mrs. Compson does not like to have her sleep in the house. The children experience the climax of her terror when, finding a sign that her husband has returned, she takes them to her cabin as a shield against his revenge. When Mr. Compson takes the children home again, leaving her alone in her cabin, she resigns herself to her fate.*

*The information about the Compson children given in several other works of Faulkner indicates that this episode is supposed to have taken place in 1902. For the real-life basis of the story, see John B. Cullen, Old Times in the Faulkner Country (Univ. of No. Carolina Press, 1961), pp. 72—73.*

Faulkner's "That Evening Sun" (1931) embodies the feeling quality of terror and impending violence more effectively than any other American short story (including Hemingway's "The Killers" and James' "Turn of the Screw"). It is a masterpiece of its genre. The terror is not at all concealed — in fact, it is heightened — for being presented from the point of view of an incomprehending nine-year-old boy and his younger brother and sister; and for the same reason it is almost purified of the racial and sexual forces that produce it. Nevertheless, for the reader who seeks not simply a vicarious emotional thrill, but insight and understanding of complex human situations that cause terror, a close reading of this story is immensely rewarding.

As the narrator, Quentin Compson, a sensitive, poetic young man, observes his home town of Jefferson, Mississippi, his meditations are rendered in highly sophisticated figures of speech: "the soiled wearing of a whole week now flees apparitionlike behind alert and irritable electric horns." Monday, laundry day, was different when he was a boy, fifteen years earlier; he recalls how Nancy, the Negro laundress, carried a huge bundle of clothes on her head with grace and balance. But he also recalls how Nancy's husband, Jesus, caused her to lose all grace and balance and to collapse into utter terror. As he tells us that story he lapses into the limited point of view and the simple language of himself as a nine-year-old boy; almost everything is told in monosyllables: "I stayed quiet, because Father and I both knew that Mother would want him to make me stay with her if she just thought of it in time." And he shifts from the generalizing verb form ("Nancy would set her bundle...") to the simple past tense ("Nancy said...").

First comes the exposition in which the background of the specific experience of terror is established in four swiftly sketched episodes: (1) Whenever Dilsey, the Compson cook and housekeeper, was ill, the children were sent to summon Nancy to take her place. Afraid of Nancy's husband Jesus ("a short black man with a razor scar down his face" — the first symbol of violence), the children refused to cross the ditch to her shack, but threw stones to arouse her attention. She was frequently in no spirit to come, a fact which the children — having no knowledge of sexuality and prostitution — attribute to whiskey hangovers. (2) But the real cause of her fatigue is implied when Nancy publicly accosts Mr. Stovall, the cashier in the bank and deacon in the Baptist church, with demands for payment for the last "three times," an obvious reference to her services as a prostitute. The violence of Mr. Stovall's response foreshadows the greater violence to come. Of course, because the episode is told from the point of view of a Southern white boy, no mention is made of the hypocrisy and injustice of the white man's treatment of the Negro and of the Negro's helplessness, the futility of any retaliation; but these ideas are dramatically established and are extremely important to the narrative to follow. (3) Nancy — and not Mr. Stovall — is jailed. Once again she is the victim of violence when the jailer beats her for attempting to hang herself. The attempt failed because her instinctive will to live was stronger than her will to die ("she didn't have anything to tie her hands with and she couldn't make her hands let go of the window ledge"). (4) Nancy, at work in the Compson kitchen, engages in an angry dialogue with Jesus, from which three significant facts emerge — Nancy is pregnant, probably by Mr. Stovall ("[This watermelon] never come off your vine"); Jesus is furious enough to commit violence ("I can cut down the vine it did come off of!"); the children who witness this strange adult behavior are puzzled ("Off of what vine?").

51

After this swiftly sketched introduction, the remainder of the story is devoted to the gradually intensifying terror of Nancy, who intuits that her husband (who had left her upon learning of her pregnancy) has returned from Memphis to kill her: "I can feel him," she says. In a magnificent, complex, sustained single line of movement Faulkner leads Nancy to a mental and emotional collapse. At first she refuses to accept responsibility for her situation ("I ain't nothing but a nigger. It ain't none of my fault") and feels that proper precautions can save her from Jesus's retribution ("If I can just get through the lane, I'll be all right then"). Jason Compson, the father, is the only one who has any real understanding and sympathy for her plight, and he tries to help her despite the whining protests of his neurotic, self-centered wife ("You'll leave me alone to take Nancy home? Is her safety more precious to you than mine?"). Mr. Compson attempts to reassure Nancy with a remark that Jesus is probably in St. Louis with another wife, and Nancy's response — "I'd cut his head off and I'd slit her belly..." — makes it clear that the punishment to be meted out to her is one which she implicitly approves. Counterpointed against the adult conversation concerning Nancy's fear is the children's dialogue: "Nancy's scaired of the dark"... "This is where Jason got scaired on Hallowe'en"... "I wasn't scaired."

In Part II, Nancy's fears become so great that she remains in the Compson house at night, sleeping on a pallet in the kitchen. But her keening rouses the family and she is permitted to sleep in the children's room, another gesture of kindness by Mr. Compson. Her eyes so widen with fear that the children see the large white orbs in the dark — the first of a sequence of physiological manifestations of terror that include tremors, muscle constrictions, and finally uncontrollable perspiration. She prays fervently ("It's the other Jesus she means," I said), but still denies her own responsibility ("I ain't nothing but a nigger"). And the counterpoint of the children's dialogue continues to play against the awful adult situation: "Jesus is a nigger," Jason said... "I ain't a nigger. Are you a nigger, Nancy?"

Part III presents a crisis when Dilsey returns to work and Nancy is dismissed to go home. She pleads for permission to stay, but "Mother said, 'I can't have Negroes sleeping in the bedrooms'." In desperation Nancy induces the children to accompany her and in the dark lane pretends to be talking to Mr. Compson so that Jesus, who may be lurking in the ditch, will not attack. Once in her house she bars the door and seeks for ways to entertain the children so that they will not leave her alone; but her mind is much too preoccupied with the danger outdoors, and she garbles her story-telling with projections of her fears: "And so this here queen come walking up to the ditch, where that bad man was hiding."

In Part IV the intensity of Nancy's terror reaches its peak. The bored children want to go home, but Nancy desperately tries to think of another story. Her concentration is so great that she does not notice her hand burning against the kerosene lamp. She offers to pop corn, and the small crises seem immense when first the popper needs mending and then she burns the seeds in the fire.

The little violence in the popper equals the greater violence that threatens Nancy, just as the children's petty quarrels are an analogue of the powerful adult strife around them. When footsteps are heard approaching the house, Nancy begins her keening and "all of a sudden water began to come out on her face in big drops, running down her face, carrying in each one a little turning ball of firelight like a spark until it dropped off her chin." The footsteps turn out to be those of Mr. Compson. Nancy collapses into hysterical, impassioned pleas for the protective company of the whites, while the boy Jason whines, "I didn't have any fun."

In Part V, Nancy's terror reaches its climax and resolution. Her awareness of Jesus's presence is no longer mere intuition; she has a sign, "a hogbone, with blood meat still on it, laying by the lamp." The compassionate Mr. Compson offers to take her to a neighbor, but Nancy is suddenly resigned to her fate: "Putting it off won't do no good." And she no longer evades her own responsibility for her plight: "I reckon it belong to me. I reckon what I going to get ain't no more than mine." None of Mr. Compson's efforts to arrange for her safety evokes a positive response.

"When yawl go home, I'm gone," Nancy said. She talked quieter now, and her face looked quiet, like her hands. "Anyway, I got my coffin money saved up . . ."

The withdrawal of the Compson family from Nancy's home in the final section marks the withdrawal of all hope and all fear. Nancy sits quietly before the fire with the door open, waiting for death. The perceptive Quentin, who has said little throughout these events and who has not participated in the children's quarrels, knows what is going to happen: "'Who will do our washing now, Father?' I said." But Caddy and Jason close the story with the leitmotif of childish bickering over the major themes: "you'd be scairder than a nigger." It is an appropriate conclusion, for the disordered world of the children always poised on the edge of infantile violence is exactly the kind of world in which Nancy suffers. All the good will in the world cannot mitigate the fear of violence aroused by a betrayal and corruption of love. However, in adopting the point of view of a child, Faulkner is able to dramatize that world without explicit moral comment. That is not to say that the dramatic action has no powerful meaning; the technique is so flawless that the moral significance is incandescently there.

1. *What is the significance of the title?*

"That Evening Sun" is a phrase from one of America's most famous blues songs, *The St. Louis Blues,* a shortened text of which is:

"I hate to see that evening sun go down, . . .
Because my baby, he done left this town.

If I'm feeling tomorrow like I feel today, . . .
I'll pack my trunk, make my getaway.
. . . . . .

>    I got the St. Louis Blues, just as blue as I can be.
>    That man got a heart like a rock cast in the sea,
>    Or else he wouldn't have gone so far from me.
>    . . . . . .
>    I'll love my baby till the day I die..."

The title is obviously ironic.

2. *By what principal means is characterization achieved in the story?*

By dialogue. There are very few sketchy descriptions of the characters, and even those must be carefully modified by what we come to know from what the characters say and by the tone in which they say it. For example, no one but Nancy and Jesus is "objectively" described, but we know that Mr. Compson is a kindly, compassionate man, concerned for Nancy's welfare (he refers to her as a "Negro" and not "nigger"), considerate but firm with his children (he carries the youngest home on his back and admonishes them against quarreling), and patient but irritated with his wife's self-pitying whining. Dilsey emerges as a masterful woman, rises prematurely from her sick bed ("If I had been a day later, this place would be to rack and ruin. Get out of here now and let me get my kitchen straight"), offers Nancy coffee and good advice ("You quit that now. You get aholt of yourself"). Of the children, Quentin is the silent, perceptive, aloof observer; Candace is the lively, inquisitive pest; and Jason the whining, complaining, selfish momma's boy (he even sleeps with his mother, although he's already five years old).

3. *Is Nancy's awareness of Jesus waiting in the ditch to kill her a hallucination?*

Superficially considered it might seem so ("I can feel him"), but she knows his violent temperament, she knows he has a powerful motive to punish her, she has been warned by him, and she has had a sign: the hogbone. It would be foolish to wonder if Nancy will actually be killed; of course she will — all the lines of force in the story move powerfully in that direction. (Incidentally, in the actual case which Faulkner used as a base for the story the murder does occur.) But Faulkner rarely dwells on scenes of violence and brutality for their own sake. In "That Evening Sun" he is concerned with complex moral forces that lead to violence and, more specifically, with the terror that precedes it.

4. *Is Jesus a pure, black villain?*

No. The fear of Jesus is established early and vividly in the story by means of the physical description of him, the children's avoidance of him, and Mr. Compson's banishment of him from the house. He is a proud man who resents the inferiority status imposed on him by the whites ("I can't hang around white man's kitchen. But white man can hang around mine... When white man want to come in my house, I ain't got no house"); he has always been kind to Nancy, whom he apparently loves ("Jesus always been good to me," Nancy said. "Whenever he had two dollars, one of them was mine"); she would be roused to a jealous fury if he betrayed her for another woman ("I'd cut his head off and I'd slit her belly") and her betrayal of him functions in the same way ("He say I done woke up the devil in him and ain't but one thing going to lay it down again"). His first response to her infidelity was to run away; only after brooding about his situation does he come back. He is a bitter, frustrated man living in a community that

offers the Negro no justice; violence is the only way he can conceive for getting justice and releasing his frustration. But since the story is told from the point of view of a child — and a white, Southern child at that — the surface impression is of a simple villain. Nevertheless, all the data of a complex character are available for the perceptive reader.
J. V. H.

Frey, Leonhard H., Irony and Point of View in "That Evening Sun", *Faulkner Studies* II, 1953, pp. 33-40 — Harrington, Evans B., Technical Aspects of William Faulkner's "That Evening Sun", *Faulkner Studies* I, 1952, pp. 54—59 — Hermann, John, Faulkner's Heart's Darling in "That Evening Sun", *Studies in Short Fiction* VII, 1970, pp. 320—323 — Hoffmann, Gerhard and Gisela, Faulkner, "That Evening Sun," *Die amerikanische Kurzgeschichte*, eds. Göller/Hoffmann, Düsseldorf 1972, pp. 247—257 — Sanders, Barry, Faulkner's Fire Imagery in "That Evening Sun", *Studies in Short Fiction* V, 1967, pp. 69—71.

## Death Drag

Text: Faulkner, *Four Stories* pp. 7—28. Schöningh

*In January 1931 three men land in their airplane on the airfield of a small Southern town. They arrange to put on a "death-defying show" for money. Jock, the pilot, is an ex-army flyer, but he lost his flying license after a fatal crash two years ago. Nevertheless they have performed their flying-show for the last five months. His partner Ginsfarb jumps from a ladder below the airplane on to the roof of a rented car running along on the ground — the death-drop — and then has himself picked up again — the death-drag. When he finds out after the beginning of the show that he is not going to get the demanded 100 dollars he is so furious that he jumps down from his ladder in mid-air — but is miraculously saved by a rotting barn roof. When the dispute is settled by Captain Warren, another veteran pilot, who lives in the town, they fly off to another place.*

"Death Drag" (written in 1931; first published in *Scribner's Magazine* January 1932) is a curious story, almost completely ignored by Faulkner critics. It represents a minor theme in the Faulkner canon, one which William van O'Connor has labeled The Folklore of Speed and which was most fully dealt with in the novel, *Pylon*. In that novel as in this story, the camaraderie and love of those involved in the bizarre life of air-show barnstorming somehow sets them off from normal people. Faulkner has always had an affection for pilots ever since he trained with the Canadian Royal Flying Corps during World War I; he and three brothers were all pilots in the twenties and thirties, but Faulkner gave it up when his brother Dean was killed in a plane crash in 1935. Strictly on the level of social history, "Death Drag" evokes a vanished period of American life — an aspect of the Jazz Age that worshiped noise, speed, and dare-devil stunts.

But this story is curious in that the dramatic setting of dare-devil flying stunts is used merely as a background for an unusual, tragi-comic treatment of the Wandering Jew. Ginsfarb, "the limping man," is the central character — a clown, a Jewish Pagliacco (Bajazzo) with the "most tragic face we had ever seen; an expression of outraged and convinced and indomitable despair." In characterizing him, Faulkner invokes all the clichés about the Jew — and more: his appearance, his voice, and his concern for money. His diction was like that of the Vaudeville comedians Weber and Fields, "making his *wh*'s into *v*'s and his *th*'s into *d*'s"; he had a nose so long that "the tip of his nose and the tip of his jaw almost touched"; and he refused a cigarette because '"I don't burn up no money.'" But Ginsfarb is no stereotype. Faulkner sees him with the eye of a Picasso. He wears breeches, and puttees and a soiled, brightly patterned overcoat; "a lateral line bisecting his head from the end of his nose to the back of his skull, his jaw, the rest of his face, was not two inches deep. His jaw was a long, flat line clapping-to beneath his nose like the jaw of a shark . . ." And his concern for money is coupled with a strict code of ethics. When it is suggested that the secretary of the Fair Association might permit them to use the airfield without charge, Ginsfarb says, "Go on and pay them;" when they are offered a ride to town in lieu of a taxi, he says, "We'll pay." Conversely, he insists on full recompense for his services and refuses to jump for less than one hundred dollars. In the brief coda at the end Ginsfarb's monetary code is revealed to have had a strict letter-of-the-law application indeed when we discover that he refused to pay for the rental of the car because he had not actually used it for his stunt.

The experiences of Ginsfarb are a hilarious combination of the traditional Yiddish joke and the Southern tall tale. Jock's story of how Ginsfarb came by his limp in a narrow escape from death only to be outraged at the cost of the fuel involved in his rescue ("Will you ruin me yet?") is similar to many Jewish tales such as the following:

Isaac the shopkeeper lay dying and asked weakly, "Where is my oldest son Irving?"

"Here I am, father," said Irving.

"And where is my second son Jacob?"

"Here I am, father," said Jacob.

"And where is my youngest son, Seth?"

"Here I am, father," said Seth.

"Then who is taking care of the store?" demanded Isaac.

And the episode of Ginsfarb realizing in the midst of his performance that he is not to be paid the full amount and becoming so indignant that he cannot wait for the plane to land, but leaps through a barn and emerges with a torn coat and bloody face to demand, "Where is that secretary?" is clearly in the tradition of the tall tale.

Nevertheless, despite these comic elements, "Death Drag" is not essentially a humorous story. The relation of Ginsfarb to the pilot Jock (who is his brother's keeper) and the contrast between the group of stuntmen and the town add serious dimensions to the meaning of the story. Although Jock, the tall man, and Ginsfarb, the short man, together evoke the image of Don Quixote and Sancho Panza and the American cartoon characters Mutt and Jeff, they are too grotesque to be simply laughable. Ginsfarb, whose face is "tragic, outraged, cold," is terribly possessed by the *idée fixe* of regaining the wealth he lost as a bankrupt merchant under the Coolidge administration. He explicitly rejects the idea of flying in a war or for heroism or glory of any kind; nor does he enjoy the thrill — "For fun? What for fun? Fly? *Grüss Gott.* I hate it..." He does his aerial stunts solely for money. As for Jock, it was not the war nor the fatal crash that killed all his passengers that left him a nervous wreck, prematurely white-haired; it was Ginsfarb's near death and his indifference to it that had so profoundly shaken Jock. Yet when Captain Warren offers him a release from his agonizing relationship, he refuses: "Who'd take care of that bestard?" He even refuses Warren's offer of an overcoat. Apparently the stuntmen live in a world apart from ordinary people and cannot enter into any meaningful relationships with them.

This idea is reinforced in many ways, both explicit and implicit. For one thing the narrative point of view is that of one of the older townspeople who knows nothing of these strangers or of flying. Hence there is considerable distance between the narrative and the narrator. The town is deliberately unnamed — it could be any small American town of the late 1920's and is typical in that it has its American Legion, Rotary Club, and Chamber of Commerce. Rooted in Anglo-Saxon, middle-class materialism, the citizens cannot possibly understand violent vitality and camaraderie of the stuntmen; they do not even realize that Ginsfarb and Jake are Jews — "they knew at once that two of the strangers were of a different race from themselves without being able to say what the difference was." The hooting and jeering and the incredulity of the crowd during the air show also underline the fact that they and the stuntmen live in separate worlds: "The rest is hard to tell. Not because we saw so little; we saw everything that happened, but because we had so little experience to postulate it with." The narrator himself is somewhat more aware than his fellow-citizens of their relative inferiority but fundamental kinship with the three strangers that have so dramatically entered their lives: "Some way we knew that that lonely, puny, falling shape was that of a living man like ourselves," but superior because he lived in full consciousness of the imminence of death while they were "interchangeable with and duplicate of ten thousand little dead clottings of human life about the land."

Though by no means typical of Faulkner's revolutionary style and technique, "Death Drag" is not an ordinary story. Apart from the bizarre, somewhat Kafkaesque subject matter, there is a shifting point of view (with an appropriate shift in diction) and a dazzling sequence of varied time perspectives. The alert reader will observe that the first section is told from the point of view of one of the elder townsmen, a man with a certain poetic sensibility. He speaks of the "apparition-like suddenness" of the plane's appearance and disappearance, of the short man's (he does not yet know his name) "limping, terrific and crablike," and of the "propeller motionless, rigid, with a quality immobile and poised and dynamic" — all favorite Faulkner adjectives (cf. Walter Slatoff, *Quest for Failure*, a study of Faulkner's characteristic diction). Since the narrator knows nothing about airplanes, he relies on the ex-army aviator in the town for the observation that the pilot was "trying to make the minimum of some specific maneuver in order to save gasoline." Part two shifts to a time after the air show is over and the narrator tells us what he heard from Captain Warren, the ex-army flyer, who was acquainted with Jock during the war fourteen years earlier. Captain Warren is not the poet that the narrator is; hence, the diction and style of this section is fairly simple, straightforward narrative. Since Warren is concerned chiefly with his old friend Jock, the pilot, we lose sight of Ginsfarb except as he is involved in Jock's life, and that involvement highlights Ginsfarb's indifference to death. Though this part of the narrative is told *after* the air show is over, it deals with events that occurred several months earlier but in such a way as to suggest the possibility that Ginsfarb may have died in the course of his dare-devil act.

The suggestion is powerfully reinforced in part three which shifts back in time to the show itself, narrated again by the poetic townsman, who speaks of the "lonely and scudding shadow upon the face of the puny and remote earth"; of the plane which "tilted and shot skyward with a noise like a circular saw going into a white oak log"; and of "the end of the delicate pen-slash of the profiled wing." Here the descriptions ("they were arguing in tense, dead voices") and the action (Ginsfarb's plunge into the barn while the plane's engine emitted a sound "like a groan, a groan of relief and despair") lead the reader to believe that the tragi-comic Jew was actually killed.

Part four shifts again to the evening in the barber shop where the prosaic Captain Warren reveals through dialogue the astounding comic denouement. The purpose of the variations in time and point of view, then, is to structure the expectation of death (in the poetic perspective of the townsman) and the comic reversal of Ginsfarb's dogged persistence (in the prosaic perspective of Captain Warren).

1. Is "Death Drag" an anti-Semitic story?

   No. Though Ginsfarb would seem to be a manifestation of the Wandering Jew, that legendary character destined to roam about the earth without rest because he struck Christ on the day of the Crucifixion, and though in many ways he is an embodiment of the anti-Semitic stereotype, he is clearly seen as superior to the dull clods that live in the town. He has vitality, daring, and bravado; he is scrupulously honest in his financial transactions; and he has inspired the devotion of Jock the pilot. He is a picaresque comic hero, reminiscent of Don Quixote or of Augie March. Captain Warren says of him: "Providence knew that he was too busy and that he deserved justice, so Providence put that barn there with the rotting roof."

2. *Faulkner has been described as an enemy of the machine age. Is there any evidence of this in "Death Drag"?*

   Although it is true that the airplane and the men associated with it are consistently described in terms related to death ("a single thin coat of dead black"...

"a dead voice"), the total action and the total balance of values do not add up to a negative view of the airmen. The townspeople who resist the world of flight ("on one side [of the airfield] is a group of trees which the owner will not permit to be felled") and jeer at the airmen ("' I got a mule Mister, how much'll you pay for a tow?'") are by comparison far less vitally alive ("dead clottings of human life"). In *Pylon,* too, the Prufrockian reporter says of the airmen, "They ain't human. Burn them ... and they don't even holler in the fire; crash and it aint even blood when you haul him out: it's cylinder oil same as in the crankcase." But the irony in that novel as in this story is that the airmen are far more dynamic, virile, and alive than the dull, normal citizens who live routine lives organized by the American Legion and the Chamber of Commerce.

3. *What unifies the three men in the airplane?*

"'Right,' the tall man said ... in his flat, dead voice, the same voice which the three strangers all seemed to use, as though it were their common language." They *do* speak the same language — they are one in their daily confrontation of death, their violation of the law, their need for money, and their loyalty to each other. We see and hear less of Jake than of the others because he has the safest job, driving the car and serving as business manager. Jock (the Scottish equivalent of Jake) is the least calm and self-controlled of the group because he is the most aware of the tremendous risks they undertake; it is he, after all, who had witnessed the death by fire of all his passengers on a commercial plane. Ginsfarb's agony shows only on his face, never in his voice or actions; he is driven by the monomania of making money by risking his life. Though these are three distinct individuals, they are solidly attached to each other in a single group.

J. V. H.

# F. SCOTT FITZGERALD

Francis Scott Fitzgerald was born on September 26, 1896, in St. Paul, Minnesota, to an Irish Catholic family. He had the early advantages of considerable travel and social life and was educated at Newman School in New Jersey and at Princeton which he left in 1917 to serve in the wartime army. While stationed in the South he met the Southern belle, Zelda Sayre, and determined to marry her as soon as he had enough money. The war terminated before he received an assignment abroad, and in the tedium of camp life he had meanwhile written his first novel, *This Side of Paradise,* which he could publish, after some difficulties, in 1920. With the profits he married and settled temporarily on Long Island before beginning a decade-long debauch with the international set that was to end with his wife's insanity and his alcoholism.

In the three years from 1920 to 1922 he established his position as historian of the younger generation of the Jazz Age, which he named and depicted with sentimental brilliance in another novel, *The Beautiful and Damned,* and a collection of short stories, *Tales of the Jazz Age*, both published in 1922. *The Great Gatsby* (1925) is perhaps the most striking fictional analysis of the age of the gang barons and of the social conditions that produced them. A second collection of short stories, *All the Sad Young Men* (1926), reveals in its title his sense of his age and the spiritual desperation and sterility of its society, which in his earlier period he had often cloaked in cynicism. As he was himself deeply involved in extravagant society life, he was only occasionally able to write at the top level of his powers.

Fitzgerald realized that the epoch with which he was identified ended with the beginning of the depression of the thirties. A new generation, characterized by social responsibility and experimentation, took the citadel of the literary world, and Fitzgerald was never able to get fully in step with it. His two later novels are also of enduring interest, although each is marred by some fault of construction. His last collection of short stories, published in 1935, announces by the title, *Taps at Reveille*, his own feeling of impending disaster. He died in 1940 after a period of spectacular decline which justified his old friend, Edmund Wilson, in choosing *The Crack-Up* as the title for the posthumous edition of essays, letters, and notes (1945).

## Babylon Revisited

Text:   *American Short Stories* VI pp. 90—114. Schöningh

*Charlie Wales returns to Paris, the scene of his years of dissipation in the 1920's, hoping that now that he has reformed and become a successful businessman, the sister of his dead wife will return custody of Honoria, his only child. The sister-in-law, still distrustful of his character and jealous of his regained wealth, very reluctantly agrees to do so. She still cannot forgive or forget that Charlie had contributed to his wife's death by locking her out in a snowstorm after a drunken quarrel. Just as Charlie is about to convince her of his worthiness, two dissipated "ghosts" from his past break in upon them, and Charlie is refused permission to take his daughter away with him. But he remains true to his new way of life, certain that some day he will regain his child.*

"Babylon Revisited", which is probably F. Scott Fitzgerald's finest short story (first published in 1931), not only evokes the mood of paralysis and defeat of the Waste Land generation following the stock market crash of 1929, but renders with understanding and compassion the purgatorial suffering of a man for whom repentence alone is not enough to redeem his past. Charlie Wales spends three days in Paris in an effort to regain custody of his daughter. He revisits the scenes of his Babylonian revels, places where he had been a "Good-time Charlie" living with the careless abandon of a playboy Prince of Wales. But "Babylon is fallen, is fallen" (Isaiah, 21:9) and is "become a desolation among nations" (Jeremiah 50:23) and Charlie finds that "the place oppressed him." He had first brought Helen to Paris; now he comes to take Honoria out.

Because the story is told from the point-of-view of Charlie Wales himself (even though it is a third-person narrative), the language appears to be sober, straightforward prose; but embedded in it, almost unnoticeably, is a rich sequence of poetic symbols — the title and the names of the central character and his daughter are obvious examples. That he is in some sort of purgatorial fire is suggested when he emerges from the Ritz bar and observes that "the fire-red, gas-blue, ghost green signs shone smokily through the tranquil rain." In Montmartre, he notices that "the Poet's Cave had disappeared, but the two great mouths of the Café of Heaven and the Café of Hell still yawned." That Charlie has experienced a rebirth and achieved a new identity is suggested not only by his control over alcohol and money, his rejection of a prostitute and of dissipated old friends, but even more subtly by his playful announcement to Honoria, "First let me introduce myself. My name is Charles J. Wales, of Prague." He is no longer from Paris, nor from Burlington, Vermont, either; he is a respectable business man from a rich cultural center in the heart of Europe. His new, sober, middle-class values are revealed in such observations as people eating dinner "behind the trim little bourgeois hedge of Duval's," the apartment of his sister-in-law as "warm and comfortably American" with "the cheer of six o'clock . . . in the eager smacks of the fire."

But it is extremely important to observe that although Charlie Wales now rejects Babylonian Paris he does not embrace the Puritanical New England values of his sister-in-law who frowns on people who go to bars, who refers to a casually-uttered "damn" as swearing, who resents anyone making money without working for it, and who cannot forgive past sins — finding it "necessary to believe in tangible villainy and a tangible villain." Although for Charlie Wales the forces of vitality had gotten out of hand during the wild twenties, Lincoln and Marion Peters "were very much in the grip of life and circumstances" and hardly models of vitality. Marion Peters and her values are also "sick" in a diametrically opposed way, and Charlie resents her legal (not moral) power. "But if he modulated his resentment to the chastened attitude of the reformed sinner, he might win his point in the end."

The story opens "with a stillness in the Ritz bar that was strange and portentous," and when it closes, again in the Ritz bar, the portents have been confirmed: he has not regained his Honoria. But though he is suffering he is not utterly defeated; Purgatory is not the Inferno. "He would come back some day; they couldn't make him pay forever." The mood is one of sadness, longing, and repentence, but not one of unutterable anguish and guilt. On his second night in Paris, Charlie Wales dreams of his wife Helen whose death he had hastened in a careless fit of pique by locking her out in a snowstorm. "She said she was glad he was being good and doing better. She said a lot of other things — very friendly things — but she was in a swing in a white dress, and swinging faster and faster all the time, so that at the end he could not hear clearly all that she said." Helen has obviously become his Beatrice figure; thus, at the end, he does not collapse into drink and despair. But his sins require more than a year or two to be purged, and he has the strength to endure more even though "he was absolutely sure Helen wouldn't have wanted him to be so alone."

There are three "vector forces" in the story: Charlie and his daughter yearning to establish the ties of paternal and filial love; Lincoln and Marion Peters, sitting in judgment over him, sanctioned by law and traditional morality; and Duncan Schaeffer and Lorraine Quarrles, emerging inexorably from his dissipated past to blast his hopes of immediate redemption. These three forces gradually converge toward the climactic scene before the denouement and give the story an admirably solid dramatic structure.

Despite the obvious symbolism of the title, critics have not generally observed that "Babylon Revisited" is a religious story — more exactly a Catholic, Dantesque story. Frakes and Traschen say that the theme is "precisely... the persistence of the past in the present," and Kent and Gretchen Kreuter say that it is determinism: "it is the acts of others that finally decide the outcome" of our lives. Neither of these two most recent commentaries is accurate. F. Scott Fitzgerald was born into a Catholic family and had a Catholic upbringing; and his most important short story, like his most important novel *The Great Gatsby*, is an evocation of a purgatorial waste land in the Dante-Eliot sense. Charlie Wales repents his sins in Babylon, but it takes more than mere repentence to gain redemption (Honoria). One need not "pay forever," but one must first endure suffering in the purgatorial fires.

1. *Cite the explicit moral comments in the story. Do they reduce the story to a mere illustration of an ethical-religious tag, as in a morality play?*

   At several points the meditations of Charlie Wales become flat statements of moral truths; for example:
   > He believed in character; he wanted to jump back a whole generation and trust in character again as the eternally valuable element. Everything else wore out.
   > ...he suddenly realized the meaning of the word "dissipate" — to dissipate into thin air; to make nothing out of something.
   > The present was the thing — work to do and someone to love. But not to love too much, for he knew the injury that a father can do to a daughter or a mother to a son by attaching them too closely...

   But these do not mean that "Babylon Revisited" is a morality play or an allegory, because: (1) these do not constitute the central meaning of the story; (2) they are the appropriate meditations of an intelligent man who has reformed; (3) the fundamental meaning here, as in all good literary art, is implicitly carried in the dramatic action and in the embedded metaphors and symbols.

2. *What references to "snow" do you find in the story? What do they mean in terms of the total context?*

   In the Ritz bar at the beginning, Charlie Wales inquires after the "Snow Bird." The term was a slang expression for a cocaine or heroin addict, and may refer to a jazz musician. It is interesting that Charlie's other old friends have left Paris after the crash, but that the dope addict and Duncan Schaeffer, "his friend" (supplier of dope?), have remained in the waste land, like the "strident queens" (homosexuals) whom nothing affects and who "go on forever."

Then, later, after Marion's *j'accuse*, Charlie recalls the horrible night when after a drunken quarrel he had locked his wife out of their home, forcing her out into a "snowstorm in which she wandered about in slippers, too confused to find a taxi," catching pneumonia from which she had recovered but which no doubt had contributed to her heart trouble that later killed her.

Finally at the end Charlie experiences a nightmarish remembrance of the past in which men "locked their wives out in the snow, because the snow of twenty-nine wasn't real snow. If you didn't want it to be snow, you just paid some money." Clearly, snow signifies death — death of the spirit and death of the body. And no one of his Jazz Age lost generation had ever honestly confronted either; "you just paid some money" and bought escape from facing the truth. But "pay" has a newer, different, spiritual meaning in the last paragraph: "they couldn't make him pay forever."

3. *The "strident queens" refers to homosexuals, but "queens" suggests royalty. Can you find other references to royalty and explain what they mean?*

After Charlie leaves the Left Bank and as Charlie rides away from the Ritz in a taxi, "the Place de la Concorde moved by in pink majesty," and he observes the "magnificent facade" of the Opera. He imagines hearing the taxi horns as "the trumpets of the Second Empire." He offers to take his daughter to a vaudeville show at the Empire, and the "ghosts" from his past think that's a grand idea. In talking to Marion, Charlie says of the old days, "it was nice while it lasted ... We were a sort of royalty, almost infallible." They were the kings of Babylon, and their ghosts have survived its destruction.

4. *What element of Paris in the 1920's not otherwise referred to in this story is suggested in the observation: "The Poet's Cave had disappeared, but the two great mouths of the Café of Heaven and the Café of Hell still yawned"?*

Paris had been the center for such writers in exile as James Joyce, Ernest Hemingway, Gertrude Stein, Sherwood Anderson, and others; but after the great depression struck, they left. Art and creative vitality had gone, but the choice of heaven or hell is always with us.

5. *Is there any progression in the appearances of the "ghosts" from Charlie's past?*

Yes. His first meeting with Duncan and Lorraine at the restaurant was a chance encounter, and he tries to avoid a future encounter by refusing to give his address. The seductive note from Lorraine was directed to him from the Ritz, and he was "glad Alix had not given away his hotel address." But he had given his sister-in-law's address, and their pursuit of him led them naturally there — to break in at an inopportune moment. One cannot simply refuse the past one's present address; one must redeem it through suffering.

J. V. H.

Griffith, Richard R., A Note on Fitzgerald's "Babylon Revisited", *American Literature* XXXV, 1963, pp. 236—239 — Gross, Seymour, Fitzgerald's "Babylon Revisited", *College English* XXV, 1963, pp. 128—135 — Kruse, Horst, Fitzgerald, "Babylon Revisited", *Die amerikanische Kurzgeschichte*, eds. Göller and Hoffmann, Düsseldorf 1972, pp. 225—234 — Male, Roy R., "Babylon Revisited": A Story of the Exile's Return, *Studies in Short Fiction* II, 1965, 270—277 — Osborne, William R., The Wounds of Charlie Wales in Fitzgerald's "Babylon Revisited", *Studies in Short Fiction* II, 1964, pp. 86—87.

# BRET HARTE

Bret Harte was born on August 25, 1836, at Albany, New York, son of a schoolmaster. As a boy he was fond of reading and began to write poetry. In 1854 he followed his widowed mother to California where during the following 17 years he worked mainly as a teacher and journalist and acquired a fund of knowledge for his writing. In 1868 he became editor of the *Overland Monthly* in San Francisco; in this journal he published the stories and poems that extended his reputation from California to the Atlantic coast and to England. In the best of these — "The Luck of Roaring Camp" (1868), "The Outcasts of Poker Flat" (1869), "Miggles" and "Tennessee's Partner" (1870) — he depicted the world of the forty-niners and gave the Far West and the gold rush a place in American literature. He developed the type of local color story in which the surroundings, the way of life and the peculiar speech-habits of the people have become an autonomous element. In 1871 Harte went back to New York, but most of his further writings lacked originality. In 1878 he went to Germany and later to England as a U. S. consul, and died in London in 1902.

## The Luck of Roaring Camp

Text:  Bret Harte, *The Luck of Roaring Camp and The Outcasts of Poker Flat* pp. 3—15. Hueber
*American Short Stories* II pp. 26—38. Schöningh

*In 1850 there were no decent women in the miners' camps. And to the rough company of gamblers and criminals at Roaring Camp it is a sensation when a baby is going to be born there. Cherokee Sal, the mother, dies and leaves the baby in the hands of the men. It is brought up with the milk of an ass and baptized Tommy Luck, because it is supposed to have brought luck to the gold miners. Slowly "The Luck" changes the appearance of the camp and the habits of its inhabitants. The camp prospers and the affection of the miners for the baby increases. The next spring, however, a sudden flood comes over the camp, and the baby dies in the arms of one of the men.*

The Wild West has provided the modern world with the setting for a type of popular "epic" — epic in the sense that characters are larger than life and motives simplified. The Wild West that is presented in innumerable books, films and television plays has, historians assure us, very little resemblance to the Wild West of rather sordid reality that existed for a short period in the last century. Bret Harte's Wild West, too, is in many respects different from the Wild West that popular media of entertainment have made familiar. In certain details Bret Harte's world seems to correspond to reality — the inhabitants of his West are described as callous rather than as picturesquely villainous or heroic, one of them has dirty personal habits (imagine the cowboy in a modern "Western" being presented as not changing his shirt often enough), they are a motley crew including a comic Cockney (not the athletic, well-paid heroes of commercial television), and so on.

In spite of these convincing details, however, this story is, in general effect, thoroughly sentimental and is designed to show that these rough diamonds have hearts of gold. Their latent goodness is aroused by the birth of a baby in the mining camp. In another story entitled "Tennessee's Partner" the same latent goodness is brought out by a funeral, and in "The Outcasts of Poker Flat" by shared hardship; in each case the same theme in different clothing. This idea of the heart of gold beneath the rough exterior, which may well have connections with the "noble savage" of Rousseau and the 18th century, plays a part in the glorification of the hero of later Wild West and cowboy stories. But in "Luck of Roaring Camp" the sentimental theme dominates and reaches its climax in the ending which is entirely in the tradition of the death of Little Paul in Dickens' *Dombey and Son*, which made a deep impression on 19th century readers and has become a symbol of Victorian sentimentality. However, in times that tend to glorify "toughness" and violence in fiction, the "touching" death scene only arouses laughter, as do the stock phrases of literary piety ("lying in sore extremity," "expiation of the sin," "punishment of the first transgression") and the consistent use of euphemism ("sinful woman," "primal curse"). These phrases mix strangely with the touches of realism. The conversion of the rough miners to the guardians of Cherokee Sal's child is made even less convincing by the fact that their roughness and wildness is treated with a humorous irony that strikes the modern reader as fairly cumbersome — "Stumpy, in other climes, had been the putative head of two families; in fact, it was owing to some legal informality in these proceedings that Roaring Camp... was indebted to his company." As the author does not take his characters seriously (he seems to regard them as hopelessly vulgar and lower-class), it would seem unreasonable to demand that their change of heart should be taken seriously. The story is, in fact, interesting from the historical and sociological point of view for the insight it gives into the attitudes and prejudices of Bret Harte's 19th century readers. It is further interesting for the glimpses it gives us of the life in the mining camps of the period and for the influence his stories had on the popular Wild West literature.

1. *Indicate some of the elements of realism in this story.*

   The opening paragraph with the fight "not novel enough to have called together the entire settlement" and the reminiscence of the gamblers who had continued playing in spite of the gun-fight. The description of the men assembled with missing fingers, toes etc. The betting on the mother's chances of survival. The burlesque Church service. The uncleanliness of Kentuck. The Camp's hostility to the outside world.

2. *Indicate some of the sentimental elements in this story.*

   Above all the ending. That the presence of the child induced cleaner habits in the miners is acceptable in the context of this story, but the idea is carried too far in the references to the regenerated camp as "fairyland" and indications of "pastoral happiness." The sentimentality is often expressed in literary clichés such as "Nature took the foundling to her broader breast."

3. *Is there a religious element in the story?*

   Apart from the pious circumlocutions in reference to Cherokee Sal which were mentioned above, the birth of "Tommy Luck" bears some resemblance to the birth of Christ. Galinsky[1] speaks of a secularized epiphany in the scene when the procession of the miners files along the table where the baby lies in a candle box, "swathed in staring red flannel." An explicit clue to this interpretation is that there is a Bible among their presents. There is also an ass in the background. And the transfiguration of the child ("there was an infantine gravity about him, a contemplative light in his round grey eyes"), the luck he brought to Roaring Camp, his civilizing influence on the miners, the "pastoral happiness" pervading the camp and Kentuck's death ("A smile lit the eyes of the expiring Kentuck. 'Dyingl' he repeated; 'he's a-taking me with him. Tell the boys I've got the Luck with me now.'") all fit into this pattern. But the religious parallel cannot be taken seriously; it comes, with regard to the whole context, near to either travesty or "Kitsch."

4. *Analyse the humorous element in this story.*

   The humor consists chiefly of irony directed at the rough characters portrayed. It sometimes takes the form of direct commentary in highly literary language, as in the passage concerning "Stumpy" already quoted. The author is laughing condescendingly at his characters, which makes their conversion less convincing and less interesting. Sometimes the characters are shown behaving in an incongruous manner, as in Stumpy's ludicrous christening address (which the author takes care to point out as ludicrous) or in the comments made by the miners on the baby's appearance ("Ain't bigger nor a derringer"). Here the humor is tinged with sentiment — the reader is intended to be touched by the incongruity of the rough men confronted by a baby.

---

[1] *Amerikanische Dichtung in der höheren Schule. Die Neueren Sprachen*, Beiheft 3, Frankfurt 1957, S. 39/40; cf. also *Praxis des neusprachlichen Unterrichts* IX (1962) pp. 107/8.

5. *What elements are present in this story that suggest later Wild West stories?*
Romantic enthusiasm for the wilderness: "the invigorating climate of the mountain camp," "that rare atmosphere of the Sierra foot-hills, that air pungent with Balsamic odor, that ethereal cordial at once bracing and exhilarating."
The tendency to glorify the rough Westerner is taken up in the later stories of the region, although in such stories the heroism and courage of the chief characters are glorified rather than any qualities of latent kindness.
Familiar features such as cowboys and sheriffs are not yet present, but the atmosphere of gun-fights and casual violence is indicated, and such figures as the professional gambler appear already in Bret Harte's stories.

W. G. C.

Boggan, J. R., The Regeneration of "Roaring Camp," *Nineteenth-Century Fiction* XXII, 1967, pp. 271—280 — Brown, Allen, The Christ Motif in "The Luck of Roaring Camp," *Papers of the Michigan Academy of Sciences, Arts and Letters* XLVI, 1961, pp. 629—633 — Ziegler, Heide, Harte, "The Luck of Roaring Camp," *Die amerikanische Kurzgeschichte*, eds. Göller and Hoffmann, Düsseldorf 1972, pp. 138—148.

# NATHANIEL HAWTHORNE

Nathaniel Hawthorne was born on July 4, 1804, at Salem, Massachusetts, son of a sea captain, who died in 1808. The novelist's great-great-great-grandfather William Hathorne had come from England to Massachusetts in 1630; his son had become infamous in history as one of the three judges in the Salem witchcraft trials of 1692. — In 1821 Nathaniel Hawthorne entered Bowdoin College with the intention of becoming an author. Henry Wadsworth Longfellow was one of his classmates there. Graduated in 1825, he returned to his mother's home at Salem and spent twelve solitary years of ascetic devotion to his literary career. Apart from *Fanshawe*, an unsuccessful novel, 36 tales and sketches appeared in periodicals between 1830 and 1837. Like many later American writers he depended on magazines for making a living, and thus was led to concentrate his production on short pieces. The publication of 18 *Twice-Told Tales* in 1837 was the first to bear the author's name and to acquire him a reputation. By that time he had written some of his best works, e. g. "My Kinsman, Major Molineux" (1832), "Young Goodman Brown" (1835), "The Minister's Black Veil" (1836). During the following years Hawthorne's financial position was improved when friends secured him employment with the harbour administration at Boston and at Salem, and in 1842 he could marry. In the same year a new edition of the *Twice-Told Tales* appeared in two volumes containing 39 stories. In 1846 another two-volume collection of short stories *Mosses from an Old Manse* was published, containing 23 pieces. In 1842, E. A. Poe had said in his famous review of the *Twice-Told Tales*, "Mr. Hawthorne's distinctive trait is invention, creation, imagination, originality — a trait which, in the literature of fiction, is positively worth all the rest..." In his review of the *Mosses* in 1847, however, Poe felt that Hawthorne's work had deteriorated and he now declared that Hawthorne was "peculiar and not original" and that he was "infinitely too fond of allegory," a judgment later echoed by Henry James.

In 1850 Hawthorne published his first great novel, *The Scarlet Letter*, one of the greatest of American novels, and in the following year the equally famous *The House of the Seven Gables*. During this time he was stimulated by a close association with Herman Melville, who in turn dedicated his *Moby Dick* (1851) to Hawthorne. The collection of short stories *The Snow Image and Other Twice-Told Tales* (1851) was the last of its kind, as Hawthorne explained, "The thought and trouble expended on that kind of production is vastly greater, in proportion, than what is required for a long story." He then wrote *The Blithedale Romance* (1852), a badly written but fascinating combination of social history (concerned with the Socialist experiment at Brook Farm), *roman à clef* (disguised negative portraits of famous New Englanders), and philosophical parable (showing the dangers of idealistic withdrawal from real life). In 1852 Hawthorne moved to Concord, but a year later he was appointed consul to Liverpool by his college friend Franklin Pierce, who had just been elected to the Presidency. Having served at Liverpool he resigned his office in 1857, traveled in England and Italy until 1860 and then returned to America. His last major work, *The Marble Faun*, a novel drawn from his experiences in Italy, was published in 1860. His last years were overshadowed by the Civil War and failing health; he died in 1864 and was buried at Concord.

The themes for most of his fiction Hawthorne found among the traditions of New England. It was the darkened outlook of Puritan faith, the sense of sin, of evil, and of the restless individual conscience that fascinated him and stirred his imagination. "Any figure... easily became with him an emblem, any story a parable, any appearance a cover" (Henry James). Hawthorne himself once ironically observed about his art[1], "His fictions are sometimes historical, sometimes of the present day, and sometimes, so far as can be discovered, have little or no reference either to time or space. In any case, he generally contents himself with a very slight embroidery of outward manners — the faintest possible counterfeit of real life — and endeavors to create an interest by some less obvious peculiarity of the subject. Occasionally a breath of Nature, a raindrop of pathos and tenderness, or a gleam of humor, will find its way into the midst of his fantastic imagery, and make us feel as if, after all, we were yet within the limits of our native earth." Mark van Doren ends his study by summing up, "The imperishable thing in Hawthorne is not, as some have said, his prose. 'I am glad you think my style plain,' he wrote to an editor in 1851. 'I never, in any one page or paragraph, aimed at making it anything else, or giving it any other merit — and I wish people would leave off talking about its beauty. If it have any, it is only pardonable as being un-

---

[1] Preface to "Rapaccini's Daughter" (1844), where Hawthorne used the pseudonym Monsieur de l'Aubépine (the French word for hawthorn); cf. Cantwell, l. c., p. 202.

intentional. The greatest possible merit of style is, of course, to make the words absolutely disappear into the thought.' His one deathless virtue is that rare thing in any literature, an utterly serious imagination. It was serious, and so it was loving; it was loving, and so it could laugh; it could laugh, and so it could endure the horror it saw in every human heart. But it saw the honor there along with the horror, and the dignity by which in some eternity our pain is measured."

## My Kinsman, Major Molineux

Text:  Nathaniel Hawthorne, *Two New England Romances* pp. 7—20. Hirschgraben

*The story is set in the capital of "a New England colony" about the year 1740. One summer evening Robin, the seventeen-year-old son of a country clergyman, arrives from his father's farm on his first visit to town. He inquires his way to his kinsman, Major Molineux (a cousin of Robin's father), who is supposed to help him to rise in the world. He is considerably surprised, however, when his inquiries are met by outbursts of annoyance or laughter. He resists the temptation of a prostitute, who pretends to be the Major's housekeeper, and continues his search, until he is advised to wait near a church, where the Major is due to pass an hour later. At the appointed time a noisy torchlight procession of grotesque figures approaches, cheered by masses of spectators surrounding a man on an open cart. This man, covered with tar and feathers, Robin recognizes as his kinsman thus exposed to public shame. Overwhelmed by pity and terror, Robin suddenly breaks into mad laughter. He wants to return to his family, but a kindly gentleman persuades him to stay and make his way without the help of his kinsman.*

This is one of the finest of Hawthorne's tales, and Hyatt Waggoner even cites it as "among the greatest stories in the language." On the surface it seems a simple tale of a young man who leaves the farm in search of a rich and powerful uncle who has promised to help him find his way in the world. According to Mark van Doren he ironically discovers the uncle at his moment of greatest defeat and humiliation, being driven by angry townspeople from the city, and turns to go home, "merely a young man over whose handsome head a storm has passed." But the story is far more complex than that. The opening paragraph invites a historical interpretation by revealing that the events occurred "not far from a hundred years ago" (the tale was published in 1832), when the Royal governors of New England were periodically driven out by popular insurrection. Presumably Major Molineux, who is tarred and feathered and driven out of the community, represents one of those governors. The descriptive details of the social setting, manners, clothing, and the political insurrection itself (carried out by citizens in weird dress and painted faces to protect themselves from retaliation by the British authorities) make up an accurate picture of colonial times.

Despite these details, the tone, structure, and point of view of the story suggest that there is more to it than a dramatic slice of colonial history. Young Robin's search for his kinsman is obviously a quest, and from the moment that the ferryman lifts his lantern to inspect his lone passenger on a moonlit night the details accumulate in such a way as to suggest an allegory. Like Christian in Bunyan's *Pilgrim's Progress* (which was standard reading in Hawthorne's day), Robin encounters Evil in various guises: the two-faced stranger with horns is the Devil, the watchman is Sloth, the innkeeper is Avarice, the woman in the scarlet petticoat is Lust, the man of authoritative bearing is Pride. In the end, before he denies his kinsman, Robin derives spiritual strength from peering into a church to see a shaft of moonlight on an open Bible. But this interpretation, too, fails to accomodate many of the strange details and reduces an eerie and compelling drama to a familiar moral pattern.

The tension and suspense mount to nightmarish proportions as Robin proceeds from one citizen to the next, inquiring for his kinsman Major Molineux and from each receives mysterious threats and abuse followed by sinister laughter. At last, waiting for his kinsman to pass, he falls into a trance-like meditation, "vibrating between fancy and reality," and wonders "if the object of his search ... were not all the time mouldering in his shroud." He is roused from his reverie by a kindly gentleman who waits with him until presently a raucous mass of people come marching down the street. In their midst is none other than Major Molineux, tarred and feathered, being pulled along in an open cart in an agony of shame. "The foam hung white on his quivering lips... The bitterest pang of all was when his eyes met those of Robin." Jeering laughter breaks out of the crowd, a riotous mirth which Robin finds irresistibly contagious — and he, too, laughs, loudest of all. Majestic in his defeat, the kinsman is carried away. Robin's feeling of guilt is immense. He wants to return to the ferry and go home, but the kind, elderly gentleman persuades him to remain in the city: "you may rise in the world without your kinsman, Major Molineux." On this level the story may symbolize the search for a father-figure and the guilty joy in the destruction of that father-figure.

Hyatt Waggoner has summarized various levels of meaning: As a psychological tale, "Major Molineux" tells us that the individual's growth to maturity is difficult and painful and involves a guilt which must be accepted. As an ethical allegory it suggests both that many snares lie in wait for the young man and that any simple dichotomy of good and evil is too simple to represent the complex facts of life. As a tale with philosophical implications, the kinsman may symbolize the past, and the denial of him, a rejection of political archaism.

Werner Hüllen (*Zeitgenössische amerikanische Dichtung*, S. 44) goes so far as to claim that the young man's learning to rise in the world without his kinsman symbolizes the way of the American nation to maturity and independence, but such a reading is too broad and too general, it is not supported by the details.

There is even a further possible interpretation suggested by Simon O. Lesser in *Fiction and the Unconscious*, namely, that Robin is not so eager to find his kinsman as he is to find sexual adventure. He is 18 years old and this is his first visit to the city. He is singularly inefficient in his mode of inquiry, first forgetting to ask the ferryman, then simply walking leisurely along the streets (including deserted back streets). The image of the woman in the scarlet petticoat haunts him and he forgets to ask the watchman, a most appropriate source of information, about his kinsman. Even when he knows that his kinsman is to pass a certain street, he seeks to go around the corner where he believes the populace is enjoying merriment, and is restrained only by the kindly gentleman who reminds him of his ostensible purpose. He even fantasies the death of Major Molineux. And the puzzling climax of the story when Robin joins in the obscene laughter at the plight of the Major makes most sense if we see it as release of suppressed wishes and a joy in seeing those wishes fulfilled with the full approval of the society around him. Says Lesser, "he would like a greater measure of sexual freedom than it is reasonable to suppose he would enjoy in the home of a colonial official . . . What he is doing is something which every young man does and must do, however gradually, prudently and inconspicuously: he is destroying an image of paternal authority so that, freed from its restraining influence, he can begin life as an adult."

1. *How is the story structured? What major parts does it have?*

a) The introductory paragraph gives historical background and setting.
b) Robin's arrival at the city and the sequence of inquiries as he wanders about the streets — the barber, innkeeper, prostitute, watchman, and the two-faced man — build tension and suspense.
c) A crisis point is reached as Robin waits for his kinsman to pass and meditates on his past and future.
d) The tension is momentarily broken by exposition in the dialogue with the kindly gentleman in which, just before the climax, we learn for the first time exactly what motivated Robin to come to the city. Perhaps this is a flaw in the structure, for there seems to be little purpose in delaying the exposition or in presenting it at a point where it interferes with the build-up to a climax.
e) The climax and most powerful emotional point of the story is when the procession arrives with Major Molineux in disgrace and Robin joins the laughter. He ironically rejects his kinsman at the very moment he finds him.
f) The denouement or resolution occurs when Robin, overwhelmed by guilt, seeks to return home but is persuaded to remain in the city.

2. *What details of the story enhance the feeling of nightmarish mystery?*

After the lantern-light inspection of the ferryman (who is faintly reminiscent of Charon who carries passengers across the Styx), Robin stops a periwigged man with "a peculiarly solemn and sepulchral intonation," whose "hems" as he answers Robin's questions have "a most singular effect, like a thought of a cold grave obtruding among wrathful passions." And the ill-mannered roar of laughter from the barber's shop is also ominous. But Robin rationalizes away the negative response to his first inquiry. The next man he questions at the inn has features "striking almost to grotesqueness..." Again his inquiry produces "a strange hostility in every countenance" and as he leaves he hears laughter. He next inquires of the prostitute (whom he really recognizes to be one, though he plays dumb in addressing her as "pretty mistress" — an ambiguous term — "I may call her so with a good conscience, since I know nothing to the contrary"). But just as she is about to draw him into her house, the opening of a door in the neighborhood startles her and she abruptly leaves him. The watchman simply ignores his belated request and Robin hears "the sound of drowsy laughter." As he proceeds down strange, dark, crooked streets, encountering muffled figures and masked strangers, the mysterious elements gradually accumulate to give an overpowering effect of a weird and grotesque experience, quite Gothic in character.

3. *What similes are involved in the descriptions and what is their effect?*

They generally add to the lurid, strange Gothic effect. The sheepish countrymen use the inn "somewhat after the fashion of a Turkish caravansary" — an allusion to remote, Oriental elements typical of Gothic literature. Eyes "like fire in a cave" on one stranger, and the sparkle of the prostitute's eye "as if moonbeams were trembling on some bright thing," both tend to relate visual effects to the mystery of the night. As Robin wandered through the town he felt that a spell was on him "like that by which a wizard of his country had once kept three pursuers wandering..." There are very few similes, the poetic effect being rendered by direct description of bizarre people and events.

4. *Is there a satisfactory "closure" to the story?*

Indeed, yes! The last page or two completes everything — the quest has been ironically fulfilled; in the crowd scene all the characters Robin had encountered during his search are recapitulated and the effects of the separate encounters are all gathered together in the convulsive merriment of the mass; and the urge to return to the ferry recalls the opening scene. The closure is perfect.

5. *When in the coda the kindly gentleman asks, "Well, Robin, are you dreaming?" how do we know that the strange procession was not indeed a figment of Robin's imagination?*

Because Robin withdraws his arm from "the stone post to which he had instinctively clung, as the living stream rolled by him" and because he says to the kind gentleman, "I have at last met my kinsman, and he will scarce desire to see my face again."

6. *How long does the action take?*

It is difficult to say exactly. "It was near nine o'clock" when Robin was crossing in the ferryboat, but after the barber-shop and inn episodes, "the ringing of a bell announced the hour of nine." Time apparently passes very slowly. Somewhat later, he is told to wait an hour for his kinsman to pass, and after a long period during which he can barely stay awake, he is joined by the kindly gentleman to whom he says, "only an hour or two since, I was told to wait here." Thus it must be about midnight when the procession finally passes.   J. V. H.

Connors, Thomas A., "My Kinsman, Major Molineux": A Reading, *Modern Language Notes* LXXIV, 1959, pp. 299—302 — Gross, Seymour L., Hawthorne's "My Kinsman, Major Molineux", History as Moral Adventure, *Nineteenth Century Fiction* XII, 1957, pp. 97—109 — Liebman, Sheldon, Robin's Conversion: The Design of "My Kinsman, Major Molineux," *Studies in Short Fiction* VIII, 1971, pp. 443—457 — Stein, William B., Teaching Hawthorne's "My Kinsman, Major Molineux", *College English* XX, 1958, pp. 83—86.

## Young Goodman Brown

Text:   (no annotated edition yet available)
Hawthorne, *Twice-Told Tales and Other Short Stories*
Washington Square Press W 580

*In Puritan Salem village, about the time of the witchcraft trials of 1692, Young Goodman Brown and his wife Faith have been happily married for three months. One evening he departs from his wife in spite of her entreaties and walks into the dark forest. He has an appointment there with the devil, who comes in the appearance of Old Goodman Brown and overcomes the young man's reluctance to follow him by referring to the services he has rendered to Brown's ancestors and to numerous worthy citizens and pious ladies. Many of them pass the bewildered Brown who still struggles to free himself and preserve his innocence. But when he sees his wife among the devil's followers he maddens with despair and hurries to the meetingplace, where he and Faith are to be taken into the communion of their race. The deep mystery of sin, Evil as the nature of mankind, is revealed to them. At the last moment before baptism Brown cries out to his wife to resist the devil. Immediately he finds himself quite alone in the wood. The next morning he returns to Salem, a changed man. He passes his joyful wife without greeting. Wherever he goes he sees sinners and hears blasphemers. Even his dying hour after many years is gloom.*

This story appeared in the *New England Magazine* for April, 1835, and was collected in *Mosses from an Old Manse* (1846).

American critics are generally agreed that "Young Goodman Brown" is an allegory and that it is one of Hawthorne's finest short stories, and there agreement ends. The meaning of the allegory is a subject of tangled controversy. Austin Warren (who must be credited with the discovery that Hawthorne's source was Cotton Mather's *Wonders of the Invisible World* (1693), where convocations of the Devil's witches in late 17th century Salem are cited as historical facts) believes that the point of the story is "the devastating effect of moral skepticism. Hawthorne educes no positive counsel from his tale; he does not bid us put our trust in God instead of in men, or in virtue rather than the virtuous. He merely depicts a state of mind· a perilous sort of disillusionment." (*Nathaniel Hawthorne*, New York 1934, p. 362)

Richard Fogle neatly distinguishes the various dichotomies of symbolism — day and night, town and forest, red and black, flame and damp, and gives specific meanings to these details. Day and Town symbolize Good; Night and the Forest symbolize Evil; red and flame symbolize the obviousness of evil; and black and damp symbolize doubt of the reality of evil. But despite the clarity of these details, Fogle finds them "harmoniously interfused" with ambiguity of total meaning; the "reconciliation of opposites" creates "multiplicity of suggestion and enriches the bareness of systematic allegory." Fogle apparently believes that the story is good not *despite*, but *because of*, the fact that it has no clear, single meaning! (loc. cit., pp. 26, 32)

D. M. McKeithan thinks it is the "story of a man whose sin led him to consider all other people sinful." Young Goodman Brown enters the forest of sin believing that he could turn back whenever he wanted to, but finds himself lured deeper and deeper until he suffers "the loss of religious faith and faith in all other human beings." (*Mod. Lang. Notes*, LXVII, 1952, 96)

Mrs. Q. D. Leavis, the British critic, says that the story "has no religious significance, it is a psychological state that is explored. Young Goodman Brown's Faith is not faith in Christ but faith in human beings, and losing it he is doomed to isolation forever." (*Sewanee Review*, LIX, 1951, 197—98)

Roy R. Male assembles a host of narrative details centered on the devil's staff and the pink ribbons to show that "Faith's ambiguity is the ambiguity of womanhood and that the dark night in the forest is essentially a sexual experience." Faith begs Goodman Brown "tarry with me... sleep in your own bed tonight," but he leaves her, unable to forget the pink ribbons which incongruously decorate her Puritan clothes. In the forest he hears that "there is a goodly young woman and a goodly young man to be taken into sinful communion that night" — and they turn out to be himself and his wife Faith. "Almost everything in the forest scene suggests that the communion of sinners is essentially sexual and that Brown qualifies for it by his marriage." (loc. cit. pp. 77—78)

Thomas E. Connolly stoutly contradicts all earlier critics in flatly asserting that "Young Goodman Brown did not lose his faith at all;" he simply purified it of its pink-ribbon promise of sure salvation in heaven. Like the minister and all the others of his congregation he had believed in the innate depravity of man and the impossibility of earning salvation, but also like them he believed that *he* was one of the rare elect. However, in the forest of sin, he sees a dark cloud cover the brightening stars at the very moment that the pink ribbon of his Faith falls. For the rest of his life he lives with a *pure* Puritan faith, absolutely certain that only "misery unutterable" is in store for him and his congregation. (*Am. Lit.*, XXVIII, 1956, 370—75)

This collection of critical summaries confirms the melancholy fact that since there is as yet no science of literary criticism a complex story will tend to function as a Rorschach ink-blot toward which each critic projects his own preoccupations and values. Nevertheless, recent critical history of this story seems to have steadily progressed toward a sound, clear interpretation. By merging the views of Roy Male and Thomas Connolly, we can achieve the fullest and richest meaning, for the story obviously deals with an experience involving religious faith *and* marriage that left Young Goodman Brown "a stern, a sad, a darkly meditative, a distrustful, if not a desperate man." Salem, Massachusetts, during the reign of King William III (1689–1702) was, as a matter of historical fact, a Puritan theocratic stronghold where the doctrine of original sin was the cornerstone of the edifice of thought. That doctrine was *both* religious and sexual — since the flesh was considered corrupt and since all men were born out of the joining of male and female, all men were corrupt, tainted with original sin, and doomed to damnation. Young Goodman Brown addresses his wife as "my love and my Faith" as he kisses her in departing on his adventure of discovery. She is indeed both — sexual and religious, and remains so. The pink ribbons, symbolizing feminine sexuality, are still on her cap when he returns after the black night, three months after his marriage, when he learned the full implications of marriage — his and his father's and of all men. When his wife whispers endearments and begs him to come to bed, she is in effect asking him to accept the fleshly consequences of marriage without probing too deeply into its implications.

And Hawthorne is apparently on her side, for he describes Goodman Brown's venture as "his present evil purpose." Too close "reasoning" along the lines of Puritan doctrine could inevitably lead to condemnation of all sexuality, even that sanctified by marriage rites, as the province of the Devil. Goodman Brown senses that; he says to the devil, who walks in the shape of his grandfather with a snake-like staff (one need not be Freudian here — the Bible makes the serpent responsible for sexuality becoming sinful in our ultimate forefather, Adam), "were I to go on with thee ... there is my wife, Faith. It would break her dear little heart." There is powerful irony in the fact that continuing with him means "keeping to the path," proceeding towards "communion," with the devil's staff to help him along (cf. Psalm 23, 4: "thy rod and thy staff they comfort me") — all religious phrases that even the most pious of the congregation (Goody Cloyse) readily accept. But Goodman Brown determines not to accept anti-sexual doctrine — "what calm sleep would be his that very night ... in the arms of Faith!" This, however, cannot be done without the sanction of the church, and along come the minister and Deacon Gookin. The deacon asserts that he would "rather miss an ordination dinner than tonight's meeting," a marriage communion; the minister agrees, "Nothing can be done you know until I get on the ground," and they hurry on. Desperately, Goodman Brown seeks a more "natural" basis for his union with Faith. He "caught hold of a tree for support" and "looked up to the sky," but the attempt fails — "a cloud ... hid the brightening stars." All the voices of the Salem community, "both pious and godly," are against him. From nature ("the branch of a tree") he can pluck only sexuality, the pink ribbon, but no whole Faith — "My Faith is gone!" He now realizes that he cannot have both sexuality and religious salvation. The "epiphany" that the dilemma is irreconcilable drives him mad. This is the turning point of the story, for Goodman Brown rushes ahead "with the instinct that guides mortal man to evil." The rest of the forest scene is a Walpurgisnacht frenzy. Other sects have accepted the

Pauline doctrine that it is better to marry than to burn, but at the heart of Puritanism to marry *is* to burn! The fires of the forest light up all the products of sexuality — there is a magnificent catalogue of all humanity. The deacon and the minister lead him to a blazing rock where he stands beside "the slender form of a veiled female," his wife.

"Welcome, my children," said the dark figure, "to the communion of your race. Ye have found thus young your nature and your destiny. My children, look behind you! [into the past] ... There ... are all whom ye have reverenced from youth [i. e., all parents who have engaged in sexuality] ...

Depending upon one another's hearts, ye had still hoped that virtue were not all a dream. Now are ye undeceived. Evil is the nature of mankind. Evil must be your only happiness. Welcome again, my children, to the communion of your race."

In this marriage ceremony Goodman Brown and his wife were "hesitating on the verge of wickedness in this dark world," about to be "partakers of the mystery of sin ... What polluted wretches would the next glance show them to each other!"

Unable to bear marriage under these conditions, Goodman Brown cries out and his night meditation is broken. He returns to Salem "more conscious of the secret guilt of others" and to Faith with the pink ribbons. With her he lives in a tormented, paradoxical love-hate. His Faith outlives him, having borne him children who in turn bear his grandchildren, but he remains forever conscious of the sin involved — "his dying hour was gloom." He knows that sexual love, even in communion with Faith, leads to damnation. Allegories are stories with messages, and such is the message of this one.

There remain several matters of technique to be considered. Richard H. Fogle has praised its clarity — "in simplicity and balance of structure, in firm pictorial composition, in contrast and climactic arrangement, in irony and detachment," and he is right. But in one aspect, narrative point of view, the story is faulty; it is the single greatest source of confusion. The story opens with a focus on Goodman Brown presented with apparently objective statements of fact and realistic details: "Young Goodman Brown came forth at sunset into the street at Salem village; but put his head back, after crossing the threshold, to exchange a parting kiss with his young wife." Everything is in visual and aural terms, until Brown turns the corner of the meeting house: "Poor little Faith!" thought he, for his heart smote him. Here the narrative mode shifts to an omniscient perspective, and when the text reads, "Goodman Brown felt himself justified in making more haste on his present evil purpose," we cannot be certain whether the judgment of the purpose as evil is the narrator's or Brown's. Perhaps it is both, since the omniscient narrator generally conforms in observation and judgment to the perspective of the central character, but the question remains a nagging one. A few paragraphs later, Brown meets the devil: "As nearly as could be discerned..." and a description follows. We ask "discerned by whom?" Why doesn't Hawthorne say "As nearly as Brown could discern..."? The problem is temporarily resolved when it is said of the devil's staff that it "might almost be seen to twist and wriggle itself like a living serpent. *This, of course, must have been an ocular deception, assisted by the uncertain light.*" It would seem that the narrator adopts the conditions and limitations of thought and perception that are experienced by Brown. Not that the narrator's judgments are identical with Brown's, but they are conditioned by the same limits. Hence, when we are told "Thus sped the demoniac on his course," the epithet is the narrator's, but it conforms to Brown's "Come devil; for to thee is this world given." Had Hawthorne maintained this discipline all might have been well, but toward the end of the story disturbing new narrative perspectives enter. As Brown surveys the forest congregation, he says "A grave and dark-clad company," and the narrator agrees, "In truth they were such." But a few lines later appears a sentence that wrenches the narrative out of its established frame: "*Some affirm* that the lady of the governor was there."

Indeed? Who are these mysterious witnesses and to whom do they affirm (with the verb in the present tense suggesting a consideration of the event after the fact) anything at all concerning the Black Wedding Ritual? And doesn't the existence of such witnesses make a mockery of the penultimate paragraph? "Had Goodman Brown fallen asleep in the forest and only dreamed a wild dream of a witch-meeting?" The limits to the narrator's knowledge are also broken when he describes one of the attendants of the veiled female as "Martha Carrier, who had received the devil's promise to be queen of hell." When and where had Martha Carrier received such a promise, and how does the narrator know?

In the last paragraphs Hawthorne shrinks the narrative perspective back to its original bounds: "Whether Faith obeyed [the cry 'Look up to heaven, and resist the wicked one'] he knew not." But here another problem enters, for it has already been established that evil is of the flesh and we know that Faith has already been married to him for three months. To be sure, the forest experience is Brown's exploration of the implications of marriage and the cry may be the expression of a fervent wish that it could be avoided. Returning to reality, he discovers that it cannot; he looks "sternly and sadly" into the face of his wife and passes "without a greeting." In terms of the effect on Goodman Brown's life, it doesn't matter whether the forest experience was a dream or not; either way the discovery of sin immanent in the human condition was an "evil omen for young Goodman Brown."

1. *What is implied about the nature of reality as this story treats it?*

    Reality is that which an individual experiences. Most of the congregation share Brown's theoretical religious convictions, but they do not experience the sense of sin as he does.

2. *Does the devil exist as a separate being?*

    Only as an allegorical figure who symbolizes the begetter of all men. In this story he takes the form of Brown's grandfather, but all the children of parents cluster around him — good and evil alike.

3. *Of what importance is the source and historical setting of the story?*

It identifies the religious creed as that of colonial New England, Puritanism, a special form of Calvinism.

4. *What oppositions or dichotomies can you isolate in the story and what meanings are attached to each?*

See the discussion of town-forest, day-night, etc., above. But note, too, that as Brown reasons with the devil the argument centers on the past ("the race of honest men and good Christians since the days of the martyrs") and the present (the minister and the congregation at Salem village); that there are two encounters en route to the ritual — with Goody Cloyse and with the minister and the deacon; that a "goodly young man" and a "goodly young woman" are to be taken into communion; that each is accompanied by two figures. Almost everything in the story is presented in two's.

5. *To what extent is the condition of Brown to be taken as "universal," as many critics maintain?*

Since the narrator generally restricts himself to the perspective of Brown, the meaning of the story applies only to those who share Brown's religious convictions, whether they carry out the logic of sinful flesh to the degree he does or not. The story, in effect, calls upon the reader to do either of two things: a) to observe what happens if one enquires too closely into the implications of one's inherited convictions; b) to accept fully or to reject fully the doctrine of the flesh as sinful.

J. V. H.

Arens, Werner, Hawthorne, "Young Goodman Brown", *Die amerikanische Kurzgeschichte*, eds. Göller and Hoffmann, Düsseldorf 1972, pp. 33—48 — Connolly, Thomas E., *Young Goodman Brown*, Columbus, Ohio, 1968 — Cook, Reginald, The Forest of Goodman Brown's Night, *New England Quarterly* XLIII, 1970, pp. 473—481 — Fogle, Richard H., *Hawthorne's Fiction: The Light and the Dark*, Norman 1952, pp. 15—32 — Lang, Hans-Joachim, How Ambiguous is Hawthorne?, *Spirit of a Free Society*, Heidelberg 1962, pp. 203—207 — Link, Franz H., *Die Erzählkunst Nathaniel Hawthornes*, Heidelberg 1962, pp. 50—57 — Robinson, E. Arthur, The Vision of Goodman Brown: A Source and Interpretation, *American Literature* XXXV, 1963, pp. 218—225.

# The Minister's Black Veil

Text: *American Short Stories* VI pp. 17—32. Schöningh

*The story begins with a sunny Sunday on which the congregation attends the familiar, routine church service, but is shocked by the fact that the Reverend Mr. Hooper is wearing a black veil. The minister persists in wearing the veil throughout the afternoon service, a funeral, and even a wedding. Since no individual was willing to confront him with a demand for an explanation, a deputation of the church visits him but find themselves unable to articulate their request. The minister's betrothed, however, has no fear; but even she fails to elicit a proper explanation or to persuade him to remove the veil, and she too succumbs to the terrors that the veil arouses. Throughout the years the veil serves to cut the minister off from the love or sympathy of his parishioners, but it makes him a much more efficient clergyman, especially for those who suffered the agony of sin. At his deathbed, he is attended by a calm physician, the deacons and other pious members of the church, and a young and zealous clergyman of a neighboring town. The latter cannot bear the mystery and attempts to remove the veil, but the dying minister's last desperate act is to keep the veil covering his face. He dies with a faint smile on his lips and is buried with the veil still on.*

"The Minister's Black Veil" is perhaps nothing but a Gothic *tour de force*, though there hovers throughout the story a heavy suggestion of a profound meaning. The Gothic elements, which no doubt attracted Edgar Allan Poe to Hawthorne's fiction, are clearly embodied in the pervading atmosphere of sinister mystery and in preoccupation with death, gloom, and suggestions of insanity. Such details as "the corpse had slightly shuddered" and "the shaded candlelight in the death chamber of the old clergyman" reinforce this effect.

The story, first published in 1836, made an impression on Hawthorne's contemporaries (a leading London critic recommended it for its "singularity"), and the strange picture of the New England clergyman with his face concealed by a veil is still well-known to modern readers. Hawthorne seems here to have struck a note that echoes in some dark place in the reader's mind — as Melville did in the white whale. The symbolism of the black veil is explained, in highly formal language, by Father Hooper on his death-bed: "What but the mystery which it obscurely typifies has made this piece of crape so awful?" In wearing the veil, the minister makes of himself a living symbol of some truth which his congregation, like most of humanity, would prefer not to face.

The meaning of the veil is not all clear; or, rather, it has too many meanings. The first meaning is revealed in the sermon that the minister preaches when he first puts on the veil: "secret sin, and those sad mysteries which we hide from our nearest and dearest and would fain conceal from our own consciousness, even forgetting that the Omniscient can detect them." Here Hawthorne comes closest to a modern, Kafkaesque psycho-moral significance. But a second meaning is suggested at the funeral when the veil hangs away from his face as he leans over the corpse: "he prayed that they, and himself, and all of mortal race, might be ready, as he trusted this young maiden had been, for the dreadful hour that should snatch the veil from their faces." The veil now seems to stand for the way we all hide from ourselves the inevitability of death. In the dialogue with his betrothed, the minister seems to reveal still another stress to the meaning of the veil: innocent sorrow as well as secret sin. Of course, at a certain level of abstraction all these significances merge into one: the ultimate mystery of life and death, which have no clear and obvious meaning or purpose. This is the theme of a great deal of modern literature, and it is no doubt our heightened preoccupation with it in the 20th century that partly explains the continued popularity of Hawthorne's obscure parable.

In a recent study Thomas F. Walsh says (*Modern Language Notes*, May 1959) that the minister's Black Veil symbolizes Reverend Hooper's failure to distinguish between indifferent actions and crime, his consequent habit of making his parishioners feel as guilty as he does, and his unknowing separation of himself from probable realization of his own hope for salvation. At the same time his smile betokens his "tenuous ties with fellow men and shaky hold on his own sanity." From the balancing of the veil-dark versus smile-light imagery arises the unresolvable ambiguity of the story, and our uncertainty of Father Hooper's fate.

Hawthorne's short stories have been described as "part essay, part tale" because of his method, which was to take some incident from history or to probe some individual problem of soul and to comment extensively on it, either directly or through the mouths of the characters. It would, however, be misleading to imagine that, because he calls the story "A Parable", he is going to give us a dogmatic demonstration of good and evil; Hawthorne did not believe in any formal system of theology. The minister demonstrates, by means of the veil, that we are all cut off from our fellows and from our Creator by some eternal mystery — either our inescapable isolation of self, the knowledge of secret sin or urge to sin, the inevitability of death. In the death scene, he sees black veils on the faces of all those standing round his bed. To him, in the darkness of night, even the Earth "had on her Black Veil."

But the minister is by no means a moral exemplar. His estrangement from the community — to whom he surely owes an explanation for his strange behavior — is possibly based on spiritual pride, though the physician, the traditional representative of science and rationality versus religion, assumes that it is a mental aberration. The theme of diseased self-contemplation runs through many of Hawthorne's short stories, and in "Egotism: or the Bosom Serpent" an obsvervation is made that would appear to apply here: "All persons chronically diseased are egotists, whether the disease be of mind or of body."

The slow movement of the tale — the horror felt by the congregation is developed at great length — and a certain grisly delight in moral death-beds and funerals mark the story as a period piece.

1. *The story bears the sub-title "A Parable". Is it a clear-cut demonstration of good and evil?*

   Hawthorne's parable is as unclear as those of Christ. He wraps his meaning in mystery, which is appropriate since his meaning *is* that there is a mystery at the heart of things. This is not a parable in the sense of a Sunday school tale for children with an obvious demonstration of good triumphing over evil. Nor is it, of course, a slice of realistic life. The tale is concerned with probing some individual problem, with comments made directly by the author ("Each member of the congregation... felt as if the preacher had crept upon them, behind his awful veil, and discovered their hoarded iniquity of deed or thought") or through the mouths of the characters ("with what horrible crime upon your soul are you now passing to the judgment?"). The tone of the story, with its deep consciousness of alienation of man from man and from the universe is appropriately reminiscent of the style of a preacher.

2. *Hawthorne said, "Think nothing too trifling to write down, so it be in the smallest degree characteristic." Has he followed this rule in the story under review?*

The story is full of slight but accurate details which serve to give depth and solidity to the moral-charged experience.

a) The behavior of the children: to church they "tripped merrily beside their parents, or mimicked a graver gait, in the conscious dignity of their Sunday clothes." The day following the strange appearance of their minister, "one imitative little imp covered his face with an old black handkerchief..." etc.

b) The reaction of the congregation: dialogue during appearance of minister ("I don't like it!" etc.) and their abashed and cowardly behavior, "pronouncing the matter too weighty to be handled, except by a council of the churches." Their original speculations as to reasons for the veil: weak eyes, madness, etc.

c) The confrontation by the minister's betrothed: her initial self-assurance, followed by realization of failure and terror and the subsequent faithfulness at a distance.

d) Realistic details: breath upon the veil, veil hanging perpendicularly as he bends over the corpse, catching glimpses of it in the mirror, the enigmatic smile appearing below the veil, gradual whitening of the minister's hair above the black veil, etc.

e) Gothic details: shuddering corpse, faint music of heavenly harp, quivering of the bride's cold fingers, minister's customary walks at sunset to the burial ground, the dying minister's heaving and rattling breath, the minister's face mouldering in the grave, etc.

3. *Does the story correspond to Hawthorne's assertion, "that in writing a romance a man is always — or always ought to be — careering on the verge of a precipitous absurdity, and the skill lies in coming as close as possible without actually tumbling over"?*

The minister with the veil is certainly dangerously absurd. But the absurdity is carried just as far as it can still serve to enhance the horror of the situation.

W. G. C./J. V. H.

Fogle, Richard H., *Hawthorne's Fiction: The Light and the Dark*, Norman 1952, pp. 33—40 — Goodman, Paul, *The Structure of Literature*, Chicago 1954, pp. 253—257 — Lang, Hans-Joachim, How Ambiguous is Hawthorne?, *Spirit of a Free Society: Essays in Honor of Senator James William Fulbright*, Heidelberg 1962, pp. 207—210 — Monteiro, George, Hawthorne's "The Minister's Black Veil," *Explicator* XXII, 1963, item 9 — Stein, William B., The Parable of the Antichrist in "The Minister's Black Veil, "*American Literature* XXVII, 1955, pp. 386—392 — Stibitz, E. E., Ironic Unity in Hawthorne's "The Minister's Black Veil," *American Literature* XXXIV, 1962, pp. 182—190 — Turner, Frederick W., Hawthorne's Black Veil, *Studies in Short Fiction* V, 1968, pp. 186—187 — Wycherley, H. A., Hawthorne's "The Minister's Black Veil," *The Explicator* XXIII, 1964, item 11.

# The Scarlet Letter

Text: Hawthorne, *The Scarlet Letter*. Braun (contains shortened versions of 15 chapters = about 25,000 words; the notes include summaries of the remaining 9 chapters)

Hawthorne, *The Scarlet Letter*. Lensing (contains shortened versions of 8 chapters = about 20,000 words)

Hawthorne, *The Scarlet Letter*. Westermann (contains 8 complete chapters = about 23,000 words)

Hawthorne, *The Scarlet Letter*. Washington Square Books (the cheapest paperback edition of the complete text of 24 chapters = about 70,000 words)

*The novel is set in the severe Puritan days of Boston, Massachusetts, in the middle of the 17th century. Hester Prynne, a young wife whose husband has been absent for two years, is sentenced to stand on the platform of the pillory in the marketplace and to wear an "A" as a mark of shame on her bosom after she has given birth to Pearl and has thus proved herself to be guilty of adultery. When her husband returns he pretends to be a physician named Roger Chillingworth and sets out to detect and revenge himself on the child's father, whose name Hester refuses to tell.*

*Hester and Pearl live as outcasts of society, the mother supporting them by her excellent needlework. After three years Roger Chillingworth finds out that the Reverend Arthur Dimmesdale is the child's father. He pretends to be attempting to cure Dimmesdale, but actually goads his conscience and derives satisfaction from Dimmesdale's growing feeling of guilt.*

*Hester Prynne gradually regains public sympathy by her demeanor of humility and helpfulness. When, after seven years, she realizes that Dimmesdale is in danger of being driven to madness by his spiritual sufferings, she persuades him to leave New England with her. But Hester soon learns that they cannot escape Chillingworth, who prepares to sail to England with them, and the Reverend finally finds the strength to stand in the only place of refuge — the scaffold of the pillory, redeeming his sin by public confession. He dies, followed within a year by Chillingworth. Hester and Pearl leave Boston, but Hester returns after some time, with the letter A still on her breast. After many years of venerated life she dies and is buried beside Arthur Dimmesdale under one tombstone bearing the scarlet letter A.*

## I

The underlying conflict in *The Scarlet Letter* is one which is not only major in American literature but which has contributed largely to the peculiar tone and point of view of that literature. It is, broadly stated, the conflict between nature and society or, more narrowly, the conflict between the natural man and the artificial structure of laws and customs that we call society. Concern with this was greatly intensified in the 19th century under the influence of romanticism and its American offspring, transcendentalism, both of which habitually and ideally resolved the conflict on the side of nature, equating naturalness with virtue and attributing to the natural the advantage of intuitive wisdom. And, with qualifications, this has been the inclination of American literature in general — nature, of course, being variously interpreted in various times.

In such a perspective, it is all too easy to romanticize Hawthorne's novel and to make of Hester Prynne simply another romantic heroine martyred by a bigoted society. The sin of adultery of which Hester is guilty is a sin of nature, of impulse and passion, of love overrunning the bounds of conventional morality. It had, Hester asserts, "a consecration of its own" (XVII). Moreover, in the contrast between the prison door and the wild rose — the harsh instrument of social justice and the indiscriminate sympathy of nature — which Hawthorne introduces in the first chapter, not only the nature-society conflict but the usual romantic resolution seems to be implied. And certainly the Puritan society in which the story is set is unattractively presented; it is narrow, somber and humorless, lacking mercy and subtlety both in its psychology and in its justice.

## II

Actually, however, Hawthorne does not allow us this romantic oversimplification. The Puritan society is unattractive — Hawthorne does not spare it either his irony or his scorn; yet, no later than the second paragraph of the novel, he takes care to remind the reader that *all* societies are radically defective because of the radical limitations of the human beings who compose them.

> The founders of a new colony, whatever Utopia of human virtues and happiness they might originally project, have invariably recognized it among their earliest practical necessities to allot a portion of the virgin soil as a cemetery, and another portion as the site of a prison. (I)

Moreover, however dour and meager of sympathy, however narrow in moral precept, the members of the Puritan community are presented as having a kind of massive dignity and a basic respect for the integrity of the individual soul which is preferable to either the almost abstract malice of a Chillingworth or the sort of frivolity that treats all human actions lightly and thereby reduces humanity to insignificance. This society could be worse as well as better. It is a gloomy background for a "tale of human frailty and sorrow" (I), but as Hawthorne writes at the end, speaking of the marker on Hester's grave —

> It bore a device, a herald's wording of which might serve for a motto and brief description of our now concluded legend; so somber is it, and relieved only by one ever-glowing point of light gloomier than the shadow: —
> "On a Field, Sable, the Letter A, Gules." (XXIV)

The society, then, against which Hester, following the impulse of nature, has transgressed, is in the end a less depressing reality than are the act of transgression and its consequences.

As for "the deep heart of Nature" (I), emblematically represented by the wild rose beside the prison door — the novel clearly suggests the inadequacy both of its sweetness and of its supposed pity. It is true that almost literally the only burst of sunshine in the entire novel occurs in the forest — in nature —

at the moment when Hester and Arthur Dimmesdale decide to accept the natural consecration of their love and flee the Puritan community that seems to them the immediate source of their sufferings. However, the whole of the forest section (chapters XVI through XIX) is so prepared for and so constructed as to suggest that what appears the one moment of happiness in the novel is, in fact, a moment charged with psychological and moral dangers for those involved.

At the beginning of chapter XVI, the reader is carefully put in mind of the fact that from one point of view — that of Mistress Hibbins, the venerable witch-lady, and to some extent of Hester herself — the forest is a place where one may expect to meet with the Black Man. The wilderness beyond the pale of the small community is traditionally the scene of evil assignations between Satan and his disciples. Again, just before the "flood of sunshine" (XVIII) which seems to burst forth both as a consecration and a promise at the moment when Hester and Dimmesdale determine to leave the Puritan community, Hawthorne tells the reader explicitly that the forest itself is the physical type of the moral wilderness in which Hester has wandered and in which she has learned "much amiss."

Consequently, a shadow of ambiguity is repeatedly cast over the whole of the forest experience. Nature might be said to recognize and accept its own; little Pearl, the elf-child, dances in the sunlight while her mother remains in shadow. In deciding to flee, Hester and Dimmesdale put their natural impulses of self-preservation and love over against the judgment and discipline of their society, and the "flood of sunshine" suggests nature's acceptance of them at that moment. But at the same time, nature is characterized in this scene as heathen, unregenerate and lawless, and its voice, in so far as it has a voice, is dark and ambiguous: the small brook that flows out of the heart of the forest babbles incoherently. It does not mean; it merely reflects the meaning that people like Hester may bring to it.

In many ways, then, for Hester and Dimmesdale the sense of exhilaration and freedom they experience in the wilderness is a dangerous delusion. For Dimmesdale certainly neither the immediate nor the potential results of the experience are good. True enough, he does draw a new vitality from the sense of freedom, from his vicarious share in Hester's rebelliousness, and from the consequent release of his pent-up emotions. But, judging by his antic behavior and perverse temptations upon returning to town (XX), the immediate result of this is simply to release the latent energies of his lower nature; for the first time he is tempted to commit deliberately what he is convinced would be evil. Moreover, Dimmesdale's physical and psychological decay is the result of the corrosive effect of his burden of unconfessed sin. His deepest need is to expiate that sin, and in leaving the Puritan community, he would cut himself off from the one place in the world where he might effectually confess and seek atonement. Roger Chillingworth, who has vowed the minister's utter destruction, realizes this and, once he has surmised the plan to flee, is eager for its fulfillment. Ironically, then, in urging the natural consecration of their love and counseling flight, Hester unwittingly makes herself the instrument of Chillingworth — the very man from whom she sought to protect the minister.

It is important here too that the behavior of little Pearl be considered. When Pearl returns from playing in the forest after the interview between Hester and Dimmesdale (XIX), she refuses with impish perversity to recognize her mother until her mother has reassumed the discarded scarlet letter and until she has confined the *natural* luxuriance of her hair beneath the *formal* severity of her cap. She denies the minister any even slight show of affection, although she does ask if he will not walk hand in hand with them into the town. Pearl is in several senses of the word a strange child. As characterized in the novel, she is a peculiarly capricious and unformed being; her nature is as wild (the adjective *wild* is repeatedly used to describe her) and unregenerate as that of the forest, knowing only "the freedom of a broken law" (X). Though there is nothing basically incredible in the idea that a child should possess some such qualities, the fact is that as a child, even an elf-child, Pearl does not have a convincing existence of her own. For she exists actually only as symbol; her whole behavior, almost her every gesture and expression, is dictated by and rigidly confined within the limits of her symbolic function. That function is complex, and because it is explicitly developed, the "essence" of the child, as Hawthorne himself might say, has evaporated. However, it is Pearl as symbol that is of interest here.

As her behavior in the forest scene suggests, there is a fundamental and deliberate ambiguity in the symbolism of Pearl's character. On the one hand, the child, so hostile and aggressive toward the human community, is completely at home and accepted in the natural world; clearly she represents the human spirit wholly delivered over to nature. Yet, on the other hand, it is she who insists that her mother and father reassume the burden of cast-off sin, the punishment imposed by a society extremely intolerant of the natural in man. From the point of view of the Puritan community and of Hester herself, this confirms the view that Pearl is the living emblem of Hester's sin and the chief instrument of her remorse, but it is at variance with the other implications of Pearl's nature. The paradox, however, on a slightly more complex level of perception is not irresolvable. From the moment when Pearl raises her arms to the minister in the first pillory scene (III) to the moment of antic rage at the end of the forest section (XIX), Pearl agitates blindly and instinctively for the public exposure of her father and the union of the family in the presence of the community. Completely natural being though she is, she will tolerate no evasion of her parents' transgression or of its consequences, for only through their complete acceptance of responsibility can she hope to assume a normal relationship to society. Thus, while Pearl represents unregenerate human nature, she also expresses the drive of the human spirit toward community with its fellows, a drive which renders the so-called state of nature intolerable. In the ambiguity of her character is symbolized the most grievous consequence of Hester's and Dimmesdale's violation of the morality of their society — that is, isolation from the human community.

## III

Not only Pearl but all the main characters in *The Scarlet Letter* suffer, according to their various natures, from this consequent isolation, and it is essentially this consequence that makes the scarlet A, the "one ever-glowing point of light" (XXIV), gloomier than the sable background of Puritanism. The resulting isolation takes several forms — psychological in Dimmesdale, intellectual in Chillingworth and practical and emotional in Hester. In all cases it threatens disaster, but it is typical of Hawthorne's general emphasis that Hester should fare best and Chillingworth by far the worst.

Chillingworth, the wronged husband, in all the obvious manifestations of his behavior leads a life of exemplary service and piety in the community which he has adopted. Though there are murmurings about his strange powers and satanic appearance, he is accepted into the highest counsels of government. Yet, while Chillingworth moves at the very heart of the Puritan community, he isolates himself from the larger community of man by destroying the bonds of humanity in himself. He undertakes a personal revenge against the seducer of his young wife, but it is from the beginning a revenge without heat, already therefore inhuman, and it is soon transmuted into a form of intellectual sadism (X) which is pursued as much for the perverse exercise of learning and power as for any satisfaction in retribution. As the Reverend Dimmesdale puts it, Chillingworth violates "the sanctity of the human heart in cold blood" (XVII), a sin which brings its own penalty by dehumanizing the guilty. In other words, Chillingworth removes himself from the community of man by assuming the role of a fiend, a purely negative and destructive agent. So completely does he lose his grasp upon what Hawthorne elsewhere calls "the magnetic chain of humanity" that when Dimmesdale finally mounts the scaffold to make his public confession, Chillingworth vanishes as if he had become totally identified with the possibility of damnation and with the negative, diseased and morbid aspects of the minister's conscience.

Arthur Dimmesdale and Hester, on the other hand, suffer isolation and ostracism respectively not because they have dehumanized themselves but because in the act of adultery they have allowed human *nature* to override the discipline of their specific society, and, while their seclusion from society involves moral and psychological perils, it also strengthens in them the bonds of sympathy with the frailty and suffering of humanity. Arthur Dimmesdale's problem is essentially that of coming to terms with his own Puritan conscience. He cannot find the courage to make the public confession that would in turn make possible the effectual expiation and atonement that is necessary to him, and though his burden of unresolved guilt deepens his sympathetic understanding of human nature and makes him a more effective preacher, his actual retreat into hypocrisy renders unreal all of the normal and apparently still effective ties of responsibility and respect with the community. Having sacrificed the substance of life for the appearances and in his cowardice substituting a subtle sort of masochism — consider his near approaches to confession in the pulpit (XI) — for open repentence, he locks himself up in a nightmare world of remorse and self-recrimination. The spirit represented by Pearl, the drive of the human spirit toward community with its fellows, is active in him, but he hasn't the strength to pay the price.

The situation of Hester is more complicated. She is, on the one hand, more fortunate than her co-sufferers, for, being unable to conceal her own guilt, she has no temptation to hypocrisy. Moreover, she is sustained by pride and by independence of will and mind, and though as a result of her ostracism her practical ties with the community are limited and strained, her relation to the community is open and realistically defined. Yet, on the other hand, her situation is a precarious one; she dwells physically and psychologically on the outer fringes of the community on the edge of the forest — the location being, as Hawthorne might say, the physical type of a spiritual reality. Further, the very pride and independence of mind that sustain her also threaten her with subtle varieties of corruption and error. It is difficult to distinguish the apparent humility of Hester's bearing in the presence of her neighbors from what may simply be a proud refusal to accept forgiveness at the hands of those who have shamed her, and certainly it is pride that underlies her temptation to project her own guilt upon other members of her society (V) and thereby to achieve a perverse justification for herself. As for the independence of mind that her seclusion develops in her — it is a doubtful quality which draws her toward the potentially disastrous rebellion of the forest scene. Hester lives, as it were, in extremity. Despite her seclusion, she is bound to humanity by her abundant sympathy and charity; yet, the harshness of her punishment and the suffering of those she loves reacting upon her pride act as centrifugal forces driving her out from the community and into the wilderness of individual speculation and self-justification.

## IV

Much of the power of *The Scarlet Letter* comes from the relentless process of analysis which, leading the reader through a maze of ambiguous situations, moves steadily toward a conclusion contrary to what the opening scene seems to imply. In this process the three pillory scenes serve to focus the implications of the analysis in a series of symbolic tableaux.

In the first pillory scene (II/III), the platform of the pillory itself seems merely the crude instrument of an inhumane justice. Hester and Pearl stand alone upon it facing the cold indignation and scorn of the crowd; the Reverend Arthur Dimmesdale sits *above* the pillory among the dignitaries of the community. He appears unimplicated in Hester's guilt; yet, in his exhortation to public confession, there is a covert appeal to Hester to save him from his false position by betraying him. Hester's courage, however, baffles his cowardice by refusing the appeal, and he is thrown back upon his own inadequate strength. Meanwhile, Chillingworth stands on the edge of the crowd, like an actor ready to assume a central place on the stage as soon as the necessary conditions for his entry have been established. He appears the wronged husband of some melodrama, but once he is drawn into the moral and psychological vortex of the action, he will come to express the satanic possibilities of human nature.

Significantly, the second pillory scene (XII) takes place at night. Arthur Dimmesdale under the compulsion of his anguished conscience makes his way to the pillory and mounts the platform. Here the platform itself, without losing the aspect of an instrument of torture, becomes at the same time an instrument of potential salvation for the minister. As Hester and Pearl pass near the scaffold, Dimmesdale calls them to him. The three now stand together, and as Dimmesdale joins hands with Pearl, a surge of vitality goes through him; he has for the moment regained his grasp upon reality, upon "the magnetic chain of humanity." In essence, however, the scene is a mockery of the minister's real need to assume his share of public shame. He is still playing a dangerous game with his conscience. For, despite his convulsive cry and the illumination of a meteor, there is little danger of discovery. He has descended from his high place but under cover of darkness, and when Pearl asks if he will stand with them in open daylight, he equivocates and she withdraws her hand. Significantly, the only person to whom the flash of the meteor reveals the family is Chillingworth, who has now moved into the center of the action by usurping the role of tormenting fiend, and, significantly too, it is Chillingworth who leads Dimmesdale away from the instrument of shame which is also the instrument of his salvation.

The third pillory scene (XXIII) comes as a rather surprising negation of the developments of the forest scenes that precede it. Feeling himself threatened as much by the impulses that Hester's rebelliousness has fostered in him as by the compassionless probing of Chillingworth, Dimmesdale finally finds strength to mount the scaffold and expose his guilt in the full view of the assembled community. On the surface the action seems disastrous, but in the stern logic of the novel, it is by far the best possible alternative. The price for Dimmesdale is death, but a less agonized and more honorable death than he would have found in following Hester's lead. Hester's hopes are defeated, but then the defeat of her hopes is synonymous with the defeat of Chillingworth's. For she has naïvely made herself an instrument of the doom which he has planned for the minister, and through Dimmesdale's confession and death, she is allowed to escape from any implication in Chillingworth's deadly sin. Moreover, by Dimmesdale's action, Pearl is finally released from her abnormal state: the drive of the human spirit toward real and vital community with its fellows is satisfied. In its broadest implications, Dimmesdale's final action is at the same time a denial of the sanction of nature, a grimly ironic rebuke to the bigoted self-righteousness of the Puritan society, and an affirmation of the human need symbolized by Pearl.

1. *What attitude is assumed toward the Puritan society in* The Scarlet Letter?
    The attitude is ambivalent, for the society is viewed both as a specific community with the peculiar characteristics of a specific time and place and as a type of all

human societies. As a specific community, it is subject to ironic rebuke for its bigotry, its self-righteousness and its inhumanity. As a type of all human societies, it is seen as defective but not without virtues; it is a reality with which the individual, because of his own psychological needs, must come to terms.

2. *Hawthorne makes frequent use of what is called his "technique of multiple possibilities"; consider, for example, the several explanations proposed for the letter A reportedly seen on the minister's breast. What seems to be the purpose or advantage of this technique?*

By this means Hawthorne is able to introduce, without straining the reader's credulity too far, implications and possibilities that a general respect for literal reality would exclude. But, more importantly, it is also a constant reminder of the fundamental ambiguity of human experience, and this is itself one of the persistent themes of all Hawthorne's fiction.

3. *What does little Pearl symbolize? Is she a convincing character?*

Broadly speaking Pearl symbolizes the psychological consequences of "sin" — the isolation of the individual from the human community. She symbolizes both the chaotic state of human nature independent of the normal bonds of love and discipline that bind the individual to his society and the drive of the human spirit toward meaningful community with its fellows. She functions to prevent Hester and Dimmesdale from evading the consequences of their actions, thus implying a close connection between the acceptance of these consequences and the satisfaction of the drive which she represents. She is not convincing as a character because she is too thoroughly and explicitly controlled by her symbolic function.

4. *Why does Hawthorne introduce Mistress Hibbins, the venerable witch-lady, into the novel?*

Mistress Hibbins, ludicrous and innocuous though she is, serves to keep before the reader the fact that a deliberate choice of evil is possible. Only Chillingworth ultimately makes such a choice, but in the encounter between Hester and Mistress Hibbins following Hester's interview with the governor (VIII), Hester confesses that, had the town fathers decided to take Pearl from her, she would have gone willingly with Mistress Hibbins to dedicate herself to Satan. This scene illuminates both the precariousness of Hester's situation and the dangers inherent in the inhumane severity of Puritan justice. The presence of Mistress Hibbins also serves to introduce the anti-romantic notion that associates the forest with the forces of evil and, thus, to prepare us for the complex ambiguities of the forest scenes.

5. *Why does Hester go to the forest (XVI—XIX)? Is she successful in her mission?*

She goes with the specific purpose of saving Dimmesdale from the doom which Chillingworth is preparing for him. She feels that she owes a greater loyalty to Dimmesdale than to anyone else, but she fails in her mission. For in talking Dimmesdale into accepting the natural sanction of their love and fleeing the community which condemns them, she unwittingly makes herself a potential instrument of that doom. The ambiguous treatment of the forest setting, the earlier exposition of Hester's and Dimmesdale's characters, the perverse temptations of Dimmesdale in chapter XX, the implicit approval of Chillingworth — all these work together to point up Hester's error.

6. *What is the function of the three pillory scenes?*

   Taken together they give the novel a firm structure. Each is a dramatic moment precipitated out of the welter of emotions, motives and impulses; together they function to project dramatically and symbolically the implications of the shifting relationships of the characters to one another and to society represented by the grotesque instrument of justice itself. Cumulatively they represent the progressive recognition of the necessity which Pearl symbolizes, which Dimmesdale because of weakness is unable to satisfy, which Hester because of pride and love is unable to see, and which Chillingworth for his own diabolical reasons attempts to deny.

7. *Why does Chillingworth attempt to prevent the minister from mounting the scaffold of the pillory in chapter XXIII?*

   Chillingworth attempts to interfere because he has dedicated himself to Dimmesdale's complete spiritual and psychological ruin, and he realizes that the one real means the minister has of escaping that ruin is public confession, public exposure of his true nature and situation.

8. *Of what sins are each of the central characters guilty? Which of these sins is presented as most grievous in its consequences?*

   Initially Hester and Dimmesdale are both guilty of the specific sin of adultery. Dimmesdale is further guilty of the sin of hypocrisy, the result of his lack of moral stamina, and Hester is further tempted through pride not only to project her guilt upon others but to evade the consequences by flight. Chillingworth is guilty of "violating the human heart in cold blood," and, though Dimmesdale's hypocrisy brings its own terrible retribution, Chillingworth's sin is clearly the most deadly of all. The sins of Hester and Dimmesdale are sins of nature, the result of love, impulse and frailty; that of Chillingworth is conscious and premeditated and involves perversion of potential good — his refined intellect and skill — to evil ends. Whereas Hester and Dimmesdale sin against the morality and discipline of society, Chillingworth sins against the claims of humanity itself by developing and exercising his powers at the expense of compassion and sympathy. The penalty for Chillingworth's sin is spiritual death, dehumanization.

9. *Why does Hester return to the Puritan community at the end of the novel?*

   Though Hester feels that through her transgression and punishment all normal ties with the community have been broken, nonetheless she remains, even in her most critical and rebellious moods, bound to the community by ties of compassion and charity. The scarlet A has the effect of setting her apart from the community; yet, by openly declaring her guilt, it also makes it possible for her to redeem herself in the eyes of the community. The process of social redemption begins early in the novel (chapter V), and her return at the end seems to imply her acceptance of the view that only in completing this process by which the significance of the scarlet letter is gradually being transformed can her life have any meaning.

10. *What relation is there between the juxtaposition of the rose and the prison door in chapter I and the juxtaposition of the gleaming red A and the sable background of the tombstone at the close of the novel?*

These two emblematic arrangements frame the action of the novel. They recall one another — the red letter, the red rose; the sable tombstone, the prison door. But the obviously opposed implications of each suggest the whole relentless development of the novel in its steady movement from illusion to reality. In the first arrangement, the prison door — emblem of the harsh discipline of society — seems merely grim; the red rose — emblem of the sympathetic heart of nature — seems full of sweetness and promise. In the second arrangement, the social reality reflected in the sable ground of the tombstone is no less grim, but the gleaming letter A, reminder of a sin committed with all the sweet sanction of nature, is said to be still gloomier. For, however easily forgiven in the light of nature, this impulsive transgression has, in the specific circumstances of the novel, entailed suffering, error, and psychological and moral disaster.

A. R. W.

Abele, Rudolph von, *The Scarlet Letter: A Reading, Accent* XI, 1951, pp. 211—227 — Cowley, Malcolm, Five Acts of *The Scarlet Letter, Twelve Original Essays on Great American Novels,* ed. by Charles Shapiro, Wayne State Univ. Press 1958 — Gerber, John C., Form and Content in *The Scarlet Letter, New England Quarterly* XVII, 1944, pp. 25-55 — Gibson, William M., The Art of Nathaniel Hawthorne: An Examination of *The Scarlet Letter, The American Renaissance, Die Neueren Sprachen,* Beiheft 9, pp. 97—106 — Haugh, Robert, The Second Secret in *The Scarlet Letter, College English* XVII, 1956, pp. 269—271 — Putzel, Max, The Way Out of the Minister's Maze, *Die Neueren Sprachen* 1960, pp. 127—131 — Sandeen, Ernest, *The Scarlet Letter* as a Love Story, *PMLA* LXXVII, pp. 425—435 — Walcutt, Charles C., *The Scarlet Letter* and Its Modern Critics, *Nineteenth-Century Fiction* VII, 1953, pp. 251—264.

# ERNEST HEMINGWAY

Ernest Hemingway was born on July 21, 1899, in a suburb of Chicago. His father was a well-known physician and passionate amateur sportsman, who taught the boy fishing and hunting in the Michigan woods. His mother was a religious and musical woman and wanted her son to devote himself to books and music. Having graduated from high school in 1917, Ernest Hemingway became a journalist, but in the following year went to Italy as an ambulance driver for the American Red Cross. Not yet 19 years old, he was severely wounded and decorated for his bravery. After the Armistice he spent a short time in the USA, then returned to Europe as a newspaper correspondent; but about 1922 he settled down with other Americans in Paris to become once and for all a writer. In 1925 he had a first book of short stories printed in New York. His novel *The Sun also Rises*, with Paris as a background, followed in 1926. In 1927 he returned to the USA and lived in Florida for the following ten years. After the publication of *A Farewell to Arms* in 1929, his interest turned mainly to bull-fighting and big-game hunting. With the Civil War in Spain, however, his passionate opposition to Fascism led him to assist the Republican cause with his money and his pen. The first-hand information he got as a correspondent in Spain was used in his most successful novel *For Whom the Bell Tolls*, published in 1940. About that time he bought a farm near Havana in Cuba, but soon went to Europe again as a correspondent in World War II and became famous for his eccentric and daring activities. After the war he traveled or lived on his farm. He was married four times and had three sons, but never made a successful husband and father. In 1952 appeared a very short novel *The Old Man and the Sea*, which is widely considered his best. The last years of his life he spent in Idaho, where, in 1961, like his father, he shot himself when high blood-pressure and diabetes threatened to break his health.

Hemingway is not essentially a novelist; he himself once said that all his novels had begun as short stories. It is in the form of the short story that Hemingway's achievements and influence on others are most conspicuous. In his art he was stimulated, among others, by Stephen Crane and Sherwood Anderson. According to Hemingway all modern American literature comes from Mark Twain's *Huckleberry Finn* (1884). In fact there are many parallels between Mark Twain and Hemingway. Both their prominent heroes, Huck and Nick, run away from home, dissatisfied with respectability, only to face life in its most dismal form, brutality and crime. Both are hurt by their experiences and end by rebelling utterly against a society that permitted such horror. More important even is the influence of Mark Twain's simple declarative style. Hemingway's prose is characterized by simplicity of diction and sentence structure. The words are normally short and common ones, the typical sentence is a principal clause, or a couple of these joined by a conjunction. Events are described in the sequence in which they occurred and with a strict objectivity. This does not mean that Hemingway is easy reading, for he is intensely implicational. He will tell us what his characters said or did, but he leaves us to our own resources in the matter of interpretation. His style is the result of calculation, not spontaneous and naïve at all, though able to create that impression. To Hemingway writing is a process of getting rid of things; strict discipline[1] is needed in this struggle for control. Terseness, understatement and meaningful omission are means of hiding and controlling emotions. When, in 1954, Hemingway was awarded the Nobel Prize for Literature "for his powerful, style-forming mastery of the art of modern narration," his enormous influence on modern writers all over the world was acknowledged.

---

[1] cf. N. Happel, Ein Beitrag zur "discipline" in Hemingways Stil; *Die Neueren Sprachen* 1957, S. 538 ff.

# Cat in the Rain

Text:  *American Short Stories of To-day* pp. 16—18. Hirschgraben
*American Short Stories* V pp. 53—57. Schöningh

*An American couple is staying at a hotel in an Italian seaside resort. As it is raining they are in their room — the husband lying on his bed with a book, the young wife looking out of the window. Suddenly she sees a kitten outside in the rain, trying to keep dry under a table. When she goes to get it, the animal has disappeared. She returns to her room, strangely disappointed and unable to control herself. The preoccupied husband remains unmoved. Then a cat is sent up by the kindly old hotel owner.*

Hemingway wrote this story at Rapallo in May, 1923, and published it first in a private print of 300 copies in Paris in July 1923. The small volume containing three short stories and ten poems was dedicated to his wife: "this book is for Hadley." The story, which shows a remarkable understanding of a woman's soul, may reflect something of Hemingway's own situation at that time. He was about to give up journalism (the break occurred in December 1923); encouraged by Gertrude Stein the ambitious young artist was reading insistently and trying to develop a style of his own, and therefore did not wish to be bothered with a family. His first son John was born at the end of 1923; the marriage ended in divorce in 1926.

"Cat in the Rain" was again published in *In Our Time* in Paris in 1924 and in New York in 1925. It is one of Hemingway's best made short stories. After an introductory paragraph that sets the scene and mood, "Cat in the Rain" is as symmetrically and as economically structured as a classic ballet. Every detail of speech and gesture carries a full weight of meaning.

In the opening paragraph we are told that the two Americans are isolated people: "they did not know any of the people they passed ..." and that their hotel room looks out on an empty square. In this isolation they are about to experience a crisis in their marriage, a crisis involving the lack of fertility, which is symbolically foreshadowed by the public garden (fertility) dominated by the war monument (death). "In the good weather there was always an artist," but the rain, ironically, inhibits creativity; there are no painters there, but the war monument "glistened in the rain."

There follows a movement of departure and return in five symmetrically arranged scenes: the hotel room, the passage through the lobby, outdoors in the rain, return through the lobby, and back in the hotel room.

In the first scene, the American wife standing at the window sees a cat crouched under a table to avoid the rain and her compassion is aroused: "the poor kitty ... I'll get it." At this stage of the story her underlying motives are not yet clear, but significant is the fact that she refers to the cat as a "kitty," sees it as a diminutive fluffy creature needing help and protection. The husband, lying on the bed reading a book, offers to get it for her, but does not rise.

As she passes through the lobby, the hotel-owner, an old man and very tall, rises and bows. There is obviously a great contrast between him and the husband, and eight times the narrator repeats "She liked ..." listing the attributes of the old man that powerfully appealed to her — he was serious, he had dignity, he wanted to serve her, he enjoyed his work, and he had an old, heavy face and big hands[1]. It would appear that these are traits lacking in her husband, but an explicit comparison does not occur to her. The story is told from her point of view, and only that which she is consciously aware of finds expression. Nevertheless the great attraction of this man is indicated by the repetitions of *she liked*. Since Hemingway is preeminently an artist of implications, we must try to discover what is implied here, a process which involves considerable speculation. We note that the old man is probably old enough to be her father and presumably arouses in her at a time of distress the feelings of comfort and protection that her father gave her. More immediately, he rises while her husband remained supine; he expresses himself with a gesture of masculine service that her husband had denied her. The further implications of this contrast become clear in the final scenes.

As she looks out into the wet empty square, she sees a man in a rubber cape crossing to the café in the rain. The critical reader seeking significance for every detail, as he must when working with a story so short and so economical as this, is encouraged again to speculate on possible meanings. The rubber cape is protection from rain, and rain is a fundamental necessity for fertility, and fertility is precisely what is lacking in the American wife's marriage. An even more precise interpretation is possible but perhaps not necessary here. At the moment she discovers that the cat is gone, she is no longer described as "the American wife," but as "the American girl" (four times); it is almost as if she were demoted in femininity by failing to have a creature to care for.

But it is not the girl's fault. "Oh," she says to the maid sent by the padrone to assist her, "I wanted it so much. I wanted a kitty." Disappointed, she again enters the lobby and again the padrone rises to bow to her, a gesture which produces a very powerful, even visceral response in her. It makes her feel "very small and tight inside ... really important ... of supreme importance," all phrases that might appropriately be used to describe the feelings of a woman who is pregnant. The conscious thought of pregnancy never enters her mind, but the feelings associated with it sweep through her.

As she returns to her room, her husband takes a moment to rest his eyes from reading to talk with her, but only briefly. He certainly does not rise or bow. The intensity of the repetitions of "she liked ..." in the lobby scene is

---

[1] The sexual significance of the reiterated "she liked" is clearly explicit in the third paragraph of Hemingway's short story, "Up In Michigan":

Liz liked Jim very much. She liked it the way he walked over from the shop ... She liked it about his mustache. She liked it about how white his teeth were when he smiled. She liked it very much that he didn't look like a blacksmith. She liked it how much D. J. Smith and Mrs. Smith liked Jim. One day she found that she liked it the way his hair was black on his arms ... Liking that made her feel funny.

here replaced by the even greater intensity of "I wanted" and "I want," phrases which occur no less than sixteen times in this very short story. And again what she really wants never reaches consciousness, but the sum total of the wants that do reach consciousness amounts to motherhood, a home with a family, an end to the strictly companionate marriage with George. She wants her hair, which is "clipped close like a boy's," to grow out, but George says, "I like it the way it is." Since the close-cropped hair styles of the twenties were preceded by matronly buns, it would appear that the American girl wants to be like her mother when she says, "I want to pull my hair back tight and smooth and make a big knot at the back that I can feel." Interwoven with this symbol of maternal femininity is her wish for a kitty, now an obvious symbol for a child. But George apparently prefers the world of fiction to the real world of adulthood: "Oh, shut up and get something to read." Darkness descends and the rain continues to fall.

The story might have ended here, but Hemingway adds a final, ironic twist. The girl's symbolic wish is grotesquely fulfilled in painfully realistic terms. It is George, and not the padrone, by whom the wife wants to be fulfilled, but the padrone has sent up the maid with a big tortoise-shell cat, a huge creature that "swung down against [the maid's] body." It is not quite clear whether this is the same cat that the wife had seen from the window — probably not; in any case, it will most certainly not do. The girl is willing to settle for a child-surrogate, but this big cat certainly cannot serve that purpose.

Hemingway has succeeded in rendering an immensely poignant human experience with all the poetry that pure prose can achieve. The simple language and brittle style simultaneously conceal and reveal a powerful emotional situation without the least trace of sentimentality. The delicacy and accuracy of the achievement is magnificently done.

1. *What does the first paragraph of the story convey?*

    It sets the scene and the atmosphere of forlornness, greyness, emptiness, wetness. And it shows the symbol of fertility and creativity (the garden) dominated by the symbol of death (the war monument).

2. *What is the meaning of the cat in the rain?*

    At first it is a poor little animal arousing the compassion and the motherly feelings of a young American wife; then a cause for her outburst of general dissatisfaction; finally a symbol for the American wife herself: her loneliness and lack of warmth. So it serves throughout to direct the reader's attention to the central figure of the story, the American wife, and her sad plight.

3. *To what effect does Hemingway employ repetition in this story?*

    Five times we are told that George is reading; any other information about him merely states a short interruption or a slight change of his position in bed. So the repetition concerns his sole interest and contrasts his absorption in reading with his wife's pleas.

With the American wife the verb "to like" is eight times repeated, stressing the great attraction of the hotel-owner for her. The expression "I want" occurs even sixteen times, the constant repetition conveying her desperate dissatisfaction with the present form of her life.

*4. Why is the story without the usual ending?*

In order to stimulate the reader's imagination who must ask himself whether the American wife can be pleased and grateful after all she has said before. She may well be shocked at realizing that this is the only result of her emotional outburst. Her words seem to have been taken too literally, her desire fulfilled too cheaply. She can hardly be in a mind to appreciate the hotel-keeper's friendly service.

J. V. H./M. D.

Hüllen, Werner, Gespräche ohne Verstehen, Versuch einer Deutung von Ernest Hemingway's Kurzgeschichten "A Day's Wait" und "Cat in the Rain", *Die Neueren Sprachen* 1957, S. 432 ff. — Kruse, Horst, Hemingway's "Cat in the Rain" und Joyce's *Ulysses, Literatur in Wissenschaft und Unterricht* III, 1970, S. 28—30 — Magee, John D., Hemingway's "Cat in the Rain," *The Explicator* XXVI, 1967, item 8.

## A Canary for One

Text: *American Short Stories* VI pp. 114—119. Schöningh

*A young American married couple is returning by night train from Italy to Paris with the intention of setting up separate residences there. An American lady is in their compartment with a canary in a cage, which she bought in Palermo and is now taking home to her daughter in New York. She wants to cheer up her daughter who has not yet got over her enforced separation from a Swiss engineer, whom she had met two years before. The American lady is convinced that "American men make the best husbands."*

The story was published in 1927, the year Hemingway's first marriage broke up.

Outwardly this is a banal incident written in the flattest of prose — it is the language of the ordinary speaker of English. The narrator, the "I" of the story, represents bare consciousness without ideas, hopes or memory. He notices, apparently in a jaded fashion, the passing scene, which includes a burning farmhouse and a wrecked train, but he does not comment on these things, they are reported in the same limited vocabulary as the view of "flat fields of grapes, with gray-stone hills behind them."

It is Hemingway's art to characterize the speakers through their unemotional style and attitude, but at the same time he unobtrusively selects the material of the narrator's everyday observations in such a way that the reader can sense the irony in the observed details and penetrate the deceptive pointlessness.

The American lady, a garrulous old woman, gabbles away, revealing her horrible self without being aware of it, to a young couple who are in no mood for conversation. The wife is obviously most distressed about the break-up of her marriage (this might well be the same couple as the one presented in "Cat in the Rain") and responds only when the daughter's marriage is being discussed. The young man's attention is focused out the window; he speaks only twice, once to poke bitter fun at the old woman who thought they were English (thus indicating his opinion of the stupidity about nationalities that underlies her objection to her daughter's love affair) — "Perhaps that was because I wore *braces*"; and once to comment ambiguously about his marriage in referring to the scene outside the train window, "Look. There's been a wreck."

The whole narrative is suddenly jarred into a new perspective in the final sentence. It is an anti-joke — the punch line does not provoke laughter, but sudden illumination of sadness. In the course of the spiritless dialogue an ironic parallel is established between the husband and wife about to separate of their own will and the enforced separation that the American lady tells them about. This old lady's firm conviction is "American men make the best husbands," which is doubly ironic as she is in the company of an American husband whose marriage is a failure.

The canary that she is taking to her daughter, who for two years has remained disconsolate over the loss of her Swiss fiancé, will obviously fail as a compensation. "A canary for one" who is broken-hearted and "doesn't care about things" because she is denied her love is not only a pitifully inadequate substitute for a husband (the American lady always refers to the canary as "him"), but also most inappropriate since the bird's behavior is ironically the exact opposite of that of the daughter: a canary sings best when it is kept alone, deprived of a mate. The poor girl will certainly be in no mood for song.

Nothing can shake the old lady's certitude, she is deaf, i. e. impenetrable in spite of her talk about "terrific presentiments." She reads the *Daily Mail* and her imagination senses disaster merely in the form of traffic accidents.

The scenes around the speeding train are all highly symbolic: the farmhouse burning, the negro soldiers, the wrecked train all are signs that normal decent home life has been broken. And as the train approaches Paris, we see that "the fortifications [of 1870] were leveled but grass had not grown," vitality had not reasserted itself. The narrator is sensitive to these scenes (though de does not tell us what they mean to him), but the "American lady pulled the window-blind down and there was no more sea, even occasionally."

Despite the skill with which Hemingway establishes a highly-charged atmosphere of unpleasantness and a gradually developing tension that finally snaps in the last sentence, the story is not a complete success. The major flaw is the fact that until almost the middle of the story everything is presented as an objective third-person narrative. Then suddenly, with the sentence "For several minutes *I* had not listened to the American lady, who was talking to *my wife*," everything is reoriented to the perspective of a subjective narrator. And the purpose of this unexpected reorientation is by no means clear, nor the reason for the delay. Furthermore, it undermines narrative integrity: how does the narrator *know* that "In the night the American lady lay without sleeping because ... she was afraid of the speed in the night" and that "the American lady lay awake and waited for a wreck"? It is true that her false imagination of catastrophe is a nice ironic contrast to her blindness to real tragedies (her daughter's and the American couple's), but the artistic gain is purchased at a high price.

1. *What does the French setting mean for the story?*

It provides a foreign environment for the characters with its consequent difficulties of communication and tendency towards distrust, which seems to have surrounded the marriage of the American couple from the beginning: they spent their honeymoon in Switzerland, and from two remarks of the narrator — "if that train *still* left at five," "if that were the way it were *still* done" — we can assume that he is very familiar with Paris traffic; his wife bought her traveling-coat in Paris. So they may not have had a normal home life so far.
As France is a country romantically connected in foreigners' minds with the idea of love, it offers a poignant background to two tragedies of love.

2. *Is the I-narrator indifferent and deprived of inwardness?*

He seems to be noticing things without interest and emotion, but from the beginning on there is a suggestion of sadness and frustration in his inactivity. He does not do anything before the arrival in Paris except speak two short sentences which are not directed to anybody in particular. From his observation that the American lady lay awake all the night we can suppose that he did not sleep either. The American lady's vitality ("looking very wholesome ... in spite of not having slept"; "she went back to the restaurant-car for breakfast") is contrasted with his lack of appetite and feeling of nausea that is somehow connected with this return to Paris: "All that the train passed through looked as though it were before breakfast." "... passing were the white walls and many windows of houses. Nothing had eaten any breakfast." They travel by night, so the references to breakfast take up the symbolic meaning of the dark night in which their marriage comes to an end: there is no beginning of a new day, there is no end to their abstaining from each other.

3. *What do we learn about the marriage of the American couple?*

It began in the fall and is dying in the hot summer, so somehow it went the wrong way. On their honeymoon they were in a fine old hotel, the "Trois Couronnes," a name which seems to denote the happiness of loving union[1]; the destruction of their hopes, the present state of their marriage is symbolized in the "three cars that had been in a wreck" which they pass while discussing the honeymoon. The last sentence before the final revelation — again in brilliant compression of the real and the symbolic — foreshadows the near future: "At the end [of their marriage] was a gate and a man [the divorce judge] took the tickets." "The train [their life together] was a *rapide* and went very fast" — it ends "in the dark" of the Paris station.

---

[1] though in reality it refers to a place which had been "famous, even classical" among Americans already half a century before (cf. the opening paragraph of Henry James' "Daisy Miller").

4. *Give an example of unconscious irony in the old lady's pointless chatter.*

She mentions that she has dresses sent to her from Paris. This has been a matter of routine for twenty years. There is a certain irony in the fact that her daughter is now getting caught up in the same routine, having been deprived of a life of her own. The old lady unconsciously sums up the hopelessness of her daughter's situation when speaking of the size of the dresses: "They had her daughter's measurements. She was grown up and there was not much chance of their changing now."

M. D./J. V. H./W. G. C.

Smith, Julian, "A Canary for One": Hemingway in the Wasteland, *Studies in Short Fiction* V, 1968, pp. 355—361.

## The Killers

Text: Hemingway, *The Killers and other Short Stories* pp. 7—18. Schöningh

*In a town named Summit two Chicago gangsters enter a lunchroom late one afternoon and wait there for a Swede, a former heavy-weight prize-fighter, with the intention of killing him when he comes in for dinner. They prepare the murder with casual, light-hearted precision, but Ole Andreson does not come, and they leave the restaurant to seek their victim elsewhere. The three witnesses of this scene, a white waiter, a Negro cook, and Nick Adams, a boy of about fifteen years, react in different ways to this dangerous experience. Nick goes to the Swede to warn him but is shocked at finding him resignedly awaiting his doom. Nick decides to leave this town.*

The story was first published in 1927. The name of the scene, Summit, is an obvious reference to O. Henry's humorous kidnapper-story "The Ransom of Red Chief," which takes place "down south in Alabama [in] a town as flat as a flannel-cake, and called Summit, of course. It contained inhabitants of as undeleterious and self-satisfied a class of peasants as ever clustered around a May-pole." The words of one of the kidnappers to his companion, "You must keep the boy amused," also turn up in Hemingway's story: "Well, I got to keep bright boy amused ..." In both stories, moreover, the gangsters proceed in a decidedly theatrical manner and appear rather unreal — and in both stories their design fails. O. Henry's intention, however, is to amuse his reader, in a style aiming at a grotesque contrast between the ridiculously overloaded language of the vagabonds and their inability to cope with a wild boy. Hemingway's story, on the other side, seems to be a grim and bitter parody on O. Henry's story; he confronts a boy with the horrifying existence of evil below the treacherous surface of normal life.

Nick Adams is a central figure in numerous stories and sketches, which can be arranged in a chronological order carefully developing Nick's character during his boyhood and young manhood. He is a very sensitive boy who, confronted with life in its roughest forms, experiences crime, brutality, prostitution and sexual perversion. From World War I he returns physically and spiritually wounded, unable to sleep. Having broken with his family as a boy, he now breaks with society. — All the heroes in Hemingway's novels resemble Nick. Many of their experiences and reactions clearly show autobiographical features.

The story has three parts: the opening long scene in the lunch room when Nick Adams becomes exposed to the threat of evil and violence; the brief scene in Ole Andreson's rooming house when Nick encounters a sense of futility in resisting such evil and violence; and the final section in the lunch room when he tries to assimilate the total experience of initiation. There are two early points at which the story might have ended, but, of course, it would have had a different meaning in each case: 1) Where Sam, the cook, says, "I don't want any more of that." Here we would have had a tension and a release, and a form would have been completed. The remainder of this scene in the lunch room focuses on Nick and serves to present alternatives of evasion and involvement to him. 2) "Nick went out. As he shut the door he saw Ole Andreson with all his clothes on, lying on the bed looking at the wall." At this point the issue of escape or submission to fate would have been presented to Ole Andreson and resolved, and Ole would have been the central figure of the story. The remainder of this scene serves, as Brooks and Warren have suggested, as a sort of knocking-at-the-gate interlude as in *Macbeth*, with Mrs. Bell serving as the porter. But it also serves to return the problem to Nick, when Mrs. Bell tells him that she's sorry Ole doesn't feel well — "He's an awfully nice man ... He's just as gentle." Nick must now somehow cope not only with the fact that Ole submits to his fate, but also with the knowledge that he is a decent fellow who doesn't deserve such a fate. In other words, Nick must learn to live with an existentialist truth about the injustice and tragedy of man's fate.

After the killers have left, George turns to Nick and says, "You better go see Ole Andreson," and the Negro cook immediately cautions, "You better not have anything to do with it at all." Nick is here faced with the choice: involvement or evasion — and he chooses involvement. When his involvement proves to be futile, he determines in his frustration to "get out of this town" ... "I can't stand to think about him waiting in the room and knowing he's going to get it. It's too damned awful." He is learning a lesson that George has apparently learned long ago. When George replies, "Well, you better not think about it," he is not reversing his stand of prudent involvement; he is merely saying *if you can't bear to think about it, don't*. George himself can bear to think about it and has pronounced his judgment: "It's a hell of a thing." Throughout the story, George has stood up to the killers within the limits of his powers. When Al asks sarcastically, "You're a pretty bright boy, aren't you?" George replies, "Sure." When they demand that the Negro cook be summoned, he resists, "Where do you think you are?" But he submits to the threat of brute force when he must. He keeps his head, constantly observes the killers and the clock, repeatedly suggests that Ole is not coming, and sends Nick to warn Ole after the killers have left. Though he is no self-sacrificing hero, his attitude and values are far more responsible and humane than the servile submission and evasion of the cook. His is the prudent wisdom that Nick must learn to acquire.

Hemingway's famous style is here appropriate to the experience of unsophisticated characters and serves also to highlight the stark reality of elemental behavior. Furthermore, the fact that Hemingway says so little — he, in fact, says nothing; he merely presents virtual action and speech — emphasizes the philosophical significance of the story, which is that there is simply nothing that man can do or say that will make any difference to the presence of evil and violence in human life.

1. *Is the story written in a simple style?*

> Words and phrases are simple, the dialogue is realistic. But the simplicity is an artistic one, intended to convey the maximum of meaning. The reader is constantly asked to cooperate. The narration is objective, but details are chosen for their significance, e. g. gloved hands, eyes on the mirror, arranging like a photographer. There is no description, no explanation, no moralizing. The style is the result of a process of omitting every word that does not help to create a certain atmosphere.

2. *What do the numerous contradictions, misunderstandings, expressions of (not) knowing and thinking indicate?*

> The repeated references to misunderstanding and ignorance make the reader realize that appearances are deceptive and must be penetrated in order to get at reality. A bare summary of the surface action does not make much sense. The conversation deals for a long time with apparently irrelevant matters — food and drink, Max keeping George amused — but the very triviality of the talk, the frequent repetitions and commonplaces help to increase the suspense and the feeling that there must be something behind it.

3. *What purposes does the reference to the clock on the wall behind the counter serve?*

> It serves two purposes — one thematic and the other developmental. When the first man (and notice that the killers remain anonymous until they reveal their own names in the dialogue) asks for a dinner and is told that dinners are not served until six o'clock, George looks at the clock and says,
> "It's five o'clock."
> "The clock says twenty minutes past five," the second man said.
> "It's twenty minutes fast."
> Thematically this suggests, as in *Hamlet* and many works of literature since, that "the time is out of joint" and that there is no dependable order or standard for men to live by. This also serves to create suspense by calling our attention to the passage of time as the killers watch both the clock and the mirror to determine the arrival of Ole Andreson who is expected at six o'clock. When the clock reads a quarter past six (really five minutes to six), "the door from the street opened." The attentive reader expects Ole, but "a streetcar motorman came in." George constantly watches the clock. At six-fifty-five (really six-thirty-five), George says (probably with great relief, or possibly merely to suggest that the killers leave), "He's not coming." At various intervals until well after seven o'clock, there are

references to the time. After the killers have left, the clock is never mentioned again; it has served its tension-generating purpose.

4. *How does the attitude of the gangsters fit into the normal world of the lunch-room?*

They are dressed like twins, both eat with their gloves on, they know exactly how to arrange the killing; "in their tight overcoats and derby hats they looked like a vaudeville team." They are the types known from crime thrillers or movies, or even from the stage. Their connection with an unreal world is stressed by Max's advice to George, "You ought to go to the movies more." And George, in fact, knows "what they kill them for." But the boys never expected such a thing to happen in reality, in the normal world. Everything is different from what is expected.

5. *What is the story really about?*

The point of view of the story is Nick's — the narrative camera follows him (except for one inconsistency when Nick is bound in the kitchen and the camera remains in the lunch counter). When Nick leaves the lunch room to warn Ole Andreson, the camera follows him and returns with him. This fact serves as structural evidence that this is Nick's story and that whatever meaning it has must relate to his experience, which is a boy's discovery of evil in the world. His reaction to it is the idea of the story. It is a story of initiation (i. e. admission to some secret knowledge).

6. *What causes the deep shock to Nick?*

At first it is the bewildering encounter with the gangsters: "He had never had a towel in his mouth before ... He was trying to swagger it off." Then he has to face the fact that Ole — "an awfully nice man" — submits to his fate, and he feels he "can't stand to think about him waiting in the room and knowing he's going to get it." To Nick this is an overwhelming experience of horror, utter hopelessness, futility, despair. He is incapable of the cook's cautious distance, and he is not yet able to bear the knowledge like George.

7. *Is Ole Andreson seen as a hero?*

Brooks and Warren suggest that Ole Andreson adheres to "the code" of the underworld which decrees that a doublecrosser must be punished by death. (Apparently, Ole Andreson had accepted a bribe from gangster gamblers to throw a fight and then had proved disloyal.) If so, he does not do so courageously; there is none of the grace or ritual gesture of the big game hunter or the bullfighter in the act of lying in bed facing the wall. It is almost as if Ole regresses to the foetal position in his helplessness. There is very little overt violence, but a tremendous atmosphere of tension is generated and can be released only by the imagination of violence. When it does come, i. e., when Ole Andreson is to be killed, he will probably be shot in his bed — a very nasty prospect. But this is only one of the many ways in which the realism of the story contrasts with the heroic ideal invoked by reference to the movies ("you ought to go to the movies more").

**8. *Is there also a symbolic level to the story?***

The name of the young boy can perhaps be seen in a symbolic light: "Adams" may refer to the first man, "Nick" (usually "Old Nick"), in the USA, is a familiar name for the devil; this would give Nick Adams a meaning like "man bedeviled." He has his initiatory experience "on a nice fall day," which, in this context, opens the perspective on the fall of man. The name Summit similarly suggests a satirical reference to optimistic belief in human advancement[1]. Nick's decision "to get out of this town" then might be seen as a rebuff to modern society.

But Hemingway's lean style puts such a burden of interpretation on the reader who demands more than a realistic little sketch that great care is required not to exceed the bounds of the narrative itself. Much interpretation must remain strictly speculative. For example, despite the limited cast of characters, Hemingway has managed to introduce, quite naturally and inconspicuously: Gentiles and Jews (Al makes a wisecrack to Max, "You were in a kosher convent. That's where you were."); Negroes and whites; Americans and foreigners (Ole Andreson is a Swede). Does this mean that the narrative is an implicit commentary on the prevalence of evil and violence in the universe and the helplessness of all men to combat it? The most that one can say is, "Perhaps."

M. D./J. V. H.

Brooks and Warren, *Understanding Fiction*, 2nd ed., New York 1959, pp. 303—312 — Carstensen, Broder, Das Zeitmoment und einige charakteristische Motive in Ernest Hemingway's Kurzgeschichte The Killers, *Jahrb. f. Amerikastudien* Band 4, Heidelberg 1959, S. 180 ff. — Evans, O., The Protagonist of Hemingway's "The Killers," *Modern Language Notes* 73, 1958, pp. 589—591 — Galinsky, Hans, und Klaus Lubbers, *Zwei Klassiker der amerikanischen Kurzgeschichte*, Frankfurt 1971, pp. 5—51 — Livingston, Howard, Religious Intrusion in Hemingway's "The Killers," *English Record* 21, 1971, pp. 42—45 — Schuhmann, Kuno, Hemingway, "The Killers," *Die amerikanische Kurzgeschichte*, eds. Göller and Hoffmann, Düsseldorf 1972, pp. 268—277 — Stone, Edward, Some Questions about H's "The Killers," *Studies in Short Fiction* V, 1967, pp. 12—17; p. 209 — West, Ray, *The Short Story in America, 1900—1950*, Chicago 1952, pp. 94—96. Cf. also the notes in *Die Neueren Sprachen* 1956, S. 307; *Die Praxis des Neusprachlichen Unterrichts* 1957, S. 98/9.

# A Day's Wait

Text: E. Hemingway, *The Killers and other Short Stories* pp. 18—21. Schöningh
*Modern American Short Stories* pp. 5—7. Diesterweg
*Great American Short Stories* pp. 35—37. Klett

*One morning a nine-year-old boy has a fever. The doctor takes a temperature of 102 degrees and diagnoses influenza. Not knowing the difference between Fahrenheit and Centigrade thermometers the boy (who had gone to school in France) naturally supposes that with a temperature of 102 degrees he will certainly die. His French schoolmates had told him that a man cannot live with 44 degrees, normal being 37. During the day's wait he manages to keep a firm and stoical grip on himself. In the*

---

[1] cf. "Zenith" in Sinclair Lewis' *Babbitt*.

*evening the father finally realizes what is troubling his boy so that he can explain the misunderstanding and tell him the truth.*

The little story was first printed in 1933. It is one of the tenderest and most delicate of Hemingway's. In it he may have rendered an experience of his own with his eldest son John, who was born in 1923 and spent some years with his parents in France. The story presents some motives that are quite characteristic of Hemingway: a young person's brave encounter with death, and the paradox of togetherness and separateness in the relation between father and son.

The story is told by the father, but it is mostly a dialogue between father and son, in which their misunderstanding reveals the boy's isolation. His terse answers, from the self-controlled "I don't worry, but I can't keep from thinking" to the sigh of relief "Oh" at the end, reflect the child's tension. Hemingway's famous "code" is here displayed at the pre-puberty level: the stoical acceptance of possible death by a nine-year-old boy: "He was evidently holding tight on to himself about something." The father, unsuspecting and only slightly alarmed, finds his diversion in shooting some quails; he trusts the learned doctor who "seemed to know all about influenza and said there was nothing to worry about . . ." The hunting episode provides a parallel of "killing" and "dying": death enters the father's mind only in connection with quail shooting, while the son envisages his own death. The homonymous use of the word "flushed" also accentuates their estrangement: the father flushed (= caused to fly up) a covey of quail, the boy's cheeks are flushed (= reddened) by the fever. The gulf between the rational world of the adults and the naïve ideas of the child is finally demonstrated in a most striking way by the different meanings of the word "it": the boy says, "You don't have to stay in here with me if *it* bothers you," and thinks of his dying; the father answers, "*It* doesn't bother me," i. e. his being with the boy. In the same way his commonplace advice "Just take *it* easy" is accepted in a profound sense, "I am taking *it* easy." With a laconic quality that nearly conceals his own emotion the father at the end observes that the next day the boy's hold on himself "was very slack and he cried very easily at little things that were of no importance." But only a loving parent will notice such a thing. His unspoken sympathy can also be detected in the affectionate term "Schatz" for his son.

1. *What has caused the boy to think he is dying?*

    "At school in France the boys told me that you can't live with forty-four degrees. I've got a hundred and two." He does not know about the difference between the Fahrenheit and centigrade (Celsius) systems: $0°$ C. = $32°$ F.; $100°$ C. = $212°$ F.; $x°$ F. = $5/9 (x - 32)°$ C.; $x°$ C. = $9/5 x + 32°$ F.

2. *How does the hunting episode function in the short story?*

    The boy is left alone when he most needs love. "Flushing" and "killing" appear in quite different contexts and thus indicate the diverging ways of thinking in father and son. The father's absence prolongs the boy's ordeal ("a day").

3. *How does Hemingway convey the boy's state of mind to the reader?*

"... seemed very detached from what was going on"; "he was looking at the foot of the bed, looking very strangely." The controlled reference to "it" (s. a.). There is no answer after the first explanation of the Fahrenheit system, he has to hear it again before he begins to grasp its meaning. His relaxation shows in his crying easily at little things.

4. *Why did Hemingway write this story?*

The trifling incident contains the elements of a tragedy: man confronting death in utter loneliness. Even a child can accomplish the same stoic indifference as an adult hero of Hemingway's pen. It is also a tragedy of the father; he obviously loves his boy, but is unable to realize and prevent his troubles.

M. D.

Bodden, H., and Kaußen, H., *Model Interpretations of Great American Short Stories*, Stuttgart 1970, pp. 100—107 — Hüllen, Werner, Gespräche ohne Verstehen, *Die Neueren Sprachen* 1957, p. 432—439 — Lubbers, Klaus, No Happy End to It, Galinsky, Hans, and Lubbers, *Zwei Klassiker der amerikanischen Kurzgeschichte*, Frankfurt 1971, pp. 66—72 — Oldsey, Bern, The Snows of Ernest Hemingway, *Wisconsin Studies in Contemporary Literature* IV, 1963, pp. 182—183.

## A Clean, Well-Lighted Place

Text: *Four Great Short Stories* pp. 5—9. Diesterweg
*American Short Stories* VI pp. 119—123. Schöningh

*Long after midnight a deaf old man is still sitting in a café in Spain. The younger of the two waiters is impatient to get home to his wife and closes the café. The older one sympathizes with the old man, for he, too, needs a clean, well-lighted place at night. As he turns home, he knows that he will lie in his bed unable to sleep before daylight.*

The scene of "A Clean, Well-Lighted Place" (published in 1933) is a café in Spain, a country which Hemingway often visited and used in his fiction (cf. *For Whom the Bell Tolls*, "Old Man at the Bridge" and other short stories).

A story which stresses the necessity of "a certain cleanness and order" in life may well demonstrate these qualities in its structure and style. "A Clean, Well-Lighted Place" is in fact a model of an almost geometrical simplicity and a style that does not admit of the slightest decorative breadth of treatment.

The opening paragraph introduces the three main characters, who are of three different age groups. The story clearly divides into three sections (three men — two men — one man), leading step by step to the final denouement, a structure which gives everything else in the story a proper place and meaning.

The relations and contrasts between the three figures in the story and the spheres they have in common can be visualized in a diagram:

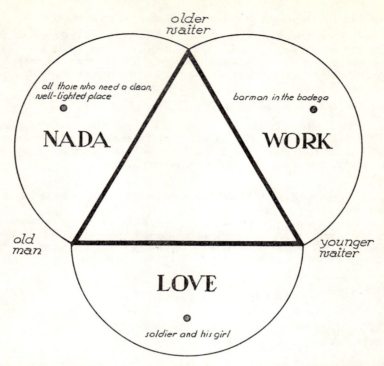

The contact between the two waiters is confined to their WORK from which the old man is excluded; indifference and incomprehension in this sphere are stressed by the figure of the barman in the bodega.

The experience shared by the younger waiter and the old man is LOVE: the waiter has a wife waiting for him, and the old man "had a wife once too." The older waiter, on the other hand, "never had confidence"; he appears to live quite alone and not even a niece looks after him. (Hence, it is not entirely true, as Robert Heilman says, that "the older waiter and the old man are in truth the same character.") The warmth and happiness offered in this sphere are stressed by the scene with the soldier who is risking arrest for love's sake. The older waiter characteristically observes the young couple in purely sexual terms — "What does it matter if he gets what he's after?"

The community between the old man and the older waiter is based on their recognition of "NOTHING" and their resulting sleeplessness. The younger waiter is impatient to get into his bed and advises his colleague to "Stop talking nonsense"; they "are of two different kinds." The bleak despair in this sphere is stressed by the reference to "all those who do not want to go to bed . . ., who need a light for the night," who need the café, who suffer from insomnia: "Many must have it."

There is an aspect to the relations between the three persons which the diagram does not yet expose: the different ways in which they participate in reality. The younger waiter is marked by the concreteness of his life, the physical character of his experience; even love is merely physical to him. The old man is marked by his resignation from reality, the spiritual withdrawal from life; even love is only a recollection to him. He has almost left the world — note his deafness, his drunkenness and his attempted suicide. The older waiter, however, partakes of both worlds, standing at the point of juncture and strain, with a view in both directions, feeling pain and pity ("Leid und Mitleid"). In order to indicate this extension into another dimension, the diagram could be divided by a perpendicular, and the left half turned up in a right angle.

The shape of the triangle not only exposes the relations between the different characters and their spheres, it also symbolizes the fact that nothing really happens in the story, it merely sketches a situation which was the same before and will be the same after this night. There is no "moment of illumination" for the older waiter, he does not "discover" the nothingness of life as Paul Foucar thinks (Hüllen - Rossi - Christopeit p. 93); the older waiter's remark "Each night I am reluctant to close up ..." and his reflections "He would lie in the bed and finally, with daylight, he would go to sleep ..." clearly express his habituation to his condition. The story is dramatic only in its mode of presentation, but not in movement.

Foucar's fundamental misinterpretation may have its origin in a careless reading of the beginning of the story. In the first section the old man is prominent as the subject of the conversation between the two waiters, and the reader's interest is directed to him. The two waiters, at this stage, are not yet clearly distinguished, because the author does not identify *which* of the waiters says *what*. But by the time the story is finished the characters of the two waiters have become contrasted so sharply and the differences in their outlook on life have been conveyed so pointedly that there can be no doubt as to the speakers. The young waiter, who is in a hurry to get home to his wife, is annoyed with the old man, treats him rudely and, knowing he is deaf, speaks to him most heartlessly ("You should have killed yourself last week"). The older waiter is sympathetic and understanding throughout the story and shares the old man's desire to spend the long hours of the night in "a clean and pleasant café." He is the one who gives all the information about the old man's attempted suicide, and the younger waiter, incapable of understanding, keeps asking blunt questions. (The older waiter never seeks information from the younger, all his questions being purely rhetorical: "What does it matter if he gets what he's after?", "How should I know?", "Why didn't you let him stay and drink?", "What is an hour?", "And you? You have no fear?") Notice that the older waiter first explains that the old man attempted suicide because he was in despair about "Nothing"; to him (as we learn at the end of the story, from "the conversation with himself") "Nothing" sufficiently accounts for a man's despair. In the conversation with the younger waiter he realizes the hopelessness of making his real meaning understood — "We are of two different kinds" — and gives the ambiguous, evasive explanation, "He has plenty of money." He rightly presumes that to the younger waiter lack of money would be the only reasonable cause for despair; to men like himself money does not help to forget, it may even increase the disgust with life[1]. When the younger waiter asks again in their next dialogue, "What did he want to kill himself for?", the older waiter simply replies, "How should I know?" If the first "Nothing" is read as "the young waiter's careless use of the word" (Theodor Wolpers in the Schöningh edition, p. 151), the full significance of the story is damaged; the older waiter's reflections would lose their full weight if they were seen as the outcome of the younger waiter's stimulation.

There is one sentence, however, that will not work in the alternating pattern of the dialogue between the two waiters.

Y. w.: "... I have a wife waiting in bed for me."
O. w.: "He had a wife once too."
Y. w.: "A wife would be no good to him now."
O. w.: "You can't tell. He might be better with a wife."
Y. w.: "His niece looks after him."
O. w.: "I know. *You said she cut him down.*"
Y. w.: "I wouldn't want to be that old..."

The solution to this puzzle presumably is that the printer of the first (magazine) edition put the sentence italicized above into the wrong line, and Hemingway never noticed or bothered to correct it. If it is added to the previous words of the young waiter, "His niece looks after him. You said she cut him down," the dialogue is not only perfectly convincing, but a grim poignancy is added to the optimistic assertion, "His niece looks after him," and the laconic answer "I know" would be suitably implicational.

The whole story is fundamentally a treatment of the older waiter and his outlook on life. Only in his words does the title of the story assume its full meaning. He knows that there are many people who cannot sleep at night and cannot bear to lie down in darkness[2]. The old man is like that, but the younger waiter is different. He has a wife. Heilman observes that the old waiter's despair is "not a private despair but one felt by others," which makes the story a philosophical and not a psychological one. Also, when the older waiter stops at a bodega for a cup of coffee, he is in effect re-enacting the experience of the old man, delaying the act of going home to a lonely bed. Loneliness, lack of human contact is one fatal experience. But there must be more. "It was not fear or dread. It was a nothing that he knew too well. It was all a nothing and a man was nothing too." When he thinks of people like the

---

[1] Cf. Andrew Carnegie: "The most miserable of men, as old age approaches, are those who have made money-making their god; ... [they have] plenty to retire upon but nothing to retire to and so they end ... passing into nothingness..."
[2] In "A Way You'll Never Be" (1933) Nick Adams says, "I can't sleep without a light of some sort."

younger waiter he realizes that "Some lived in it[1] and never felt it," but he cannot escape from it, "he knew it all was nada."

In saying that "It was all a nothing" the old waiter denies any value at all in life; he has no confidence in anything, he is cynical about marital love — "You have no fear of going home before your usual hour?" —, he has no faith in God. He remembers the prayers he was taught as a child, but they have become empty: "Our nada who art in nada, nada be thy name ..." The situation of the older waiter is thus seen as the utter loneliness of the godless, unbelieving man. Robert Penn Warren has said, "The sleepless man — the man obsessed by death, by the meaninglessness of the world, by nothingness, by nada — is one of the recurring symbols in the work of Hemingway. In this phase Hemingway is a religious writer. The despair beyond plenty of money, the despair that makes a sleeplessness beyond insomnia, is the despair felt by a man who hungers for the sense of order and assurance that men seem to find in religious faith, but who cannot find grounds for his faith..."

This cruelly hopeless view of life is hardly mitigated by the wretched consolation, the little alleviation man is granted: he can bear his insight with dignity ("that is all that is provided for these hours"); so the older waiter likes the old man for his dignity and poise ("He drinks without spilling. Even now, drunk ... a very old man walking unsteadily but with dignity.") and he himself smiles and tries "to make a joke" in all his obsession with nada. — Sympathy with the fellow-sufferer is possible: each night the older waiter is "reluctant to close up because there may be someone who needs the café." — And a little rest is offered at night to "all those who do not want to go to bed" in the light and the cleanness and the pleasantness of a café. "He disliked bars and bodegas. A clean, well-lighted café was a very different thing." "... you do not want music. Nor can you stand before a bar with dignity ..."

Outwardly he appears composed, but the interior dialogue reveals the bleakness of his despair, which is sharply underlined by his stoical attempt, in the last two sentences of the story, to shrug off his inability to stop thinking as being "probably only insomnia."

1. *By what principle does Hemingway select specific details?*

> He does not describe the looks and clothes of the men at all. All the details in the story are selected to give us the quality rather than the appearance of the characters. Only a repeated most careful reading will reveal the implications of numerous statements. The emphasis upon visual and audible detail creates a strongly visual image which permits us to fill in such other details as we need to give us the illusion of full scene.

2. *How far does the story approach play form?*

> It consists almost entirely of stage directions and dialogue, including "the conversation with himself." The way the characters speak is not indicated, it is left

---

[1] "it" does not refer to "cleanness and order," as Foucar suggests, but to "nothing."

to the reader-actor's imagination. There is an occasional passage where the narrator steps out of his reserve, e. g.: he classifies the younger waiter from his way of "speaking with that omission of syntax stupid people employ when talking to drunken people or foreigners."

3. *How can you find out which waiter says what?*

a) from the reference to the waiting wife; b) from the growing acquaintance with the two waiters, the younger one asking all the unappreciative questions (eight) about the old man, the older one knowing and understanding him; c) from the end of the story when we realize what "nothing" means to the older waiter; d) from the expressions of hurry; Hemingway distinguishes "the unhurried waiter" from "the waiter who was in a hurry." From this observation the sentence, "They went by five minutes ago," in the episode with the soldier would best fit into the younger waiter's mouth: he is impatient and therefore keeps looking at his watch and counting the minutes. Even the words, "He had better get off the street now," may not express consideration but annoyance: everybody should get off the street now so that he can close the café. The older waiter then ("What does it matter if he gets what he's after?") speaks in his mood of kind-hearted cynicism; later on he confirms his appreciation of "youth and confidence": "those things are very beautiful."

4. *Why does the old man sit in the café every night?*

He is very old; he is deaf; he has no wife any more. "Plenty of money" and a niece who cares for his soul are all he has. His deafness cuts him off from human society — he does not hear what the impatient waiter says to him, he cannot talk with anybody; ten words is all he says, and their monotony speaks for his situation: "Another brandy... A little more... Thank you... Another brandy... Another." The silence and isolation are most painful at night: "at night it was quiet and he felt the difference" does not mean that he enjoys the stillness, on the contrary; with the noises of the day, the world around him penetrates his deafness, at night he is completely shut off. As he is one of those who cannot sleep he likes to sit in a café. There is light, he can sit in the liveliness of the moving shadows. There he can drink and try to forget.

5. *In which ways does the older waiter occupy a central position in the story?*

His age. His participation in and understanding of both worlds: the active life of WORK and the contemplative life of the recognition of NADA. He knows more about LOVE than the younger waiter ("He might be better with a wife") and he knows more about NADA than the old man ("I have never had confidence."). He has managed to live with his insight and to bear it with dignity. He does not only suffer himself, but suffers with his fellow-beings. His WORK provides him with the pleasantness of light and "a certain cleanness and order," and he offers it to others who need it.

6. *What realistic details are used on two levels?*

Irony and symbolic usage usually combine to accentuate the deeper meaning of the scene. Darkness and light have a symbolic value, of course, so has the old man's deafness. Light is experienced in two forms: "In the daytime (God's light) the street was dusty," but at night when the dew settled the dust it is man's electric light that defines order[1]. The bed is seen in two sharply contrasting ways — it offers either love or unbearable loneliness. The normal desire for "a certain cleanness and order" becomes of vital importance in the context of the older waiter's facing nothing, i. e., chaos. — The apparently meaningless "nothing" assumes its weight in the course of the story; "confidence" is at first used in a joking reference to the younger waiter's wife, then reflected upon by the older waiter on a philosophical level; "insomnia" is a most effectful example of ironical understatement. Note the pun in "waiter".

7. *Why is "A Clean, Well-Lighted Place" a religious (or antireligious) story?*

The experience of NADA is not only shared by the older waiter and the old man in the story, but repeated references to "all those who need a light for the night" reveal it as a problem of our time. The key line of the story, "It was all a nothing and man was nothing too," denies any value, and the parodied prayers demonstrate the emptiness of faith. The experience is seen as suffering, which causes a strong desire for "a certain cleanness and order."  M. D.

Bache, William B., Craftsmanship in "A Clean, Well-Lighted Place," *Personalist* XXXVII, 1956, pp. 60-64 — Baker, Carlos, *Hemingway*, Princeton 1952, pp. 123-125 — Foucar, Paul, Hemingway, "A Clean, Well-Lighted Place," Hüllen-Rossi-Christopeit, *Zeitgenössische amerikanische Dichtung*, Frankfurt 1960, pp. 91—95 — Gabriel, Joseph, The Logic of Confusion in "A Clean, Well-lighted Place," *College English* XXII, 1961, pp. 539—546 — Henss, Herbert, Eine verbindende Interpretation..., *Die Neueren Sprachen* 1967, pp. 334—338 — Lodge, David, Hemingway's Clean, Well-Lighted, Puzzling Place, *Essays in Criticism* XXI, 1971, pp. 33—56 — Lubbers, Klaus, No Happy End to It, Galinsky and Lubbers, *Zwei Klassiker der amerikanischen Kurzgeschichte*, Frankfurt 1971, pp. 72—83 — May, Charles, Is Hemingway's "Well-Lighted Place" Really Clean Now? *Studies in Short Fiction* VIII, 1971, pp. 326—330.

## The Old Man and the Sea

Text: Hemingway, *The Old Man and the Sea*. Hueber (Silva) (abridged)

*Santiago, an old Cuban fisherman, has not caught a fish for 84 days. Nevertheless he tries again and rows far out to sea quite alone, since the boy Manolin, who admires him, is no longer allowed by his parents to accompany him. He hooks a huge marlin at noon, which keeps pulling him out to sea for 48 hours before he can kill him. While he is sailing home with the prize, a big Mako shark is attracted by the blood. Santiago can kill him, but loses his harpoon. With a knife tied to one of the oars he kills three of the shovel-nose sharks which follow, then the blade snaps. He hurts two more with an oar, but finally cannot prevent them from eating the fish. Early in the morning of the fourth day he returns to port exhausted and with only the skeleton of the fish to show.*

---

[1] cf. Wallace Stevens, "The Idea of Order at Key West": "... the glassy lights ... As the night descended ... Mastered the night, and portioned out the sea, Fixing emblazoned zones and fiery poles, Arranging, deepening, enchanting night." (Hüllen - Rossi - Christopeit, *Zeitgenössische amerikanische Dichtung* p. 223).

*The Old Man and the Sea* (published in 1952) develops a familiar Hemingway theme — the theme of the undefeated. Like other Hemingway treatments of the same theme, this one presents the story of a moral triumph which has as its absolutely necessary condition an apparently smashing defeat. The literary lineage of the old fisherman, himself, goes back to several earlier Hemingway "code heroes," and, as Philip Young has observed,

"Particularly he is related to men like Manuel Garcia, 'The Undefeated' bullfighter, who lose[s], in one way, but win[s] in another. Like Manuel, Santiago is a fighter whose best days are behind him and, worse, is wholly down on his luck. But he still dares, and sticks to the rules, and will not quit when he is licked. He is undefeated, he endures, and his loss, therefore, in the manner of it, is itself a victory."

This, in effect, is what it means to be a Hemingway "code hero," but the manner of Santiago's loss and of Hemingway's presentation of it is such that it sets the old fisherman apart from all predecessors. He is the apotheosis of the code hero; his experience is not only a confirmation of personal dignity and courage but what is perhaps best called a *ritual of transfiguration*.

The sense of ritual accompanies the whole action from the opening dialogues between Santiago and Manolin (in which catachetical question and response serve to sustain an innocent illusion of uncompromised respect and dignity) to the final disposal of the remains of the great fish. This sense of ritual action is fostered by the simplicity of the style, by verbal repetition, by the deliberateness with which even small acts are performed, and by the old fisherman's own sense of mystery. Furthermore it is reinforced by what might be called Reminiscences of Christianity, present in the story sometimes as symbol, sometimes as direct allusion and sometimes merely as a matter of tone. The transfiguration that is at the heart of the story, however, is no Christian mystery; it is "in the manner of it" fundamentally and essentially pagan.

This is not to say that there isn't something of the Christian saint about Santiago. He has achieved the most difficult and saintly of all Christian virtues, humility, a humility so absolute that it involves "no loss of true pride." There is even in him a suggestion of Saint Francis, in his response to animal life and especially to birds — the "small delicate black terns" and the small warbler that comes to rest on his fishing line. Moreover, at various moments in the story Santiago affirms the major Christian virtues: *faith* — "'He hasn't much faith.' 'No ... But we have'"; *hope* — "It is silly not to hope, he thought. Besides, I believe it is a sin"; and *charity* — his general but unsentimental love of men and animals. But as the old fisherman moves away from the shore and out into the sea, it becomes apparent that his "sainthood" is of a non-Christian order.

His "charity" arises, not from the feeling that all are God's creatures, but from a sense that he and all natural creatures participate in the same pattern of necessity and are subject to the same judgment: "'Take a good rest, small bird,' he said. 'Then go in and take your chance like any man or bird or fish.'"

His relation to the sea and to the life of the sea is intensely personal and pagan. The sea is "la mar"; it is feminine, not quite personified, but capable in a moment of fantasy, of taking a lover beneath a blanket of yellow seaweed. It gives forth life and reabsorbs it: the old man is fascinated by the sight of a dead fish growing smaller and smaller as it sinks. Moreover, for him the realm of nature and the realm of morality are co-existent; the creatures of the sea express for him all that he knows about life — the falseness of the Portuguese man-of-war, the playfulness of the dolphin, the nobility and endurance of the marlin. If there is a god in Santiago's life (he says he is not religious), it is the sea, and the sea, as traditionally, is life itself, which Santiago both loves and mistrusts but to which he can commit himself because he knows "many tricks" and because he can endure. Though he does not consider his tricks a grounds for superiority, he has, nonetheless, his intelligence and his will.

Similarly, Santiago's faith and hope rest, not upon any belief in a just and benevolent God, but upon his belief in man's ability to endure suffering. This basis of hope is implicit even in the early pages of the story. When we first see Santiago, he appears immensely old, he has been 84 days without catching a fish, and he carries a sail which, furled, "looked like the flag of permanent defeat." Yet, "his hope and his confidence had never gone"; he only needs luck, and in the past he has been lucky. Significantly, the signs of that luck are visible in the old man's hands: "... his hands had the deep-creased scars from handling heavy fish on the cords. But none of these scars were fresh. They were as old as erosions in a fishless desert." Clearly in Santiago's world luck and pain are closely related. Luck is something that comes and goes, and a man may hope for it from day to day, but it is meaningless unless he can endure pain.

In the first few pages of the story the word faith appears twice — once, when the old fisherman affirms that he has faith, and then again later, in a very different context. During a conversation about baseball, Santiago says to Manolin, "Have faith in the Yankees my son. Think of the great DiMaggio." A bit later this attitude is further elaborated in talk between the boy and the fisherman:

"'In the American League it is the Yankees as I said,' the old man said happily.
'They lost today,' the boy told him.
'That means nothing. The great DiMaggio is himself again.'
'They have other men on the team.'
'Naturally. But he makes the difference.'"

One can have faith in the Yankees, because DiMaggio makes the difference. In just what way he makes the difference becomes clear only later.

During the long ordeal of his struggle with the great fish and then against the sharks, the old man thinks repeatedly of DiMaggio, wondering whether or not DiMaggio would approve of the way in which he has fished and endured. Behind this is not merely the child-like idolization of a baseball player. The

DiMaggio of these reveries is first of all a man with a mysterious and painful ailment, a bone spur; he is, in other words, a man who performs well against the handicap of pain. And it is this that makes the difference. One can afford to place his faith where he finds the power to endure suffering, and this power Santiago finds in himself and in other men. In the end, for him, pain becomes literally the means of distinguishing reality from unreality — "... He had only to look at his hands and feel his back against the stern to know that this had truly happened and was not a dream"; and it is all but synonymous with life itself — "He put his two hands together and felt the palms ... and he could bring the pain of life by simply opening and closing them." The power to endure suffering, then, which is in man, gives the power of mastery over life and thus a basis for hope and faith.

In a sense, *The Old Man and the Sea* is a study in pain, in the endurance of pain and in the value of that endurance. The old fisherman fishes as much for a chance to prove himself as he does for a living, and, though he fails to bring the giant marlin to market, he wins the supreme chance to prove himself in the terms he best understands. Starting in simple physical pain, he transcends, through his agony, his own heroic ideal, personified in DiMaggio, and ends in the attitude of the crucified Christ: "... he slept face down on the newspapers with his arms out straight and the palms of his hands up." All this he endures without compromising his code either as man or fisherman; he succeeds in showing "what a man can do and what a man endures."

Hemingway's story, however, does not place a final emphasis upon endurance as a value in itself. Within the pattern of the story, endurance like pain is a necessary condition, not so much of victory but of being "undefeated." Hemingway's Santiago is equal to Camus's Sisyphus. The fundamental qualities of the old man's character — his humility, his simple and pagan reverence for the conditions and processes of life, and his capacity for suffering — serve to transform his struggle into something which he himself vaguely feels to be a mystery, and his defeat into a triumph much as the divinity of Christ transforms the terror and sorrow of the Crucifixion into the promise of life.

Before the old fisherman is himself identified by obvious allusion with the crucified Christ, he is identified with Cain and with the crucifiers of Christ. Once he has hooked the great fish, all of his generalized sense of humble brotherhood with other creatures of the sea concentrates upon this one magnificent marlin. Repeatedly, he addresses the fish as "brother"; the taut line that connects them becomes an expression of an equally strong bond of suffering and, on the fisherman's part, of love. Yet, at the same time, he is relentlessly determined to capture and kill the marlin, as Cain killed his brother and as the Roman soldiers killed Christ. That the great fish is somehow to be associated with Christ is not left to conjecture based on traditional symbolism. "'Christ,'" Santiago exclaims in wonder, "'I did not know he was so big. I'll kill him though. In all his greatness and his glory.'" Significantly this is the only place in the story where the expletive, Christ, is used, and the echo in the second sentence is unmistakable — "for thine is the kingdom and the power and the glory forever." When Santiago does slay the fish, he drives the harpoon into his side behind the chest fin "that rose high in the air to the altitude of the man's chest," and pierces the heart. Then, the fish rises into the air and hangs there a moment, and there is "some great strangeness" in it.

The old fisherman is not unaware of the paradox of his situation. He thinks, "... it is good that we do not have to try to kill the sun or the moon or the stars. It is enough to live on the sea and kill our true brothers." He thinks on occasion that perhaps he should not have been a fisherman; yet the question is scarcely admissible. He was born to be a fisherman; he is a fisherman of necessity, and he must kill the giant fish out of necessity that is deeper than hunger.

Santiago is, of course, incapable of articulating just what this necessity is, but the pattern of the story makes it clear enough. All the qualities which Santiago sees in the great fish — beauty, nobility, courage, calmness and endurance — are the qualities which he values most; they are the qualities which *redeem* life from meaninglessness and futility (this is perhaps the fundamental link in the story between the fish and Christ); and they are the qualities that Santiago wishes to confirm in himself. Paradoxically the only means he has of confirming them in himself is by exercising them in opposition to the fish. He must, symbolically, slay the lord of life, in order to achieve a spiritual identity with him.

Thus, the central event of the story is one in which the redemption of life and the destruction of life, affirmation and guilt are locked in a single action. While he is actually battling the great fish, there is some thought of injustice but none of guilt in the old man's mind. There is only the bond of love and suffering and the sense of mystery, the sense of some deep necessity that the old man cannot quite bring into consciousness. But after the first shark, the Mako shark, has mutilated the fish, thoughts of sin come to tease the old man's mind.

"Perhaps it was a sin to kill the fish. I suppose it was even though I did it to keep me alive and feed many people. But then everything is a sin. ... everything kills everything else in some way."

The old man, who has said he is not religious, cannot quite believe in sin in the orthodox Christian understanding of the word; yet, he cannot evade the sense of sin in connection with his killing of the fish. He has chosen "to go there to find him beyond all people." He may argue, "... I did it to keep me alive and feed many people," but he knows, as he confesses, that the boy Manolin keeps him alive, and he has said earlier that no one is worthy to eat of the great fish. Here again in the idea of worthiness with its suggestion of communion, the Christian allusion is clear, but in the context of the story worthiness is something acquired in action, by being great in the same way the fish is great.

The old man cannot resolve the question of guilt for himself; he can only oppose to it his conviction of necessity: "You were born to be a fisherman as the fish was born to be a fish." And in the fight against the sharks, the feeling of sin is lost and replaced by something more congenial to the spirit of the old man, something like the idea of *hybris*.

"And what beat you, he thought.

'Nothing,' he said aloud. 'I went out too far.'"

While the question of sin and guilt persists, however, the old man tries to deal with it honestly, and having counseled himself against rationalization, he leans forward, almost unconsciously tears a piece of the flesh from the giant, and eats of the fish of which no one is worthy to eat.

It is only after this act, which the reader has been prepared to recognize as a kind of communion, that we meet the first of the allusions that serve to refer the old man's experience to the Passion of Christ. As he sees the first of the shovel-nose sharks approaching, the old man utters a cry: "'Ay,' he said aloud." And the reader is told,

"There is no translation for this word and perhaps it is just a noise such as a man might make, involuntarily, feeling the nail go through his hands and into the wood."

Before this, all symbols associated with and all allusions made to Christ's Passion have been applied to the giant fish. Now begins a process of transfer from the fish to the man. As he leaves the skiff, the old man falls and lies for a moment with the mast across his shoulders; he must sit down five times before he reaches his shack on the hill, and when he reaches the shack, he lies down in the attitude of the crucified Christ.

The point of this accumulation of allusions is not simply, as Philip Young has suggested, that life crucifies even the strong and noble in the end and that the important thing is how one takes it when it comes. The transfer of Christian symbols and allusions from the great fish to the fisherman is, in fact, only part, perhaps the most obvious part, of a fairly complex process through which identity is established between them.

Santiago fights and kills the great marlin "out of pride," out of the desire to show that he is like the great fish. What he seeks is identity. He affirms continually his own feeling of brotherhood, but, in another sense, brotherhood can be affirmed only in a struggle that must end in the death of the fish. In a moment of semi-delirium just before he kills the fish, the old man's sense of identity with him becomes so intense that he thinks,

"Never have I seen a greater, or more beautiful, or a calmer or more noble thing than you, brother. Come and kill me. I do not care who kills who."

After the fish is dead, the old man has a strong desire to touch him, to confirm the reality of the fish and, thereby, the reality of what he has proved about himself. The delusion of confused identities persists as the old man, seeing the giant carcass of the fish alongside, wonders, ". . . is he bringing me in or am I bringing him in?" When the fish is hit and mutilated by the first shark, the old fisherman feels "as though he himself were hit." Later, when, without pride, almost unconsciously, the old man eats of the fish, the fish becomes a part of his life. Almost immediately the *galanos* approach, and we encounter the first of the allusions that refer the old man's experience to the

Passion of Christ. The pattern is extremely tight and neat: just as the great marlin in his noble but futile struggle to preserve his life becomes identified symbolically with the crucified Christ, so the old man in his noble but futile struggle to preserve the fish from the sharks becomes identified with the same figure.

Seen as a part of this general pattern, the fact of crucifixion no longer suggests either, on the one hand, the vague evocation of Christianity or, on the other, merely the supreme experience of "the pain of life" and the supreme test of endurance. It is the final seal of the old man's triumph. Through the tragic image of Christ in his agony, the identity of the fisherman with the fish, that is, with the essentially pagan virtues which the fish represents, is finally affirmed. The justification for this non-Christian use of Christian symbolism stems not only from the fact that the giant marlin expresses in action all those qualities that, for the old man, redeem life, but from the fact that the Crucifixion is a consummate metaphor for the medium of suffering, endurance and apparent defeat through which the old man achieves his at least momentary transfiguration.

When the old man reaches shore, he has only the skeleton of the marlin. The experience has been stripped of its practical and material aspects, and even the great skeleton is at the last only so much more garbage waiting to go out with the tide. At most it serves to give the other fishermen a clue as to what the struggle must have been; to the outsiders, the man and woman tourists who look down from the terrace, it is all but meaningless. They perceive some strange beauty in the thing itself, but they cannot distinguish even the elementary terms of the experience.

"'I didn't know sharks had such handsome, beautifully formed tails.'

'I didn't either,' her male companion said."

Having lost his fish to the least worthy of opponents, the shovel-nosed sharks that are just moving appetites, even the old man is unclear about what he has accomplished, and the boy, Manolin, whose admiration and pity counter-point the old man's humility, must order the experience for him.

"'They beat me, Manolin,' he said. 'They truly beat me.'

'*He* didn't beat you. Not the fish.'

'No. Truly. It was afterwards.'"

Finally the old fisherman seems almost indifferent to the great struggle; he is beyond it; it is complete in itself, and the others may take from it what they can: the head of the marlin to Pedrico, the spear to Manolin, the uncomprehending glimpse of the skeleton to the two tourists. But the gap between what the experience has actually been and what the others can gather from the remains is strongly suggested by the total lack of connection between their concern with the skeleton and the dream of the lions which fills the old man's sleep at the close of the story.

In a sense, the old man's final reward for having endured is the freedom which he finally has to dream, uninterrupted, of the lions that he had once seen playing like cats upon the shores of Africa and that somehow now are "the main thing that is left." The dream has come before during the story, but always before the old man has been called back to a reality of further action and further suffering. Now, that reality is held at a distance. For the old man there is a child-like happiness and reassurance in seeing the great beasts at play. What the lions represent beyond this is broadly suggested by the details of the dream in their relation to the general pattern of action and symbol. The lions, traditionally, are the noblest of the great beasts in comparison with which man, according to the old fisherman, "is not much." They are the kings of the jungle, primal nature, which they dominate by their courage, their strength, their fierceness and their supposed pride. They are both like and unlike the great marlin: like him in that they have the qualities that redeem life and are in this way the lords of life; unlike him in that their beauty and nobility is compounded with fierceness and therefore, inspires not only awe but fear. In the dream, however, the lions come out from the jungle and down onto the beach to play on the sand; they have put aside their majesty and have grown domestic and familiar. It is as if they gave themselves up to the old man, to his love, without the necessity of further trial or guilt or suffering.

As the lions come out of the jungle and fill the old man's sleep, their cat-like playfulness, free of threat or challenge, suggests a harmony between the old man and the heroic qualities which the lions possess and the giant marlin possessed and which the old man has fought to realize in himself. Most simply, perhaps, they suggest an achieved intimacy between the old man and the proud and often fierce heart of nature that for him is the repository of values.

1. *This story is not divided into chapters; yet, there are definite points at which such divisions might logically be made. Where do these occur?*

    The first section ends when the old man bids Manolin good luck and sets out from shore. The second section ends when the old fisherman succeeds in hooking the giant marlin, and the third section ends with the killing of the marlin. The fourth section presents the old man's battle with the sharks and is followed by a brief fifth section, beginning with the old man's admission that he is beaten. The fifth section reads much like an epilogue to the entire action.

2. *What does the boy, Manolin, contribute to our understanding of the old man and of his experience?*

    Manolin serves to highlight for us the character of the old fisherman. His admiration both affirms and counterbalances the old man's humility; his presence and concern create an occasion for the dramatization of this humility that "involves no loss of true pride" and at the same time provide an initial point of view from which the old fisherman can be seen as something more than an old man since he was not, after all, defeated by the fish. It should also be noted that during his long fight with the marlin the old man wishes often that Manolin were with him. The absence of the boy, the absence not only of practical help but of the support that love and respect can give, stresses the loneliness of the man, the fact that he has indeed ventured out "beyond all people."

3. *Before the fisherman hooks the giant marlin, we are shown him fishing under more or less normal conditions, and we are given at some length his impressions of and response to the sea and the life of the sea. What, in general, is the function of this section?*

Whereas the first section serves to introduce most of the elements that recur in the story — the cut hands, Di Maggio, the lions —, the second section serves as an exposition both of the old man's integrity as a fisherman (despite the urgency of his need, he would rather be exact than lucky) and of his intensely personal response to the sea. Through his reaction to a variety of sea life, we learn that for him the realm of nature and the realm of values are co-existent, not in any mystical sense but in the sense that for him, as for the pagan mind, all living things are subject to the same laws and liable to the same sort of censure or praise. He observes and judges the sea animals as if there were no essential difference between them and him.

4. *The old man makes quite a point of the difference between those who speak of the sea as "el mar" and those who speak of it as "la mar". What, basically, is the difference?*

Those who think of it as masculine, "el mar," are the fishermen who have prospered and adopted progressive methods. They experience the sea merely as something opposed to their prosperity and security. Those who speak of the sea as feminine, "la mar," are fishermen, like Santiago, who have not abandoned the old ways and therefore have not lost their primitive contact with the sea which they mistrust but also love. In a sense, the difference is basically the difference between a sterile and a potentially fruitful relationship.

5. *Throughout the story, the old man speaks and thinks frequently of DiMaggio, a famous American baseball player. Is this purely a reflection of the old man's enthusiasm for baseball, or are there other, less obvious reasons for this obsession?*

Di Maggio would, of course, have no place in the old man's thoughts, if the old man were not a baseball enthusiast; yet, the old man thinks of DiMaggio not so much as a ball player but as a man who is great (notice that the name DiMaggio literally means "the great one") despite the mysterious affliction of a bone spur. That the old man should constantly measure himself against the idolized image of such a man indicates the importance of suffering in his view of human experience and of individual achievement. Only through suffering, as the total pattern of the story suggests, can a man discover the depths of himself and possibly achieve that additional dimension — nobility.

6. *Why does the old man call the great fish his "true brother"?*

Most simply, this is the fisherman's way of expressing the love and wonder that the great marlin inspires in him. At the same time, in calling the fish "brother," the old man places the fish on the same plane of being with himself and implicitly recognizes in the fish all the claim to respect, love and responsibility that a human being would have in similar circumstances. Moreover, this way of addressing the marlin is a spontaneous affirmation of the old fisherman's desire to be like him, to share his virtues.

7. *If the old man considers the fish his "brother" and if, as he says, "it is unjust," why does he feel that he must kill the fish?*

The only way in which the old man, a simple fisherman, can prove that he is worthy of the brotherhood that he feels with the fish, is by battling the fish — opposing calmness to calmness, courage to courage, endurance to endurance.

8. *In the primitive Christian church the fish was a symbol representing Christ himself. Is there anything in this story to suggest that such a symbolistic view of the giant marlin is appropriate?*

Yes (see analysis). But it should not be assumed that this makes the story specifically Christian in point of view. The most obvious link between the fish and Christ in the story is the experience of crucifixion. Beyond this, the virtues the fish possesses and the fisherman seeks to acquire are in a sense redeeming virtues, but they are not specifically Christian virtues.

9. *In view of what we are shown of the old man's character, how are we to understand his statement that he is not religious?*

Clearly the statement in context refers directly to the old fisherman's nominal religion, Catholic Christianity. In saying that he is not religious, the old man seems to be saying both that he does not feel this orthodox religion to have a significant effect upon his way of life and that he does not ordinarily look to it either for support or for assurance. Actually he seems to stand between the Christian and the pagan. The sea, which rules his life and has shaped his moral sensibility, is not quite personified in his mind, and the general reverence which he feels toward life flows on the one hand into superstition and on the other into familiar orthodox Christian forms. This fact is extremely important to the way in which we interpret the Christian symbols and allusions in the story.

10. *What is the effect of the repetition, especially in the third section of the story, of the phrase "the water that was more than a mile deep"?*

Though it appears with variations, the repetition suggests the poetic tags that one is accustomed to meet in epic poetry. As such it contributes to the tone of epic or ritual action which, in turn, prevents us from reading the story as a simple fishing tale. On the other hand, the fact of the mile deep water leads into the idea of hybris, of having exceeded one's proper limits, which later comes to replace the old man's sense of guilt and defeat.

11. *Why does the old man say that he is not sure that he believes in sin? If he does not believe in it, why is he unable to put it out of mind after the great fish has been mutilated by the Mako shark?*

If one reads the whole passage about sin carefully, he will note that the orthodox concept of sin is incompatible with the old man's sense of necessity involved in his killing of the fish. Given such a fish and such a fisherman, any other alternative seems to the old man inconceivable, and to burden a man with guilt for having fulfilled his destiny seems unreasonable. Yet, the fact that he has not only killed the great fish that he has called "brother" but has exposed him to mutilation by his unworthy enemies, naturally leads to a feeling of guilt.

12. *First the fish and then the fisherman are related by means of symbol and allusions to Christ's Passion. What does the use of these symbols and allusions contribute to the realization of the story?*

Generally speaking what is involved here is a technique of heightening; the symbols and allusions provide a means of connecting suggestively one level of experience with another — in this case the level of practical action with what we can only rather vaguely call the moral, religious, or spiritual level. More specifically, through these symbols and allusions the "brotherhood" of the fish and the fisherman is affirmed in defeat as well as in victory. The old man is beaten by the sharks, and the fact that in his practical defeat he assumes the attitude of the crucified Christ expresses both the depth of indignity and the intensity of suffering that he has endured, but it also implies that, through his suffering and endurance, he has achieved a final identity with what the fish represents.

13. *Why does the author carefully contrast the two different kinds of sharks that attack the fish — the Mako, that comes first, and the shovel-nosed sharks?*

This contrast makes clear that the old man is not outmatched in those qualities that he admires in the marlin and can also recognize in the Mako shark. What beats him is sheer number and appetite.

14. *What effect is gained by introducing the comments of the two tourists at the end?*

The comments of the tourists, naïve outsiders capable of only the most superficial perceptions, amount to a final reduction of the actual, concrete experience to meaninglessness. The effect of this ironic reduction is to emphasize for the reader the significance that is in the experience but not in any physical reminder of it.

15. *What are the implications of the last paragraph of the story?*

Unlike the other fishermen and the tourists who are preoccupied with the skeleton (literally the mere bones of the experience), the old man in his dream of the lions is detached from the experience. It is behind him, complete in itself, but through it he has earned the freedom to enjoy the happiness and reassurance that come to him from seeing the great beasts at play.

A. R. W.

Baker, Carlos, ed., *Ernest Hemingway: Critiques of Four Major Novels*, New York 1962, pp. 132—172 — Buchloh, Paul G., Bedeutungsschichten in Ernest Hemingways *The Old Man and the Sea*, *Amerikanische Erzähler von Hawthorne bis Hemingway*, Neumünster 1968, pp. 224—241 — Burhans, Clinton S., *The Old Man and the Sea: Hemingway's Tragic Vision of Man*, *American Literature* XXXI, 1960, pp. 447—455 — Cooperman, Stanley, Hemingway and Old Age: Santiago as Priest of Time, *College English* XXVII, 1965, pp. 215—220 — Dupee, F. W., Hemingway Revealed, *Kenyon Review* XV, 1953, pp. 150—155 — Kopp, Richard, *Hemingway: Der Alte Mann und das Meer*, München 1964 — Moseley, Edwin M., *Pseudonyms of Christ in the Modern Novel*, Pittsburgh 1962, pp. 205—213 — Sylvester, Bickford, Hemingway's Eternal Vision: *The Old Man and the Sea*, PMLA LXXXI, 1966, pp. 130—138 — Wandruszka, Mario, Strukturen moderner Prosa, *Der Deutschunterricht* IX, 1957, pp. 89—104 — Weeks, Robert P., Fakery in *The Old Man and the Sea*, College English XXIV, 1962, pp. 188—192 — Zabel, Morton D., *Craft and Character in American Fiction*, New York 1957, pp. 321—326.

# WASHINGTON IRVING

Washington Irving (named for the general who had driven the British from his native city) was born on April 3, 1783, in New York, the youngest son of eleven children of a prosperous merchant who had come from Scotland. He was well educated and at 16 began to study law, but preferred life in the literary Bohemia. In 1804 he was sent on the traditional "grand tour" of Europe and traveled for two years in Holland, France, Italy and England. After his return he was admitted to the New York bar, but practiced little. Soon he became well known as a writer of humorous commentaries on New York society and of a humorous *History of New York, by Diedrich Knickerbocker* (1809). He joined his brother's firm in 1810 and went on business to Europe in 1815. In 1818, however, the failure of the Irving firm led him to pursue a literary career. The *Sketch Book* was published serially in 1819 and 1820, and Irving became the first American author to achieve an international success; the end of the first installment was marked by the famous "Rip Van Winkle". His interest in German romanticism led him to visit Germany where he found many sources for his writings. From 1826 to 1829 he was in Spain on diplomatic business, giving his heart to the romantic past of Spain. After seventeen years abroad he returned to the United States and devoted his studies to the history of his own country. From 1842 to 1845 he was again in Spain, as ambassador, then settled down to write a five-volume *Life of George Washington*, which he finished just before his death in 1859.

Irving was a great friend and admirer of Sir Walter Scott, but he surpassed his master in becoming one of the great prose stylists of American romanticism and the first great American humorist. The scope of his life and his writing was international, and his influence abroad, as writer, as visitor, and as diplomat, was that of a gifted cultural ambassador, at home on both continents, at a time when his young country badly needed such representation.

# Rip Van Winkle

Text:  Washington Irving, *Rip Van Winkle*. Velhagen (the references are made to this edition)
Washington Irving, *Stratford-on-Avon and Rip Van Winkle*. Hueber
*American Short Stories* I pp. 11—28. Schöningh
*Humorous American Short Stories* pp. 6—19. Hueber (Gottschalk)
Washington Irving, *Rip Van Winkle*. Lensing (abridged and much simplified)

Rip Van Winkle is a descendant of the early Dutch settlers of New Amsterdam and the country along the Hudson River. He lived "many years since, while the country was yet a province of Great Britain" (3:35-36), in the quiet, peaceful days of "His Majesty George The Third" (6:35). Though Rip is a kind-hearted, good-natured fellow and loved by everybody — not even the dogs bark at him — he cannot find peace at home because of the sharp tongue of Dame Van Winkle. He tries to escape her whenever possible, idling about the village or roaming through the woods, always willing to lend a helpful hand to a neighbor and "ready to attend to anybody's business but his own." (5:10-11)

One day, when his ramble has taken him high up to the Kaatskill Mountains, he has the strange adventure of meeting the spirits of Hendrick Hudson and his crew playing at nine-pins in a deep ravine. According to legendary lore, this "first discoverer of the river and country kept a kind of vigil there every twenty years, ... being permitted in this way to revisit the scenes of his enterprise, and keep a guardian eye upon the river and the great city called by his name." (18:9-14) Rip is made to wait upon the company and pour them liquor. His initial fear soon subsides and he cannot resist tasting the beverage again and again until he falls into a deep sleep.

On waking and finally returning to his village, Rip finds the world and himself strangely changed. He gradually realizes that he has really slept for twenty long years and that he is an old man as unfamiliar with the ways of the new generation as with those of old Hendrick Hudson and his crew. In the meantime the Revolutionary War has taken place, and whilst "the country had thrown off the yoke of Old England, ... he had got his neck out of the yoke of matrimony" (19:4-12), a fact yielding enough consolation for Rip to spend the rest of his days happily "as one of the patriarchs of the village and a chronicle of the old times 'before the war'." (18:36-37)

As Washington Irving states in his prefatory remarks[1] which relate the tale to "a posthumous writing of Diedrich Knickerbocker," he was interested (1) "in the Dutch history of the province, and the manners of the descendants from its primitive settlers," (2) in "legendary lore, so invaluable to true history," and (3) though he "did now and then [want to] kick up the dust a little in the eyes of his neighbors, and grieve the spirit of some friends, .... he never intended to injure or offend."

Much of the *Sketch Book* in which this story appeared is of secondary interest and contains highly sentimental pages strongly marked by their time.

---

[1] not contained in any of the annotated editions.

"Rip Van Winkle" is the freshest of the stories in this collection, free from sentimentality; and as in a genuine fairy tale, there is no straining after effect. The author has concentrated his skill in the invention of telling details — such as the rusty gun that Rip finds on waking up, the afternoon thunder of Hendrick Hudson's game of nine-pins — that make the reader willing to believe that he is in the presence of an authentic tradition, not of an invented story. The illusion of tradition is maintained by the use of old and tried devices — the theme of the long sleep is an old folk-tale motif and the recognition scene on Rip's return to his native village recalls similar scenes from older literature, especially the return of Odysseus. The author, however, translates these traditional elements into native American terms. Here again telling detail creates the illusion of realism; especially striking are the inn sign with George III roughly transformed into George Washington and the encounter with the oldest inhabitant. The ne'er-do-well hero who has a termagant wife but who is loved by dogs and children is a traditional figure, and an old and tried way of rousing the reader's sympathy, but Irving makes him into a specifically American figure.

This story is, above all, marked by Irving's strong sense of locality. Like his friend Walter Scott, Irving creates an atmosphere rich in associations and reminiscences. In *Bracebridge Hall* (1822) he does this for rural England, in *A Chronicle of the Conquest of Granada* (1829) for Spain — a comparatively easy task, because, as Irving himself expressed it, "Europe held forth the charms of storied and poetical association." As a visitor to London he was entranced by old alley-ways and searched for the site of the Boar's Head Tavern. In this story Irving wreathes the American scene in the mists of antiquity (a recent "antiquity" only dating back to the War of Independence) and creates legend where none has existed.

What gives the story literary value and fully justifies its inclusion in an anthology of the best American short stories is the skill with which the author combines all details: the folk-lore motif of the long sleep, the realistic description of the country round the Kaatskill Mountains and its inhabitants, the dilemma of the hen-pecked husband, the mysterious atmosphere of Rip's adventure and, last not least, the political events that have changed not only the inn sign, but "the very character of the people ... There was a busy, bustling, disputatious tone about it, instead of the accustomed phlegm and drowsy tranquillity." (14:18—21) The fact that to the completely stupefied Rip the changes do not appear to the better, implies a criticism of Irving's time and contemporaries which gives the harmless, humorous folk-tale a somewhat ironic quality. The very "tree that used to shelter the quiet little Dutch inn of yore" has changed into "a tall naked [flag-] pole" (14:4—6), and in place of the wise 'philosophers' and 'sages' of the village club, Rip finds "a lean, bilious-looking fellow, ... haranguing vehemently about rights of citizens — elections — members of congress — liberty — Bunker's Hill — heroes of seventy-six — and other words, which were a perfect Babylonish jargon to the bewildered Rip Van Winkle." (14:25—30) Rip is addressed by "a knowing, self-important old gentleman ... in an austere tone" — all the by-standers regard him full of mistrust, even as a "culprit" (15:4—21). But the underlying humor, exaggerating this scene almost to the grotesque, does not allow any bitter feeling to come up. Poor Rip, trying to protest his harmlessness by stating that he is "a loyal subject to the king" is at once considered "A tory! a spy! a refugee!" appearing at the election "with a gun on his shoulder, and a mob at his heels," probably intending "to breed a riot in the village" (15: 11—15). Later, when he is driven to doubt his own identity, people believe he is merely out of his wits. "A drop of comfort" (17:16) is given to Rip in the answer to his last question, "put ... with a faltering voice": Dame Van Winkle is dead, "she broke a blood-vessel in a fit of passion at a New-England peddler." (17:14—15) Thus the development of the story, having almost touched the tragic in the suddenly aged man who finds himself alone in a strangely altered world, leads back to the abundant humor of the initial pages.

There is a level of meaning in "Rip Van Winkle" usually missed by those who concentrate exclusively on its folk tale qualities, namely, the importance and inevitability of CHANGE and the priority of private to political life. The epigraph is ironically significant: an oath "by Woden" that truth will be preserved until the day of death. But Woden (Wotan) is no longer a viable god (nor was he in Irving's day) and truth like marriage and government is subject to the inevitable metamorphosis of time. The opening description of the Catskills includes this important sentence: "Every change of season, every change of weather, indeed, every hour of the day produces some change in the magical hues and shapes of these mountains..." (3:10—13). And at the end of the story Rip, at his wits' end, exclaims, "I'm not myself ... I was myself last night, but I fell asleep on the mountain, and they've changed my gun, and everything's changed, and I'm changed and I can't tell what's my name, or who I am!" (16:21—26) Those around Rip tap their fingers against their foreheads, indicating that they believe Rip has gone mad; but Rip's peculiar experience has given him an insight into a truth that ordinary mortals rarely face. It is, in fact, the experience of TIME, of "enormous lapses of time" (16:7). Rip's romantic adventure in the Kaatskill Mountains permits the author to treat three epochs of American history as seen from the perspective of a single human being.

Furthermore, the importance of change to Rip is hardly political, even though he wakes up to a world that had undergone an immense political convulsion: "Rip, in fact, was no politician; the changes of states and empires made but little impression on him; but there was one species of despotism under which he had long groaned, and that was — petticoat government. Happily, that was at an end ..." (19:7—11). And some, at least, of Rip's new neighbors come to realize the importance of this kind of change. The story ends on this significant note: "it is a common wish of all henpecked husbands in the neighborhood ... that they might have a quieting draught out of Rip Van Winkle's flagon." (19:31—34) Here is the real heart of the story — a fantasy of escape from marital strife and marital responsibility.

1. *How does Irving create the atmosphere of the locality he is dealing with?*

He touches on the history of the Dutch colonizers (e. g. Peter Stuyvesant) and at considerable length on the scenery of the Catskill Mountains. There is much detailed description of the village where Van Winkle lived and of the costumes and appearance of the Dutch players of nine-pins. The domestic aspect of life (Rip's wife, all the goodwives of the village, the family squabbles, the neighbors, the idle 'philosophers' and 'sages' of the village club) is emphasized to create a Dutch atmosphere.

2. *How does W. Irving's humor work?*

a) By comic contrasts, comic situations and unexpected comparisons: Rip's ancestors had "a martial character," but he is a simple, good-natured fellow and henpecked husband; he is a favorite among all the goodwives of the village, but not with his own wife; Dame Van Winkle is ironically referred to as belonging to "the amiable sex"; Rip "would never refuse to help a neighbor even in the hardest work," but he has "an insuperable aversion to all kinds of *profitable* labor"; after the long sleep it is not quite clear who is more amazed — the young generation at the sudden appearance of the remnant of the old one or Rip at the completely incomprehensible new world; the mountains are regarded as "perfect barometers," whereas old Nicholas Vedder leads such a slowly moving and regular life "that the neighbors could tell the hour by his movements as accurately as by a sundial"; etc., etc.

b) By casual remarks and attributes, even names: "Derrick Van Bummel, the schoolmaster, a dapper learned little man, who was not to be daunted by the most gigantic word in the dictionary" (7:6-8).

c) By using a choice vocabulary in a deliberately contrasting everyday context, drawing from learned language (e. g. "The great error in Rip's composition was an insuperable aversion to all kinds of profitable labor" 4:33-34); military expressions (his reaction "always provoked a fresh volley from his wife; so that he was fain to draw off his forces..." (6:9-10) and "From even this stronghold the unlucky Rip was at length routed by his termagent wife" 7:28-29); references to Shakespeare ("more in sorrow than in anger" (preface) in *Hamlet* (I, 2, 232), "an unkind cut" (13:28) in *Julius Caesar* (III, 2, 182), "shrews" (4:12) in *The Taming of the Shrew*, "much ado" (5:30) in *Much Ado About Nothing*; proverbial wisdom ("a tart temper never mellows with age, and a sharp tongue is the only edged tool that grows keener with constant use" 6:28-30); far-fetched similes ("a rod as long and heavy as a Tartar's lance" (4:36-37), "a hollow, like a small amphitheatre" 9:34).

d) By continually puzzling and surprising the reader's mind.

3. *Is Rip a "comic" hero?*

Yes, he is, in the proper sense of the word, and not merely a burlesque figure. Reasons:

a) The order of the universe is never disturbed, neither through Rip's unmanly "meekness of spirit" which makes him the plaything of his wife and the whole village and leads him into the temptation of tasting the bewitched beverage (other persons, e. g. Peter Vanderdonk's father, have watched the strange beings without any harm), nor by his sad experience of having lost twenty years of his life by one night's sleep. For actually Rip cannot be blamed for his weaknesses, which are due to a "great error in Rip's composition" (4:33), so that responsibility is transferred to higher powers. And, in the end, Rip is quite contented with his lot — "Whenever [Dame Van Winkle's] name was mentioned, ... he shook his head, shrugged his shoulders, and cast up his eyes; which might pass for an expression of resignation to his fate, or joy at his deliverance." (19:14-17)

b) Throughout the story the reader is able to maintain the "knowing" attitude necessary for the humorous effect: he can be sure that whatever happens, things will turn out right, even ironies or sad human experiences flow back into the stream of relaxing humor.

4. *What are the "Romantic" characteristics of this tale?*

The attempt to capture the atmosphere of a particular locality, the love of the supernatural. An appeal to the irrational borderland of experience in the traditional folk-tale motifs.

The scene of Rip lying musing "on a green knoll, covered with mountain herbage, that crowned the brow of a precipice," watching "the lordly Hudson, far below him, moving on its silent but majestic course, with the reflection of a purple cloud, or the sail of a lagging bark, ... losing itself in the blue highlands," whereas "on the other side he looked down into a deep mountain glen, wild, lonely, and shagged, the bottom filled with fragments from the impending cliffs, and scarcely lighted by the rays of the setting sun," (8:15-27) might pass for a masterpiece of Romantic landscape description. Besides, the homely life of the village so far described provides a good contrast to the mysterious atmosphere which is now slowly, but convincingly built up by such details as the majestic surroundings, the loneliness of the place, the gradually advancing evening, Rip's "uneasy feelings," the sound of a voice when he can see "nothing but a crow winging its solitary flight across the mountain" (8:35:36), Wolf's queer behavior, the "vague apprehension stealing over" Rip, finally the strange outward appearance of the unknown figure suddenly emerging, and even more so the complete stillness and mysterious silence in which the company of nine-pin players amuse themselves, only interrupted by "the noise of the balls, which, whenever they were rolled, echoed along the mountains like rumbling peals of thunder." — What again makes this "Romantic" scene typically Irving and maybe 'American' is the never-ceasing strain of realistic detail, continually balancing the "supernatural" and keeping it within its limits. So that, e. g., the "Romantic," mysterious atmosphere of this scene is ghastly, though realistically, reflected in the forlorn desolateness Rip finds at his return; "he called loudly for his wife and children — the lonely chambers rang for a moment with his voice, and then all again was silence." (13:33-35)

5. *This story is often praised for its simplicity. Comment.*

The plot is simple, as is the life it describes, and prolixity is avoided. The structure seems simple, consisting of three major parts,

a) the introduction into the life and manners of the Dutch settlers and the humorous characterization of the title figure;

b) the exploitation of the folk-lore motif and the Romantic experience of the supernatural or irrational;

c) the ironic criticism of the patriotic present.

These three parts, however, are interwoven into an extremely complex **whole**, held together by the leitmotif of "change" involving the problem of the lapse **of** time, by contrasts and comparisons — Rip and his wife, the inhabitants of **the** village before and after the war, the atmosphere of "drowsy tranquillity" and that of bustling, disputatious haste as well as that of awe-inspiring mystery etc. The humorous perspective which checks all apparent transgressions allows for a truly ironic suspense and a kind of game with such weighty subjects as change, **time**, truth, reality, and the irrational.

That Irving's style with its manifold possibilities of producing humorous **effect** is far from 'simple' need hardly be mentioned.

6. *Compare "Rip Van Winkle" with "The Devil and Daniel Webster"!*

Both create synthetic tradition, using telling detail and age-old motifs (pact with Devil, long sleep). Both have a central vein of humor (Irving's less obtrusive and rather simpler — for example, the comic Dutch name Van Winkle). Benét's story has an explicit moral and a patriotic message, while Irving, more endearingly, tends to laugh at conventional patriotism. Irving's love of his native land is implicit, where Benét, born in an age of advertizing, feels that implication is not enough. Their treatment of thunder is revealing. Irving attributes thunder on summer afternoons to a gigantic game of skittles played by the old Dutch settlers — this is homely yet mysterious and a fine imitation of the anthropomorphism of the genuine folk tale. Benét uses his thunder, like an advertizing copy-writer, to underline Daniel Webster's might.

W. G. C./M. D./J. V. H.

Day and Bauer, *The Greatest American Short Stories*, New York 1953, pp. 349-359 — Fiedler, Leslie A., *Love and Death in the American Novel*, New York 1960, pp. 332—336 — Link, Franz, *Stilanalysen amerikanischer Erzählkunst*, Bonn 1970, pp. 13—20 — Lubbers, Klaus, Irving, "Rip Van Winkle", *Die amerikanische Kurzgeschichte*, eds. Göller and Hoffmann, Düsseldorf 1972, pp. 25—35 — Schik, Berthold, Irving, "Rip Van Winkle," *Interpretationen zu Irving, Melville und Poe*, ed. Finger, Hans, Frankfurt 1971, pp. 7—21 — Young, Philip, Fallen from Time: The Mythic Rip Van Winkle, *Kenyon Review* XXII, 1960, pp. 547—573.

# SHIRLEY JACKSON

Shirley Jackson was born on December 14, 1919, in San Francisco and spent most of her early life in California. In 1940 she married a literary critic and settled in Vermont. She published her first novel *The Road Through the Wall* in 1948, and soon afterwards a collection of short stories *The Lottery; or the Adventures of James Harris*. Several more novels appeared later, apart from a collection of essays and numerous short stories in magazines. When she died in 1965, the obituary notice of *Studies in Short Fiction* (III, 1) closed, "The fact, is, however, that the rigorously objective point of view... of her fiction can bring the fullest pleasure to only the most sophisticated sensibility."

# The Lottery

Text:   *American Short Stories* VIII pp. 50—60. Schöningh.
*Contemporary American Short Stories* II pp. 33—43. Hueber.

*The whole community of a small American settlement gathers on the morning of June 27th for the traditional lottery, the origins of which go back to the time of the first settlers. Mr. Summers, who has time and energy to devote to civic activities, calls upon every grown-up man of the village to draw a slip of paper from a black wooden box. Bill Hutchinson gets the one slip with a black mark. Now the members of his family have to draw lots, and this time Mrs. Hutchinson picks the black mark. Although much of the ritual is forgotten, the most important part is still carried out: the victim is stoned to death by all the other villagers.*

Shirley Jackson's "The Lottery" was first published in The New Yorker magazine in 1948 and has been reprinted in many anthologies of modern American short stories. It can easily be misread simply as a tour-de-force shocker, and there is no doubt that within the limits of such a genre it is a masterpiece. The whiplash reversal in the last 15 sentences has a more powerful effect than even the narratives of Ambrose Bierce. But if that were the only quality of the story, it would be simply something to chuckle at, a bit of *Schadenfreude*. A deeper insight into the story, however, reveals it to be a very shrewd fantasy-parable on a specific sociological mechanism in modern life and in human nature.

On the purely narrative level, "The Lottery" has a very simple plot: a small American community[1], mostly Anglo-Saxon but including its French (Delacroix) and Italian (Zanini) elements, gathers for an annual summer ritual and carries it out. The focus is on the community event, and characterizations are very slight, just enough to render the individuals and the families as specific (even if typical) people rather than pure abstractions, but not enough to make any specific person (not even the victim, Mrs. Hutchinson) a central character. This is not a psychological story; nobody suffers any carefully-delineated internal conflict, nobody has a crucial choice or decision to make, nothing unexpected happens. But what is to this community a familiar, ordinary event is suddenly revealed to the reader as a tremendous shock.

The style is magnificently controlled. Matter-of-fact details of a perfectly credible situation are presented in a calm tone, and that tone is maintained even when the situation becomes incredible. But, as we shall see, only the specific *form* of the scapegoat ritual is incredible in this socio-historical context. The *fact* that such scapegoat sacrifices actually occur even in modern society is a truth that is brilliantly dramatized by the technique of this story. The opening paragraph stresses pleasant details: the morning is "clear and

---

[1] There is nothing that indicates it to be a New England village as Brooks and Warren state it is — it could be any small American town in a farm area.

sunny, with the fresh warmth of a sunny day," and preparations are being casually made for an ordinary, annual ritual. The gathering of stones is drained of any possible sinister significance by the play of children, the shyness of adolescents, the farm talk of the men and the gossip of the women. The lottery is to be conducted by a "round-faced, jovial man," who also supervises the square dances, teen-age club, and Halloween program.

The forward motion of the story is interrupted by three paragraphs of exposition, revealing that the lottery is an ancient tradition which has considerably degenerated — "much of the ritual had been forgotten or discarded," preparations are described as "a great deal of fussing," slips of paper have been substituted for the original chips of wood, and the chant and the ritual salute have been abandoned. These details tend to counter-act later signs of uneasiness and fear when the lottery begins: some of the people "were quiet, wetting their lips"; "They grinned at one another humorlessly and nervously"; Mr. Adams, after drawing his slip, "stood a little apart from his family, not looking down at his hand"; Mrs. Delacroix "held her breath while her husband went forward"; etc. Signs of calm and reassurance are balanced against signs of fear in a powerful tension which is released only when we discover that even though the procedures of the ritual have decayed, the chief purpose of it has remained terrifyingly intact.

Robert Heilman has asserted that the story is extremely weak in its structure because it "gives us the sinister *after* the innocuous, instead of the two simultaneously," but this is surely inept reading. Only the most insensitive reader could fail to observe the gradual accumulation of ominous details: Mr. Graves "greeted Mr. Summers gravely," before drawing his slip; the sporadic laughter of the crowd is quite nervous; and always in the background is the pile of stones especially gathered in the village square. The most portentous sign of all is the shift in attitude of Mrs. Hutchinson from playful humor to terror: "It wasn't fair!"

As the lottery proceeds, there is a discussion between Mr. Adams and Old Man Warner about the possibility of abandoning the lottery as other communities have done. Old man Warner is typical of the older generation clinging to outmoded rituals — "there's *always* been a lottery" — and by his logic that fact alone bestows value on it and sanctions its continuance. Only "fools" (and presumably radicals, Communists, troublemakers) would want to change the established way of life of a community. Whereas Mrs. Hutchinson had accepted the lottery in the careless optimism of the naive and the innocent, Old Man Warner accepts it as a veteran of 77 years of living with it; it is he who recalls its original purpose: "Lottery in June, corn be heavy soon." Obviously, the sacrifice of a human scapegoat is part of a fertility rite, an appeasement of the forces of nature or the gods to ensure a rich harvest. (Details of many primitive scapegoat rituals can be found in Sir James Frazer's *The Golden Bough*[1], which is the standard work on the subject.) As with many

---

[1] paperback edition by Macmillan, London.

modern survivals of ancient rituals, the original purpose may have been lost, but some need of the community is fulfilled. Here, apparently, the dammed-up urge for violence and bloodshed, tightly inhibited by the mores of a small farm community in which nothing ever happens, finds release in a traditional act. Fasching and Mardi-Gras are similar in that they permit strongly Catholic communities with powerful sexual taboos to find a socially sanctioned release for pent-up drives.

But Shirley Jackson's story does not merely illuminate social processes described by anthropologists; it also reveals the cruelty that can be inflicted on innocent people whenever a community acts irrationally in concert. Whenever a society encourages or rewards the persecution of an individual in the name of religion or patriotism — as in the Inquisition, or under Nazism and Communism, or during the McCarthy era in America — it is behaving in precisely the way Shirley Jackson's community does.

The *meaning* that is dramatized in "The Lottery" and the *way* that it is dramatized work beautifully together. Probably the best critical comment on the story is that of Brooks and Warren: "The contrast between the matter-of-factness and the cheery atmosphere, on the one side, and the grim terror, on the other, gives us a dramatic shock. But it also indicates that the author's point in general has to do with the awful doubleness of the human spirit — a doubleness that expresses itself in the blended good neighborliness and cruelty of the community's action. The fictional form does not, therefore, simply "dress up" a specific comment on human nature. The fictional form actually gives point and definition to the social commentary."

1. *Why are details of time stressed in the first paragraph?*

    To communicate the sense that the events to occur are standard, carefully regulated, and community-sanctioned, and to establish a tone of calm and normality that later becomes bitterly ironic.

2. *What significance is there in the fact that Delacroix is pronounced "Dellacroy"?*

    It shows that the French family has been integrated into the community and has become Anglicized. The fact that Mrs. Delacroix picks up the first and heaviest stone does *not* mean that she represents the outsider seeking an opportunity for personal or family vengeance on the Anglo-Saxon community.

3. *What does it mean when Mrs. Hutchinson arrives late explaining that she "clean forgot what day it was" and then jokes that the others "Wouldn't have me leave m'dishes in the sink"?*

    Three possible meanings are involved here. 1) Mrs. Hutchinson subconsciously rejects the ritual of the lottery and really doesn't want to participate in it; 2) but she is an "other-directed" person who doesn't dare even to admit to consciousness the possibility of rebellion against tradition — she wants to be a "normal" member of the community; 3) and there is great irony and a touch of pathos in the fact that this cheerful wife and mother rebels only when she is the victim, the scapegoat, and that she will never wash dishes again.

4. *What is the strongest evidence that the ritual is completely accepted by the community?*

Not simply the fact that Mrs. Delacroix, who had joked with Mrs. Hutchinson, picks up the first stone, but the fact that even members of Tessie Hutchinson's own family do not for a moment even consider sympathizing with her or protecting her from the consequences of her "winning" the lottery. The daughter's schoolfriends say, "I hope it's not Nancy," but there is no doubt that if it were Nancy who drew the black dot she would be stoned to death by her own schoolfriends. The children "both beamed and laughed" when they drew blank slips; they were saved even if one of their parents is to die. Bill Hutchinson forces the slip of paper out of his wife's hand and holds it up to the crowd.

5. *Is the ending a reversal of the tone of the entire story?*

No, not at all. It is an appropriate culmination, however shocking, of the gradually accumulating tensions and details which clearly foreshadow some kind of terrible event.

J. V. H.

Brooks and Warren, *Understanding Fiction*, 2nd edition, New York 1959, pp. 72-76 — Gordon and Tate, *The House of Fiction*, 2nd edition, New York 1960, pp. 72—76 — Heilman, R. B., *Modern Short Stories*, New York 1950, pp. 384—385 — Lainoff, Seymour, Jackson's "The Lottery," *Explicator* XII, 1954, item 34.

# HENRY JAMES

Henry James was born on April 15, 1843, in New York City. His father, a well-to-do philosopher and theologian, took great care with the education of his children. After being privately tutored in New York, James received special schooling abroad between 1855 and 1860, when the family lived in London, Switzerland, France, and Germany. For a short time he studied painting, then began to study law at Harvard, but soon decided to become a writer. In a long short story "Passionate Pilgrim", published in 1871, he first dealt with his favorite theme of the cultural attraction and repulsion between Europe and America. In 1875 a first collection of short stories followed, *A Passionate Pilgrim and Other Tales*, and his first novel of consequence, *Roderick Hudson*, appeared as serials in the *Atlantic Monthly*. From 1876 on he lived permanently in England, at first in London, later in Sussex. Spending much time in Paris, he came to know Flaubert and Turgenev. The French and Russian realists and naturalists influenced his style, but he never adopted the naturalist's unselective zeal to report everything observed.

With *The American* (1877), *The European* (1878), *Daisy Miller* (1879) and *The Portrait of a Lady* (1881), James was recognized as a master of the international novel. J. W. Beach, whose study *The Method of Henry James* first appeared in the year of James's death, observed, "It was his tendency always to subordinate incident to character, to subordinate character as such to situation — or the relation among the characters; and in situation or character, to prefer something rather out of the ordinary, some aspect or type not too obviously interesting but calling for insight and subtlety in their interpretation."

For a period of almost 50 years James wrote many more novels, novelettes and short stories, but became also famous as a literary critic (e. g. *Hawthorne*, 1879) and a writer of essays (e. g. "The Art of Fiction", 1888). From 1907 on he carefully revised and edited his works for the New York Edition (26 vols.). One year before his death in 1916, he became a British subject, as a protest against the neutrality of his native country in the early years of World War I.

James has been profoundly influential on the generations since his death, particularly on Lawrence, Joyce, Conrad, Edith Wharton, Virginia Woolf, Willa Cather and T. S. Eliot. By utilizing psychological devices for a more intense realization of character and situation he was a pioneer in the development towards the "stream of consciousness"-technique.

## Daisy Miller

Text: *American Short Stories* IV pp. 12—79. Schöningh

*The story begins in a summer about the year 1875 and ends in the following April. Frederick Winterbourne, a rich American of twenty-seven years, who has grown up in Geneva, visits his aunt, Mrs. Costello, in Vevey. There he makes the acquaintance of a charming American girl, Daisy Miller, who is traveling in Europe with her mother and her brother Randolph. He is perplexed but also attracted by her "laxity of deportment" and wonders whether "she was only a pretty American flirt." They have a pleasant trip to the Château de Chillon together, but then Winterbourne returns to Geneva. They meet again in Rome the following January, and Winterbourne is worried when he finds her making herself impossible in society by her eccentricities. One midnight he meets her in the Colosseum with an Italian friend of hers. He warns her of the danger for her health, but loses all respect for her. When she dies from Roman fever a few weeks later, however, he learns from the Italian that she was quite innocent and then realizes his mistake.*

In this "study", Henry James says (in the 1909 preface), he tried to concentrate on "an object scant and superficially vulgar — from which, however, a sufficiently brooding tenderness might eventually extract a shy incongruous charm." The first editor to read the story could see only the vulgarity and refused to publish it, but it went on to become one of James's most famous novelle and one of the indispensable works in American short fiction.

The story has an hour-glass structure with two fairly symmetrical halves (published in consecutive issues of *Cornhill Magazine*, 1879). Vevey is balanced against Rome; the flirtation with Winterbourne is balanced against the flirtation with Giovanelli; the protests of the European courier and of Mrs. Costello against those of Winterbourne and Mrs. Walker; the trip to the Château de Chillon against the trip to the Colosseum. But the story is not made up of a simple, repeated inversion, for the incipient love relationship between Daisy and Winterbourne is developed into a triangle involving Giovanelli and is tied in with complex social forces and ironies.

Despite the fact that the story is told in the third person, the point of view is strictly that of Winterbourne; only his inner thoughts supplement the action and dialogue. And since Winterbourne's outlook is distorted by his character and background, the reader must make careful adjustments to understand motivations that Winterbourne cannot understand. Even at the end when Daisy's innocence is explicitly established, there remains the question of why she and the other characters behaved precisely as they did.

The story is not, as has often been claimed, fundamentally a tale of Europe versus America, even if Daisy Miller and Giovanelli may be said to draw from their national inheritances: Daisy an independent self-reliance, and Giovanelli a devotion to aesthetic values. The central conflict is between Daisy and Winterbourne. It is true that Winterbourne's trouble stems partly from the fact that he is neither a "real American," nor a German or Swiss either: "He felt that he had lived at Geneva so long that he had lost a good deal: he had become dishabituated to the American tone." He now pays too much attention to the voices of a displaced American code of social conventions — "He had imbibed at Geneva the idea that one must always be attentive to one's aunt" — and this is a sterile source. So the immediate background of the story is in a way that of a contrast between Daisy's innocent naturalness and Winterbourne's barren, stiff artificiality. The relations between the Millers and the other Americans in the story are also to be seen as part of a class struggle — the manners and morals of a Europeanized American *haut-monde* versus those of the American *nouveaux riches*.

Since characterization and motivation are at the heart of the drama, perhaps the most useful discussion of the story is in terms of the central figures, Winterbourne and Daisy. Name symbolism is important here, as in most of James's fiction. Winterbourne is a man whose spirit is in the bourne (realm, domain) of winter. He is a twenty-seven year old man who ever since he was a little boy had lived and was educated in Geneva, "the little metropolis of Calvinism." As a result Daisy can hardly take him for a "real American" —

"he seemed more like a German." His Christian name Frederick is quite in accordance with this impression. His outstanding trait is that he is extremely sensitive to social customs and inclined to "accuse" people of "actual or potential *inconduite*, as they say at Geneva." Uncertain of his ability to evaluate Daisy, he consults his aunt, Mrs. Costello, who is properly shocked and, thinking him "too innocent," warns him of making "some great mistake." Winterbourne is "vexed with himself that, by instinct, he should not appreciate her [Daisy] justly." Nevertheless, attracted by her charm, he is quite prepared to take advantage of her innocence and escort her in a boat by moonlight to the Château de Chillon — despite the protest of Eugenio, her European courier, who doesn't think it proper. When, two days later, they do make the trip, he takes "much satisfaction in his pretty companion's distinguished air," though he at first feels disappointed that "she was not fluttered." Her interest in him, however, obviously increases and she even asks him to stay with her when he announces that he must return to Geneva, keeping his obligation there mysterious; but he promises to see her in Rome the following winter when he is to visit his aunt.

In Rome he holds back from calling upon Daisy, even though he defends her from his aunt's charge that she is "hopelessly vulgar." Meeting her quite by chance, he protests against her constant sightseeing with Giovanelli whom he regards as a fortune-seeking imitation of a gentleman. However, to Mrs. Walker he insists that one must not "make too much fuss about it." "Vexed at his want of instinctive certitude as to how far her eccentricities were generic, national, and how far they were personal," Winterbourne abandons her to Giovanelli when the chips are down. Discovering her by chance with Giovanelli in the Colosseum at night, he is outraged that she should thus expose herself to the Roman fever and he hurries her home. She dies a few weeks later, and at the funeral he learns from Giovanelli that "she was the most beautiful young lady... and the most amiable... and she was the most innocent." Later he expresses to his aunt the realization that Daisy "would have appreciated one's esteem," only to be corrected by her observation that "she would have reciprocated one's affection." "I was booked to make a mistake," says Winterbourne. "I've lived too long in foreign parts."

This, in essence, is Winterbourne's experience. From it we can safely draw several conclusions. One is that he is a moral coward — James says at one point that "he felt quite ready to sacrifice his aunt, *conversationally*," implying, of course, that he could not do so in action. Related to this trait is the fact that, like so very many of James's heroes (and, perhaps, like James himself), Winterbourne is almost sexually inert; his sexual attraction to a woman is not strong enough to overcome class conventions. (Or, as a psychologist might put it, he subconsciously uses social conventions as a shield against any intimate and sustained heterosexual commitments.) Isn't it significant that he does not dance? And, again as with so many of James's heroes, insight into the worth of the woman and the real possibility of love comes (safely) too late. Furthermore, it is one of the greatest psychological flaws of James's narratives that insight often comes from the outside; the hero does not internally struggle through to crucial knowledge, but is simply informed by a friend, acquaintance, or total stranger that he has not understood the truth.

Complex though the character of Winterbourne is, Daisy Miller seems to be much more difficult to understand. It is generally assumed that James's first editor was wrong, that the story is *not* critical of American womanhood, and that Daisy's "inexperience and innocence had made her a victim of the evil around her" (C. G. Hoffmann, loc. cit. p. 19). Some critics give her an even more positive role: "Daisy is a tribute to the American girl ... In her instinctive way she has demonstrated — almost with her life — a point of morality, vindicated the individual against the group, the spirit against the letter" (F. W. Dupee, loc. cit. p. 93). However, although the expatriate American community in Rome is certainly wrong in assuming that Daisy is a depraved horror, it does not necessarily follow that she is either simply a sweet young thing or a poor man's Joan of Arc; and what she finally appears to be to Winterbourne is not necessarily what she must seem to the perceptive reader.

Daisy Miller is *not* a representative American girl (whatever that may be); she is an "uncultivated" girl from a wealthy provincial family in Schenectady and would be equally out of place in the sophisticated circles of the Boston, New York, or New Orleans of her day. However, she has spirit, wit, and social ambition, and she is shrewd and perceptive in everything except Winterbourne. She thinks he is a normal young man who would respond appropriately to her invitation to make advances to her and whose jealousy would be aroused by her attentions to other men, but she is baffled and frustrated by his fundamental coldness and stiffness and adopts more and more desperate tactics to snare him. Her desperation finally leads her too far; she contracts Roman fever from a midnight visit to the Colosseum and dies, not a tragic heroine but an ordinary girl with ordinary drives who simply miscalculated. James is very careful not to romanticize or idealize her. She is never described as "beautiful," but quite consistently as "pretty" — and even this is curiously qualified: [her face] "was not at all insipid, but it was not expressive; ... [it had a] want of finish." Yet she is a girl with spirit:

"I never heard anything so stiff! If this is improper, Mrs. Walker ... then I'm all improper, and you must give me up. Good-bye; I hope you'll have a lovely ride!"

with wit:

[on Winterbourne's solemn face] "If that's a grin, your ears are very near together."

"It has never occurred to Mr. Winterbourne to offer me any tea," she said ... "I have offered you advice." ... "I prefer weak tea!"

with social ambition:

"I know just what *your* aunt would be; I know I should like her. She would be very exclusive; I'm dying to be exclusive myself."

Her purpose in Europe is to get a man; from the beginning she herself chatters quite candidly on the subject — "Europe was perfectly sweet ... [but]

there isn't any society. ... I'm very fond of society ... I have always had a great deal of gentlemen's society." She invites Winterbourne's attentions, encourages the moonlight trip to the Château de Chillon, and then — not wishing to be too easy a catch — reneges with "That's all I want — a little fuss!" Later she says openly "I want you to come [to Rome] for me," and she becomes teasingly indignant when she intuits that he has an amour in Geneva. In Rome, she protests that flirting "seems to me much more proper in young unmarried women than in old married ones," invites Winterbourne to accompany her to the Pincio to meet Giovanelli in an obvious effort to rouse his jealousy: "Tell me if Mr. Giovanelli is the right [gentleman]." She teases him with little barbs: "You are always going round by yourself. Can't you get anyone to walk with you?" and "she showed no displeasure at her tête-à-tête with Giovanelli being interrupted." A crisis in these tactics is reached when she teasingly announces (with a calculated policy of deception) that she is engaged to Giovanelli. But her tactics misfire; a week later when Winterbourne spots her with Giovanelli in the Colosseum, "it was as if a sudden illumination had been flashed upon the ambiguity .... She was a young lady whom a gentleman need no longer be at pains to respect." (In terms of Winterbourne's character, it is interesting that this resolution of doubts is not accompanied with regret, but "with a sort of relief.") Their last dialogue of the story marks the climax of Daisy's perverse pursuit of Winterbourne — she realizes that she has failed:

"I believe that it makes very little difference whether you are engaged or not!"

He felt the young girl's pretty eyes fixed upon him through the thick gloom of the archway; she was apparently going to answer...

"I don't care," said Daisy, in a little strange tone, "whether I have Roman fever or not!"

The resolution of her struggle is revealed in her death-bed message of regret: "She says she's not engaged. I don't know why she wanted you to know; but she said to me three times — 'Mind you tell Mr. Winterbourne.' And then she told me to ask if you remembered the time you went to that castle in Switzerland." It is poignant enough, but James has carefully avoided a death-bed confrontation scene — one of the many tactics by which he toughens the fiber of his narrative, removes it from the class of romantic grand-passion fiction. James drily comments, "A week after this the poor girl died," to which the proper response is not "Oh, the tragedy of it all!" but simply, "Too bad!" And there is more than a touch of irony in the final lines of the story: "Nevertheless, he went back to live at Geneva," resuming the same old life which gave rise to the same old rumors. Camellias, not daisies, are the appropriate flowers for romantic fiction.

1. *What is the character and function of Giovanelli?*

   He serves as foil and as source of revelation to Winterbourne. Mrs. Walker's circle is just as mistaken in their evaluation of him as they are of Daisy. Winterbourne gradually comes to learn better. His first opinion of the Italian is that "he is not a gentleman, he is only a clever imitation of one. He is a music-master, or a penny-a-liner, or a third-rate artist." But later, after he has made enquiries, he is able to report to his aunt that Giovanelli is a "perfectly respectable little man... *a cavaliere avvocato*. But... [he] knows that he hasn't a title to offer." There is no evidence that he has ever deceived anyone or ever behaved in any way but with perfect propriety. "Giovanelli, from the first, had treated Winterbourne with distinguished politeness... He carried himself in no degree like a jealous wooer." He does not try to boss Daisy around; even when he doesn't approve of her wishes he tries to fulfill them: "when was the Signorina ever prudent?" And he does all this either for the pure pleasure of her company or because he is a confidante and co-conspirator in her plot to make Winterbourne jealous, for he confesses at the end, "If she had lived I should have got nothing. She never would have married me." It would seem, in fact, that of all the characters in this "study," Giovanelli is the most exemplary.

2. *How unexpected is Daisy Miller's death? Is there any foreshadowing?*

   Perhaps the first inkling is when, in Vevey, Daisy intimates her mother's poor condition, "She suffers dreadfully from dyspepsia... she doesn't sleep... she's dreadfully nervous." The idea of sickness in the family is more firmly planted when, in Rome, Randolph blurts out that his mother has dyspepsia — "I've got it too. Father's got it. I've got it worst!" — At the happy visit to the Château de Chillon Winterbourne's "grave" expression of face causes Daisy to tease him, "You look as if you were taking me to a funeral." Daisy's final "message" to Winterbourne recalls the time they went to that castle — shortly before her own death and funeral in Rome. — Then the threat of Roman fever is carefully developed. Dr. Davis in Schenectady warned them. They are provided with medicine and pills against it. Daisy is warned by her mother, "You'll get the fever as sure as you live"; and she announces quite casually, "We are going to stay all winter — if we don't die of the fever." Finally, when Winterbourne is walking in the Colosseum before encountering Daisy and Giovanelli, he observes that "if nocturnal meditations in the Colosseum are recommended by the poets, they are deprecated by the doctors... the historic atmosphere, scientifically considered, was no better than a villainous miasma." Thus, the foreshadowing of her death has been firmly established by the time Daisy is rushed home and Winterbourne meditates that even "if she were a clever little reprobate? That was no reason for her dying of the *perniciosa*."

3. *What characteristics of Daisy's speech suggest that she is not completely well-bred?*

   The constant recurrence of the interjection "well":
     "Well, I guess I know my own mother."
   The use of "real" as an intensifier:
     "I think he's real tiresome."

The use of unrefined interjections:
"Gracious me!" "Oh, dear; I can't say all that!"
The use of "don't" with the 3rd person singular:
"He don't care much..."

**4. What flaw is there in the characterization of Randolph?**

This beastly little boy is certainly not one to stay out of the way of his sister's relations with men — at least, certainly not when it involves a trip to a castle: "he don't care much about old castles."

J. V. H.

Deakin, Motley, "Daisy Miller," Tradition and the European Heroine, *Comparative Literature Studies* VI, 1969, pp. 45—59 — Draper, R. P., Death of a Hero? Winterbourne and Daisy Miller, *Studies in Short Fiction* VI, 1969, pp. 601—608 — Dupee, F. W., *Henry James* (rev. ed.), Garden City 1956, pp. 91—97 — Grant, William, "Daisy Miller": A Study of a Study, *Studies in Short Fiction* XI, 1974, pp. 17—25 — McElderry, B. R., The "Shy, Incongruous Charm" of "Daisy Miller,", *Nineteenth Century Fiction* X, 1955, pp. 162—165 — Stafford, William T., ed., *James's Daisy Miller: The Story, The Play, The Critics*, New York 1963 — Wegelin, Christof, *The Image of Europe in Henry James*, Dallas 1958, pp. 61—64.

# RING LARDNER

Ring Lardner was born on March 6, 1885, at Niles, Michigan. Having graduated from High School in 1901, he drifted from one job to another until, after some apprenticeship, he became a sports writer and columnist with various newspapers in Chicago, St. Louis, and New York. Soon he began to experiment with the composition of weekly letters, which he gradually developed in the form of an epistolary novel, and later published as a book in 1916 (*You Know Me, Al: A Busher's Letters*). During the following decade, Lardner's stories, sketches, and topical articles appeared in numerous magazines and won him a great reputation as a humorist and a vernacular critic of American life. In 1924 he selected ten of his best stories in *How to Write Short Stories* to "illustrate in a half-hearted way what I am trying to get at." From then on he was acknowledged as a genuine artist, a satirist of the false standards of material success in the society around him, particularly in the world of sports and the theater. And there is a deep undercurrent of sadness, if not tragedy, underlying his humor. In 1933 he died of tuberculosis, having just completed a volume of sardonically humorous sketches *Lose with a Smile*.

He has two sets of readers: those who only laugh, and those who are shaken with horror and regard him as "the greatest and sincerest pessimist America has produced" (*Twentieth Century Authors*, 1942, p. 791).

# Haircut

Text: (no annotated edition yet available)
*The Pocket Book of Short Stories* PB 91, pp. 174—186.

*While cutting a customer's hair a garrulous small-town barber relates the story of how Jim Kendall got killed. He praises Jim's rough sense of humor and his amusing habits, although some people in the village were hurt by the callousness of his jokes. Doctor Stair resented Jim's neglect of his family, and his practical jokes on a mentally-defective boy named Paul Dickson and on Julie Gregg, a young spinster who was in love with the doctor. One day when Jim was duck-shooting with Paul Dickson he was killed by the half-wit. Doctor Stair, who was the coroner, declared "it was a plain case of accidental shooting."*

Although "Haircut" has frequently found an anthology place[1] beside stories by such masters as Melville, James, Kafka, Joyce, and Faulkner, it has generally been considered a rather simple piece of fiction. The subtlety and complexity of Lardner's craft in his most famous short story is underestimated by assuming that Jim Kendall, the practical joker of "Haircut", occupies the central position and brings about his own death.

Lardner employs a frame device of having a garrulous barber who feels that he "shouldn't ought to be gossipin'," but nevertheless tells his silent customer (the reader) a tale of paranoid cruelty, frustrated love, and death by shotgun blast. Since these are events he has observed or heard about from his vantage point in the barber shop, the point of view is that of the "I as Witness," a technique which Norman Friedman has described in these terms: "The natural consequence of this narrative frame is that the witness has no more than ordinary access to the mental states of others; its distinguishing characteristic, then, is that the author has surrendered his omniscience altogether regarding all the characters involved, and has chosen to allow his witness to tell the reader only what he as an observer may legitimately discover. The reader has available to him only the thoughts, feelings, and perceptions of the witness narrator; he therefore views the story from what may be called the wandering periphery."

Mr. Friedman's category ought to be subdivided into (1) "I as Reliable, Perceptive Witness", and (2) "I as Unreliable, Obtuse Witness." The barber certainly fits into the second group, for Lardner has chosen "the one man perhaps least qualified by knowledge and insight to tell [the story], in order to underline the pathos of the tragedy through the insensitivity of the narrator."[2] The consequences of the narrator's unreliability, however, are far-reaching and affect the meaning in more significant ways than merely "to underline the pathos of the tragedy." The technique adopted by Lardner requires that we scrutinize everything the barber says in order to discover not

---

[1] e. g. Gordon and Tate, eds., *The House of Fiction*, New York 1954, pp 424-32
[2] Gordon and Tate, op. cit., p. 632

only what really happened — the true plot — but also who the central character really is, i. e. the one who contributes most to the main action.

The barber is a pigmy Balzac. Before he tells us his little tragedy, he introduces us to the small town setting ("We ain't no New York City or Chicago") and to the principal characters. He considers Jim Kendall a great comic and "a good fella at heart," but gradually we realize that Jim's practical jokes which so amuse the barber are manifestations of an appalling sadism, especially towards his wife who would have divorced him "only they wasn't no chance to get alimony and she didn't have no way to take care of herself and the kids." All readers immediately catch the irony in the characterization of Jim Kendall, but it seems not so evident that similar ironies are involved in the depiction of the other characters as well.

The next character is Doc Stair, presented as the complete antithesis of Jim Kendall — an educated, sensitive, kind human being, a healer. We are told, for example, that he treated Jim's wife and children to the circus after Jim had cruelly left them waiting at the gate. But we have other, more puzzling details that depart from the stereotype of the kindly small-town doctor. He wears expensive, custom-tailored clothes and goes to Detroit several times a year, even though "he never dunned nobody for what they owed him and the folks here certainly has got the owin' habit." It is rumored that he has come to this small town, despite the fact that there are already two general practitioners, in order to forget a woman and to become a good, all-round doctor. We are led to believe that it is his nursing of an old love's wounds — and not Julie Gregg's age, appearance, and aggressive pursuit of him — that explains his refusal to respond to Julie Gregg's advances. In the light of subsequent events, however, Doc Stair may well be a totally different sort of person than the barber takes him for. And his becoming coroner assumes a sinister significance.

Julie Gregg is a young spinster, daughter of a merchant ("who got to drinkin' and lost most of his money" before he died) and of a semi-invalid mother who kept her in the small town against her wishes. The barber's references to her education in Chicago and New York and to her being "too good for the young people around this town" suggest that she is a cousin of Carol Kennicott, the culture-vulture of Sinclair Lewis's *Main Street*. It is no wonder that the doctor wants to keep her at a distance.

In addition to this curious triangle, there is Paul Dickson, the standard small-town idiot of fiction. He is the constant butt of Jim Kendall's practical jokes (he is sent on errands to fetch a left-handed monkey wrench or the key to the pitcher's box), but is befriended by Doc Stair and Julie Gregg.

Once this cast has been introduced, the action begins. As the barber tells it — and as most readers accept it, Julie Gregg develops an unrequited love for Doc Stair and is, in turn, vainly pursued by Jim Kendall. After she fights off the latter's attempts to thrust himself upon her, Jim vows revenge. He tricks her into visiting the doctor's office late at night only to be mocked and jeered by Jim's cronies who are hidden under the stairs. The idiot boy, resenting this cruelty to his female protector, informs the doctor, who swears he'll "make

Jim suffer." But before he can achieve his revenge, Jim takes the idiot boy hunting, presumably to have sadistic fun at his expense. Jim is accidentally killed when he lets Paul take the gun to shoot at some ducks: "Paul hadn't never handled a gun and was nervous. He was shakin' so hard that he couldn't control the gun."

To most readers the final irony of the story is that the barber fails to appreciate fully the poetic justice of Jim's fate. His monumental understatement is, "It probably served Jim right, what he got. But we certainly miss him round here. He certainly was a card!" However, one measure of the quality of fiction is the extent to which all the details fit into a soundly-structured, meaningful pattern. If "Haircut" is merely a folksy little tale for barber shop amusement, we need not probe for significance in the barber's asides and peripheral comments. But once we seek for a whole that incorporates the maximum number of details, we can discover a fascinating and complex human experience within the barber's narrative. Since the barber is oblivious to the meaning of his own story, it is up to the reader to order the various scattered fragments that will reveal it.

For example, early in the story during the introductory description of Julie Gregg, the barber tells us that Doc Stair had taken a professional interest in the idiot boy: "Doc done all he could to improve Paul's mind and he once told me that he really thought the boy was gettin' better, and they was times when he was as bright and sensible as everyone else." Further, the barber conjectures upon hearing of the outrage Jim had perpetrated on Julie Gregg: "It's a cinch[1] Doc swore he'd make Jim suffer ... He was goin' to do somethin', but it took a lot of figurin'." The "figurin'" may have been necessary merely to avoid becoming Julie Gregg's public champion while ridding the community of that monstrous social cancer, Jim Kendall. The reader can link together motive and means. Doc Stair knew that under his ministrations Paul Dickson had come to have moments of lucidity "when he was bright and sensible as anybody else." During one of those moments, the idiot "had told him about the joke Jim had played on Julie. He said Paul had asked him what he thought of the joke and *the Doc had told him that anybody that would do a thing like that ought not to be let live.*"

Either this physician had become so emotionally aroused and so careless in the presence of a mentally-deficient patient as to utter irresponsible and inflammatory remarks, or he was a crafty, Iago-like person intent on a deed that "took a lot of figurin'." The maximum meaning of the details is that Doc Stair deliberately planted the idea of murder in the mind of Paul Dickson, knowing that he had the legal power as coroner to protect the half-wit from the consequences of his act. The doctor first covered up for himself by appearing nervously at the barber shop to inquire about Jim and Paul on that fatal morning, feigning bewilderment that they would go hunting together "because Paul told him that he wouldn't never have no more to do with Jim as

---

[1] sl. for 'a sure thing'

long as he lived." Then, called to the scene of the crime as coroner, he immediately exonerated the boy, declaring that there was "no use callin' a jury, as it was a plain case of accidental shootin'."

Thus, the central character is not Jim Kendall, but the enigmatic doctor who is in the town "to hide himself away and forget" something in his past. His mysterious background, unexplained wealth, and periodic trips to the big city have a sinister suggestiveness. Furthermore, unless there is a connection between his background, his motivation to "get even," his strong hold over the mind of the half-wit, his peculiar relationship with Julie Gregg, the maliciousness of Jim Kendall, and the doctor's fortuitous position as coroner, the story would have to be considered a failure for having introduced so much unrelated and irrelevant material. The stupid narrator, of course, cannot see the relationship. Such is the nature of Lardner's craft that we must, so to speak, reverse the lenses of his viewing instrument — minimize the details that loom large to the barber and magnify those details whose significance he does not understand. Surely the continued popularity of this tale among discriminating readers is not to be explained by something so elementary as the simple irony of the barber's failure to see the horror of his "comic hero," but rather by the intriguing and tantalizing appeal of a complex human situation with sinister undertones and subtly delineated motivations.

1. *What is the advantage of having the story told by the barber?*

    He can give the detailed observations of a witness who is well acquainted with all the inhabitants of the little village and the gossip concerning them, and whose shop was a regular meeting-place on Saturday afternoons, when Jim Kendall used to think up his practical jokes. But as he does not realize the meaning of the little tragedy and fails to appreciate the justice of Jim's death, he does not anticipate the reaction of the reader, who is, on the contrary, left unsatisfied and thus set to thinking.

2. *Who is the central character in this story?*

    From the beginning the barber is talking about Jim Kendall (". . . we have pretty good times. Not as good, though, since Jim Kendall got killed."), he entertains his customer with the report of Jim's jokes and finally sums up his tale with Jim, "But still we miss him round here. He certainly was a card!" When the reader finds out how unreliable and insensitive the narrator is, however, he will begin to doubt whether Jim's death merely occurred because "he was a sucker to leave a new beginner have his gun." Looking for a figure who contributes more compellingly to the main action and gives a meaning to numerous otherwise irrelevant details, he has to re-examine the information received about Doctor Stair, which will reveal his dominating part in the events reported.

3. *How did the Doctor manage to "make Jim suffer"?*

    He had "done all he could to improve Paul's mind." Since the "boy was crazy about Julie," it did not need much from the doctor's side, whom he regarded as "a real friend," to fix the idea in the boy's mind that Jim "ought not to be let live." When opportunity offered he took care to prevent any suspicion and, as coroner, protected the boy.

J. V. H.

Brooks and Warren, *Understanding Fiction*, 2nd edition, New York 1959, pp. 145-150. Goldstein, Melvin, A Note on a Perfect Crime, *Literature and Psychology* XI, 1961, pp. 65—67.

# HERMAN MELVILLE

Herman Melville was born on August 1, 1819, in New York. His parents were both of well-to-do families of Scottish and Dutch descent, whose fortunes, however, declined. At the age of 13, Melville had to leave school and, after unsuccessful attempts at different jobs, went to sea in 1839. His experiences as a sailor and ashore in the slums of Liverpool were later recalled in *Redburn* (1849). In 1841 he joined the crew of a whaling-ship bound for the Pacific and was absent for almost four years. His first publication *Typee: A Peep at Polynesian Life* (1846), which catapulted him into fame, was based in part on his own adventures after jumping ship and living among the savages of the South Seas. In the following year Melville married the daughter of a Boston chief justice and settled down in New York. During eleven years (1846—57) Melville wrote ten major volumes with diminishing popularity until his fiction writing suddenly ceased. The most important novel of this period is *Moby Dick* (1851), which is not merely a vivid and stirring account of a whaling voyage, but a poetically-rendered allegory representing the struggle of man against his destiny at various levels of experience. It is perhaps the greatest American novel of the nineteenth century.

In 1850, Melville had established a residence on a farm in Massachusetts, where he formed a stimulating friendship with Hawthorne. With the year 1857, however, Melville's literary career came to an end. After some hard and bitter years he settled down humbly in 1866 as a customs inspector in New York. Only in *Billy Budd*, written from 1888 to 1891, did he recover his literary powers. The manuscript of this novelette was not yet fully prepared for press when Melville died in 1891, and was not published till 1924.

For many years after his death his work was neglected, but about the time of his birth centenary there was remarkable revival of interest in his books, and he is now reckoned one of the greatest of American authors.

Interpretations of his work continue to be highly controversial, though. Some critics take him to be a precursor of twentieth-century atheistic existentialism; others see him struggling toward an affirmation of Christian faith. But the volume of Melville scholarship attests his continuing importance for the modern world.

## Bartleby the Scrivener

Text:  *American Short Stories* VI pp. 32—74. Schöningh
*Seven Anglo-American Short Stories* pp. 64—102. Diesterweg

*An elderly lawyer relates his recollections of Bartleby, the strangest copyist or scrivener he had ever employed in his office. At the beginning Bartleby was a reliable and industrious worker but could not be brought to do any work apart from copying. When the lawyer finds out one day that Bartleby has made the office his home and lives there all friendless and joyless, he is overcome by pity for Bartleby's miserable life, but also feels annoyance at his stubborn refusal to behave reasonably. When Bartleby even stops copying, the lawyer vainly tries to get rid of him. For some time he persuades himself to put up with him although he is entirely useless. But then he tries to escape by changing his office. Bartleby does not leave the old premises, and soon the new tenant complains to the lawyer. When another attempt fails to make Bartleby see reason, the landlord has him evicted by the police. The lawyer feels obliged to look after Bartleby in prison and, after a few days, finds him dead. He cannot get the desired information about Bartleby's former life, but a rumor says that Bartleby had been employed in the Dead Letter Office at Washington, burning letters that could not be delivered or traced to their senders.*

"Bartleby the Scrivener," published in *Piazza Tales* in 1856, is probably Melville's finest short story and probably the most "modern" short story to come from 19th century America. The point of view of the "I" narrator is perfectly maintained throughout the tale, the setting and characters are all symbolic without ever quite transgressing the bounds of realism, and the existentialist meaning is dramatically embodied in the action. Not quite as macabre or fantastic as Kafka (another "drawer-up of recondite documents of all sorts"), Melville nevertheless captures a Kafkaesque quality in the eccentric scrivener's puzzling behavior. However, Bartleby himself is not the central character, despite the fact that he is the focus of the narrator's attention, the "strangest [scrivener] I ever saw, or heard of." It is not Bartleby's experience, fascinating though it be, that is the most dramatic event, but the *effect* of it on the narrator who tells "what my own astonished eyes saw of Bartleby." Shaken to the depths, the lawyer tries to compose himself and to tell calmly and clearly about the most profound experience of his life, his encounter with the "pallidly neat, pitiably respectable, incurably forlorn" creature who exasperated him, aroused his pity, drove him to distraction, infuriated him, and finally initiated him to the brotherhood of those who know the sad truth about the human condition.

After the prologue of the opening paragraph, the lawyer feels obliged to "make some mention of myself, my employees, my business, my chambers, and general surroundings, because some such description is indispensable to an adequate understanding..." And he is, indeed, correct. Only on second reading, however, can we fully grasp the tone and significance of this exposition. For example, we might assume on first reading that the narrator is a pompous ass, convinced that "the easiest way of life is the best," dedicated to ease, comfort, money, and the good opinion of such robber-barons as John Jacob Astor whose name "hath a round, orbicular sound to it and rings like unto bullion." But knowing the whole story we can see the bitterly ironic amusement with which he mocks himself with his legal "imprimis" and his "all who know me consider me an eminently *safe* man." Bartleby has already taught him the shallowness and stupidity of his earlier values, but we must first see him as he was in order to understand the full impact of what he has learned.

With the description of the lawyer's chambers the recondite symbolism of the story begins to emerge. The subtitle, "a story of wall street," has two meanings: a story of life among those dedicated to financial profit, and a story of the walls that separate men from each other and from the essential truth about the human situation. At one end the lawyer's chambers look out upon a white wall of a sky-light shaft (heaven), "deficient in what landscape painters call 'life'"; at the other on a "lofty brick wall, black by age and everlasting shade" (hell). Later Bartleby is placed mid-way between these views, isolated by a high green folding screen (life) and next to a small window that presented "no view at all." If we remember that "such description is indispensable to an adequate understanding" of Bartleby's peculiar behavior, we realize that Bartleby has no vision of heaven or hell, but only of meaningless death that renders life absurd. Again and again, we are told that Bartleby was "standing in one of those dead-wall reveries of his," surrounded by his green screen; and at the end of the story, Bartleby is in The Tombs (the city prison of New York, otherwise ironically known as The Hall of Justice), "in the enclosed grass-platted yards, . . . his face towards a high wall." There he dies, "asleep . . . with kings and counselors," and the lawyer adds a postscript "with a certain suggestive interest" — Bartleby had once been a subordinate clerk in the Dead Letter Office. This fact gives the lawyer the key to understanding not only Bartleby but all men (the final sentence of the story is "Ah, Bartleby! Ah, humanity!") who are "the sons of Adam," equally the prisoners of an irrational universe in which they are condemned to death. The story ends with the lawyer's — and the reader's — moment of illumination. Bartleby himself had had that insight long before he sought employment in Wall Street; it explains his reiterated and frustrating "I would prefer not to" — first to proofreading copy, then to the copying itself, and finally to quitting the premises. The morose scrivener prefers not to pretend that the usual activities of life are meaningful and rational, and, as the lawyer says, "Nothing so aggravates an earnest person as a passive resistance" . . . "he begins to stagger in his own plainest faith."

The lawyer's other three employees are Turkey, Nippers, and Ginger Nut — food, drink, and spices. They represent the usual run of humanity, often rebellious, generally agreeable; their frustrations are balanced and cancel each other. "Their fits relieved each other, like guards." Turkey's reiterated "with submission, sir" is the antithesis to Bartleby's "I would prefer not to."

The lawyer's charity (motivated by his religion) and his indignation (motivated by the social pressure of his colleagues) alternate in gradually-increasing swings of his spiritual pendulum, but neither Christian charity nor social indignation can solve the problem posed by Bartleby. Nothing can.

When the lawyer says that "for the first time in my life a feeling of overpowering stinging melancholy seized me... presentiments of strange discoveries hovered round me," he means that his faith in the Christian conception of the universe is about to be shaken. He almost says so literally: "It is not seldom the case that, when a man is brow-beaten in some unprecedented and violently unreasonable way, he begins to stagger in his own plainest faith. He begins, as it were, vaguely to surmise that... all the justice and all the reason is on the other side." On his way to Trinity Church one Sunday morning he stops by the office in Wall Street, "deserted as Petra," and discovers the plight of his scrivener—"what miserable friendlessness and loneliness are here revealed!" Since he is a "sensitive being," he perceives that "pity cannot lead to eventual succor," and feels disqualified "for the time from church-going." The elemental loneliness and ultimate absolute death of man are not compatible with Christian doctrine.

For some time the lawyer struggles against this insight and continues to fluctuate between the "self-interest" of following the commandment to love one another and the "old Adam of resentment." A temporary resignation to Bartleby's refusal to move follows the lawyer's reading of "[Jonathan] Edwards on the Will and [Joseph] Priestley on Necessity"—basic texts on the Calvinist notion of predestination, but again the "relentless remarks" of his friends prevail and he comes to the absurd conclusion, "Since he will not quit me, I must quit him." He moves to new premises, leaving the stubborn Bartleby behind. The new tenants have him forcibly evicted by the police, and Bartleby "silently acquiesced" to being conducted to The Tombs. The conscience-stricken lawyer visits him there, and makes one last futile attempt to reconcile him to the human situation: "It is not so sad a place as one might think. Look, there is the sky and here is the grass." But Bartleby replies, "I know where I am." His final act of rebellion against God's universe is to refuse to eat until he dies. As the postscript makes clear, the "good tidings" (i. e., Gospel) can never reach "those who died stifled by unrelieved calamities. On errands of life, these letters speed to death."

As Newton Arvin has said, in one of the finest studies of Melville's works, "what Bartleby eventually dramatizes... is the bitter metaphysical pathos of the human situation itself; the cosmic irony of the truth that men are at once immitigably interdependent and immitigably forlorn."

1. *Explain the references to a) Byron, b) Cicero, and c) the man struck by lightning in Virginia.*

   a) Just before Bartleby first announces that he "would prefer not to" verify copy, the narrator tells us that such a job is "a very dull, wearisome, and lethargic affair.... I cannot credit that the mettlesome poet, Byron, would have contentedly sat down with Bartleby to examine a law document..." There are two levels of meaning to this — realistically, of course, Byron was a romantic rebel with a fiery temperament with no patience for such petty mundane uses of time; symbolically, the law document equals God's law with which the atheist Byron would have nothing to do. Bartleby also rebels against God's law, but unlike Byron he does so passively.

b) When the narrator is faced with Bartleby's refusal, it is the fact that there is not "anything ordinarily human about" the scrivener which prevents him from dismissing the obstinate employee immediately. In comparing him to his "pale plaster-of-paris bust of Cicero," which he would never think of turning out of doors, he does not only see Bartleby as a being as lifeless as the pale plaster-of-paris bust ("a motionless young man," writing on "silently, palely, mechanically"); he also senses "something about Bartleby that not only strangely disarmed me, but, in a wonderful manner, touched and disconcerted me" — a philosopher's understanding of the human condition.

c) After the lawyer delivers his first ultimatum to Bartleby, he is "thunderstruck" to find the scrivener still in the office:

> "For an instant I stood like a man who, pipe in mouth, was killed one cloudless afternoon long ago in Virginia, by summer lightning; at his own warm window he was killed, and remained leaning out there upon the dreamy afternoon, till some one touched him, when he fell."

This has something of the same meaning as the passage from T. S. Eliot's "The Love Song of J. Alfred Prufrock":

> "Shall I say, I have gone at dusk through narrow streets
> And watched the smoke that rises from the pipes
> of lonely men in shirt-sleeves, leaning out of windows?"

Both are images of men who are dead while having the semblance of life. The lawyer here is moving toward his shattering insight into the fact that all life is death-bound.

2. *Cite the most salient references to vision and explain the meaning.*

When Bartleby first announces that he will do no more writing, the lawyer demands to know the reason. Bartleby indifferently replies, "Do you not see the reason for yourself?" Looking into Bartleby's dull and glazed eyes, the lawyer immediately assumes that too much copying had impaired Bartleby's vision. The irony is that Bartleby sees the truth about life and death all too well, and it is the lawyer who will come to have the scales fall from his eyes.

3. *What is "the doctrine of assumptions"?*

"Without loudly bidding Bartleby depart — as an inferior genius might have done — I *assumed* the ground that depart he must," says the lawyer; and for several pages we find a continual play with the words assume, assumed, assumption, ending with: "It was hardly possible that Bartleby could withstand such an application of the doctrine of assumptions." The word *doctrine* has religious implications, and in terms of the whole meaning of the story it is interesting that no doctrine (e. g. that of *elections* or of *predestination*, both invoked in the next few pages) is true simply because convention assumes they are true.

4. *Who is Monroe Edwards and why is he mentioned in the story?*

The grub man at The Tombs says he thought Bartleby was like Monroe Edwards a gentleman forger, because "they're always pale and genteel-like, them forgers." The only other reference to an Edwards in the story is to "Edwards on the Will." The implication is that Jonathan Edwards's Christian doctrine was also a forgery. (cf. a similar ironic play on the name James in *Billy Budd*.)

5. *How sensitive a man is the lawyer-narrator?*

On first introduction to him, we might assume that he is a rather insensitive person; like a Browning monologist, he seems unaware of how much he betrays himself. For example, he tells us that he seldom loses his temper but proceeds to narrate how incensed he was when his sinecure as Master in Chancery (a beautifully ironic title), "not a very arduous office but very pleasantly remunerative," was cancelled. But his urge to treat Bartleby kindly, though rationalized in various ways — "he means no mischief ... a valuable acquisition" — is evidence of compassion and understanding: "There was something about Bartleby that not only strangely disarmed me, but, in a wonderful manner, touched and disconcerted me." In remorse for abandoning Bartleby, he is ready to take him into his own home. Compare this treatment with that of the lawyer's successors in the Wall Street chambers. It is this compassionate response to the misery of Bartleby that ultimately redeems him and makes possible his final insight.

6. *Are religion and social pressure at opposite poles as forces acting upon the lawyer?*

Yes and no. The first calls for charity and the application of the principle "Love thy neighbor"; the second for prudence — "common sense bids the soul be rid of pity." But neither works as a basis for dealing with Bartleby; neither can cope satisfactorily with death, the basic evil of the universe.

7. *What role do Turkey, Nippers, and Ginger Nut play in the story?*

They serve two functions: to show how ordinary men adjust and accept the human condition that is intolerable, and to introduce comic relief into a story which would otherwise be unbearably gloomy.

J. V. H.

Abcarian, Richard, The World of Love and the Spheres of Fright: Melville's "Bartleby the Scrivener," *Studies in Short Fiction* I, 1964, pp. 207—215 — Felheim, Marvin, Meaning and Structure in "Bartleby," *College English* XXIII, 1962, pp. 369—376 — Fogle, Richard H., Melville's "Bartleby": Absolutism, Predestination, and Free Will, *Tulane Studies in English* IV, 1954, pp. 124—135 — Gibson, William M., Herman Melville's "Bartleby the Scrivener" and "Benito Cereno," *Die Neueren Sprachen*, Beiheft 9, 1961, pp. 107—116 — Kopetzki, Robert, *Weltfreude und Todesnähe*, Frankfurt 1967, pp. 81—94 — Link, Franz, Melville, "Bartleby the Scrivener," *Die Amerikanische Kurzgeschichte*, eds. Göller/Hoffmann, Düsseldorf 1972, pp. 118—128 — Marx, Leo, Melville's Parable of the Walls, *Sewanee Review* LXI, 1953, pp. 602—627 — Vincent, Howard, ed., *The Melville Annual 1965, A Symposium: Bartleby the Scrivener*, Kent 1966 — Widmer, Kingsley, Melville's Radical Resistance: The Method and Meaning of *Bartleby*, *Studies in the Novel* I, 1969, pp. 444—458.

# Benito Cereno

Text: Melville, *Benito Cereno*. Diesterweg
(shortened by one third; in the following discussion, the symbol (–) indicates that the cited passage is not included in the Diesterweg edition)

*In the year 1799, the United States trading vessel Bachelor's Delight touches port at an uninhabited island off Chili to get water. Also at anchor in that remote place is a Spanish merchantman, the San Dominick, carrying Negro slaves. The American captain Amasa Delano pays her a visit and is surprised by the strange condition of the Spanish captain, Benito Cereno, and the general disorder on board. The sick captain, waited upon by a Negro servant named Babo, explains that storms had damaged his ship and that scurvy and a malignant fever as well as lack of food and water had caused the loss of the owner of the ship and almost all his crew. He praises the loyalty of the Negroes, but Captain Delano is puzzled by scenes of insubordination which remain unpunished. He promises to help the Spaniard, but feels mistrust and suspicion at the mysterious atmosphere, which is increased by some disguised warnings. After doling out water and food, Captain Delano leaves the Spanish ship, whose captain refuses to return the visit. Suddenly, however, Captain Cereno leaps overboard into the American boat, soon to be followed by his servant with a dagger in his hand. Now "the scales drop" from Captain Delano's eyes — he sees the Negroes have been conducting a mutiny. When the San Dominick tries to escape from the harbor, Delano gives chase, attacks, and seizes control of the ship from the Negroes. After two days the ships sail to Lima in Peru, where the whole affair comes before court. Benito Cereno is nursed by monks, but cannot recover from his horrible experiences and dies. In a document he gives evidence of the revolt that had brought his ship into the hands of the Negroes, who were seeking to gain freedom in the Negro state of Senegal. Babo, the ringleader, is hanged.*

"Benito Cereno" was published together with "Bartleby the Scrivener" in *The Piazza Tales* (1856). As in "Bartleby" and in *Billy Budd,* Melville has here developed a relatively simple action, but so hedged it about with qualifications in structure, setting, characterization, and symbolism that we can take nothing at face value. And as usual, the narrative is presented from the point of view of one who does not fully understand what is happening, is compelled to puzzle out the meaning: "if I could only be certain that, in my uneasiness, my senses did not deceive me" (–) . . . "ah, these currents spin one's head round almost as much as they do the ship" (–). What happened aboard the San Dominick is finally revealed: "That moment, across the long-benighted mind of Captain Delano, a flash of revelation swept, illuminating, in unanticipated clearness, his host's whole mysterious demeanor, with every enigmatic action of the day, as well as the entire past voyage of the San Dominick" (38:34–37). Buth this resolves only the suspense about the action; it does not resolve the *meaning* of that action. Hence, there follows a court scene and an epilogue which take up one-third of the story; but even in these the ambiguities are not clearly resolved, and Melville explicitly warns the discerning reader that "the nature of this narrative, besides rendering the intricacies in the beginning unavoidable, has more or less required that many things ... should be retrospectively, or *irregularly* given; this last is the case with the following passages" of epilogue (50:29—33). From the opening mists of the grey dawn, "Shadows present, foreshadowing deeper shadows to come" (5:18), there emerge a clear action and a shrouded meaning. The wise reader who has, "along with a benevolent heart, more than ordinary quickness and accuracy of intellectual perception" (5:30—31) can see beneath the shroud.

No doubt the mystery surrounding the first part of the story has an aesthetic purpose, the time-honored device of suspense which is resolved the moment Benito Cereno leaps over the side of his ship. The mystery of the epilogue is not so easily explained; one can only conjecture that once again, as with *Moby Dick,* Melville felt a necessity to conceal all but the simple adventure from a 19th century New England public that would have no proper appreciation for his "evil book." For all of Melville's major fiction deals with the theme of cosmic rebellion against the inevitable evil in the world, but pious Christians could not be expected to sympathize with Melville's angry conviction that God was responsible for that evil and that no glossing over that fact can deceive or mollify any perceptive and compassionate human being. The average Yankee Protestant could safely be expected to identify with Amasa Delano, the simple, good-hearted merchant sea-captain, to rejoice in his saving a fellow Christian from the hands of evil black savages, and to share his incredulous puzzlement when Benito Cereno is grateful but languishes in mournful melancholy to his death. However, the title character is Benito Cereno, and it is his insight — cryptically communicated when he answers simply, "The Negro," to Delano's astonished and pained question, "What has cast such a shadow upon you?" (52:16—17) — that is the essential meaning of the story. What does he mean by "the Negro," and why doesn't Delano understand him? All of the subtle hints and recondite symbolism imply that Benito Cereno has learned from the Negroes that Christianity itself is fundamentally evil and corrupt — and Delano is "a person of a singularly undistrustful good nature" (5:26) ... "incapable of sounding such wickedness" (49:23).

That some sort of Christian significance is involved is clear from the names and descriptions that recur throughout the story. (It is further significant that these were introduced when Melville adapted his source, *A Narrative of Voyages and Travels in the Northern and Southern Hemispheres* (1817) by Captain Amasa Delano.) The *San Dominick* is named after the saint who at the beginning of the 13th century exterminated the Albigenses, a Manichean sect that believed Satan was a co-ruler of the universe, equal in power with God. They denied the value of the church and advocated simply, "Follow Christ your leader" (cf. Matthew 16:24—25). But Christian elements are treated with powerful irony. The captain of this ship, Benito Cereno, is hardly a man characterized by "blessed serenity" and when Delano first sees the ship through shreds of fog, it "appeared like a white-washed monastery," manned by "a shipload of monks ... of Blackfriars pacing the cloisters" (6:20—27).

These Blackfriars, i. e. Dominicans, are of course mutinous Negro slaves — a fact which suggests that the dominical ship of Christ is manned by impostors. Such meanings are like the ship itself — they "hoard from view their interiors, till the last moment" (7:27—28).

Aboard the *San Dominick*, Amasa Delano proves to be amazingly stupid. He observes several instances of "insubordination" only to assume that Cereno "is one of those paper captains ... who has little of command" (—); he is the dupe of Babo's transparent charades — "Faithful fellow! ... Don Benito, I envy you such a friend; slave I cannot call him" (13:3—4); he receives many hints and covert signals which his childishly innocent mind cannot comprehend, as when the aged sailor tosses him a knot saying, "Undo it, cut it, quick" (22:39), and he simply stands mute, "knot in hand and knot in head" (23:4). Melville's ironies are directed as much at Delano's beliefs as at the man himself, for every time Delano dismisses the doubts and suspicions that creep into his shallow mind he does so with serene religious faith: "Who would murder Amasa Delano? His conscience is clean. There is some one above" (—) and "Once again he smiled at the phantoms which had mocked him and felt something like a tinge of remorse that ... he should ... have betrayed an atheist doubt of the ever-watchful Providence above." (—) Indeed, Delano's innocence is maintained to the very end; he never does see the agonizing truth that tortures Cereno: "Yes, all is owing to Providence, I know" (51:24).

Melville's ironies are quite Voltairian, and Delano is his Candide, blissfully certain that he lives in the best of all possible worlds. To him the Negro slaves are as faithful as "Newfoundland dogs" (27:18); "they are natural valets and hair-dressers" (27:2—3); and he never dreams that these noble savages, "pure tenderness and love" (—), might ever feel a drive for freedom powerful enough for them to mutiny, seize ship, and demand to be carried to Senegal, a free Negro country. "When a mulatto has a regular European face, look out for him; he is a devil" (30:21—22); that is to say, the Negroes have learned their cruelty from the whites. A fact which has consistently escaped short-sighted critics of this story is that the Negroes *do not* represent evil, that their violence is purely retaliatory, their motive for revolt as praiseworthy as Thomas Jefferson's. In fact, the Negroes are in revolt against evil; but because Melville is working in cosmic-religious, rather than political-social, terms, the revolt cannot ultimately succeed. The white man, like the white whale, is indomitable; the evil in the universe cannot be overcome, and it is inextricably linked with Christianity.

Sequence after sequence of symbols carry this meaning. For example, as Delano steps from the poop-deck where lie Negro mothers and their children "unsophisticated as leopardesses, loving as doves" (—) to the starboard quarter-gallery, he moves from pagan vitality to morbid Christian civilization. And his glance falls on a "row of small, round dead-lights ... like coppered eyes of the coffined" and a "cabin door ... like a sarcophagus lid" (—). The deck cabin where Babo shaves Cereno contains a thumbed missal, a crucifix, "some melancholy rigging, like a heap of poor friars' girdles," two settees like "inquisitors' racks," a misshapen arm-chair like "some grotesque engine of torment," and a washstand "like a font" (—) — the elements of the Church and the Inquisition, death and evil are curiously amalgamated. Even details of religious ritual and Biblical narratives are mocked. In a grotesque version of the communion ceremony, Delano distributes bread and water, but he "would have given [them to] the whites alone, and in chief Don Benito; but the latter objected" (24:34—35). Cereno (whom Babo ironically refers to as "master") and Delano sit down to a "last supper," which the American seizes as an occasion for discussing "the pecuniary part of the business (31:21), i. e., the remuneration for his good Samaritan act of charity in aiding a ship in distress. Perhaps most daring of all is the parody of the crucifixion in the rebellion described in the Official Version of the mutiny (which, like the "authorized naval chronicle" in *Billy Budd* and the court judgment against Bartleby, naturally presents the case in terms of the vested interest of the society). Don Alexandro Aranda, owner of the slaves, is murdered on deck and his body carried below for three days; then he is "resurrected" and his skeleton is "substituted for the ship's proper figurehead — the image of Christopher [i. e. Christ-bearer] Colon, the discoverer of the New World" (45:20—21). Then Babo warns Cereno to "keep faith ... or you shall in spirit, as now in body, follow your leader" (45:25—26). These last words are, in a sense, a *leitmotif* of the story, occurring first when Delano observes "*Seguid vuestro jefe*" (7:8) rudely painted beneath the shrouded figure-head; he sees the words again when the skeleton is exposed (39:19), he hears a mate cry the words as the whites seize the *San Dominick* (41:19), and they are echoed at the very end when the head of Babo, leader of the revolt against Christian slavery, is fixed on a pole in the Plaza and looks "unabashed ... towards St. Bartholomew's church, in whose vaults slept ... the recovered bones of Aranda: and ... towards the monastery, on Mt. Agonía ... where, three months after being dismissed by the court, Benito Cereno, borne on the bier, did, indeed, follow his leader" (52:34—39). Melville seems to be asking us to consider where we shall end if we take the Christian injunction seriously, and he maliciously suggests that slavery and death are the consequences. In the end Benito Cereno, unable to face Babo again, is well aware that "malign machinations and deceptions impose" (51:38) on even the most innocent of men, and when Delano urges him to forget it as do the sun and the sea and the sky, he replies "They have no memory ... because they are not human" (52:8—9). There is not the slightest hint of reconciliation or redemption for the man aware of the human predicament; only the naïvely innocent, like Delano, can "smile at the phantoms which had mocked him" (—).

1. *Explain the broad structure of the story and the function of each main section.*

> The story has three parts: (1) Delano's experience aboard the *San Dominick*, a narrative with the classical unities of time, place, and action — twelve hours

aboard the *San Dominick* with gradually mounting mystery until the climax of Cereno's leap and the moment of illumination when Delano sees Babo attempting to stab his master; (2) the court deposition of Benito Cereno, which shifts the point of view from the innocent Protestant American to the official "objectivity" of the Catholic Spanish Court to reveal the exact details of the mutiny and to show "that it was impossible for the deponent and his men to act otherwise than they did" (—), i. e., to justify the white Christian perspective; and (3) the epilogue, revealing from a neutrally objective point of view the execution of the unrepentant Babo ("since I cannot do deeds, I will not speak words" — 52:25-26), the sustained ignorance and innocence of Delano ("all is owing to Providence" — 51:24), and the final agony of the enlightened Cereno who knew at last the meaning of the Negro.

2. *What is the dominant color symbolism of the story?*

Gray, white, and black. The gray mists through which Delano first sees the *San Dominick* suggest not only the mystery of the ship but also the American's lack of clear vision. White is the color of Christianity ("white-washed monastery"), of the slave-drivers, and of the bleached bones of Aranda — a curious configuration suggesting that conventional color symbolism is being violated: white is the color of evil and of death. Black is the color of the oppressed, who become violent in order to cast off their chains; in doing so, they adopt the means of the whites (they appear to be Black Friars). It is significant that in the court deposition the leaders of the revolt are all Negroes who have some white blood or at least prolonged association with white civilization (cf. *Jb. f. Amerikastudien* 5, Heidelberg 1960, pp. 159 ff.).

3. *Explain the major ironies for each of the "ritual scenes" of the story!*

a) The Greeting Scene. Delano believes Cereno to be responsible for disorder aboard the *San Dominick;* looks upon Babo as a shepherd dog faithfully serving his master. "Did he but know the particulars of the ship's misfortunes, he would, perhaps, be better able in the end to relieve them," says Delano (10:18-19).
b) The Pardon Scene. The gigantic Atufal, ("a king in his own land"), in false chains, begs the pardon of Cereno. Delano finds the padlock and key to be "significant symbols, truly" (17:4) and fears that Don Benito is "at bottom ... a bitter hard master" (34:18-19).
c) The Gordian Knot Scene. (Ironies obvious)
d) The Communion Scene. Delano provides sustenance to those who are plotting his murder and the seizure of his ship.
e) The Shaving Scene. Babo and Cereno ironically play at their former roles of master and servant, but with the flag of Spain as the barber's cloth ("It's well it's only I, and not the King, that sees this," says Delano, "but ... it's all one, I suppose, so the colors be gay" (—); and Babo is amused by the remark). The basin resembles a headsman's block, and Babo's razor draws blood — "See, master ... here's Babo's first blood" (28:22), says the wily Negro; and we learn in the deposition scene that this is literally true (neither Babo nor Atufal committed murder with their own hands (49:1). The shave ended, the servant completes the toilet and stands back to survey "the creature of his own tasteful hands" (29:15) ...

"But neither sweet waters, nor shampooing, nor fidelity, nor sociality, delighted the Spaniard" (29:18-19).
f) Communion Meal: again, Babo, the attentive servant; Cereno, the sullen host; Delano, the irritated guest.

J. V. H.

Canaday, Nicholas, A New Reading of Melville's "Benito Cereno"; *Studies in American Literature*, ed. by McNeir and Levy, Baton Rouge 1960, pp. 49—57 — Ensslen, Klaus, Melville's "Benito Cereno," *Die amerikanische Kurzgeschichte*, eds. Göller/Hoffmann, Düsseldorf 1972, pp. 103—117 — Pasternak, Dieter, Melville, "Benito Cereno," *Interpretationen zu Irving, Melville und Poe*, ed. Finger, Hans, Frankfurt 1971, pp. 22—36 — Rosenthal, Bernard, Melville's Island, *Studies in Short Fiction* XI, 1974, pp. 1—9 — Runden, J. O., ed., *Melville's Benito Cereno* (text and criticism), Boston 1965 — Vanderhaar, Margaret, A Re-examination of "Benito Cereno," *American Literature* XL, 1968, pp. 179—191 — Widmer, Kingsley, The Perplexity of Melville: "Benito Cereno," *Studies in Short Fiction* V, 1968, pp. 225—238 — Yellin, Jean Fagan, Black Masks: Melville's "Benito Cereno," *American Quarterly* XII, 1970, pp. 678—689.

## Billy Budd

Text: Melville, *Billy Budd*. Braun
Melville, *Billy Budd*. Velhagen und Klasing (slightly condensed)
The quotations in the following analysis refer to this latter edition.

*In the year 1797 a handsome young sailor named Billy Budd is impressed into the King's service on H. M. S. Indomitable, which is on her way to join the Mediterranean fleet. He is made a foretopman and is soon well liked among the crew but arouses the envy and antipathy of Claggart, the master-at-arms. One night another impressed man tries to persuade Billy to join their conspiracy. He refuses, stuttering with excitement, but does not report the occurrence, although several mutinies have recently shaken the British Navy.*

*Choosing a time when the Indomitable is detached from the fleet after contact with an enemy frigate, Claggart addresses Captain Vere and accuses Billy Budd of conspiring to mutiny. When he is confronted with Billy, the innocent foretopman, unable to speak, kills Claggart by a blow on the forehead. Captain Vere, in spite of his fatherly feelings for Billy, calls a drumhead court, which, under the law of the Mutiny Act, condemns Billy Budd to death. The following morning he is hanged, and buried at sea. Owing to Captain Vere's authority martial discipline is maintained among the crew and soon confirmed in an engagement with the French fleet. Some time later, Capt. Vere is killed by a musket ball from the French ship, Athéiste.*

Full of passionate brooding and dark vision, *Billy Budd* is Melville's final and most ambiguous novella. Though immensely popular, it is by no means widely understood; Melville's involved and crabbed style, characterized by abstruse allusions, obscure qualifications, and sly hints, shrouds the meaning of his narrative with mystery. Again and again, Melville warns us that we must be shrewd, discerning and alert if we are to understand the complex of motives and morals that wind through what is otherwise a relatively simple action. "But at heart and not for nothing, as the late chance encounter *may indicate to the discerning,* down on him... [Claggart] assuredly was" (35:6—8); "with an added hint or two... the resumed narrative must be left to vindicate as it may, its own credibility" (37:17—20); "he there let escape an ironic inkling" (38:1); "whether Captain Vere... was really the victim of any degree of aberration, one must determine for himself by such light as this narrative may afford" (60:30—31, 61:1—2). If *Billy Budd* is in some sense a "Testament of Acceptance" or an analogue of the Christ Passion or simply a morality play with a conventional display of good and evil in the universe, what need is there for these recondite innuendoes? Either they are a blemish or they alert "the discerning" reader to a level of meaning which, if it were plainly presented, would be inacceptable to a general public that had also rejected *Moby Dick* and *Pierre,* and it would behoove a critic to seek a perspective from which he can see every detail as a smoothly joined part of a total pattern. It is not good critical practice to ignore a particular set of important facts (as Rolf Lorenz does in the introduction to the Velhagen & Klasing edition) in order to force out of the story a conventional Christian interpretation. The bare action itself could be explained in a wide variety of ways; hence the real meaning must lie in the historical setting, characterizations and motivations that make up the substance of most of the chapters.

The story is by no means perfectly executed; the narrator, who stands apart from and above the events, fluctuates between omniscience and a limited point of view. Although he was not himself a party to the private confrontation scene in which Claggart accused Billy of inciting his shipmates to mutiny, he is able to give us a vivid and detailed account of it, but he confesses to be ignorant of exactly what happened when Captain Vere tells Billy that he is condemned to die. He transmits the authorized version of the whole affair (Chapter 26) from "a publication now long ago superannuated and forgotten," but knows nothing of Claggart's — or Billy's — past life. In other words, Melville's narrator has no stable perspective. Furthermore, he is unnecessarily garrulous, constantly speculating about the meaning of specific events in ambiguous terms — either because he does not dare to tell the truth as he sees it, or because he is not quite certain what the truth is. Nevertheless, the "discerning reader" can see an over-all pattern that contains his specific utterances in a single meaningful whole.

The pivotal action of the story concerns a mutiny, or at least the temptation, accusation, and fear of one aboard the H. M. S. *Indomitable.* The ship is rightly named, for no mutiny actually occurs; but the whole point of the historical setting, powerfully suggested in the Preface, is that *revolt is perfectly justified.* And it is a revolt specifically against political tyranny and symbolically against Christianity. Far from being a "testament of acceptance," Melville's novella is a bitter lament over the futility of revolt. The year is 1797, a time of "crisis for Christendom" and a "rectification of the Old World's hereditary wrongs," and although under Napoleon the revolution itself became a tyranny "to some thinkers ... it has ... turned out to be a political advance along nearly the whole line for Europeans." In His Majesty's Navy, the specific context of the events in *Billy Budd*, the spirit of revolt took the form of mutinies (at Spithead and Nore) "against real abuses" and "prompting the most important reforms in the British Navy." Or, as he says in Chapter 3, "reasonable discontent" grew "out of practical grievances," and the mutineers gained absolution at Trafalgar. Since discontent survived the two mutinies at Spithead and Nore, "it was not unreasonable to apprehend some return of trouble sporadic or general." (22:26—27)

With this background in mind, the careful reader should be able to sense at once Melville's ironic treatment in the first two chapters of "the welkin-eyed Billy Budd or Baby Budd," who at the age of 21 when he should have been a man "made no demur" at being forcibly impressed into naval service. His former "shipmates turned a surprised glance of silent reproach at the sailor" who genially waved goodbye to the *Rights of Man*. There are a number of powerful implications in that gesture. For one thing Billy himself has no conception of the rights of man; with his "lingering adolescent expression," he is "a child-man" (46:3) more "like the animals" (16:29—30) and, indeed, animal imagery in the description of Billy is sustained throughout the story: "a blood horse" (19:13), "a dog of St. Bernard's breed" (19:23—24); "a young horse" (43:20), "a dog of generous breed" (65:26—27). Furthermore, Thomas Paine's famous book, *The Rights of Man*, was a plea for a non-Christian, humanist way of life. Although "to deal in double meaning and insinuations of any sort was quite foreign to [Billy's] nature," it is quite in keeping with the narrator's mode of expression! Billy's one blemish, his stutter, Melville says, "should be evidence that he is not presented as a conventional hero, but also that the story in which he is the main figure is no romance."

Another set of allusions in the characterization of Billy, equally effective in undermining any notion of his masculinity, is to his feminine traits. "Something about him provoked an ambiguous smile in one or two harder faces among the bluejackets" (18:9—10). "Like the beautiful woman in one of Hawthorne's minor tales, there was just one thing amiss in him ... a vocal defect" (19:29—32); "... face like that of a condemned vestal priestess" (57:8). He is twice compared to an angel, and in this connection the narrator thinks of "Fra Angelico's seraphs some of whom ... have the faint rose-bud complexion of the more beautiful English girls." (not contained in the Velhagen edition; Braun p. 97) And it is interesting that during Billy's trial, Captain Vere argues against clemency by equating it with femininity: "the heart, sometimes the feminine in man ... must here be ruled out." (68:35—69:2) It would be shrinking the wide significance of the story to interpret it, as Leslie Fiedler suggests, as a struggle against homosexual urges within Captain Vere. Such a meaning is, of course, not at all impossible, but to leave it at that would be to rule out the political, historical, and religious elements that loom very large. Nevertheless, Captain Vere's attitude here is extremely important; it is part of a total characterization that shows him to be fundamentally a weak man who, unable to trust his own humanity, protects himself with the armor of the rigid code and traditions of the British navy.

He is "a bachelor of forty or thereabouts"; that is to say, he has refused to commit himself to love and marriage. Melville's attitude to bachelors is clear from his little allegory, "A Paradise of Bachelors and a Tartarus of Maids," and from many of his tales. Vere was a humorless man (23:21) and despite his military bearing he "would at times betray a certain dreaminess of mood" (24:3—4). Like everything else in the story, the description of Vere is given by a narrator who seems to have no firm conclusions of his own, trying to be fair and impartial, but who in the process piles up detail after detail that damns Captain Vere. For example, Vere is a reader of books, an intellectual, and in this respect an extraordinary sea captain. But what and how does he read? Certainly no poetry and fiction, but history, biography, and unconventional writers, like Montaigne. But he is such a bigoted man that he cannot learn from what he reads; he reads to find "confirmation of his own more reserved thoughts ... His settled convictions were as a dyke against those invading waters of novel opinion social political and otherwise, which carried away as in a torrent no few minds in those days, minds by nature not inferior to his own" (25:21—31). Vere's reading, then, is another aspect of his rigid, reactionary, Calvinistic and aristocratic temperament.

In terms of the religious analogy of the story, Vere ("Starry Vere") equals God, just as Billy Budd equals Adam and Claggart equals the serpent Satan. It is not a pure analogy because Melville is trying to condemn such religious concepts as they find expression in human society. But, as far as it goes, God-King-Captain are a complex of authoritarian power that paradoxically demands loyalty and obedience with threat of dire punishment at the same time that it asks for such loyalty out of the free will of the subject. From Melville's point of view, men who valued their humanity could never submit to such harsh and irrational conditions; but rebellion could never succeed. Hence, Melville is America's most dramatic nineteenth-century existentialist. In *Benito Cereno*, he portrayed the active revolt of Negro slaves against tyranny and the failure of that revolt; in *Bartleby the Scrivener*, he portrayed the passive revolt of the gloomy and haunted copy clerk and the failure of that revolt; in *Billy Budd* he portrays the refusal to revolt of the innocent young sailor, and the failure of that refusal. Melville's final work is a complex and dissonant *nunc dimittis*.

Like Milton's God, Melville's Vere lacks the companionable quality, has no sense of humor, is a strict and retributive authoritarian, and in the area of his responsibility permits evil (Satan, Claggart) to do his work.

Men such as John Claggart were "secure, because once enlisted aboard a King's-Ship, they were as much in sanctuary, as the transgressor of the middle ages harboring himself under the shadow of the altar" (28:24—26). The careful reader will observe that, however much the narrator qualifies his negative portrayal of Claggart by comments on the irresponsibility of opinions of the crew who dislike him, he nevertheless states as a fact that promotion to positions of power can be achieved by such a "true madman" (36:34) through "constitutional sobriety, ingratiating deference to superiors, together with a peculiar ferreting genius" (29:8—11). That Claggart acts on behalf of the highest powers is made explicitly clear: "a nature like Claggart's... [is] the scorpion for which the Creator alone is responsible" (39:6—7). He is a Satan figure — "the first mesmeric glance was one of serpent fascination" (56:28—29) and the removal of his body "was like handling a dead snake" (58:1). Vere is responsible for Claggart just as God is responsible for Satan, however much either may dislike the agent of evil under his command; and both authorities are equally implacable in meting out punishment to those who are provoked into wrong-doing by the agent.

The first six chapters are devoted to introducing the three central characters in a highly suggestive historical setting. With chapter 7 the central drama begins to move. The innocent Billy, enjoying his life in the foretop and horrified at the punishment for dereliction of duty, strives to please everyone. The Old Dansker, the Teiresias figure of this tragedy (note that he is "an Agamemnon man"), warns Billy that the master-at-arms is "down" on him, but the boy-child cannot believe it. The old veteran with a "certain grim internal merriment" and a "pithy guarded cynicism" (attitudes which Melville, also an old veteran, no doubt, shared), speculated on what would happen to a nature like Billy's in a world "where such innocence as man is capable of does yet in a moral emergency not always sharpen the faculties or enlighten the will." It is Billy's "harmlessness itself" that maddens Claggart, who is naturally depraved — in Plato's, not Calvin's sense; i. e., Claggart is one of those among men who is born evil. But the narrator makes it clear that his evil, the "mystery of iniquity" in him, is *not* Calvinistic (36:8—9) or Biblical (37:11—15), for if it were it would be merely a trait which he shares with all mankind.

As Dansker explains it, the master-at-arms arranges for one of the afterguardsmen to attempt to bribe Billy into joining a mutiny of the impressed men. Billy, of course, indignantly refuses; but he is not so offended as to strike the man (his only way to articulate extreme indignation) and he plays the safest possible game by neither joining nor reporting the supposed mutiny. "Innocence was his blinder" (47:34). Events then move at a swift pace. Claggart delivers his *j'accuse,* Captain Vere arranges for a secret confrontation in his cabin, and the outraged and inarticulate Billy lashes out with his fist, killing the master-at-arms. "Fated boy," says the Captain (57:32), and after the Surgeon verifies that Claggart is dead, "Struck dead by an angel of God. Yet the angel must hang!" (59:12—13). This is, as the three judges of the drumhead court-martial later realize, "a prejudgment on the speaker's part" (65:31—32). The Surgeon, an objective, dispassionate, scientific observer, suspects the Captain of being "affected in his mind" (59:31; 60:9) in this peremptory judgment and in forcing the issue by holding an immediate trial. Like him, the officers of the court "seemed to think that such a matter should be reported to the Admiral" (60:18—19).

The trial itself takes up the longest chapter of the novella. Vere, as sole witness, accuser, and final judge, makes a mockery of human justice by turning "the matter over to a summary court of his own officers, reserving to himself as the one on whom the ultimate accountability would rest, the right of ... interposing" (62:19—23). Billy confirms the captain's factual account of the death of Claggart, but in his naive and primitive way attempts to introduce the question of motive and protests his loyalty to the King (63:28—30; 64:3—8). The irony of this will not escape the discerning reader, but since it is "a spiritual sphere wholly obscure to Billy's thoughts" (65:3—4), Billy cannot cope with Vere's obstinate dismissal of the question of motives. The captain employs every possible argument to win over his handpicked jury, paralyzed by "troubled indecision" (66:31); he frankly drops the role of witness to become their "coadjutor" (67:27). He argues that motives are a matter for "psychologic theologians"; "military duty" takes precedence in any choice between Nature and the King; clemency is effeminate and cowardly; and the danger of mutiny threatens if severe discipline is not applied. (Melville specifically alludes to his source, the *Somers* conviction, which he heartily detested (71:20—30).) Reluctantly, the court yields and Billy is sentenced to hang.

Vere endures the agony of Abraham in communicating the sentence to Billy; to pious Christian readers this would seem to redeem the captain, but to those of a more humanist persuasion the comparison condemns Abraham along with Vere. The crew listens to the captain's announcement "in a dumbness like that of a seated congregation of believers in hell listening to the clergyman's announcement of his Calvinistic text" (74:17—19). According to Vere, the decision was required by the exigencies of war, and what the narrator thinks of war is clear from a not very adroitly introduced allusion to the war merchants: the prisoner Billy is illuminated by a lamp "fed with the oil supplied by war-contractors (whose gains, honest or otherwise, are in every land an anticipated portion of the harvest of death)" (76:12—15). The chaplain who visits Billy is equally condemned as a man who has "a stipend from Mars" (77:5); "the worthy man lifted not a finger to avert the doom of such a martyr to martial discipline" (78:12—13); "a chaplain is the minister of the Prince of Peace serving in the host of the God of War — Mars" (78:17—19). As for Billy, the Christian interpreters of this tale consistently fail to confront his attitude to the chaplain: "futile were [the chaplain's] efforts to bring home to him the thought of salvation and a Saviour" (77:25—27). "He kissed on the fair cheek his fellow man, a felon in martial law, one who though in the confines of death he felt he could never convert to a dogma" (78:8—9). In short, chapter 22 alone would be sufficient to reveal the fundamentally anti-Christian nature of Melville's so-called "Testament of Acceptance". Billy's final "God bless Captain Vere" must be read in either of two ways: either Billy remains the naïve innocent to the very end, loyal to the evil of authority; or he is delivering a bitterly ironic accusation. It is in Billy's conscious intention probably the former; nevertheless, the crew's "resonant sympathetic echo" (80:3) is after a few moments followed by a "revulsion of thought and feeling ... a sullen revocation on the men's part of their involuntary echoing of Billy's benediction" (81:6—9). The mystical vision of "the Lamb of God" (80:15—16) at the moment of Billy's execution hardly justifies the comforting interpretation of an "ascension to heaven" — like a lamb he is sacrificed on God's command, without guilt and without rebellion. The following "prodigy of repose in the form suspended in air" (82:9—10) causes the Purser, "a ... person more accurate as an accountant than profound as a philosopher," to attribute the phenomenon to Billy's "will-power" and to mystify his death as "a species of euthanasia" — both which views the Surgeon in his "discreet causticity" flatly refutes as being "at once imaginative and metaphysical" and having no authenticity in scientific terms. (This passage is not contained in the Velhagen edition.)

In a similar way the ignorant crew, "being of all men the greatest sticklers for usage" (74:34—35) and tending to be superstitious, see great spiritual significance in the fact that the sea-fowl hover over the spot where Billy's body entered the sea; but the narrator is careful to remind the discerning reader that "the action of the sea-fowl [is] dictated by a mere animal greed for prey" (82:11—12). In Melville's original version the story ends with the religious rites of burial and everything proceeds as usual aboard the *Indomitable*. That ending is perfectly good, having every element of closure; but Melville, aged and utterly forgotten by the literary public, apparently lacked confidence in his powers of ironic communication and tacked on three chapters of epilogue that reinforce an anti-Christian reading of the narrative:

"The symmetry of form attainable in pure fiction cannot so readily be achieved in a narration essentially having less to do with fable than with fact. Truth uncompromisingly told will always have its ragged edges ..." (83:17—20).

Political and religious elements dominate the epilogue. It is appropriate that retribution against Captain Vere comes not from a Christian monarchy, but from an atheist republic. Captain Vere is killed by a musket ball from the main cabin of a French ship formerly named the *St. Louis*, but renamed the *Athéiste*; and as he dies he mutters the name of Billy Budd, but not in accents of remorse. Remaining true to his principles, he nevertheless seems to recognize that all the forces of individual freedom he had fought against were now achieving a kind of revenge.

The "authorized version" of the incidents aboard the *Indomitable,* like the official version of the mutiny in *Benito Cereno* and of all rebellions against tyranny from Adam's against God to the French Revolution, is false. It is not to be trusted. But neither is the glorification of Billy by the "ignorant" crew. The narrator clearly dissociates himself from the crew's belief that Billy is some sort of Christ figure: "*To them* a chip [of the mast on which he was hanged] was as a piece of the cross." The final vision of Billy (in the ballad that ends the novella) is not of one who has "risen," but of one who has rejected the chaplain and who lies at the bottom of the sea: "the oozy weeds about me twist" (87:32). The ballad has a "certain grim internal merriment" (31:20) that makes the final view equal to that of the Old Dansker with his "pithy guarded cynicism" (33:13).

1. *How and where is Billy Budd's violent reaction to Claggart's accusation foreshadowed? What does it reveal about Billy's character and value as a man?*

   When Billy is first impressed, Captain Graveling of the *Rights of Man* tells Lieutenant Ratcliffe about how Billy once reacted to an insulting dig in the ribs by Red Whiskers: "Quick as lightning Billy let fly his arm. I dare say he never meant to do quite as much as he did, but anyhow he gave the burly fool a terrible drubbing" (14:27-29). He rebels without reflection at overt personal insult, but he has no conception of the common good or of the need to join his abused and oppressed shipmates in action for the general welfare. Billy acts only out of "blind feeling" (64:30) and shows us the danger of utter innocence in the complex world of good and evil. "He is not presented as a conventional hero ... he is the main figure in no romance" (20:9-11).

2. *When the narrator says: "One person excepted, the master-at-arms was perhaps the only man in the ship intellectually capable of adequately appreciating the moral phenomenon presented in Billy Budd" (38:28—31), whom does he mean by the one person excepted?*

   Apparently the Dansker, "the salt seer" (32:21), who took a "certain philosophic interest" (32:3) in Billy, saw that such innocence was dangerous. He always substituted Baby for Billy (32:13).

3. *What special meanings are there to the names of the men and the ships in this story?*

   *Billy Budd:* The diminutive "Billy" — originally "Baby" — indicates that he is not quite a full man. Only in the official version, chapter 26, is he referred to as William Budd. "Budd," of course, refers to that stage of growth of a flower when it has not yet bloomed. This image is taken up in the reference to the "rose-bud complexion of the more beautiful English girls" (see analysis). For a powerful young man of twenty-one, the name is, of course, quite ironic.
   *Captain the Honorable Edward Fairfax "Starry" Vere:* He is "honorable" only by the standards of the Royal British Navy defending tyrannical monarchy against popular revolt; he is not very "fair" in insisting that only the superficial "facts" be considered at Billy's secret trial; he is deemed "starry," though without "brilliant qualities" (24:12), by a relative of like rank in the navy. "Vere" suggests "revere" — to worship as God, and "veer" — to turn sharply or suddenly, as he does against Billy Budd, whom he admired and had considered for promotion.
   *John Claggart:* Rhymes with "blackguard," and has phonological associations with "clabber" (to become thick in souring), "black art" (magic derived from the devil), and "clogged" (to hinder or obstruct, especially by sticky matter) — all words of a distinctly negative significance.
   *Old Dansker,* the Agamemnon-man, also referred to as "old Merlin" and the old

sea-Chiron, has a combination of names all of which suggest the wisdom of the ages, universal and ancient truth. It is he with his "eccentric unsentimental old sapience primitive in its kind" (31:21-22) who represents Melville's point of view — he sees the truth, accepts the inevitable, and never romanticizes or sentimentalizes.
*Captain Graveling:* looks "gravely" upon the loss of Billy from the *Rights of Man*.
*Lt. Ratcliffe:* is the "rat" who performs cheerfully the task of impressing Billy.
*Mr. Mordant*, the Captain of Marines: there is something "caustic" or "sarcastic" in Melville's naming this chief officer of the drumhead court who was for leniency but who succumbed to Captain Vere's "logic" with a name that has a homonym, "mordent," in music a rapid alternation of a principal tone with another tone one degree below it.
The ships, *Rights of Man, Indomitable, St. Louis,* and *Athéiste,* have obvious allegorical significances.

4. *What explanation, other than Rolf Lorenz's ("Melville verwechselt ihn hier mit dem Marinehistoriker William James") is possible for the confusion of a romancer (G. P. R. James) with an objective naval historian (21:15)?*

Irony. William James' failure to deal with the details of the Nore Mutiny ("Nor are these readily to be found in the libraries" (21:19)) makes him no better than a fiction writer. Melville wants "truth uncompromisingly told" (83:19). Cf. a similar ironic play on the name Edwards in "Bartleby."

5. *Why did Melville choose Montaigne to typify the writers read by Captain Vere?*

There are two points of view on this question. One is that although Montaigne was basically a great humanist, there was for him no contradiction between his humane ideals and his almost Macchiavellian political ideas. For Montaigne, as for Vere, the state was supreme; for each of them it was necessary, for the greatest common good, to preserve the order of the state even at the expense of the individual and of ideal justice: "The public Good requires that a man should betray, and lie, and murder..." ("Of Profit and Honesty"). Although he realized that "there is nothing so much, nor so grossly, nor so ordinarily faulty as the *laws*" ("Of Experience"), he feared changes even more since they would necessarily involve a loss of authority. So for him, it became "the rule of rules, and the general law of laws, that everybody should observe those of the place wherein he lives" ("Of Custom and Law")[1]. So Montaigne stands for "those books to which every serious mind of superior order occupying any active post of authority in the world, naturally inclines" and for the writers who, in Captain Vere's opinion, "in the spirit of common sense philosophize upon realities" with results that offer "confirmation of his own more reserved thoughts" (25:14-22).
A contradictory point of view is offered by Lawrance Thompson, who believes that Montaigne's essays involve a powerful irony, especially in the "Apology for Raimond Sebond," which is directed against all the values of religion and politics that Vere stands for and which he characteristically fails to see[2].

---

[1] cf. Kilbourne, "Montaigne and Captain Vere"; in *American Literature XXXIII* (January 1962), pp. 514-517.
[2] cf. Thompson, *Melville's Quarrel with God*, Princeton, N. J., 1952.

6. *What is Captain Vere's idea of social order?*

"With mankind," he would say, "forms, measured forms are everything." (82:35) Like "Orpheus with his lyre spell-binding the wild denizens of the woods" (83:2) he applies "music and religious rites" on his ship — but to a very different purpose: "subserving the discipline and purpose of War"! (83:9-10) His idea of "measured forms" becomes clear in the following passage:

> True martial discipline long continued superinduces in an average man a sort of impulse of docility whose operation at the official sound of command much resembles the effect of an instinct. (82:17-20)

Billy is a man after his own heart — easily guided like "the wild denizens of the wood," as long as he does not submit to any stronger "instinct." He fights against "the disruption of form going on across the Channel *and the consequences thereof*" (83:3-4), which, as the Preface said, "turned out to be a political advance along nearly the whole line for Europeans."

7. *What are "the rarer qualities of our nature" Captain Vere and Billy Budd are said to be "each radically sharing in" (72:8)?*

With Billy it is stated explicitly: "as elsewhere said, a barbarian Billy radically was" (77:21—22; cf. 19:25—26). His state is "so rare indeed as to be all but incredible to average minds however much cultivated" (72:8—10): he is "one to whom not yet has been proffered the questionable apple of knowledge" (19:18), "of self-consciousness he seemed to have little or none" (19:22) and there is only a thin cover of civilization on him, "in the nude he might have posed for a statue of young Adam before the fall" (53:23—24).

In the communication scene both men find "much the same spirit" (72:17) in each other; a few lines later the narrator may refer to more than the difference in age in saying that Captain Vere "was old enough to have been Billy's father." He, too, is able to act according to "what remains primeval in our formalized humanity" (72:26), i. e. according to the spirit of the Old Testament: to sacrifice his son "in obedience to the exacting behest" (72:29).

The whole scene is kept ambiguous, but the bitter irony is too obvious to be denied; the narrator "conjectures" that Billy, after the Captain's frank disclosures, "Not without a sort of joy indeed ... might have appreciated the brave opinion of him implied in his Captain making such a confidant of him" (72:18—20). Joy indeed! But Billy would only fulfill Captain Vere's expressed expectation: "I take him to be of that generous nature that he would feel even for us on whom in this military necessity so heavy a compulsion is laid" (71:1-3), in other words that the victim would feel sorry for the executioner.

Billy and the Captain are also described as "two of great Nature's nobler order" (72:32—33); apart from the noble blood in their veins (cf. 19:12 and 23:8) there seems little justification for this statement — if it is not an ironic reference to their agreement in lacking humanity.

8. *Is there a "diviner magnanimity" in Captain Vere's dealing with Billy Budd?*

Melville is careful in making it quite clear that the Captain is very fond of the foretopman; in the private interview he may even have developed a feeling of "passion" (72:23) for Billy. But imperturbably he remains "the austere devotee of military duty" (72:25), who successfully strives "against scruples that may tend

to enervate decision" (67:31—33). He thinks that the king's officers have "ceased to be natural free-agents" (68:20) and are obliged to suppress their warm hearts (68:31—69:2) and their "private conscience [which must] yield to that imperial one formulated in the code" of martial law (69:7—8). So he is resolved, "however pitilessly that law may operate, we nevertheless adhere to it and administer it" (68:28—29).
At the climax of the court scene, however, he finally admits that even were clemency "clearly lawful for us under the circumstances" (70:13), he would insist on capital punishment and not risk the consequences of clemency, since "'The people' (meaning the ship's company) . . ., 'long moulded by arbitrary discipline, have not that kind of intelligent responsiveness that might qualify them to comprehend and discriminate'" (70:14—21); but "arbitrary discipline" is exactly the system of order he administers (cf. question 6). "The agony of the strong" (73:5) then turns out to be the agony of one who is caught in his own cage of a radically inhuman system. There is no evidence of a "diviner magnanimity" (73:2).

J. V. H./M. D.

Braswell, William, Melville's *Billy Budd* as "An Inside Narrative," *American Literature* XXIX, 1957, pp. 133-146 — Freeman, F. Barron, *Melville's Billy Budd*, Cambridge Mass. 1948 — Lang, Hans-Joachim, Melvilles *Billy Budd* und seine Quellen, eine Nachlese, *Festschrift für Walter Fischer*, Heidelberg 1959, pp. 225-249 — Miller, James E., *Billy Budd:* The Catastrophe of Innocence, *Modern Language Notes* LXXIII, 1958, pp. 168—176 — Rosenberry, Edward T., The Problem of *Billy Budd*, *PMLA* LXXX, 1965, pp. 489—498 — Stafford, William T., *Melville's Billy Budd and the Critics*, San Francisco 1961 — Sühnel, Rudolf, Melville's *Billy Budd*, Sprache und Literatur Englands und Amerikas Bd. III, Tübingen 1959, pp. 125—144 — West, Ray B., The Unity of *Billy Budd*, *Hudson Review* V, 1952, pp. 120—128 — Zink, Karl E., Herman Melville and the Forms: Irony and Social Criticism in *Billy Budd*, *Accent* XII, 1952, pp. 131—139.

# ARTHUR MILLER

Arthur Miller was born on October 17, 1915, in New York City, son of Isidor Mahler, a well-to-do manufacturer from Austria. He received the usual public school education and then worked some time in a New York warehouse (setting of *A Memory of Two Mondays*). As a student at the University of Michigan he began his career as a dramatist; in 1938, when he graduated, he received the Theater Guild National Award. In the next few years he wrote radio plays and collected background material for the film *The Story of G. I. Joe*. In 1944 he published a commentary on the war, *Situation Normal,* and in 1945 a novel, *Focus*, which had anti-Semitism as its theme.
After the failure of his first Broadway production, *The Man Who Had All The Luck* (1944), success came to him in 1947 when *All My Sons* was awarded the New York Drama Critics' Circle Prize and the Pulitzer Prize for drama.

*Death of a Salesman* (1949) brought him the same awards and even higher critical praise. In 1950 Miller adapted Ibsen's *An Enemy of the People* for modern audiences. *The Crucible*, a play with the Salem witch-hunts of 1692 as its subject, but with the then current un-American activities investigations obviously suggested, was produced in 1953. In 1955 he wrote two one-act plays, *A Memory of Two Mondays* and *View from the Bridge*, and afterwards expanded the latter to full-length. During his marriage to Marilyn Monroe, his second wife, Miller produced only a film script *The Misfits* with a leading role for her. His divorce from Marilyn Monroe in 1961, her subsequent suicide and his remarriage all apparently engendered a spiritual crisis which Miller embodied in a highly autobiographical, controversial, and formless play, *After the Fall* (1964). His observations of the German Auschwitz trials were transformed into a long one-act play, *Incident at Vichy* (1964). In 1967 he published a collection of eight stories written between 1951 and 1966, *I Don't Need You Any More;* in 1968 a play *The Prize* followed.

About his aims as a playwright Miller wrote in the introduction to his *Collected Plays* in 1957: "they are one man's way of saying to his fellow men, 'This is what you see every day, or think or feel; now I will show you what you really know but have not had the time, or the disinterestedness, or the insight, or the information to understand consciously.' ... I regard the theater as a serious business, one that makes or should make man more human, which is to say, less alone."

## All My Sons

Text: Arthur Miller, *All My Sons.* Hueber (Silva)
Arthur Miller, *All My Sons.* Diesterweg

*Joe Keller, a successful Chicago manufacturer of 61, sold cracked cylinder heads to the U. S. Army Air Force in 1943. When as a consequence twenty-one pilots crashed and were killed, he and his partner and neighbor Steve[1] Deever were convicted and sent to a penitentiary. In the court of appeal Joe was exonerated and all the blame was put on his partner, whose family then moved to New York. Steve Deever's daughter Ann was in love with Larry, Joe Keller's eldest son, but Larry was reported missing as a pilot after his father's conviction.*

*Three years later Joe Keller's younger son, Chris (who has returned from the war and, believing in his father's innocence, now works in the family business) invites Ann to come to Chicago. Convinced that his brother is dead, he wants to marry Ann, but his mother, insisting that Larry is still alive, violently objects to the proposed marriage. Then Ann produces Larry's last letter which announced his intention to commit suicide after reading about his father in the papers. Chris is deeply shocked at realizing his father's guilt when Ann's brother George accuses Joe Keller of his betrayal of his partner. Chris wants to make his father confess and go to prison again, but Joe Keller shoots himself.*

---

[1] In the first version his name was Herb; in the 1957 edition of the *Collected Plays* Miller changed it to Steve, but overlooked one mention: Diesterweg 28:17, Silva 34:21

Looked at superficially, Arthur Miller's *All My Sons* may appear to be simply a social problem or social thesis play. Such classification — a valid one if severely qualified — is suggested both by the timeliness of the story and by the presence of considerable overt social criticism. The story itself is obviously calculated to engage the audience's social conscience. Stated in the simplest terms, the play dramatizes the process by which Joe Keller, a small manufacturer, is forced to accept individual social responsibility and, consequently, to accept his personal guilt for having sold, on one occasion during World War II, fatally defective airplane parts to the government.

However, while this bare-bone synopsis is essentially accurate, it does, in fact, do violence to the actual complexity of the play. Like all of Miller's plays, *All My Sons* demands of the reader an awareness of the deviousness of human motivation, and understanding of the way in which a man's best qualities may be involved in his worst actions and cheapest ideas, and, in general, a peculiarly fine perception of cause and effect. Nowhere is it suggested that the social realities and attitudes that are brought within the critical focus of the play can be honestly considered outside of some such context of human aspirations and weaknesses as is provided by the play; and nowhere is it suggested that the characters are or can be judged strictly on the basis of some simple social ethic or ideal that might be deduced from the action. The characters do not simply reflect the values and attitudes of a particular society; they use those values and attitudes in their attempt to realize themselves. And it is these characteristics that give *All My Sons* and other Miller plays a density of texture so much greater than that of the typical social thesis play, which seeks not only to direct but to facilitate ethical judgments upon matters of topical importance.

There is no difficulty in assenting to the abstract proposition which Chris puts to his mother at the end of the play: "You can be better! Once and for all you can know there's a universe of people outside and you're responsible to it ..." And there is no problem either in giving general intellectual assent to the morality of brotherhood for which Chris speaks. There is, however, considerable difficulty in assenting to the actual situation at the end of the play, in accepting it as a simple triumph of right over wrong. For the play in its entirety makes clear that Joe Keller has committed his crimes not out of cowardice, callousness, or pure self-interest but out of a too exclusive regard for real though limited values and that Chris, the idealist, is far from acting disinterestedly as he harrows his father to repentence.

Joe Keller is a successful small manufacturer, but he is also "a man whose judgments must be dredged out of experience and a peasant-like common sense." Like many uneducated, "self-made" men, he has no capacity for abstract considerations; whatever is not personal or at least immediate has no reality for him. He has the peasant's insular loyalty to family which excludes broader responsibility to society at large or to mankind in general. At a moment of decision, when his business seemed threatened, the question for him was not basically one of profit and loss; what concerned him was a conflict of responsibilities — his responsibility to his family, particularly his sons to whom the business is to be a legacy of security and joy, versus his responsibility to the unknown men, engaged in the social action of war, who might as a remote consequence suffer for his dishonesty. For such a man as Joe Keller such a conflict could scarcely exist and, given its existence, could have only one probable resolution.

When the worst imaginable consequence follows (21 pilots killed in Australia), Keller is nonetheless able to presume upon his innocence as established before the law. His ethical insularity — symbolized in the play by the hedged-in backyard setting — protects him from any serious assault of conscience and allows him to let Steve Deever be imprisoned for his crime so long as he can believe that anything done in the name of the family has its own justification. Yet, he is not perfectly secure within his sanctuary. His apparently thick skin has its sensitive spots: he is afraid, for reasons that become clear later, to oppose his wife's unhealthy refusal to accept her son Larry's death, and in his protest to Ann Deever's cold rejection of her father, in his insistence that he does not believe in "crucifying a man," and in his insistence that Chris should use what he, the father, has earned "with joy ... without shame ... with joy," he betrays a deep-seated uneasiness. His appeal on behalf of Steve Deever is, in fact, partly a covert appeal on his own behalf, an appeal for merciful understanding, called forth by the shocked realization that some considerations may override and even destroy the ties of family upon which his own security rests.

It is Chris Keller who, in reaching out for love and a life of his own, first undermines and then destroys this security altogether. Chris has brought out of the war an idealistic morality of brotherhood based on what he has seen of mutual self-sacrifice among the men whom he commanded. But he has not survived the war unwounded; he bears a still festering psychological wound, a sense of inadequacy and guilt. He has survived to enjoy the fruits of a wartime economy, and he fears that in enjoying them he becomes unworthy, condemned by his own idealism. Even his love for Ann Deever, the sweetheart of his dead brother, has seemed to him a guilty desire to take advantage of the dead to whom he somehow owes his life.

As the play opens, however, he has decided to assert himself to claim the things in life and the position in life which he feels should rightfully be his, and as the initial step he has invited Ann to his family home. His decision brings him into immediate conflict with his mother, who looks upon the possible marriage between Chris and Ann as a public confirmation of Larry's death. At first Joe Keller seems only peripherally involved in this conflict; his attempt to evade Chris' demand that Kate be forced to accept Larry's death carries only ambiguous suggestions of insecurity. However, at the end of Act II, Kate is emotionally exhausted by the fruitless effort to use George's accusations as a means of driving out Ann, and, opposed for the first time by declared disbelief of both husband and son, she breaks down and reveals the actual basis of her refusal: if Chris lets Larry go, then he must let his father go as well. What is revealed here is that Kate is fundamentally like her husband; only what is personal or immediate is real for her. If Larry is alive, then, in a sense, the war has no reality, and Joe's crimes do not mean anything; their consequences are merely distant echoes in an unreal world. But if Larry is dead, then the war is real, and Joe is guilty of murder, even, by an act of association, guilty of murdering his own son. Her own desperate need to reject Larry's death against all odds and upon whatever flimsy scrap of hope has been the reflex of her need to defend her relation to her husband against whatever in herself might be outraged by the truth about him. Actually, however, Kate has "an overwhelming capacity for love" and an ultimate commitment to the living which makes it possible for her to "let Larry go" and rise again to the defense of her husband at the end.

Chris, on the other hand, is incapable of any such surrender of the letter of morality in the name of love or mercy; he cannot, as his father would have him, "see it human." At the rise of the curtain in Act II, Chris is seen dragging away the remains of Larry's memorial tree. The action is clearly symbolic: Chris, because of his own needs, has determined to free the family of the shadow of self-deception and guilt cast over it by the memory of Larry, to let in the light of truth. Yet, when the light comes, he is less able to bear it than the others. Ann, in the hope of love and marriage, rejects the seeds of hatred and remorse which her brother, George, offers her; and Kate sacrifices the dead son to the living father. But Chris has too much at stake; his life must vindicate the deaths of those who died in the war, which means that he must maintain an ideal image of himself or else be overwhelmed by his own sense of guilt. Because he is closely identified with his father, his necessary sense of personal dignity and worthiness depends upon his belief in the ideal image of his father; consequently, he can only accept the father's exposure as a personal defeat.

It becomes clear in the exchange between Chris and George Deever that Chris has suspected his father but that he has suppressed his suspicions because he could not face the consequences — the condemnation of the father whom he loves, and the condemnation of himself as polluted by sharing in the illicit spoils of war. Yet, this is precisely what the exposure of Joe Keller forces upon him, and Joe's arguments in self-defense — that he had expected the defective parts to be rejected, that what he did was done for the family, that business is business and none of it is "clean" — all shatter upon the hard shell of Chris' idealism not simply because they are, in fact, evasions and irrelevant half-truths, but because they cannot satisfy Chris' conscience. Consequently, even after Larry's suicide letter has finally brought to Joe a realization of his personal responsibility, Chris must go on to insist upon a public act of penance. The father becomes, indeed, a kind of scapegoat for the son; that is, if Joe expiates his crimes through the acceptance of a just punishment, then Chris will be relieved of his own burden of paralyzing guilt. His love of his father and his complicity with his father will then no longer imply his own unworthiness. In insisting that Joe must go to prison, Chris is, in effect, asking Joe to give him back his self-respect, so that he may be free to marry Ann and assume the life which is rightfully his. But Chris' inability to accept his father "as a man" leads Joe to believe that not only have his defenses crumbled but that the love of his son and family — the whole basis of his life — is gone, and he kills himself.

Because it forces upon the reader an awareness of the intricacies of human motivation and of human relationships, *All My Sons* leaves a dual impression: the action affirms the theme of the individual's responsibility to humanity, but, at the same time, it suggests that the standpoint of even so fine an ideal is not an altogether adequate one from which to evaluate human beings and that a rigid idealism operating in the actual world of men entails suffering and waste, especially when the idealist is hagridden by his own ideals. Moreover, the corruption and destruction of a man like Joe Keller, who is struggling to preserve what he conceives to be a just evaluation of himself in the eyes of his son, implies, in the context of the play, a deficiency not only in Keller's character but in the social environment in which he exists. Keller's appeal to the general ethics of the business community —

"Who worked for nothin' in that war? .... Did they ship a gun or a truck outa Detroit before they got their price? ... It's dollars and cents, nickels and dimes; war and peace, it's nickels and dimes, what's clean? —"

is irrelevant to his personal defense; yet, it is an indictment of that community nonetheless. For it indicates that the business community failed to provide any substantial values which might have supplemented and counterbalanced Keller's own limited, family based ethics. From the business community came only the impulse to which Chris also responds when he feels prompted to express his love for Ann by saying, "... I'm going to make a fortune for you!"

Furthermore, there is a sense in which Kate's words, "We were all struck by the same lightning," are true; the lightning was the experience of the Second World War — a massive social action in which they were all, willynilly, involved. It was the war that made it possible for some to profit by the suffering and death of others and that created the special occasion of Joe Keller's temptation, which led in turn to his son Larry's suicide and his wife's morbid obsession. Chris Keller and George Deever brought something positive out of the war, an ideal of brotherhood and a firmer, more broadly based ethic, but George, as he appears in the play, is paying in remorse for the principles that led him to reject his father, and Chris' idealism is poisoned at the source by shame and guilt which are also products of his war experience and which make it impossible for him to temper justice with mercy either for himself or anyone else.

1. *At the beginning of the play Joe Keller is reading the "want ads" section of the newspaper; when Chris appears, he takes the book review section. What is the significance of these different preferences on the part of father and son?*

    The choice is appropriate to the character of each and provides the first cryptic insight into an important difference between them. Joe's declaration, "... I don't read the news part any more. It's more interesting in the want ads," is a minor statement of a major theme — that is, Joe's moral, intellectual, and emotional isolation from the world that lies beyond the boundaries of family and business. The specific interest in the "want ads" suggests that, in thinking about people in general, Joe is dominated by the business man's curiosity about material desires and needs. Chris' interest in the book review section also hints at what we later come to know of him; though he is very much his father's son and in no sense intellectual, he inclines toward the world of ideas and imagination. Not only has he had a broader experience of the world than has his father, but he has derived from that experience general concepts, values, which are beyond his father's grasp.

2. *What does the setting of the play contribute to the expression of the theme?*

The "secluded amosphere" of backyard setting implies both the solidarity and the isolation of the Keller family, which is also resonant in their name: Keller = cellar. The thickly grown poplar hedge is particularly important in this connection; it stops all vision at the property line, the edge of the family domain, and it conceals the house next door, once occupied by Steve Deever, the partner whom Joe Keller betrayed. The importance of the setting is pointed up at the end of the play when Chris says to his mother, "once and for all you can know there's a universe of people outside..."

3. *What use does the apple tree serve in the play?*

Broadly, it functions as a foreshadowing and focusing device. The apple tree was planted as a private memorial to Larry Keller. As we first see it, it has been shattered by the wind, but the fruit still clings to its branches. Though the broken tree immediately becomes a subject of speculation among family and neighbors, it has no particular meaning for anyone but Kate who sees in its destruction a sign that the acceptance of Larry's death had been premature. Actually, the destruction of the memorial tree foreshadows the final acceptance that Kate has so long evaded. Ann has just arrived, armed, as we learn later, with a letter that puts the fact of Larry's death beyond all dispute. Larry, like the tree, has been a living presence, kept alive by Kate's unhealthy refusal to "let him go," and now Ann and Chris are alike determined that Larry be buried once and for all, so that he will no longer stand between them. However, because of the curious connection that exists in the minds of both Kate and Joe between Larry's death and the question of Joe's guilt, the attempt is unexpectedly but necessarily accompanied by a straining and tearing apart of relationships and loyalties which is the psychological counterpart of the storm that shattered the memorial tree.

4. *Chris tells Ann that he has loved her for some time. Why, then, has he waited so long before declaring his love?*

Though Chris has believed all along that his brother is dead, his mother's assumption that Chris has no right to claim Ann has worked upon his own deep-seated fear that he will fail to be worthy of the dead, that he will somehow betray them by taking advantage of them. Chris half confesses this to Ann when he tells her that he felt ashamed in the civilian world to which he returned after the war (Act II), and Ann points to the same thing when she accuses Kate of making

Chris feel guilty with her (Act III). Furthermore, Chris cannot ask Ann to marry him unless he can somehow assume a normal, settled position in society, and only when he has assured himself that sharing the profits of his father's business involves no comprise of his ideals, is he free to do so.

5. *What is it that makes Keller a sympathetic character despite the fact of his guilt?*

Though he is certainly no Othello, Joe Keller might justly be spoken of as "one that loved not wisely but too well"; and the fact that his crimes were committed out of a misguided and too exclusive concern for the love of father and son keeps him from slipping into the category of villain. (See the analysis of his character in the preceding discussion of the play.) Moreover, underneath all of Keller's specific lines of self-justification runs a single appeal to a realistic and charitable view of human nature. He asks Ann and Chris, with reference to Ann's father, to "see it human"; he insists that he does not "believe in crucifying a man"; and he tells Chris, "A man can't be a Jesus in this world." To Chris, of course, to be human means something quite different; it implies an ideal of responsibility. Neither view, however, excludes the other, and if there is a competition between them, Chris' view is likely to be handicapped by a certain intellectual chill that clings to it.

6. *Why does George Deever come to the Keller home, and what does he contribute to the thematic and dramatic development of the play?*

George Deever comes to the Keller's to prevent Ann's marrying Chris. Like Chris, George is a young man of severe principles that have been re-enforced by his war experience, and what has happened to him is a variation upon the theme of father and son and serves to foreshadow, in a general way, what Chris is yet to experience. Out of the rigor of his convictions, George has rejected his father, but as he appears in the play, he is a man overwhelmed with remorse for his own callousness. Shaken by the realization of his father's suffering, he has come to prevent Ann's further betrayal of the rejected father. Moreover, though George does not himself succeed in exposing Joe Keller, he prepares the way for that exposure. Actually, George is easily overborne by Joe; the general character of George's father will not support much confidence and the temptation to evade remorse and to avoid casting off the Kellers is strong. He is, in fact, on the verge of capitulating when Kate makes the slip that gives away the truth. This slip is so clumsy as to be suspect, especially when one considers that the arrival of George has placed Kate in a peculiar position. She must defend her husband; yet, George's accusations, if true, seem to provide at the moment the best means of getting Ann to leave. Ann, however, refuses to let the past destroy the future, and Kate, frustrated and opposed on every side, breaks down and reveals the truth to Chris. (For further discussion of this last point see the analysis of the play.)

7. *Why, when he is threatened with exposure, does Joe insist that "Larry never flew a P-40" (end of Act II)?*

The statement is a spontaneous rebuttal of Kate's implied accusation that he has killed his own son, but the very spontaneity of it suggests that he too has sensed and feared some obscure connection between Larry's death and consequences of his own actions. This connection he must immediately deny because, whereas the deaths of unknown men in remote Australia may be dismissed as a mistake, guilt for his son's death cannot be evaded.

8. *Why does Keller say, "I'm his [Chris'] father and he's my son, and if there's something bigger than that I'll put a bullet in my head"?*

There is in this, of course, a bit of obvious foreshadowing. But further, it is a final confirmation of the fact that all of Joe's values, his aspirations and decisions, have been based upon the assumption that family ties and especially the love and mutual loyalty of father and son are sacred and paramount. If this assumption is false, then Joe's life becomes meaningless and his decision to save the business becomes unjustifiable.

9. *Why at the end of the play does Chris insist that Joe must go to prison?*

The cause of Chris' insistence is most directly revealed in the following passage. "Chris *(to his father)*: I know you're no worse than most men but I thought you were better. I never saw you as a man. I saw you as my father. *(Almost breaking)* I can't look at you this way, I can't look at myself!"
Chris is closely identified with his father — practically, by his share in the profits of the business, and psychologically, by his love and admiration for his father; consequently, Chris shares his father's guilt and is dependent upon his father to expiate for both of them. For further discussion, see the analysis of the play.

10. *What is the effect of Kate's declaring at the end of the play that "the war is over"?*

Though Kate's intention is to dissuade Chris from sending his father to prison, her remark actually serves to emphasize the fact that, in a sense, the war is *not* over, that the whole action of the play may, in fact, be seen from one point of view as an aftermath of the war.

11. *How do the minor characters — Sue and Jim Bayliss, and Frank and Lydia Lubey — function in the play? What do they contribute?*

Generally speaking, these characters provide variations upon the main themes of the play and serve as reflectors for the main characters. Frank and Lydia reenforce in an obvious way the important theme of guilt derived from the war; they have been "lucky" in that Frank was not directly involved in the war and was, consequently, able to marry and develop a normal family life. However, they have not survived the war without damage; both Frank and Lydia feel guilty about their good fortune; they are uneasy in the presence of those who have suffered and sacrificed, and Frank, in particular, has been undermined by the imperfectly repressed suspicion that he has evaded his responsibility. His interest in astrology is a barely adequate attempt to shift his burden of guilt to impersonal forces beyond his control.

Sue and Jim Bayliss dramatize in their relationship the uneasy marriage of practicality and idealism which is one of the alternatives theoretically available to

Chris at the end of the play. Jim's ambition has been to devote himself to medical research, but he has given in to Sue's practical insistence that his primary responsibility is to provide comfort and security for his family. Significantly, while Jim quietly idolizes Chris and covers his sense of self-betrayal with a sardonic but charitable cynicism, Sue resents Chris' influence. For Chris' idealism, which she believes to be phony, is a threat to her security; it sets a disquieting example for her husband, making him dissatisfied with himself and with his life.

Whereas Frank and Lydia serve to broaden the theme of the peripheral, psychological effects of the war, Sue and Jim serve to suggest that the central problem in the play — the accomodation of idealism to practical reality — has no *necessary* connection with the war.

A. R. W.

Dotzenrath, Theo, Arthur Millers *All My Sons* als Schullektüre, *Die Neueren Sprachen* 1959, pp. 33—40 — Lerner, Max, *Actions and Passions*, New York 1949, pp. 20—28.

## Death of a Salesman

Text: Arthur Miller, *Death of a Salesman*. Diesterweg

*After working as a traveling salesman for a New York company for 36 years Willy Loman is on the edge of a nervous breakdown. He hardly earns any money any more and has to borrow from his neighbor Charley. His mind often wanders into the past and people think him crazy — but his wife Linda still loves him and silently bears his irritability.*

*His two sons, Biff (34) and Happy (32) have not done well — Biff has been restlessly moving around as a farm laborer for more than ten years, and Happy is assistant to an assistant buyer and a notorious philanderer. Some obscure event in the past makes Biff and his father constantly quarrel with each other. But Willy Loman still idealizes his sons and, when they come for a visit, all make plans for a great future. The following day, however, Willy loses his job, Biff doesn't get the financial support he had hoped for, and Happy goes off with his brother and two girls when they are supposed to have a celebration dinner with their father. In a dramatic scene Biff tries to wake his father out of his dreams and make him face the truth about the failure of his values and the corruption of his family love. He fails but touches his father's heart with his desperate tears. Willy Loman commits suicide in his car in order to give his boys a good start with his 20,000 dollars life insurance money.*

Ever since the evening of February 10, 1949, when Willy Loman, weighed down with his two sample cases, first shuffled across the stage of the Morosco Theatre in New York City, *Death of a Salesman* has had a tremendous impact on audiences the world over and it has stimulated one of the most intense literary controversies of modern times. Brooks Atkinson, the dean of American drama critics, has described it as "by common consent, ... one of the finest dramas in the whole range of the American theater"; but Eleanor Clark has said that "it is a very dull business which departs in no way that is to its credit from the general mediocrity of our commercial theater." W. David Sievers says that *"Death of a Salesman* may prove to be the finest American tragedy thus far in the twentieth century," but George Jean Nathan insists that "it does not measure up by a very considerable margin to a tragedy of real artistic stature." The play has also been described variously as a *drame bourgeois* (John Gassner), a celebration of the importance of the family in a fragmented culture (Wm. J. Newman), an Ibsenesque attack on corrupt materialistic society (Walter Kerr), a discussion of the effects of the passing of the old frontier (London Times Literary Supplement), an exposure of a vicious man who has no ideals and no moral values (John Beaufort), a sentimental play based not on ideas but on self-contradictory and arbitrary melange of social and moral clichés (Richard J. Foster), a confused mixture of a tragedy of the common man and a social protest (Eric Bentley), and a masterful psychoanalytic exposition of the unconscious forces that determine our lives (Daniel E. Schneider). It is impossible here to summarize adequately the various interpretations and the complex range of arguments for and against the play. Almost every critic of modern literature and a great many historians, psychologists, sociologists have published analyses and commentaries on the play; a complete bibliography would run to hundreds of items in more than a dozen languages.

Arthur Miller himself considers *Death of a Salesman* to be his finest work and has published articles, prefaces, and interviews in its defense. In the *New York Times* (Feb. 27, 1949) he asserted his belief that "the common man is as apt a subject for tragedy in its highest sense as the kings were ... the tragic feeling is evoked in us when we are in the presence of a character who is ready to lay down his life, if need be, to secure one thing — his sense of personal dignity." In an essay entitled "On Social Plays," Miller argued that all good drama is essentially social drama, depicting man in a struggle to wrest from his society some recognition of his existence and worth not as a customer, draftee, machine tender, ideologist, or whatever, but as a human being. Modern society refuses to grant him that recognition, and any determined effort to secure it is bound to end tragically. "The reason *Death of a Salesman* ... left such a strong impression was that it set forth unremittingly the picture of a man who was not even especially "good" but whose situation made clear that at bottom we are alone, valueless, without even the elements of a human person, when once we fail to fit the patterns of [social] efficiency." The fullest discussion of the genesis, form, and meaning of all of Miller's plays to date is in his introduction to the *Collected Plays* (New York, 1957; all page references are to this edition), where Miller takes various of his critics to task for misreading *Death of a Salesman* as an anti-capitalistic propaganda play or as a document of futility and pessimism. Perhaps the most revealing comment is Miller's belief that "Willy Loman has broken a law [i. e. of modern culture just as Oedipus had of Greek culture] without whose protection life is insupportable if not incomprehensible to him and to many others; it is the law which says that a failure in society and in business has no right to live. Unlike the law of incest, the law of success is not administered by statute or church, but it is very nearly as powerful in its grip upon men ... My attempt in the play was to counter this [law] with an opposing system which, so to speak, is in a race for Willy's faith, and it is the system of love which is the opposite of the law of success. It is embodied in Biff Loman, but by the time Willy can perceive his love it can serve only as an ironic comment upon the life he sacrificed for power and for success and its tokens." (pp. 35—36)

As a statement of the author's intentions concerning the abstract meaning of *Death of a Salesman*, these remarks are valuable. However, if the basic meaning of a play lies in its form, in the human experience shaped out of language and gesture, they are misleading. Furthermore, Miller and all his critics have assumed that the central character of the play is Willy Loman; and this, too, is false — if we believe that the central character must be the one who most struggles for understanding, who faces the most crucial question, who achieves the most transforming insight, and whose motives, decisions, and actions most influence the total situation. By those criteria the main figure of *Death of a Salesman* is not Willy (whose understanding and values change not one iota from the beginning to the end), but Biff Loman who must "find himself," make an anguished choice between clear-cut alternatives, and who finally does so — redeeming himself, achieving vitality at the sacrifice of his father and his father's false values. Willy is simply a man to whom things happen and who responds with bewilderment and a desperate clinging to his old faith; Biff is a man who makes things happen, who responds to the great shock in his life first with a paralyzing emotional and moral confusion, and then with a determined effort to face the truth and to establish a satisfying order in his life at whatever cost.

Probably the chief reason why audiences and readers have difficulty in seeing this pattern of dramatic meaning is that Miller has used a revolutionary technique by incorporating into drama the two major innovations of modern fiction: stream of consciousness, and the controlling intelligence or limited point of view. Although Eugene O'Neill, Tennessee Williams, and others had experimented in this direction, Miller is the first to be such a thoroughgoing success. But he has made the frame far too large, too fascinating and he has paid the price of having audiences respond emotionally to the new medium itself rather than to see through it to the drama that it contains. As a consequence the life of an unsuccessful salesman, toiling at a task that provides too little income and no sense of creative fulfillment, becomes the focus of attention — far too much attention has been paid to this man!

Miller has worked with artistic intuition rather than critical intelligence, for his remarks on the form of *Death of a Salesman* suggest that he does not fully understand his own accomplishment. "The first image that occurred to me ...," he says, "was of an enormous face the height of the proscenium arch which would appear and then open up, and we would see the inside of a man's head. In fact, *The Inside of His Head* was the first title ... I wished to create a form which ... would literally be the process of Willy Loman's way of mind." (p. 23) Even without the physical image of the huge head, Miller has succeeded in making the action of the play largely the stream of consciousness of Willy; through a fluid stage setting and bold use of lighting, he renders the memories and hallucinations of Willy as happenings of the present, not as "flashbacks" to earlier times objectively seen. Almost all the *exposition* is presented as the product of Willy Loman's mind.

But Miller also says, "What was wanted ... was not a mounting line of tension, nor a gradually narrowing cone of intensifying suspense, but a bloc, a single chord presented as such at the outset ... to hold back nothing ... even at the cost of suspense and climax." (p. 24) To be sure, in so far as Willy is not merely the medium but the subject of the drama, Miller has achieved his aim. The very first image of Willy is of a man utterly defeated and one of his first lines is "I'm tired to the death. I couldn't make it. I just couldn't make it, Linda." His death at the end is merely physical confirmation of the psychological fact established at the outset.

However, in so far as Willy's mind is the frame, the controlling intelligence, the stream of consciousness within which is enacted *the drama of Biff*, there is a magnificently structured line of mounting tension. To a large extent, the movement of the play is exactly like that of Sophocles' *Oedipus Rex*; the drama moves forward by accumulating significant moments of the past and every single one of the past moments directly or indirectly has to do with the conflict between the father and the oldest son. Exactly what is that conflict? what brought it about? how will it be resolved? — these are the questions that are involved in the central movement of the play. The very first dialogue between Willy and Linda begins to shape "the gradually narrowing cone of intensifying suspense":

> WILLY, *worried and angered:* There's such an undercurrent in him. He became a moody man...
> LINDA: ... I think if he finds himself, then you'll both be happier and not fight any more.
> . . . . . .
> WILLY: Why did he come home? I would like to know what brought him home.
> LINDA: I don't know. I think he's still lost, Willy. I think he's very lost. (pp. 133–34)

Biff is indeed lost, and he has come home to make one final effort to resolve the inner conflict; but at this stage we still do not know what the conflict is all about. The dialogue suggests that it somehow has to do with his relations with his father, and this notion is strengthened in Biff's first dialogue with Happy:

> HAPPY: ... What happened, Biff? Where's the old humor, the old confidence? (*He shakes Biff's knee. Biff gets up and moves restlessly about the room.*) What's the matter?
> BIFF: Why does Dad mock me all the time? ... / ... Everything I say there's a twist of mockery on his face. I can't get near him. ...

HAPPY: I think the fact that you're not settled, that you're still kind of up in the air...

BIFF: There's one or two other things depressing him, Happy.

HAPPY: What do you mean?

BIFF: Never mind. Just don't lay it all to me. (pp. 137–38)

No suspense? No mounting line of tension? Only the most insensitive member of the audience would not at this point feel a rising curiosity focused precisely on Biff.

In the ensuing dialogue, Biff recapitulates his misery in trying to establish a foothold in the business world just after leaving high school and the contrasting peace and content he experienced while working on a ranch out West: "There's nothing more inspiring or — beautiful than the sight of a mare and a new colt" (p. 138) — an effective symbol of his urge to vitality and creativity. Then why, as Willy had asked earlier, did he come home? Because his family is the arena of his unresolved conflict. Biff then listens in amazement to his father's hallucinatory recapitulation of the idyllic past when Willy was still the idolized god for his sons, inculcating in them the false values that he persisted in holding despite the fact that they did not work for him. That long scene ends with Willy's immense feeling of guilt concerning his philandering; the worst consequence of his pursuit of economic success is the betrayal of what he loves most in the world — his family. The connection between this and Biff's problem is explicitly established later in Act II; here the Woman accepting Willy's gift of silk stockings while Linda mends her old ones serves as a foreshadowing of the crisis in the Boston hotel room.

Again and again the first act thrusts relentlessly toward illumination of the fundamental father-son conflict. Every dialogue occurring in the present sooner or later touches on it. When the neighbor Charley comes over to calm Willy after his raving hallucination, Willy says, "I can't understand it. He's going back to Texas again... I got nothin' to give him, Charley," (p. 154) and his kindly neighbor advises him to forget it, to release the boy, to let him live his own life according to his own code. Then, after Charley leaves and Willy decides to go for a walk, the two sons come down to discuss their father's plight with their mother and again the father-son issue is faced.

LINDA: When you write you're coming, he's all smiles... And then the closer you seem to come, the more shaky he gets... He can't bring himself to — to open up to you. Why are you so hateful to each other? Why is that? (p. 161)

Biff is evasive and conciliatory, but the mother insists that the son must have respect for his father, be concerned about his distraught and pitiable condition — "What happened to the love you had for him?"

BIFF: ...I know he's a fake and he doesn't like anybody around who knows!

LINDA: Why a fake? In what way? What do you mean?

BIFF: Just don't lay it all at my feet. It's between me and him — that's all I have to say. (p. 164)

Again, the revelation of the cause of the conflict is avoided, but it is foreshadowed when Linda, describing Willy's attempts at suicide, refers to a woman and Biff sharply interrupts with a tense question, "What woman?" before Linda can explain that the woman witnessed Willy's deliberate smashing of his car. Finally, this powerful dramatic line culminates at the end of the first act in a tremendous confrontation scene between father and son. The clash between their *social* values, which has been clear since the opening dialogue between Biff and Happy, is openly faced, but the more powerful discord — the *private*, secret anguish caused by the awareness of both father and son that Willy has betrayed the love of his family — is only darkly suggested:

BIFF: ... They've laughed at Dad for years, and you know why? Because we don't belong in this nuthouse of a city! We should be mixing cement on some open plain, or — or carpenters...

. . . . . .

WILLY: Why do you always insult me?

. . . . . .

BIFF: Oh, Jesus, I'm going to sleep!
WILLY: Don't curse in this house!
BIFF: Since when did you get so clean? (pp. 166–67)

But Biff succumbs to the forces of family reconciliation and reluctantly agrees to make an attempt to fulfill his father's dream for him. However, the first act ends ominously with Biff in the cellar holding the rubber tubing with which Willy has been planning to commit suicide, while Linda timidly asks the key question of the play, "Willy, dear, what has he got against you?" (p. 171)

Act II opens late the following morning with Willy announcing that he has "slept like a dead one" but feeling very optimistic. The catastrophes begin to mount when (symbolically foreshadowing the climax of the play) the son of his former boss (and his own god-son) fires him from his job. This is not the only rejection of a father by a son that will occur. In desperation he calls upon Charley in order to borrow money for the payment of his insurance premium, and in Charley's office the key question is again posed by Bernard, but this time narrowly focused in time and place:

WILLY: ... There's something I don't understand ... His life ended after that Ebbets Field game. From the age of seventeen nothing good ever happened to him ... / ... Why did he lay down?

. . . . .

BERNARD: ... I got the idea he'd gone up to New England to see you. Did he have a talk with you then? ... / ... I knew he'd given up his life. What happened in Boston, Willy? (pp. 188–90)

Willy is unable to face that question. At the restaurant where the victory banquet with his two sons turns into a shambles when it is revealed that not only has Willy lost his job but that Biff was unable to get one, Willy interrupts

Biff's attempt to explain with the outburst: "I'm not interested in stories about the past." (p. 199) However, as inexorably as in Sophocles, the past must be faced. It rises in Willy's fantasies to collide head on with the present that it has led to. As in Freudian psychotherapy, well-being can be restored only when the suppressed traumas of the past can be raised to consciousness and abreacted. Thus the penultimate crisis of the play (and the answer to the intensely persistent question raised in the beginning: "What happened, Biff?") is reached when through Willy's consciousness we see enacted the shocking confrontation of the penitent son and the philandering father in Boston fifteen years earlier. (It is a scene which is structurally and dramatically as important to *Death of a Salesman* as the herdsman scene is to *Oedipus Rex:* Both serve to reveal the moral impostume hidden in the past that must be uprooted before wholeness and order can be restored.) Biff's idol is shattered: "You fake! You phony little fake! You fake!" (p. 208) It is this discovery that had poisoned their relations and had rendered Biff incapable of reconciling himself to his father's values. But neither had been able to reject him and thus cut himself off from the strongest source of love he had ever known. He pleads with his brother, "Help him! Jesus . . . help him . . . Help me, help me, I can't bear to look at his face!" (p. 204) He realizes that however much his father has been a failure, he has also suffered.

Nevertheless, the ambivalence must be resolved, and the final crisis occurs when Willy and Biff meet at home that evening. Biff announces to his mother, "with absolute assurance, determination: 'We're gonna have an abrupt conversation, him and me.'" (p. 211) Biff does not intend to expose his father, as Willy fears, but he is resolved to break with him, to declare his independence, to assert his own identity and his own values:

> BIFF: I'm saying good-by to you, Pop . . . / . . . Today I realized something about myself . . . To hell with whose fault it is or anything like that. Let's just wrap it up, heh? (pp. 213–14)

But Willy cannot believe that there can be a rejection without hatred, and provokes a scene that for emotional tension and dramatic illumination is one of the finest in modern drama. The discovery of the self and the honest assertion of it regardless of the consequences has always been the high point of the greatest tragedies. Here it has tragic consequences, but not for the protagonist; hence, *Death of a Salesman* is — in the highest sense as explained by Susanne Langer in *Feeling and Form* — a comedy, because the forces that obstruct the development of Biff's vitality are grappled with and overthrown. However, Arthur Miller has created such an elaborate dramatic frame in Willy Loman that even such a powerfully dynamic story as Biff's is obscured and almost in the tidal waves of tragic feeling that wash over it. That is perhaps why there is so much critical controversy over whether or not *Death of a Salesman* is a tragedy. Even with Willy as protagonist, despite the immense sadness of his experience, there is a legitimate question; to be sure, *Hamlet, Samson Agonistes,* and other tragedies do open with the central character already in a posture of defeat, but they at least achieve some insight and face their deaths with some degree of understanding about why they are dying. Willy Loman goes to his death still blindly committed to his false ideals. The fact that he does so out of an overwhelming love for his son makes his action deeply pathetic, but hardly tragic. Within this frame of pathos is the experience of Biff in which we see an action that is serious, complete, and of sufficient magnitude, including a dynamic plot with ascending crises, epiphany, peripeteia, ethos, and dianoia. Arthur Miller himself has been so preoccupied with his pathetic salesman that he does not realize that his own play does contain ethos (the moral decision of a character) and dianoia (the ability of a character to say what is fitting in a given situation); he claims that *"Death of a Salesman* is a slippery play to categorize because nobody in it stops to make a speech objectively stating the great issues which I believe it embodies." (p. 32) What then are we to make of Biff's climactic speech which reveals that he has gained insight into himself, that he understands the issues involved in the conflict, and that he has made the morally and psychologically right decision?

BIFF: No! Nobody's hanging himself, Willy! I ran down eleven flights with a pen in my hand today. And suddenly I stopped, you hear me? And in the middle of that office building, do you hear this? I stopped in the middle of that building and I saw — the sky. I saw the things that I love in this world. The work and the food and time to sit and smoke. And I looked at the pen and said to myself, what the hell am I grabbing this for? Why am I trying to become what I don't want to be? What am I doing in an office, making a contemptuous, begging fool of myself, when all I want is out there, waiting for me the minute I say I know who I am! (p. 217)

In his desperate fury to make his father understand, Biff seems on the verge of attacking him, but he breaks down sobbing, pleading for release from his father's phony dream. Willy, wild with relief at discovering that his son, far from hating him, truly loves him despite everything, relapses into his old dream: "That boy — that boy is going to be magnificent!... / ... Can you imagine that magnificence with twenty thousand dollars in his pocket?" (pp. 218—19) He rushes off to commit suicide, certain that with the insurance money Biff will "be ahead of Bernard again."

In the brief epilogue, "Requiem", the dialogue at Willy's funeral reveals that only Biff truly understood his father: "He had the wrong dreams. All, all wrong... / ... He never knew who he was... / ... I know who I am."

There is then in *Death of a Salesman* a play within the play. The outer drama, daringly experimental in technique, has properly been described as social criticism — "a challenge to the American dream... the death of Arthur Miller's salesman is symbolic of the breakdown of the whole concept of salesmanship inherent in our society" (Harold Clurman). The inner drama, quite classical in form and technique, has not been sufficiently appreciated as a uniquely American manifestation of the eternal, humanizing struggle of a man to discover his own identity.

1. *What exactly is Willy Loman's code of values? How firmly does he believe in it?*

In the first evocation of the past, Willy instructs his son: "the man who makes an appearance in the business world, the man who creates personal interest, is the man who gets ahead. Be liked and you will never want." (p. 146) In the long dialogue with Ben in Act II, Willy asserts: "it's not what you do, Ben. It's who you know and the smile on your face! It's contacts, Ben, contacts." (p. 184) But like an atheist Christian, he wills to believe what he knows isn't true. Faced with Linda's family budget, he confesses that the code doesn't work. Furthermore, his greatest personal joy comes from creative work with his hands — putting up a new ceiling or making a cement porch. There was a man behind the futile mask that Willy wore, but he never had the courage to tear it off and face the truth about himself and about the world around him.

2. *Is the play an anti-capitalistic play?*

Arthur Miller himself has denied it. "A play," he says, "cannot be equated with a political philosophy ... / ... To speak of a play as though it were the objective work of a propagandist is an almost biological kind of nonsense, provided, of course, that it is a play, which is to say a work of art." (pp. 36—38) He says further, "The most decent man in *Death of a Salesman* is a capitalist (Charley) whose aims are not different from Willy Loman's. The great difference between them is that Charley is not a fanatic." (p. 37) And it must be admitted that in its larger dimensions, this play is not primarily concerned with politics or economics. Nevertheless, *to the extent that it is concerned with these matters*, the play is clearly an indictment of the profit motive, and competitive salesmanship, and planned obsolescence (the deliberate manufacture of goods which, for reasons of style or quality, will need to be replaced after a short time) — the three principal factors of capitalistic society that distinguish it from any other dehumanizing industrial mass society. When Willy is cruelly deprived of his job after some forty years with the firm, Howard explains, "It's a business, kid, and everybody's gotta pull his own weight ... business is business." (p. 180) And Willy rightly protests against planned obsolescence: "Once in my life I would like to own something outright before it's broken! I'm always in a race with the junkyard! I just finished paying for the car and it's on its last legs. The refrigerator consumes belts like a goddam maniac. They time those things. They time them so when you finally paid for them, they're used up." (p. 174)

Miller has said also that the exponents of socialism cannot take heart from his work. "There is no such thing as a capitalistic assembly line or drygoods counter. The disciplines required by machines are the same everywhere and will not be truly mitigated by old-age pensions and social-security payments. So long as modern man conceives of himself as valuable only because he fits into some niche in the machine-tending pattern, he will never know anything more than a pathetic doom" ("On Social Plays," p. 10). There is truth in this, and *Death of a Salesman* is also an indictment of all modern industrial society; but, again, in specifically attacking the profit motive, competitive salesmanship, and planned obsolescence, this play does directly hit at the capitalistic form of modern society.

3. *"When asked,"* said Miller, *"what Willy was selling, what was in his bags, I could only reply, 'Himself'."* (p. 28) *Obviously he was speaking metaphorically. Is it possible to determine exactly what Willy was selling?*

Yes. There are several clues in various places of the text to indicate that Willy Loman was a dry-goods or clothing salesman. We first see him carrying two large sample cases similar to those which salesmen take to the offices of buyers in large department stores. He presents stockings to The Woman who is secretary to a buyer in Boston; the stockings are apparently from his stock of samples. When Biff suggests that his father's confusion with traffic lights may be due to color-blindness, Happy responds with "Pop? Why he's got the finest eye for color in the business. You know that." (p. 137) Finally, Willy's references to the companies he does business with — F. H. Stewart's, Brown and Morrison, Filene's, Slattery's — are all to well-known department stores in New England.

4. *Trace the pattern of father-son relationships in the play.*

The frequent mirroring of father-son relationships reinforces the fact that *Death of a Salesman* is primarily a drama about the conflict between Willy and Biff. In the dim past there was Willy's father and his two sons; the father was an itinerant flute-maker, a creative man who traveled to the western frontiers and to Alaska. The older brother Ben followed in his footsteps and became rich, but Willy remembers him only as "a man with a big beard, and I was in Mamma's lap." (p. 157) When Linda soothes Willy to sleep with a lullaby, we see that Willy has never been able to wean himself from the need of a mother-figure — he drinks milk to soothe his nerves. And he suppresses the artisan in him, the skill of making things with his hands that he inherited from his father. When Biff resolves to break with his parents and go to Texas, he is reverting back to the healthy drives of his grandfather; but Happy remains in the grip of his Oedipal ties — he denies his father in the restaurant scene, but resolves to fulfill his father's dream in the Requiem scene. And his attachment to his mother is so strong that he cannot genuinely love another woman.

Two other father-son relationships figure in the play: Old Man Wagner and his son Howard, and Charley and his son Bernard.

5. *What elements serve as transitional devices from present to past and back again in Will's hallucinations? What function do they serve?*

Willy has five hallucinatory experiences — two in Act I and three in Act II. The first four of these are similar in that they are all re-enactments of past experiences in Willy's life, but the fifth breaks the pattern when the ghost of Ben appears not as an image out of the past but as a symbol of death encouraging Willy to commit suicide. It is as if Willy felt so strongly the need of some sanction for such an act that he invoked the one person in his life whose power and authority he respected to approve of it. Furthermore, it is ironically appropriate that dying as a way of gaining money should follow the living death of a life dedicated to the making of money.

Of the re-enactments of the past, the first is the most complex for there is a time-shift within the time-shift. Willy, having had to return home because he was unable to control his car on the trip to New England, reminisces about the days when the car was an object of love and security — "The way Biff used to simonize that car?" (p. 136) — and he is suddenly in that idyllic past. But the past was not as idyllic as Willy wishes. He is soon recalling his failures and Linda, as usual, tries to comfort him with flattery: "Willy, darling, you're the handsomest man in the world —." (p. 149) This provokes a memory of another woman's flattery and he is in the Boston hotel room with the buyer's secretary who says, "... you've got such a sense of humor, and we do have such a good time together, don't we?" (p. 150) He is jolted out of that memory when the woman thanks him for his gift of stockings as he notices Linda mending her old ones. And when Happy comes down the stairs to calm down his father's ravings, Willy's sense of guilt over his betrayal of Linda is so powerfully in his consciousness that the first thing he says upon returning to present time is, "Why did she have to wax the floors herself? Every time she waxes the floors she keels over." (p. 152)

The second re-enactment of the past occurs when Willy's neighbor, Charley, offers him a job and Willy recalls his brother Ben who had also offered him a job in Alaska. This time his troubled recollection of Ben's visit and his missed opportunity is broken by Linda, who has come to see what's wrong with her husband. As Willy returns to the present he asks her about a diamond watch fob that Ben had given him during that visit.

In Act II, just after he has been dismissed from his job by Howard, Willy once again recalls his missed opportunity with Ben, who had warned him that he wasn't building anything that he could lay his hand to. Now that the substantial foundations of his life have collapsed, he relives his desperate defense of them to Ben on the day when Biff played his last football game. And as Willy is approaching Charley's office, he recalls the insult he interpreted in Charley's goodnatured joking about the unimportance of a game of football.

The final and most crucial re-enactment of the past begins in the climactic restaurant scene when Willy, hearing of Biff's failure to get a job, recalls Biff's failure in mathematics. It was that which had prompted Biff to rush to seek his father's aid in Boston where he experienced the powerful trauma that lies at the heart of the play. At the moment when Biff abandoned him in the hotel room, Willy is returned to the present to discover that his sons have abandoned him in the restaurant. This hallucination scene is appropriately the last, for once this past experience is revealed we know all we need to know in order to understand the anguished relationship between Willy and his son.

Dramaturgically as well as psychologically, these evocations of the past are brilliantly executed. The motivation for each is clearly established, and each is perfectly placed in the total structure of the play. The only difficulty is that they do displace the focus of attention too much from Biff, the true protagonist, to Willy, who is the medium through which we observe Biff.

6. *What are the most important symbols of the play?*

(a) Before any action begins, we hear a melody played on a flute, telling, according to the stage directions, "of grass and trees and the horizon." (p. 130) It recurs every time Willy recalls the idyllic past, and assumes greater significance when we learn that Willy's father was an itinerant flute-maker. Hence, it refers to one-ness with nature, the wide plains of the west, a strong, bold, secure father, and the joy and satisfaction of the creative life.

(b) The refrigerator, car, washing machine, and all the gadgets that continually break down seem to symbolize the essential futility of materialistic values in general, and the corruption of capitalism in particular.

(c) The huge apartment houses built on either side of Willy's home, blocking the sun and making it impossible for anything to grow in his garden show how modern urban life inhibits creativity. Willy's futile persistence in planting seed there is thus contrasted with Biff's decision to return to Texas where he enjoys the beautiful and inspiring sight of a mare and a new colt.

(d) Just after the powerful double rejection scene in the hotel-restaurant, Willy rushes to buy seeds, saying, "Nothing's planted. I don't have a thing in the ground." This is clearly symbolic of his awareness of failing vitality and of the fact that his "seed," his two sons, have also failed him. Significant, too, is the way he plants the seeds after he has bought them:

> WILLY: Carrots ... quarter-inch apart. Rows ... one-foot rows. *(He measures it off.)* One foot. *(He puts down a package and measures off.)* Beets. *(He puts down another package and measures again.)* Lettuce. *(He reads the package and puts it down.)* ... (p. 212)

It is obviously impossible for him to plant anything any longer.

(e) Willy's encouragement of Biff's athletic activities is mocked by Charley (the chorus figure of the play): "Willy, when are you going to grow up." (p. 186) Athletics are not only childish, but they are a perfect analogue of sales activity — tremendous energy is expended in both for a success that is measured in mathematical terms (numbers of points = numbers of dollars); neither requires intellectual training or creative skill; and neither produces any tangible, permanent good. Since Charley and his son are the norms against which Biff and Willy are measured, it is interesting to note that at the height of his professional career Bernard, who was too puny to engage in glamorous mass athletics in school, carries two tennis rackets with him to Washington. Obviously for him, the stress is on the first term in the adage, *mens sana in corpore sano*.

(f) Several of the names have symbolic significance. "Willy" is in English the diminutive form, suitable for little children but not for adults; it suggests that Willy is infantile, and indeed Charley, Howard, and others often address him as "kid": "Now, look, kid, enough is enough," (p. 191) or "Look kid, I'm busy this morning." (p. 182) *Loman* is equivalent to Low Man, and Willy is indeed lowman on the totem pole of the business world. *Biff* is American slang for a blow or a punch; it is he who strikes down his father and unwittingly drives him to his death by his rejection of him. *Happy* is clearly an ironic name:

> BIFF: ... Are you content, Hap? ...
> 
> HAPPY: Hell, no! ... / ... All I can do now is wait for the merchandise manager to die. (p. 139)

J. V. H.

The following essays and reviews are conveniently available in *Two Modern American Tragedies: Review and Criticism of "Death of a Salesman" and "A Streetcar Named Desire,"* edited by John D. Hurrel, New York, 1961:

Atkinson, Brooks, Review of *Death of a Salesman*, pp. 54-56 — Clark, Eleanor, Review of *Death of a Salesman*, pp. 61-64 — Clurman, Harold, Review of *Death of a Salesman*, pp. 65-67 — Foster, Richard J., Confusion and Tragedy: The Failure of Miller's Salesman, pp. 82-88 — Miller, Arthur, Tragedy and the Common Man, pp.

38-40 — Miller, Arthur, On Social Plays, Introduction to *A View from the Bridge*, pp. 41-48 — Newman, William J., Arthur Miller's *Collected Plays*, pp. 68-71 — "Our Colossal Dad" from *Times Literary Supplement*, pp. 72-75 — "A Matter of Hopelessness in *Death of a Salesman*," A Symposium with Arthur Miller etc., pp. 76-81.

Bentley, Eric, *In Search of a Theater*, New York 1953, pp. 84—88 — Goetsch, Paul, Arthur Miller's Zeitkritik in *Death of a Salesman*, Die Neueren Sprachen 1967, pp. 105—117 — Jochems, Helmut, *Death of a Salesman* — eine Nachlese, *Literatur in Wissenschaft und Unterricht* I, 1968, pp. 77—97 — Krutch, Joseph, *Modern Drama*, Ithaca 1953, pp. 124—129 — Lübbren, Rainer, *Arthur Miller*, Velber bei Hannover 1966, pp. 45—59 — Mennemeier, Franz Norbert, *Das moderne Drama des Auslandes*, Düsseldorf 1961, pp. 96—110 — Moss, Leonard, *Death of a Salesman*: Verbal and Symbolic Technique, Itschert, ed., *Das Amerikanische Drama von den Anfängen bis zur Gegenwart*, Darmstadt 1972, pp. 378—384 — Rössle, Wolfgang, *Die soziale Wirklichkeit in Arthur Millers Death of a Salesman*, Freiburg/Schweiz 1970 — Silkenat, Anne Lore, Miller, *Death of a Salesman*; Hüllen-Rossi-Christopeit, *Zeitgenössische amerikanische Dichtung*, Frankfurt 1960, pp. 158—164 — Szondi, Peter, *Theorie des modernen Dramas*, Frankfurt ⁶1969, pp. 154—161 — Welland, Dennis, *Arthur Miller*, Edinburgh 1961, pp. 51—73 — Wiegand, William, Arthur Miller and the Man Who Knows, *Western Review* XXI, 1957, pp. 85—103.

# EUGENE O'NEILL

Eugene O'Neill was born on October 16, 1888, in New York, the son of a well-known actor of Irish descent. He was educated by tutors and in Catholic boarding-schools. He also attended Princeton University for one year, but had to leave in 1904 because of an undergraduate prank. After working variously as a seaman, in offices and as a gold-seeker in Honduras he took minor parts for a time in his father's company and then became a reporter. Recuperating from tuberculosis in 1912 he read the classic repertoire of the theater and in 1914 took part in George Pierce Baker's famous dramatic workshop at Harvard University. The next year he was a member of the Provincetown Players in Cape Cod and wrote several one-act plays, some of which were also published in a magazine.

For his first long play, *Beyond the Horizon* (1919), he was awarded the Pulitzer Prize. Within the next two years, the production of such plays as *The Emperor Jones*, *Anna Christie*, and *The Hairy Ape* left no doubt that a dramatist of great power had appeared. Before long these and later plays of O'Neill were being performed in the capitals of Europe, and he became an international influence.

Between 1924 and 1931, O'Neill produced nine plays, most of them tragedies with complex psychological implications. *Mourning Becomes Electra* (1931) exploited the Greek tragedies of the Agamemnon family in a trilogy dealing with a New England family of the Civil War period. *Ah, Wilderness* (1933) was a brilliant domestic comedy, his only venture in this field.

O'Neill was awarded the Nobel Prize in 1936, two years after he was stricken with a fatal malady. During intervals of improved health he completed four full-length plays and worked on a cycle of eleven plays dramatizing several successive generations of a family, of which only two were completed.

He left an autobiographical drama, *Long Day's Journey into Night* (written in 1941), which was produced after his death in 1953 and proved to be his great masterpiece. He had postponed writing it, he said, until I could "face my dead [parents] with pity, understanding, and forgiveness." It won the first Pulitzer Prize ever awarded posthumously, and was the fourth of his plays to win that award.

O'Neill was foremost among the playwrights, who, from 1916 to 1924, brought about in American drama a revolution which fundamentally changed its character. He enriched his art by an enlarged awareness of all conscious and subconscious realities and by using experimental techniques in stagecraft and acting which completely ignored the conventions of the "well-made" play and called directly upon the subconscious responses of the audience.

## Beyond the Horizon

Text: Eugene O'Neill, *Beyond the Horizon*. Westermann

*Andrew and Robert Mayo are the two sons on a small farm somewhere north of New York near the Atlantic coast. Robert, the younger one, who went to College one year, likes to read poetry and dream of "the beauty of the far off and unknown ... of the secret which is hidden over there, beyond the horizon." Andy is "a Mayo through and through ... wedded to the soil." Both love Ruth Atkins, their neighbor's daughter, but they have an even greater respect and affection for each other.*

*Robert, who was a sickly boy, is supposed to join his uncle, Captain Dick Scott, on a three years' voyage, but stays at home and lets his brother go instead, when Ruth returns his love.*

*Three years later, when Andy comes home, he finds the farm in a very poor state and Robert's and Ruth's love, in spite of their having a little daughter, turned into hatred. He has changed, too; he leaves the farm again and goes to Buenos Aires for a job in the grain business.*

*Another five years later he returns after losing most of the money he had made by speculating. He arrives just before Robert dies of tuberculosis, eight months after his little girl's death. Robert realizes that Andy's guilt in leaving the farm and becoming a speculator in grain is greater than his own and Ruth's failure and asks his brother to marry Ruth after his death, for "only through contact with suffering ... will you — awaken."*

Eugene O'Neill's plays make rather thin reading, and this is particularly true of his realistic dramas such as *Beyond the Horizon*. Plays are, of course, written for stage presentation, and O'Neill's plays are for the most part "good theater." Yet there is something inevitably pejorative in such a judgment, for it stresses the importance of spectacle and of the immediate impact upon the audience of the actors on the stage and, thereby, hints at the triteness or confusion of vision which so often appears once this immediacy has been eliminated.

Such realistic O'Neill dramas as *Beyond the Horizon, The Emperor Jones*, and *Desire under the Elms* are relatively free from the injudicious eclecticism of *The Great God Brown* and from the hasty, unassimilated intellectual enthusiasms which account for such daring and, in retrospect, crude plays as *The Hairy Ape* and *Strange Interlude*. However, precisely because they are naked of the formalistic and expressionistic elements that characterize his experimental drama, O'Neill's more realistic plays often suffer from weaknesses that non-realistic treatment elsewhere serves to mask. For one thing, there is O'Neill's heavy reliance upon stage stereotypes. In *Beyond the Horizon*, admittedly a very early play, not one of the characters escapes easy classification under some trite but, in this case, adequate heading: the dreamy romantic, the man of the soil, the old salt, and so on. For another thing, there is O'Neill's inability to suggest the actual rhythm and accent of the spoken language. As the characters are themselves theatrical clichés, so their language — and this is particularly obvious in *Beyond the Horizon* — seems derived from the theater rather than from any personal awareness. The sometimes grotesque rhetoric of Robert's longer speeches and the clumsy attempts at reproducing the rural New England dialect in *Beyond the Horizon* are symptoms of an ear very little aware of the actualities of the spoken language, and they are particularly awkward in a play committed to the restraints of verisimilitude.

This deficiency of language or style can, of course, be overcome to a certain extent in the theater by skillful directing and acting; on the printed page, however, it cannot be disguised. As for his dependence upon stereotyped characters — O'Neill, in *Beyond the Horizon,* draws from it both advantages and disadvantages. The advantages lie in the very simplicity of such pre-established characters. Because they are simple and known quantities, once their identities have been made clear, O'Neill is free in the construction of the play to concentrate upon the dynamic results of combining these characters in a particular way under particular circumstances. Moreover, in as much as the fundamental theme of the play has to do with the consequences that follow when one violates his own nature, the oversimplified natures of the characters involved make for greater force and clarity of thematic statement. The disadvantages lie in the fact that such characters rarely convince us of their significance. The sense of tragic waste that should apparently accompany the decline and fall of Robert Mayo issues merely in pathos because there is nothing to convince us of the inherent worth of his aspirations. That he is the only character in the play who possesses a sense of the largeness of life and a desire to penetrate its mystery is in a way obvious; yet, his aspirations are so thoroughly bound up with the love of adventure and exoticism characteristic of the naïve romantic stereotype of which he is an embodiment that one can never quite take them seriously.

When the structure of *Beyond the Horizon* is examined in detail, it becomes immediately apparent that it is essentially a very simple and somewhat mechanical one. As has already been suggested character, motive, and circumstance are broadly sketched, and such dramatic power as the play has comes from the relentlessness and directness with which a single line of dramatic force is developed from beginning to end. Though it is not in any technical sense a tragedy, it belongs among those plays sometimes loosely called "domestic tragedies," and within this category, it achieves distinction by its strictness of form and by a straightforward treatment of causal relationships that remotely suggest classical Greek drama. Stated in the most general terms possible the story of the plays is this: the three main characters — Robert, Ruth and Andrew — are all confronted with the necessity of making a specific choice. The choice in each case involves electing one way of life as against another, and, for various reasons, all three choose in such a way as to violate their basic natures and, consequently, to entail suffering for themselves and others.

Each act of *Beyond the Horizon* consists of two scenes, alternating between roadside and farmhouse, farmhouse and hilltop, farmhouse and roadside; and this alternation establishes a basic rhythm in the play as it comes to express more and more obviously the vaccillation between hope, on the one hand, and frustration and despair, on the other. The farmhouse represents, of course, the narrow, enclosed provincial existence from which Robert longs to escape, and in its progressive deterioration, it registers the failure, the frustration, and the demoralization of Robert and his wife, Ruth. The road leads toward and the hilltop looks out upon the wider prospect; they are associated with the possibility of freedom and with the hope of a more satisfying life, a hope which for one character and another is repeatedly frustrated and reborn until it finally issues in the emotional and moral anesthesia of Ruth and the fevered illusions of Robert.

The first act is built upon a simple but ominous reversal of situation. The main characters partly choose and partly are forced by the choices of others to change positions. At the beginning, Robert Mayo, out of the urgency of his romantic longing for the mysteries beyond the horizon and out of a desire to escape the strain of a supposedly unrequited love for Ruth Atkins, has committed himself to a three-year sea voyage; at the end, he has decided against the voyage and has committed himself to the farm which he despises. And Andrew Mayo, who loves the farm and is fully and satisfyingly expressed in the labor of the farm, has assumed his brother's position, volunteering to substitute for him on the voyage. The precipitating agent of this abrupt and total reversal is Ruth Atkins. Of the three main characters, Ruth is furthest from having achieved any degree of self-knowledge. She is attracted to Robert by the rhetoric of a high-flown romanticism that is, in fact, opposed to her basically practical, materialistic, and duty-bound nature. Yet, acting upon this attraction, she offers her love to Robert instead of to Andrew, who has believed it to be his almost by natural right.

From a situation defined essentially by the basic needs and inclinations of the characters involved, the first act, then, develops toward a situation defined by delusion and supposed necessity. Only in the case of Andrew is the falseness of the new position immediately apparent. When his uncle, Captain Dick Scott, who has planned upon compensating for the sterility and loneliness of his bachelor life by borrowing the youngest son of his sister, protests against the sudden dashing of his plans, Andrew seizes upon the protest as an opportunity both to escape his own embarrassment and to sacrifice himself for his brother, that is, to make sure that the love between Robert and Ruth is in no way qualified or disturbed by his presence. However, Andrew's quarrel with his father, which is in effect a quarrel with himself, dramatizes the extent to which his decision forces him to betray and even deny his basic nature. From Ruth and Robert, the fallacies in their decision are hidden by the illusion that they have found a love which answers their deepest needs and by the very lack of mutual understanding which makes their love possible.

The second act presents the climactic moment in the relationship between Ruth and Robert, the moment in which, under the pressure of three years of accumulated experience and of the imminent return of Andrew, they are forced to face and accept the consequences of their choices. The act opens in the farmhouse which for both Ruth and Robert has become a trap, a place of futile drudgery. It opens with a conversation between Mrs. Mayo and Mrs. Atkins in which are foreshadowed the stages of selfish vindictiveness and will-less despair through which Ruth is yet to decline. Under the scourge of deprivation and failure, Ruth's fundamental nature has begun to assert itself — her preeminent desire for practical security and comfort, her admiration of the masculine efficiency and skill that make such a life possible, and her lack of any basic respect for, in fact her sense of inferiority in the presence of intellect and imagination.

The suspicion of mutual betrayal has already scattered the seeds of hatred between Ruth and Robert, but both have attempted to hide from themselves the fact that they have been duped by love into trapping and imprisoning one another. However, with the expectation of Andrew's return, Ruth's hope for a better life centers once more in him. To this hope, Robert is now an obstacle, and in her desperate though not fully conscious need to drive him out, she turns upon him viciously, attacking not only his inadequacies as a "man" but everything he values as well. Just as Andrew's prosaic response to the Orient has served to remind Robert of all the fine, if rather vague, spiritual profits that he had dreamed of finding in such a voyage, so Ruth's violent rejection with its implicit confession of smallness and meanness reveals to him the full extent of the bad bargain which he has made with life.

Essentially, what Ruth attempts to do in Act II is re-establish the situation with which the play began, a situation that has come to seem infinitely preferable to the one which she herself has chosen. The current of events stemming from the original choice is, however, too strong for her. For she is opposed not only by Robert who refuses to give up either what satisfaction he has found in the love of his daughter or to allow his brother's sacrifice to be rendered meaningless, but also and far more effectually by Andrew who has found in his wanderings what he believes a wider field for the exercise and fulfillment of his nature. He now thinks in terms of the 10,000 acre wheat farms of Argentina, and in the sweep of that vision both the family farm and the woman he had loved have ceased to have personal meaning for him. The shift in Act II from farm to hilltop expresses simultaneously Robert's return to his now hopeless dreams and Ruth's reaching out for new hope. The hill still looks out upon the promise of distant horizons, but Andrew's obvious lack of personal interest closes those horizons as firmly to Ruth as they are closed to Robert.

The third act follows much the same pattern as the second; it moves from the farmhouse interior, now expressive of the final stages of squalor and demoralization, to the out-of-doors, this time the roadside. Again there is an attempt to re-establish the pattern of relationships existing at the beginning of the play, but this time the attempt is made by Robert who, in facing his own death, comes to a more charitable understanding of all of them. Robert, however, succeeds no better than Ruth in altering the configuration of events or forestalling their consequences. Though the final scene in many ways recapitulates the first scene of the play, in terms of implied potentialities it is a bleak mockery of what might have been.

Robert, himself, dies happy but only because his fever-ridden imagination clothes even death in the somewhat gaudy trappings of a naïve romanticism. Before he dies, Robert perceives that Andrew, who appears to have come through it all far better than the rest, has actually sustained the most thoroughgoing defeat.

> ROBERT: ... You — a farmer — to gamble in a wheat pit with scraps of paper. There's a spiritual significance in that picture, Andy. *(He smiles bitterly.)* I'm a failure, and Ruth's another — but we can both justly lay some of the blame for our stumbling on God. But you're the deepest-dyed failure of the three, Andy. ... You used to be a creator when you loved the farm. You and life were in harmonious partnership. And now — ... your gambling with the thing you used to love to create proves how far astray — So you'll be punished. You'll have to suffer to win back — ... (p. 114)

And Robert attempts to extract a promise that Andrew will marry Ruth after he, himself, is dead. The gesture is almost impersonal, as if Robert were a priest assigning penance or an artist arranging figures in an allegorical painting: Andrew must embrace suffering and despair (Ruth), because only through suffering and despair will he come to know the extent of his self-betrayal and, thereby, possibly regain his true nature. As the final curtain falls, Andrew is fumbling for the meaning of what his brother has said, but there is little hope now of any meaningful relationship being realized between him and Ruth, between the shrewd man of affairs and the woman who is sunk in "that spent calm beyond the further troubling of any hope." (p. 124)

1. *What is the main point of the first act of* Beyond the Horizon?

The first act makes clear that the main characters choose their own dooms, by choosing ways of life in which their dominant needs are least likely to be satisfied. They choose blindly, of course, but nonetheless freely, and in choosing they condemn themselves to the series of destructive experiences elaborated in the play.

2. *In what way does the alternation of scenes between roadside or hilltop and farmhouse help to express the theme of the play?*

Each act of *Beyond the Horizon* consists of two scenes — one within the farmhouse; the other by the roadside or on the hilltop. In general, the road and the hill are associated with the hope of freedom, especially the freedom to seek the meaning of life beyond the narrow confines of the farm; the farmhouse, itself, in its progressive deterioration is associated with confinement, failure and frustration. Only the first act shifts from the roadside to the farmhouse interior, emphasizing Robert's fateful abandonment of his dreams and his commitment to a world that is worse than meaninglessness to him. Act II moves from farmhouse to hilltop thus reflecting both Robert's despairing return to his original dreams and Ruth's illusory hope that Andrew on his return will offer her the possibility of a better life. Act III also moves from the farmhouse to the out-of-doors, from farmhouse to roadside, as Robert finds a kind of delirious hope in the approach of death. Death is at least an escape for him from the meanness and demoralization of the life reflected in the delapidated farm.

3. *To what extent is Ruth responsible for the pathetic waste of life which the play depicts?*

Ruth is so little developed as a personality that is is scarcely possible to attribute to her any sort of personal responsibility; moreover, her shallowness and her naïve selfishness amount almost to a sort of innocence. Her lack of self-knowledge and her lack of understanding of the two brothers is certainly accountable for much, but what is responsible, above all, is the promise of love which both brothers see in her. When she, in what she supposes to be good faith, confers her love upon Robert, she unwittingly leads both brothers to violate their basic natures by committing themselves to ways of life in which their deepest needs cannot be satisfied. Then, when she discovers that Robert cannot provide her with what is necessary to fulfill her own desires, she naïvely attempts to withdraw her love from him in order to give it to Andrew. The result is that, while failing to attain her own ends, she deprives Robert of the one thing that might have sustained him in the face of his inadequacy and dissatisfaction and, thus, hastens for them both the decline into spiritual disintegration and despair.

4. *How do the minor characters — Mr. and Mrs. Mayo, Captain Dick Scott, and Mrs. Atkins — contribute to the play?*

All the minor characters are bare, undisguised stereotypes. Their contribution to the play is almost purely mechanical; that is, they are simply devices by means of which various dramatic necessities are satisfied and the machinery of the plot is made to operate. Thus, Captain Scott in his querulous disappointment over Robert's change of heart, inadvertently opens the door for Andrew's immediate flight; Mr. Mayo is a kind of alter ego for his son, Andrew, and his stubborn opposition to Andrew's decision to leave serves to dramatize the violence which Andrew is doing to the demands of his own nature; the invalided Mrs. Atkins is the practical embodiment of the fatal ties which bind Robert to the farm that he despises and which are implicit in his choice of love over the search for mystery; and Mrs. Mayo and Mrs. Atkins, as they appear at the opening of Act II, foreshadow Ruth's alternative responses to defeat by life — selfish vindictiveness and abject despair.

5. *What does Robert mean when he says that Andrew is "The deepest-dyed failure of the three" (Act III, scene 1)?*

   Ruth and Robert have failed both to fulfill their responsibilities and to satisfy their most fundamental needs; they have, in effect, destroyed one another; yet, their mistakes were made in the name of love, which they had believed would somehow compensate for all deficiencies and all sacrifices, and have been paid for in suffering and degradation. Andrew, on the other hand, has been fortunate in that, in being forced out into the world, he has found better opportunities for self-fulfillment. However, in pursuing these opportunities, he has been led by greed to betray himself. He has divorced himself from the land, from the most vital part of himself which was expressed in his love of the land. Yet he does not recognize his failure because he has ceased to know himself.

6. *Why does Robert attempt to force Andrew to promise to marry Ruth?*

   Robert's intention is perhaps best termed allegorical; it seems to have nothing to do with love or even with providing for Ruth. The proposed marriage is a kind of recipe for salvation, and in it Ruth, herself, seems little more than a personification of suffering and defeat. Mechanical and unconvincing though Robert's formulation is, the implication would seem to be that he has come to the conclusion that it is better to be defeated and borne down by life than to succeed at the expense of self-betrayal, and he offers Ruth to Andrew both as the price and the means of Andrew's rediscovering himself.

7. *What dramatic effect is achieved by making the final scene of the play reminiscent of the first scene?*

   By making the final scene echo the situation at the beginning of the play, O'Neill intensifies our awareness of the moral and psychological distance that the main characters have traveled. The general effect is not to renew the hopes and expectations of the first scene but to deepen the sense that life for these people has exhausted itself. What was for Robert the promise of a voyage in pursuit of the mysteries of life has become the necessity of accepting death. What was for Andrew and Ruth, at least in the eyes of others, the expectation of love and marriage has become the possibility, and that a remote one, of some sort of relationship based, not upon love, but upon suffering and pity.

A. R. W.

Falk, Doris V., *Eugene O'Neill and the Tragic Tension*, New Brunswick, N. J., 1958, pp. 37—45 — Kracht, Werner, *Beyond the Horizon*, in Hüllen-Rossi-Christopeit, *Zeitgenössische amerikanische Dichtung*, Frankfurt 1960, pp. 170—180 — Woolcott, A., *Beyond the Horizon*, in Cargill-Fagin-Fisher, *O'Neill and His Plays*, New York 1961, pp. 135—139.

# DOROTHY PARKER

Dorothy Parker was born on August 23, 1893, at West End, New Jersey, daughter of Henry Rothschild. Educated at a convent in New York, she turned to journalism and became a well-known book-reviewer. Her first book of light verse (1927) was well received, and in 1929 she was awarded the O. Henry Prize for her short story "Big Blonde". During the following ten years she published several more books of poetry and short stories and also wrote for the screen.

Her style is modeled on Ernest Hemingway's, who is her favorite author. Her sense of humor has been called "bitter-sweet," and she is a satirist rather than a humorist. She herself once wrote, "The humorist has never been happy, anyhow. Today he's whistling past worse graveyards to worse tunes." She has taken active interest in the political and economical developments of her time and visited Spain during the Civil War.

Edward Weeks sums up, "As we see the work *in toto*, with its laughter, its wit, its silly sophistication, and its heartburn, we realize that there are limitations, the chief of them being a lack of depth and a lack of cordiality."

## You Were Perfectly Fine

Text: *American Short Stories* V pp. 110—113. Schöningh

*A young man, suffering badly from a hangover and a dim feeling of having misbehaved on the previous night's party, is consoled by his girl friend. He may have disgusted everybody else, but she happily remembers their intimate relationship at the end of the night, in the course of which he seems to have committed himself more than he meant to.*

This brief vignette is a fine example of sophisticated, hard-boiled New Yorker wit, and it gives a swift insight into the behavior of the disorganized, valueless "lost generation" of the jazz age (the 1920's). Dorothy Parker's short stories might be described as the distilled essence of Ernest Hemingway and F. Scott Fitzgerald — distilled, that is, into a dialogue of carefully modulated ironies. The author remains objective and detached; William Plomer has said of her that "there is something clinical, something of the probing adroitness of the dentist: the fine-pointed instrument unerringly discovers the carious cavity behind the smile."

The mood, tone, and pace of the piece are those of a vaudeville sketch — a swift series of jokes and wisecracks told in the "he said — she said" rhythm of the comic entertainer. The technique of the humor is chiefly that of the girl's statements of soothing reassurance immediately followed by damning qualifications: "I don't think anybody at the other tables noticed it at all.

Hardly anybody." The young man's horrible, drunken behavior of the night before (which he has completely forgotten) is revealed in a series of such statements, which make the title obviously ironic. The young man is apparently a rather decent fellow and is shocked at his own behavior: "Clam juice down that back. And every vertebra a little Cabot. Dear God. What'll I ever do?" (The reference to Cabot here is not, as the editor of *Am Sh St* V suggests, to the 15th century explorer, but to the distinguished upper-class family of New England: the popular New England jingle is

> "And this is good old Boston,
> The home of the bean and the cod,
> Where the Lowells talk to the Cabots
> And the Cabots talk only to God.")

But there is a double involution to the irony of the title, for the most humorous revelation of the story is the sense in which the young man *was* "perfectly fine" after his "fall". The story changes direction at the point where the young man's name is first mentioned: "Ah, now, Peter! ... You can't sit there and say you don't remember what happened after that!" Up to that point his behavior toward *others* has been revealed; but after that, his behavior toward *her* is revealed. Also, after that the girl's feelings and behavior become a focus of attention. Peter had thrilled the girl so much by his confessions and embraces in the taxi that she can neither believe that he doesn't remember at least that much of the previous night's events nor blame him for his outrageous conduct toward the others. The young man is now caught; he has thoroughly compromised himself. It is too late for him to "go join a monastery in Tibet." The young man's first line of dialogue, "Oh, dear ... Oh, dear, oh, dear, oh, dear," was a lament over his hangover, the physiological consequences of his drunken debauch; its repetition at the end is a lament over the psychological and moral consequences. Though the story belongs to one of the lighter genres of American fiction, it is magnificently executed — not a word is wasted — and it must not be lightly dismissed.

1. *What is the double irony of the title?*

    a) the young man's behavior was in fact abominable; b) the young man was too nice to the girl and now faces an undesired commitment.

2. *What is the double significance of the young man's fall?*

    See the commentary above.

3. *At what point does the story change direction? What is the main significance of each half?*

4. *What increase of meaning has been attached to the young man's first line of dialogue when it is repeated at the end?*

5. *Why does the girl not criticize him for his behavior toward others on the night before?*

6. *What is witty about the reference to Walt Whitman?*

   The young man feels that his head is not his own, but that of someone old, gray, fuzzy, and bearded.

7. *Is there a German equivalent of "The hair of the mastiff that bit me"?*

   Den Teufel mit Beelzebub austreiben.

8. *At what point does Peter, who understandably refused the first offer of a drink, finally ask for one?*

   When he realizes at last the awful consequences of his previous night's behavior.

J. V. H.

# EDGAR ALLAN POE

Edgar Poe was born on January 19, 1809, in Boston, the son of itinerant actors. His English-born mother died soon after his father had deserted her, in 1811, and the child was unofficially adopted by John Allan, a tobacco exporter in Richmond, Virginia, whose name he later adopted. When business interests took Mr. Allan abroad, Poe lived with the family in England and Scotland from 1815 to 1820. The good education he had received there was continued on their return to America, including one year at the University of Virginia, where he had to leave for excessive drinking and gambling.

Unable to come to terms with Mr. Allan, who wanted to employ him in his business, Poe ran away to Boston, where he published his first collection *Tamerlane and Other Poems* (1827). While serving in the army Poe produced two more volumes of poetry, and in 1831, causing a break with his fosterfather, decided to depend on his pen for a livelihood. In 1832 his first short stories appeared in print, and in 1833 "MS Found in a Bottle" won him a prize and subsequently various editorial employment. In 1836 Poe married a thirteen-year-old cousin, who died of tuberculosis in 1847.

In the last decade of his life he became well known in literary circles for his editorial articles, his poetry and his short stories (*Tales of the Grotesque and Arabesque* 1840, *Tales* 1845). He was the first to attempt a definition of the short story, in his review of Hawthorne's *Twice-Told Tales* (1842) and of literary standards in general, in "The Poetic Principle" (1848, published 1850).

His fame was assured by the success of "The Gold-Bug" in 1843 and the poem "The Raven" in 1845; nevertheless, Poe's life was mostly one of instability and consequent escapes into eccentricities, a tragedy of frustration in a society and period with which he was wholly discordant. His reputation was bismirched by gossip, and he died in drunkenness in 1849 — "the saddest and the strangest figure in American literary history."

"During a short life of poverty, anxiety, and fantastic tragedy Poe achieved the establishment of a new symbolic poetry within the small compass of forty-eight poems; the formalization of the new short story; the invention of the story of detection and the broadening of science fiction; the foundation of a new fiction of psychological analysis and symbolism; and the slow development, in various stages, of an important critical theory and a discipline of analytical criticism.

The literary tradition of Poe, preserved by European symbolism, especially in France, played a considerable part in shaping the spirit of our twentieth-century literature, particularly in its demand for the intellectual analysis and controlled perception of emotional consciousness." (Bradley-Beatty-Long, *The American Tradition in Literature* I)

## The Gold-Bug

Text:   Edgar Allan Poe, *The Gold-Bug.* Hueber
Edgar Allan Poe, *Two Fantastic Tales* pp. 4—29. Diesterweg (contains a shortened version)

*Infected with misanthropy, William Legrand has taken up his residence at Sullivan's Island, off the coast of South Carolina, where he lives with a Negro servant and devotes himself to hunting, fishing and completing his entomological collection. One day his friend and physician — the narrator — comes over from the mainland and finds him in high spirits after having found an unknown species of beetle, with golden scales. When Legrand finds out that a piece of paper he coincidentally picked up on the beach contains a secret message of pirates concerning a hidden treasure he regards the beetle = bug as the index of the fortune he is going to regain. As soon as he has deciphered the message he invites his friend to join him on an expedition, but does not divulge his secret.*

*Unable to make any sense of Legrand's conduct and suspecting him to be mad, the narrator reluctantly complies. They make their way to a high tree on top of an almost inaccessible hill. A skull nailed to one of its branches leads them to a place where, after excessive toil, they find a chest containing a treasure of incalculable value. Having taken it safely to Legrand's hut the latter informs his friend of the ingenious way in which he solved the mystery of the message he had found.*

"The Gold-Bug" (1843) represents the intellectual trend in the mystery story. It is usually classified, according to Poe's own definition, as a tale of ratiocination, i. e. reasoning, exact thinking. Another story not dealt with here,

"The Mystery of Marie Rogêt", is an even better example of a solution that is reached by sheer logical deduction. That story consists of newspaper cuttings from a genuine case (with the names changed) and has no formal ending, as it stops when the process of deduction can take the author no further. Years later the general lines of argument were shown to be sound by the confession of the parties involved in the real case. "The Gold-Bug" is not so purely deductive as this; the narrator is astonished by the antics of his friend and is kept in the dark until after the discovery of the treasure, when the cipher is presented to the reader. Interest in the strange character of William Legrand is one of the features that make the story interesting to the general reader, where "Marie Rogêt" is rather a connoisseur's piece. The mystery in "The Gold-Bug" arises from grotesque elements combined with a Romantic melancholy landscape and suggestions of horror. The theme of madness that obsessed Poe is here, too, though it turns out to be feigned madness. Death and decay are present in the skull on the branch, and, even more characteristic of Poe's horrors, the mass of human bones uncovered by the dog just before the treasure is found. There is even a hint of Poe's theme of burial alive in the theory advanced that the pirate king struck down his helpers with a mattock and interred them with the loot. Even a touch of the revenge theme (which Poe occasionally carries to extremes) can be detected in the behavior of William Legrand in his feigned madness, intended to punish his friend for his suspicions.

The grotesque element, however, is merely a back-cloth to one of the first detective stories ever written where the reader is given the material, in this case a cryptogram, to work out for himself. There is no "cheating," no withholding of clues until the end (as there often is in the Sherlock Holmes stories). Needless to say, this type of tale has a large element of pure technique — it improves with time and accumulated experience like a mechanical invention. But Poe, who invited the readers of his magazine to submit similar cryptograms to him and solved most of them, must be honored as an innovator, although he shares this honor (as is always the case with inventions) with others, principally Voltaire and his "Zadig," a *conte* written as early as 1747 with strong detective elements. There are other elements that would not satisfy the modern reader; the narrator's tedious insistence that his friend should seek medical advice and the over-lengthy speeches of the Negro servant with the "comic" dialect are suspense devices that have lost their effectiveness. The convention of the buried treasure is an acceptable convention, but no modern reader of detective stories is going to swallow the accidental finding of the parchment with instructions leading to the hiding-place, much less the invisible ink that survives long immersion in sea-water and wet sand. But we owe our sophistication in these matters largely to Poe who was a founder of the whole detective-story industry. He wrote few analytical stories, probably realizing that the field was not of large importance.

A more serious matter is the clumsiness of language, very noticeable where Poe is not fascinating us with his strange and terrible images. In the first sentence of this story the phrase "I contracted an intimacy" is a typical example of this style, reminiscent of a 19th century provincial newspaper, where a burglar never breaks in but invariably "effects an entry." This disease, which was especially prevalent in American writing at the time of Poe and Cooper, is generally considered to have been cured by Mark Twain who, in his best works, closed the breach between vernacular and literary language.

1. *What mystery story elements does Poe employ here?*

    The reader can help to solve the mystery (here by unraveling a cryptogram — no clues are withheld). Suspense (the narrator's refusal to regard Legrand's excitement as anything but a mental aberration, the slow accumulation of detail in the halting narrative of the Negro servant, the scythe and spades in the boat leading to the finding of the treasure). Background (remote region, romantic landscape, suspicion of madness in the main character.

2. *In what ways has the technique of the mystery story advanced since Poe's day?*

    The mystery that the reader has to solve is no longer a simple cryptogram, but a complicated web of times, places and clues. In a similar way suspense is achieved by more sophisticated methods than the simple refusal to take the story seriously that Poe employs. The improbabilities of this story are of a type that no modern reader would accept (finding of parchment on seashore, invisible ink unaffected by exposure to sea-water). The detective with the keen analytical brain who is at the same time a bit of a queer fish is one of Poe's most effective strokes that has been extensively imitated. The character of the hero and the choice of an interesting or exotic background to the mystery tale has become a separate branch of the industry — there are tales that concentrate on these features to the exclusion of the "ratiocinative" aspect of the story. In richness of background material Poe has not been exceeded by present-day writers of mystery stories.

3. *Discuss the sequence of events in this story.*

    The suspense elements are succeeded by the finding of the treasure as a central climax of the story. Only afterwards do we learn the steps by which Legrand solved the mystery. This arrangement is necessitated by the fact that the gold-bug (which provides the title) has only a tenuous connection with the treasure-hunt. If the narrator (the "I" of the story) had followed the steps of the solution, the mystification with the gold-bug would have been ludicrous.

W. G. C.

Becker, Jens-Peter, Edgar Allan Poe: "The Gold-Bug," *Interpretationen zu Irving, Melville und Poe*, ed. Finger, Hans, Frankfurt 1971, pp. 59—73 — Goldhurst, William, Edgar Allan Poe and the Conquest of Death, *New Orleans Review* II, 1969, pp. 316—319 — Hassell, J. Woodrow, The Problem of Realism in "The Gold-Bug," *American Literature* XXV, 1953, pp. 179—192.

# The Tell-Tale Heart

Text: *American Short Stories* I pp. 59—65. Schöningh
*Great American Short Stories* pp. 19—23. Klett

*The narrator tries to convince the reader that he is not mad by demonstrating how cunningly he prepared and executed the murder of a harmless old man whose "vulture eye" frightened him. What people take for madness he attributes to an overacuteness of his senses. For seven nights he silently entered his victim's room and found him sleeping. Having awakened him in the eighth night by a slight noise and waiting in silence, with a ray of his lantern directed on the "vulture eye," he hears the beating of the old man's heart growing quicker and louder until he can bear it no longer and kills the old man. He dismembers the corpse and deposits the parts under planks of the floor. When three police officers search the house in the morning he dispels their suspicions — until his ears begin to ring and the beating of the old man's heart gradually grows into such an unbearable noise that he admits the deed.*

As a tale of terror this story stands in contrast to a purely deductive mystery story like "The Mystery of Marie Rogêt". The interest here is psychological and centered in the state of mind of the madman who narrates the story. Tautness is achieved in the presentation by allowing the madman to tell the story himself in wild and whirling words containing vehement denials of his own madness. The plot and the murderer's mental state are conveyed more neatly than by exposition by a third person.

The narrator opens the story by explaining the acute state of his senses, especially that of hearing, a motif that is taken up again at the end when he, and only he, can hear the beating of the heart. After the opening paragraph he moves directly on to the time when he was considering the murder of the harmless old man, so that there is no doubt that the narrator is indeed mad (in other stories of this nature tension is achieved by allowing the reader to have doubts as to whether the narrator or those around him are insane). By any sane standards, however, the motives of Poe's madman are ridiculous; the act that is out of all proportion to the cause creates a nightmare atmosphere with an element of melodrama — an atmosphere that is met with again in "The Cask of Amontillado" where the deed is everything and the motive barely hinted at. The madman has, in fact, persuaded himself that his victim's eye is a symbol of evil and he compares it to the eye of a vulture — one of the images that go to create the atmosphere of the story. The evil and the vulture quality are rather in the madman himself and projected to the outside world — an acute piece of observation on Poe's part at such an early date. The eye is also, further, a symbol of watchful censure that prepares the reader for the murderer's final self-betrayal so that the story does not degenerate into a mere unconvincing "Right will always win." The madman's satisfaction at his victim's terror on the night of the murder is psychologically convincing, while the incident of the ray from the lantern falling on to the old man's eye is dramatically telling and in keeping with the extravagant events narrated here.

The madman's feeling of supreme confidence ("hybris") combines the psychological and dramatic elements of the narrative. It is worth observing, too, in connection with the psychological accuracy of the tale, that the madman revels in the long-drawn terror of his victim and puts off committing the murder for seven nights; the talk of the Evil Eye is plainly to some extent a pretext masking more primitive lusts. On the eighth night, that of the murder, the motif mentioned in the title emerges, at first naturally, but symbolically, in the ticking of the death-watch beetles in the wall, then, departing from the world of naturally observed phenomena, as the beating of the old man's heart that the overacute senses of the madman alone can apprehend. This sound, which is to lead to the murderer's self-betrayal, is at this point in the story the signal for the murder, described briefly but with lurid details that convey insanity at the expense of overstepping the boundary separating the gruesome from the ridiculous ("A tub had caught all [the blood] — ha! ha!"). The heart-beat motif re-emerges even less probably here — it is heard while the victim is being suffocated under a "heavy bed." The police who afterwards arrive do not actively discover the murderer, but simply enable him to reveal himself by means of the heart-beat that has now passed over entirely to the realms of the imagination. As on the previous night the beating becomes intolerably loud, and as he was then impelled to commit murder, so he is now impelled to confess. The Romantic theme of the death-wish has expressed itself here in the form of a punishment and self-betrayal that arise from the moral nature of the criminal.

Commentators like to speak of this story's "influence" on the "stream of consciousness technique" of later writers. "Influence" is difficult to prove without minute investigation, and "stream of consciousness" in the sense of an attempt to reproduce what passes through a character's mind, is as old as story-telling. What can be said on this score is that Poe's story reflects an awareness of hitherto hidden regions of the mind and of the nature of men's motives and moral imperatives such as were becoming apparent to acute observers at the time when this story was written (1843).

1. *Where does Poe reveal his psychological acuteness in this tale?*

   The madman's refusal to recognize his own insanity; the projection of his own evil on the outside world (the old man's "Evil Eye"); the partial recognition of objective reality (the old man is admitted to be harmless); the self-punishment by the moral nature of the criminal himself; the satisfaction and pleasure at killing hinting at primitive lusts of uncivilized man; the enormous and laborious cunning of insanity.

2. *What are the dramatically telling elements in this story?*

   The use of the first person (state of mind and action are communicated at the same time without cumbersome explanation — tautness); the atmosphere of the dark house with death-watch beetles and the lurking murderer; more specifically, the ray of the lantern falling on the "Evil Eye" already dwelt on as the cause of the madman's murderous feelings; the dwelling on the preparation for the murder — the murder itself being disposed of in a few swift lines.

3. *The events in this tale could appear arbitrary. How does Poe attempt to avert this danger?*

By preparing the reader for the denouement. The accusatory "Evil Eye" foreshadows the eventual self-betrayal. The heartbeat motif is prepared for with the deathwatch beetles, after which it becomes less and less probable as an objective phenomenon. After the death of the victim it is confined entirely to the madman's imagination, and leads to his self-betrayal after he has observed with satisfaction that the eye could trouble him no more. The increasingly loud beating of the heart leads, on the first occasion to murder, on the second to discovery of the murder.

4. *Examine the imagery employed in this story.*

The old man's eye is compared to that of a vulture, the ray from the murderer's lantern to a spider's web. The beating of the heart is called a "hellish tattoo." This helps to create the atmosphere of this story and is understood by the reader as a projection of the nightmare mental state of the narrator (advantage of first-person narrative — two birds with one stone).

5. *What associative links connect this story to others by Poe?*

Broadly speaking the themes of murder and madness. Nearly all Poe's stories deal with murder and violent death. "The Cask of Amontillado" repeats the device of having the tale told by the insane murderer. The motive is revenge (in our story there is no normal motive), but the murder itself is far more important than the deed that provoked it. The eye motif occurs elsewhere ("The Black Cat") together with the theme of the apparently successful murderer who betrays himself. The dismemberment of corpses is another favorite motif (notorious are "The Facts in the Case of M. Valdemar" and "The Murders in the Rue Morgue"). The concentration on the psychology of the murderer is a distinguishing feature of this tale. "The Cask of Amontillado" dwells on the details of the murder, while other tales provide a richly described Gothic back-cloth ("The Fall of the House of Usher," "The Gold-Bug").

6. *Comment on Poe's language.*

High-flown as ever. But expressions from melodrama, such as "Villains!... dissemble no more!" seem less incongruous in the mouth of a madman.

W. G. C.

Bodden-Kaußen, *Model Interpretations of Great American Short Stories*, Stuttgart 1970, pp. 62—70 — Gargano, James W., The Question of Poe's Narrators, *College English* XXV, 1963, pp. 177—181; The Theme of Time in "The Tell-Tale Heart," *Studies in Short Fiction* V, 1968, pp. 378—382 — Quinn, Patrick F., *The French Face of Edgar Poe*, Carbondale 1957, pp. 232—236 — Robinson, E. Arthur, Poe's "The Tell-Tale Heart," *Nineteenth-Century Fiction* XIX, 1965, pp. 369—378.

# The Cask of Amontillado

Text: Edgar Allan Poe, *Short Stories and Poems* pp. 27—33. Vandenhoeck

*Fifty years after the incident Montresor, an Italian nobleman, confides to a friend how he revenged himself for the injuries and insults he had suffered from Fortunato. During the carnival season he took advantage of his weak point and lured Fortunato into the vaults of his palazzo in order to sample a cask of Amontillado wine. In the remotest recess of the family catacombs he suddenly chained him to the rock and then walled up the entrance of the small room. He was gratified to hear the screams and pleading of the hated man, but when sudden silence followed, he realized with dismay that he had not achieved the perfect revenge he had hoped for.*

The revenge theme of this story links it with others by Poe — with "The Black Cat" (1843), where the idea of walling up a body had occurred, without the refinement of entombing the victim alive, and with "Hop-Frog" (1849). "The Cask of Amontillado" (1846) lies between the other two revenge stories not only in time but also in treatment of the theme. In "The Black Cat" the murderer is apparently about to escape the consequences of his crime (as in "The Tell-Tale Heart," published in the same year) before he feels compelled to confess his guilt. The compulsion to confession is obviously by no means as strong in "The Cask of Amontillado," in which the narrator tells of his deed some fifty years after the murder. On the other Hand Quinn is obviously wrong when he implies that the murderer is thoroughly satisfied with his vengeance, thus placing the action on a par with the simple sadism of "Hop-Frog."

It is generally believed that none of Poe's stories illustrate his own philosophy of composition better than "The Cask of Amontillado." In a review of Hawthorne's *Twice-Told Tales* (1842) Poe declared that "a skilfull literary artist ... having conceived, with deliberate care, a certain unique or single *effect* to be wrought out ... then invents such incidents — he then combines such events as may best aid him in establishing this preconceived effect. If his very initial sentence tend not to the outbringing of this effect, then he has failed in his first step." And in his later "Philosophy of Composition" (1846) he asserted that "nothing is more clear than that every plot, worth the name, must be elaborated to its *denouement* before anything be attempted with the pen."

Poe has achieved these aims in "The Cask of Amontillado" only if the "effect" and the "denouement" are merely those of a first-rate Gothic story — only if a susceptible reader is expected to feel chills run down his spine and exclaim, "Ugh!" The serious difficulty with this story is that it suggests so much more, but offers nothing more. For once a serious reader becomes alerted to the possibility that a profound psychological and moral study is involved, he is frustrated by the opacity and confused ambiguity of the tale. The fact of the matter is that there are two mutually contradictory, but equally plausible readings beyond the level of Gothic horror: (1) that Montresor, making a confession fifty years after his grisly murder of Fortunato, shows the ultimate effect of his remorse and prays for the soul of his victim; (2) that Montresor, speaking intimately with a confidant, shows that after fifty years he is still galled by the fact that he had failed to achieve the perfect revenge in the murder of Fortunato.

The initial sentence of this story gives us both the motive and intention of Montresor, the narrator; he tells us that when Fortunato added insult to injury he vowed revenge. Hence, "The Cask of Amontillado" is a revenge story, and every step leads brilliantly and ironically to the fulfillment of that revenge. However, unless we know more about Montresor's motives, the story — however brilliantly it is executed — must remain at the level of melodrama. As Montresor leads his victim inexorably toward his doom, their dialogue indirectly reveals something of their relationship to each other. For example, Montresor says, "You are rich, respected, admired, beloved; you are happy, *as once I was*. You are a man to be missed. For me it is no matter." This may suggest that in some way Fortunato is responsible for Montresor's loss of happiness. (Since it is presumably the Lady Fortunato that will miss him, is it possible that Montresor may have been Fortunato's unsuccessful rival for her hand? Poe gives no hint.) Then we get an insight into the sort of injuries that have galled Montresor when Fortunato says that he does not remember Montresor's coat of arms or his family motto and when he declares it impossible that Montresor can have been accorded the honor of admittance to the brotherhood of the Freemasons. These confirmations of the fact that Fortunato does indeed insult Montresor imply that the murderer is not simply a paranoid madman.

Nevertheless, it may be crucially important to the story that Montresor never explains to his victim precisely why he is killing him. For, as in *Hamlet*, where proper revenge also calls for more than simply dispatching one's victim, the goal cited in the very first paragraph is punishment *with impunity*: "A wrong is unredressed when retribution overtakes its redresser. It is equally unredressed when the avenger fails to make himself felt as such to him who has done the wrong." Therefore, at the end, although Fortunato is dead, Montresor has *not* achieved his goal. Before setting the final stone in the wall covering the aperture where Fortunato is chained, Montresor wants a last word with his victim:

... I hearkened in vain for a reply. I grew impatient. I called aloud:
"Fortunato!"
No answer. I called again:
"Fortunato!"
No answer still ... My heart grew sick — on account of the dampness of the catacombs.

Clearly the dampness is not the real reason for his sickness of heart. Had he candidly told the truth, what would he have said? "My heart grew sick with remorse at what I had done"? Possibly. But also possible — and perhaps more in keeping with Poe's "Philosophy of Composition" which says that the opening of a story must lead directly to the conclusion — is that he would have said, "My heart grew sick with the realization that Fortunato was dead before I had a chance to explain to him precisely why he was dying, because 'a wrong is unredressed when the avenger fails to make himself felt as such to him who has done the wrong.'" The fact that the intoxicated Fortunato has submitted so gullibly to Montresor's grisly deception and that, suddenly sober, he tries at the end to laugh it off as a "very good joke, indeed — an excellent jest" clearly suggests that he does not see himself as the object of a justified revenge, but as the victim of a madman who might yet be jollied out of a senseless act. On the first level of ironic inversion, the joke is on the man dressed in motley; but in another sense the joker wins by dying prematurely and thus depriving Montresor of his proper revenge. In the image on Montresor's coat of arms, "the foot crushes a serpent rampant *whose fangs are imbedded in the heel;*" i. e., though Fortunato is crushed, he does, in a sense, bite back!

Such dramatic irony is perfectly in keeping with the story's technique of progression. Three times Montresor pretends to dissuade Fortunato from proceeding any further into the damp catacombs, but continues to ply him with drink and to refer to the rival connoisseur Luchresi, thus goading him on. (Incidentally, it would appear that Fortunato was no genuine connoisseur at all despite the comment that "in the matter of old wines he was sincere," because en route to passing judgment on the Amontillado he guzzles down draught after draught of Medoc and De Grâve, then both cheap wines that would surely diminish the sensitivity of his taste buds.) There is marvellous irony in the dialogue:

"... the cough is a mere nothing; it will not kill me. I shall not die of a cough."
"True — true," I replied ...
. . . . . .
"I drink," he said, "to the buried that repose around us."
"And I to your long life."
. . . . . .
"I forget your arms." ...
"*Nemo me impune lacessit.*"
"Good!" he said.

If we consider that Montresor is still relishing these ironies in telling the tale fifty years after the murder, we must conclude that he is not experiencing remorse. His final utterance, *"In pace requiescat,"* must then be taken as sardonic. Still galled at having been cheated out of a perfect revenge, he is deriving all the satisfaction he can out of his half-century-old cleverness.

But it may simply be that Poe was utterly unaware of this possible interpretation of the story, or that it is merely a technical convention that the narrator while telling about the events that happened fifty years before, temporarily lapses into the attitudes he held then. The gradual growth of the remorse that began when his heart felt sick and concluded with the confession and the prayer, *"In pace requiescat!"* had not begun until Fortunato died.

There is only one clue concerning the audience of Montresor's confession. The second sentence of the story says, "You, who so well know the nature of my soul, will not suppose, however, that I gave utterance to a threat." Here Poe's mathematical precision fails him, for the line does not yield enough data by itself and is not supplemented explicitly or implicitly in any way that leads to secure conclusions. Who would know the nature of the speaker's soul so well? His priest? Is this story, then, by way of a death-bed confession? Possibly, but he goes on to say that anyone who knows his soul would not suppose that he gave advance warning of his intent to kill! Then perhaps he is confessing to an intimate, perhaps his wife, possibly even to the Lady Fortunato herself whom he married after the mysterious disappearance of her husband? Such a situation would be in keeping with the psychology of the confessor and with the cynical ironies of the story, but unfortunately there is insufficient evidence to permit that interpretation. Poe's perfection is as a craftsman of horrifying Gothic effects, and not as an analyst of subtle problems in psychology or morality. Hence, he is fundamentally a second-rate artist.

1. *In what historical period does this story take place?*

> The cynical manipulation of the victim by the murderer, the ironic comments, and the Italian background with carnival costume and palazzo all vaguely suggest the Italy of Macchiavelli. Closer inspection shows that the story takes place in Poe's present. The reference to "British and Austrian millionaires" in the third paragraph makes this plain. The British millionaire was, of course, a characteristic part of the nineteenth-century scene, and Austrian millionaires would also be chosen as examples of the breed because Italians in the 19th century were beginning to resent Austrian rule in Northern Italy. Amontillado is a Spanish wine, a variety of Sherry, while the other wines in Montresor's cellars appear to be French (Médoc, De Grâve). Such a variety of foreign wines argues a late date, and indeed the distinction between Amontillado and other types of Sherry appears to belong to the early 19th century.

2. *What is appropriate about the time-place setting of the story?*

> Carnival season when vitality is celebrated in Rome is an ironic setting for death; it makes credible the absence of the servants, the disguises and masks, the intoxication of Fortunato. That Fortunato wears the conical cap and bells makes him the fool or jester, who ironically does fulfill that role even though it is he that is fooled.

3. *Is there any significance to the names of the characters?*

> They all in one way or another refer to riches: Fortunato = fortune, Montresor = my treasure, and Luchresi = lucre, money. It is not perfectly clear why Poe rang changes on this motif in his name symbolism, except perhaps simply to suggest that all the characters involved belong to the aristocracy.

4. *What evidence, other than his skill in luring Fortunato into the catacombs, is there for Montresor's Iago-like cleverness?*

He had told his servants that he should not return until morning and had given them explicit orders not to stir from the house, knowing that they would immediately disappear as soon as his back was turned.

5. *Is there any progression in the physical contact between the two men in the catacombs?*

Yes. When they first meet, they shake hands warmly. Then as they enter the vaults, "Fortunato possessed himself of my arm." After his first coughing spell, "he again took my arm and we proceeded." As they reach the inmost recesses, "I paused again, and this time I made bold to seize Fortunato by an arm above the elbow." Thus Montresor conditions his victim not to be alarmed at being firmly grasped; hence, he is able to fetter him to the wall quite swiftly and efficiently.

J. V. H./W. G. C.

Foote, Dorothy N., Poe's "The Cask of Amontillado," *The Explicator* XX, 1961, item 27 — Fossum, Richard H., Poe's "The Cask of Amontillado," *The Explicator* XVII, 1958, item 16 — Freehafer, John, Poe's "Cask of Amontillado": A Tale of Effect, *Jahrbuch für Amerikastudien* 13, 1968, pp. 134—142 — Mabbott, Thomas O., Poe's "The Cask of Amontillado," *The Explicator* XXV, 1966, item 30 — Rea, J., Poe's "The Cask of Amontillado," *Studies in Short Fiction* IV, 1966, pp. 57—69 and 266—268.

# KATHERINE ANNE PORTER

Katherine Anne Porter now admits that she was born on May 15, 1890, at Indian Creek, Texas. She was orphaned at an early age and then raised by her grandmother, the most important influence in her life. Having eloped from a convent school in her teens, she has had little formal education, but she has been visiting professor at a number of major universities. She wrote about herself: "As soon as I learned to form letters on paper, at about three years, I began to write stories, and this has been the basic and absorbing occupation, the intact line of my life which directs my actions, determines my point of view, and profoundly affects my character and personality, my social beliefs and economic status, and the kind of friendships I form. I did not choose this vocation ... I made no attempt to publish anything until I was thirty, but I have written and destroyed manuscripts quite literally by the trunkful ..."

She has lived in New Orleans, Chicago, Bermuda, Mexico City, New York, Paris and Berlin. She was married twice, but both times divorced after a few years. In the late 1920's her short stories in the more distinguished literary magazines began to attract attention. In 1931, after the publication of her first collection of short stories, *Flowering Judas*, she received a Guggenheim fellowship for studying abroad. In the thirty years since, she has published two more volumes of short stories, five short novels, and a collection of essays. Her first long novel, *The Ship of Fools*, on which she had been working for 20 years, appeared in 1962. The title is taken from Sebastian Brant's fifteenth-century moral allegory *Das Narrenschiff*. The main theme in it, the budding of evil in the German ethos that permitted Hitler's regime, serves to demonstrate the point "that evil is always done with the collusion of good" — as Miss Porter said in an interview (Washington *Post and Times Herald*, April 1, 1962).

The setting of most of her stories is the south-west of the USA; she is one of the leading representatives of the so-called Southern Renaissance. About her art she wrote: "My one aim is to tell a straight story and to give true testimony. My personal life has been the jumbled and apparently irrelevant mass of experiences which can happen, I think, only to a woman who goes with her mind permanently absent from the place where she is. My physical eyes are unnaturally far-sighted, and I have no doubt this affects my temperament in some way. I have very little time sense and almost no sense of distance or of direction. I lack entirely a respect for money values, and for caste of any kind, social, intellectual, or whatever..." She is considered one of the foremost stylists among American writers and has been compared favorably to Katherine Mansfield, whose work she has praised.

## The Jilting of Granny Weatherall

Text: *American Short Stories* V pp. 93—103. Schöningh

*Mrs. Weatherall, a grandmother nearly eighty years old, is dying. As she was an energetic and tough woman all her life she is surprised to feel dead tired and removed from events. She cannot hear and see clearly any more, and her thinking is interrupted by periods of unconsciousness. Among many memories of her childhood one experience returns to her mind which "for sixty years she had prayed against remembering": as a young bride she had been jilted by her bridegroom on the day of their marriage. Although she had found another husband and had born him five children and lived in a house of her own, a wound remained deep in her heart. Even in her last hour she thinks of her children and her possessions — the things that had helped her to forget for sixty years. But suddenly she realizes that her soul is sinking into complete darkness: there is no sign of God; and with the bitter resentment, "there is nothing more cruel than this," she dies. — The setting of the story is the rural South some time after the Civil War.*

Granny Weatherall has truly "weathered all" — all but the end of life itself, and in this exquisitely shaped story we see her finally achieving the "all." There remains, however, one final, painful disillusionment, the ultimate jilting, to be experienced. For sixty years she had prayed against two things: against remembering that her first fiancé had left her on her wedding day, and "against losing her soul in the deep pit of hell." And now both her prayers fail her. She had been jilted by George and had weathered that with a successful marriage which had helped her to bury the memory; but now she is jilted by God— "again no bridegroom and the priest in the house"—and this jilting she will never forgive.

The story, which was first published in 1929, is magnificently structured. All the lines of force—the realization that she is dying, the memory of her first jilting, and the final awareness of the endless darkness to come—move toward a single, quietly powerful climax. The story progresses from day to night, from light to dark, from hope to despair, from life to death. And the progression is studded with metaphorically charged details: "Her eyes closed of themselves, it was like a dark curtain drawn around the bed"; "The dust that lion could collect in twenty-four hours!" "The lamp was lit, they didn't have to be scared ... She stretched herself with a deep breath and blew out the light."

The theme is one which runs through many of Katherine Anne Porter's eighteen short stories and six novelle (her production is slight only because she destroys everything she writes except that which she feels is as near perfection as she can achieve). James W. Johnson has described it as the theme of "man's slavery to his own nature and subjugation to a human fate which dooms him to suffering and disappointment," as exemplified in "Noon Wine", "Maria Concepción", "Magic", "He", and "Hacienda". And the theme, as another critic, Charles Allen, has said, is "given extraordinary power through a rich and complex characterization. ... Though the characters are typical, recognizable types, they are also particular flesh and bones — somewhat fluid, unpredictable, elusive, contradictory." Granny Weatherall is in many ways a "typical" grandmother, tough, crotchety, and self-sufficient; but like all of us she has a unique, personal past which she hides and a future which she fears. Miss Porter evokes both with beautiful artistry, giving us the hard-fact details of the death-bed scene and the equally hard-fact details of the rich, full life she has lived. It is all rendered as a single experience. But the distinguishing mark of this story is the compressed, poetic presentation, one step removed, of Granny Weatherall's stream of consciousness. The poignancy of her experience never lapses into sentimentality; it is embodied and objectified in form and language that we can contemplate with the joy of insight into truth.

1. *Who tells the story?*

> A narrator observing and reporting the stream of consciousness of the central character.
> 
> *From whose point of view?*
> Strictly from the point of view of the dying woman.
> 
> *Does the author ever intrude with information not immediately and directly available to Granny Weatherall?*
> No. Every sentence with a "she" referring to Granny Weatherall could be changed to an "I".

2. *Are exposition and dramatic action separate elements?*

No, exposition is dramatically embodied as the crucial reminiscences of Granny W.
*How old is Granny W.?*
Nearly 80 — see third paragraph, p. 93.
*How many children does she have?*
Five — see bottom of p. 98; her first son is significantly named after her first fiancé.
*About how old are they?*
The youngest, Cornelia, who is looking after her, is already married. The oldest, Hapsy, has been dead for a long time — cf. last paragraph, p. 99. Twenty years before, she had taken farewell trips to see her children *and grandchildren* — cf. p. 95. Thus, her children must now be at least in their mid- or late forties, all now older than their father was when he died — cf. p. 96.
*Who is absent from the death-bed?*
Hapsy, who is dead.
*How old is the doctor?*
In his 30's — see last paragraph p. 93.
*How is all this information conveyed to the reader?*
Not through mechanical exposition, but through clues given in dramatic dialogue and dramatically functional reminiscences.

3. *When Granny W. insists that "there's nothing wrong with me," how soon and from what details can we know that she is wrong?*

By the end of. p. 93, we know that she is very old and very ill. The "not that she was tired" on p. 94 is plainly a rationalization. First explicit reference to her facing the possibility of death is on p. 95. When the spirit of Hapsy welcomes her to death, the reader can be certain that she will die — cf. p. 99.
*When does she realize the truth?* On bottom of p. 102.

4. *"It was good to have everything clean and folded away," she thinks, and she has carefully folded away the memory of her having been jilted. But the memory becomes more and more vivid and painful as we approach the climax of the story. Trace the specific steps by which it is developed.*

When Granny W. refers to George's letters, which she doesn't want her children to see (p. 95), the attentive reader will remain alert to have him identified. But the thought is rigidly suppressed until p. 98 — "It's bitter to lose things ... For sixty years she had prayed against remembering him." And there comes the first reference to a jilting. Then the remembrances come more frequently and explicitly; "she had changed her mind after sixty years and she would like to see George" — p. 100 —; "What if he did run away and leave me to face the priest by myself?" — p. 102 —; "Again no bridegroom and the priest in the house" — p. 103.

5. *What is the first reference to God and religion?*

"... thank God there was always a little margin over for peace; then a person could spread out the plan of life and tuck in the edges orderly" — p. 94.

*What other references follow? How are they merged with references to the first jilting?*
Like the references to George, these are suppressed until we begin to approach the end. "God, for all my life I thank thee" — p. 97 — is, like the first reference to God, ironic. "She prayed against losing her soul..." — p. 98; "a shuffle of leaves in the everlasting hands of God" — p. 99. Father Connelly arrives — p. 100 — to administer the last rites, and the cluster of religious references is thick to the end.

*What is the double meaning of "bridegroom" in the last paragraph?*
The bridegroom is, of course, both George and Christ — cf. Matthew, Chapter 25, 1—13. There was a priest in the house for both the wedding and the death, but the proper bridegroom did not appear on either occasion.

6. *In what ways does the story function as a poem? Cite some representative images, similes, and metaphors.*

By the compression of a complex life experience and the metaphoric merging of various elements of that experience into a single unity. "Tuck in the edges [of life] orderly" (p. 94) is a perfect image for a housewife; "... like a dark curtain drawn around the bed" (p. 94); the modulation of leaves rustling to newspapers swishing to voices whispering (p. 94) is a microcosmic example of the large, experiential modulations of the entire story. Rummaging around in the attic for letters and finding death (p. 95); "A fog rose over the valley ... time to go in and light the lamps" (p. 97) is a metaphor of approaching death fended off by light, and it is a basic poetic element of the story (see ending); "pick all the fruit this year and see that nothing is wasted" (p. 97) is metaphoric for living a rich, full life; Hapsy, who had evidently died in childbirth, welcomes her mother to death (p. 99); agony of birth equated metaphorically with agony of death (p. 100) and emphasizes the poignant cosmic pessimism of the entire story; storm (p. 102) equals fog (p. 97); unfinished chores (p. 103) make ironic the demand for neatness in life (p. 94); and the merging of light, wedding, death, and religious images draws the poetic elements to a final unity as the story ends.

7. *Is there an explicit moral?* No. *Is there an implicit one?*

The implicit moral seems to be that the universe has no order, the proper bridegroom never comes — to expect him will inevitably lead to cruel disillusionment. Perhaps, however, it is possible to live a full, rich life with a substitute, a human adjustment with human love that can compensate for the lack of a divine one. But such a reading is only very tenuously suggested and must not be stressed so strongly as to minimize the basic pessimism of the story.

J. V. H.

Becker, Laurence A., "The Jilting of Granny Weatherall": The Discovery of Pattern, *English Journal* LV, 1966, pp. 1164—1169 — Hoffman, F. J., *The Art of Southern Fiction: A Study of Some Modern Novelists*, Carbondale 1967, pp. 39—50 — Weber, Robert W. Porter, "The Jilting of Granny Weatherall," *Die amerikanische Kurzgeschichte*, eds. Göller/Hoffmann, Düsseldorf 1972, pp. 216—224 — Wiesenfarth, Joseph, Internal Opposition in Porter's "The Jilting of Granny Weatherall," *Critique* XI, 1969, pp. 47—55.

# The Old Order

Text: *Twentieth Century American Novelists* pp. 13—20. Hirschgraben (shortened by more than one third)
Katherine Anne Porter, *The Old Order:* Ten Stories of the South, Harvest Books HB 6 (95 cents), pp. 11—33

*In the story an idea of 'The Old Order' in the Southern States is developed in a large number of reminiscences from the life of Grandmother Sophia Jane. Like Katherine Anne Porter's own grandmother, she is the great-granddaughter of Kentucky's most famous pioneer, and the daughter of a notably heroic captain in the War of 1812. After her husband's death Grandmother moves to Louisiana first, then to Texas and raises her family of nine children there. Her role becomes that of authority administered according to a fixed code. With the new generation of grandchildren growing up, Grandmother's quaint old-fashioned ways tend to cause her family acute discomfort. In her love of the past she has a like-minded companion in her Negro maid Nannie, who has been with her since her fifth year.*

"The Old Order" (from *The Leaning Tower*, 1944) is not a short story by any ordinary definition of the term, but Katherine Anne Porter is never one for ordinary definitions of any terms. Ordinarily, of course, we expect a short story to have a *plot*. Miss Porter despises that requirement. Recalling that one of the most beautiful stories she had ever read anywhere was rejected by the author's agent with a merry little note, "No plot, my dear, — no *story*. Sorry," Miss Porter registers a snort against plots:

"There are all sorts of schools that can teach you exactly how to handle the 197 variations on any one of the 37 basic plots... They can teach you the O. Henry twist... But there are surer and much more honest ways of making money... Except in emergencies, when you are trying to manufacture a quick trick and make some easy money, you don't really need a plot...

A short story needs *first* a *theme*, and then a point of view, a certain knowledge of human nature and strong feeling about it, and style — that is to say, his own special way of telling a thing that makes it precisely his own and no one else's... The greater the theme and the better the style, the better the story, you might say." (*The Days Before*, pp. 134—35.)

The theme of "The Old Order" is, of course, the title. Miss Porter has always been attracted to it; in 1944 she published an essay, "Portrait: Old South" which was also a celebration of her grandmother, and in 1961, nearing the end of her long career, she announced, "I would like to write about two wonderful old slaves who were my grandmother's companions, but someone is always giving a low name to good things and I suppose the N. A. A. C. P.[1] would say I was glorifying Uncle Tomism." (*Time*, July 28, 1961, p. 65.) —

---

[1] National Association for the Advancement of Colored People.

Lumber has no grain; only an individual piece of wood, a board, shows a grain. History is like lumber; only the individual character has grain. (Unfortunately, much of the detail is removed in the cut version of *Twentieth Century American Novelists*, Hirschgraben, 1960.)

The opening passage reveals Grandmother and old Nannie, her devoted former slave, "cutting scraps of the family finery, hoarded for fifty years, into strips and triangles, and fitting them together again in a carefully disordered patchwork." There could be no more perfect analogue to what Katherine Anne Porter is doing — cutting and reshaping scraps of family history. And many a modern reader responds exactly as do the grandchildren "who had arrived at the awkward age when Grandmother's quaint old-fashioned ways caused them acute discomfort."

Grandmother is, of course, the Old South — resentful of change, eager to preserve the fixed code of the past even though the past had been bitter. Nannie, the ancient Negro, had lived a lifetime without making any decisions of her own; hence, in her view of the past as in all matters of policy "she had all her life obeyed the authority nearest to her." But there is an enormous difference in the ways they remember the past: for Grandmother the *abstract pattern* has paramount importance ("masses of dates in her mind, and no memories attached to them"), but for Nannie the *detailed individual experience* without reference to any particular order dominates her memory. Except for this basic difference in their attitudes toward history, the two women are alike in being "firm, critical, and unbewildered" on such subjects as religion, the decline of the world, the decay of behavior, and youth. Friendship is not strong enough a word and love is too passionate a word to describe the relationship of the imperious grand dame of the declined aristocracy and the black woman who was given to her as a gift when, at the age of five, she had pointed to the scrawny bright-eyed pickaninny and had demanded, "I want that little monkey." Like positive and negative electrons, these two opposite elements of a vanished way of life clung to each other, each supporting and confirming the other's past and, hence, the other's existence. Not so much affection, but interdependence bound them together.

At opposite ends of the social scale, they grew up together, married together, "started their grim and terrible race of procreation" together, watched their children marry and die together, while they refused to die. The specific episodes are described in vivid detail in the text, and need not be recalled here. What must be stressed is the characterization. Allen Tate has observed that in Katherine Anne Porter's stories "character is taken as a fixed and inviolable entity, predictable only in so far as a familiarity may be said to make him so, and finally unique as the center of inexhaustible depths of feeling and action." The two central characters of "The Old Order" are not merely illustrative abstractions on which to hang an account of the old South; they are people of integrity and judgment who rule if they can, but who will never be ruled — neither by prejudice nor by social custom. For example, would anyone expect that a Negro raised in slavery would turn to her white mistress and say of a white judge: "Look lak a jedge might had better raisin'... Look lak he didn't keer how much he hurt a body's feeling" — and to hear the mistress apologize for the judge? Or — and such is the power of Katherine Anne Porter's calmly assertive style that we are neither shocked nor incredulous — would anyone ordinarily believe that a Southern white mistress would, despite the protest of her husband and her mother, suckle at her own breast the black baby of her slave when that slave is too ill to do so herself? (One wonders what led to the suppression of this episode in the Hirschgraben edition.) The outstanding trait of these people is their dogged preservation of vitality. To be raised in grandeur, to lose it in war, to be plunged into poverty, to become displaced persons — these have become all too commonplace experiences in the twentieth century. Grandmother and Nannie bear it as the elementally strong have always done. As Miss Porter describes her own grandmother in the essay, "Portrait: The Old South":

> "The long difficulties of her life she regarded as temporary, an unnatural interruption to her normal fate, which simply required firmness, a good deal of will power and energy and the proper aims to re-establish finally once more. That no such change took place during her long life did not in the least disturb her theory."

Her vitality is active to the final moment of her life: "Grandmother came into the house quite flushed and exhilarated, saying how well she felt in the bracing mountain air — and dropped dead over the doorsill."[1] No sentimentality, no melodrama, no labored explanation or apology; instead, a direct rendering of character and event with complete assurance that the design of the grain has value and interest to the discerning reader. Other readers do not matter.

1. *In terms of "The Old Order" describe the three elements — theme, point of view, and style — that Miss Porter claims are essential to a short story.*

    *Theme:* a complex one, involving social and individual forces, the preservation of vitality and individuality in the face of social and historical opposition and the passage of time.
    *Point of view:* objective, but not dispassionate; presenting the broad sweep of events with a panoramic view, focusing occasionally on some particularly significant dramatic event.
    *Style:* Predominantly the voice of the narrator, speaking calmly, expanding and contracting narrative elements as she goes along, frequently mimicking the voice of her characters in especially dramatic situations.
    a) Example of narrator's own voice: "She dreamed recurrently that she had lost her virginity (her virtue, she called it), her sole claim to regard, consideration, even to existence, and after frightful moral suffering which masked altogether her physical experience she would wake in a cold sweat, disordered and terrified."

---

[1] "dead" has to be inserted in the German school edition.

b) Example of narration in indirectly presented voice of character: "It was not that there was anything seriously damaging to be said against any of them; only — well, she wondered at her son's tastes. What had each of them found in the wife he had chosen?"

2. *Is the grandmother a lovable old woman?*
No.
*Does the narrator love her?*
Yes.
*Explain.*

It is not simply that the "Grandmother's quaint old-fashioned ways cause [her grandchildren] acute discomfort," but that she is a strongwilled woman absolutely certain that her way is best and must be imposed on those about her, if possible. On the other hand, the ways of those about her are obviously wrong — socially, economically, and morally. The history of the American South proves that. Nevertheless, Grandmother's integrity is strong enough to tolerate opposition from those with an equally strong will and integrity of their own. She never issues ultimatums or threats, never seeks revenge; she is scrupulously fair in providing educations, dowries, inheritances, etc., for her children. And her relationship with Nannie is, for its time and place, probably the very finest kind of Negro-white association ever depicted in American literature. (These things are not explicitly stated in the narrative, but such beliefs and judgments obviously guided the selection of details that went into the story.)

3. *What philosophy of life informs the narrative?*

Katherine Anne Porter is an existentialist of the school of Albert Camus; this is not to say that she deliberately shaped her public utterances to conform with Camus', but those values are implicit in almost everything she has written. The grandmother lives in a universe whose values she cannot fully accept, but she has a job to do and gets on with it as best she can: "they had questioned the burdensome rule they lived by every day of their lives, but without rebellion and without expecting an answer. This unbroken thread of inquiry in their minds contained no doubt as to the utter rightness and justice of the basic laws of human existence, founded as they were on God's plan; but they wondered perpetually, with only a hint now and then to each other of the uneasiness of their hearts, how so much suffering and confusion could have been built up and maintained on such a foundation ... Her own doubts and hesitations she concealed ... she reminded herself, as a matter of duty."

J. V. H.

Emmons, Winfred S., *Katherine Anne Porter: The Regional Stories*, Austin 1967, pp. 10—12 — Mooney, Harry John, *The Fiction and Criticism of Katherine Anne Porter*, Pittsburgh 1957, pp. 17—19 — Nance, William L., *Katherine Anne Porter and the Art of Rejection*, Chapel Hill 1964, pp. 88—100 — West, Ray B., Jr., Katherine Anne Porter and "Historic Memory," *Southern Renascence*, ed. by Louis D. Rubin, Jr., and Robert D. Jacobs, 1953.

# Holiday

Text: K. A. Porter, *Holiday*. Velhagen

*A sensitive young woman is advised by a friend to forget her troubles by spending a spring holiday on a farm of German peasants in Texas. In the course of a few weeks she gets well acquainted with the large family and its patriarchal way of life. There is birth, marriage and death on the farm while she is there, she watches healthy and crippled life and is drawn into reflections on life and death which make her forget her own troubles.*

Katherine Anne Porter's fiction has generally impressed critics as embodying an essentially negative view of life. "Incomprehension and incompatibility — these are her governing themes," says Vernon A. Young; "usually her theme is the betrayal of life through the hostility that develops if physical and social needs are repeatedly and consistently frustrated," says Charles A. Allen; "Miss Porter's world is a black and tragic one, filled with disaster, heartbreak, and soul-wrecking disillusionment," says James William Johnson. But Miss Porter's latest story, "Holiday," which was published in December 1960, reveals her tragic perspective in a new light.

Like many first-person narratives, this is a double story: it is a richly detailed, naturalistic account of German peasant life in the remote plains of Texas ("my South, my loved and neverforgotten country"), and it is the epiphany experience of a young woman who goes there to escape certain undefined personal troubles, but gains instead a profound insight into the human condition. The unnamed narrator seeks the advice of a former schoolmate, Louise, about an inexpensive place for a spring holiday and receives an enthusiastic description of the Müller farm. Louise, however, was famous for "amusing stories that did not turn grim on you until a little while later, when by chance you saw and heard for yourself." Such phrasing understates the grimness of the experience she is about to have.

She arrives at the "sodden platform of a country station" and is taken on a "broken-down spring wagon" through "soaked brown fields" along "scanty leafless woods" to the "gaunt and aching ugliness" of a farmhouse where she is to occupy the attic room. Her gloomy forebodings are dissipated when she shakes hands with each member (except one) of the bustling, energetic Müller family as they stream out of the house for their evening chores. "These were solid, practical, hard-bitten, landholding German peasants who stuck their mattocks into the deep earth and held fast wherever they were, because to them life and the land were one indivisible thing..."

They include the patriarchal Father Müller, who reads *Das Kapital*, refuses "to pay a preacher goot money to talk his nonsense," and invariably wins at chess; strong-boned Mother Müller, who is worshiped by her children; three sons — Hans, Fritz, and one unnamed; three daughters — Annetje, Gretchen, and Huldah (Hatsie); two sons-in-law, soon to be joined by a third; and eight grandchildren under the age of ten. As Louise said, "everybody was so healthy and good-hearted," and the narrator becomes absorbed by "the hysterical inertia of their minds in the midst of this muscular life." She is sure that "there could be nothing here more painful than what I had left," but she does not reckon with Ottilie, "a crippled and badly deformed servant girl," a mute whose "whole body was maimed in some painful, mysterious way."

The movement of the story becomes a rhythmic counterpoint between the sequence of marriage, birth, and death in the Müller family and the gradually increasing intensity and intimacy of the narrator's relations with Ottilie. The more she becomes absorbed with the vital, elemental family life, the more she forgets her old troubles; but the more she gets to know Ottilie, the closer she comes to a staggering realization of a fundamental truth of life. At her first supper with the family she notices Ottilie: "no one moved aside for her, or spoke to her, or even glanced after her when she vanished into the kitchen" after serving the meal. And like everyone else, she, too, soon ignores Ottilie. After a *Turnverein* dance, it is announced that Hatsy will be married the following Sunday. There is a tremendous wedding at which Ottilie serves the guests. "Her face was a brown smudge of anxiety, her eyes were wide and dazed. Her uncertain hands rattled among the pans, but nothing could make her seem real, or in any way connected with the life around her."

But the next morning, Ottilie does a remarkable thing; she pulls the narrator by the sleeve to her dingy, bitter-smelling, windowless room and produces a faded yellow photograph of a pretty, smiling, five-year-old German girl — Ottilie! "For an instant some filament lighter then cobweb spun itself out between that living center in her and in me, a filament from some center that held us all bound to our inescapable, common source, so that her life and mine were kin, even a part of each other, and the painfulness and strangeness of her vanished." For some time thereafter, the narrator suffers a tortured perplexity as she observes the family, so kind to each other and even to the animals about the farm, remaining indifferent to their own flesh in the horribly grotesque and misshapen Ottilie. She even wishes that Ottilie might die at once rather than keep on cooking and serving for that cruelly insensitive family. But gradually she adjusts and even comes to see that the Müllers "with a deep right instinct had learned to live with her disaster on its own terms."

A lesser artist would have ended the story here, but Katherine Anne Porter continues to tighten the tension to a tremendous burst of insight. Some time later Gretchen bears a child, but a storm cuts short the celebrations. Lightning, thunderbursts, and flood assault the farm, driving the entire family into heroic efforts at salvaging goods and chattels. The mother, who had hoisted a calf to the hayloft and milked the cows in the rising water, collapses and dies, as the weeping father shouts, "A hundert tousand tollars in the bank . . . and tell me, tell, what goot does it?" Two days later the neighbors join the muddy procession to the cemetery, as the narrator lies numbly in her attic room. In a half-sleep she hears the howling of a dog, goes to the kitchen to discover that it is Ottilie, who, left behind, apparently longs to join the mother's funeral procession. The narrator manages to harness a pony to a dilapidated wagon and tries to take Ottilie through the churned mud to the cemetery. At this human gesture of communion with her, Ottilie "gave a choked little whimper, and suddenly she laughed out, a kind of yelp but unmistakably laughter, and clapped her hands for joy, the grinning mouth and suffering eyes turned to the sky." The narrator realizes that it is hopeless either to try to get to the cemetery or to expect that the ceremony there and its concomitant family unit could possibly include Ottilie, and she turns back. "Ottilie was beyond my reach as well as any other human reach, and yet, had I not come nearer to her than I had to anyone else...? Well, we were both equally the fools of life, equally fellow fugitives from death."

The meaning of "Holiday" is exactly that of all the fiction of Albert Camus (as an artist, Katherine Anne Porter is as superior to Camus as she is his inferior as an eloquent philosopher). It is simply this: that man lives in a universe without shape or meaning. He is therefore obligated to project a meaning, to shape and form his own life in an effort that is ultimately doomed since it will end with death and chaos. But while he is making the effort, he can be sustained by love — even love for a twisted, mute, half-beast of a human being like Ottilie. Since we are all prisoners of the universe together, let us love one another.

It is a meaning dramatized, but the drama is filtered through the consciousness of a sensitive, searching young woman who is quite a contrast with the nature-bound Müllers. The Müllers are not detached enough from nature to be able to contemplate it or extract a meaning of life from it. The narrator, however, is alienated not only from the land but from the society of the land. She does not understand Plattdeutsch, and hence feels a sense of "freedom from the constant pressure of other minds and other opinions and other feelings, that freedom to fold up in quiet and go back to my own center..." The story is therefore a process of discovery of the essential humanity at the center of herself, and as she says in the opening paragraph her former troubles are no longer important: "It no longer can matter what kind of troubles they were, or what finally became of them."

1. *By what device does the narrative gain a cosmic significance?*

> By the firm and detailed natural setting, and especially the season when the "moribund coma" of nature comes to an end and "the earth revives and bursts into the plenty of spring with fruit and flowers together"; and by the life cycle of birth, marriage, and death that various members of the Müller family endure.

2. *What symbolic details are embodied in the story?*

> The detailed description of the harness and the wagon symbolize man's inadequate adjustment to nature; the cheap literature of escape (Ouida, Ella Wheeler Wilcox, etc.) stored in the attic of a house where real life goes on; the predominance of animal imagery in the story seems to underline the essentially animal quality of life among the Müllers. Even small details have large significance: at the wed-

ding ceremony, Ottilie's hand is steady — "when I set my pitcher on the stove, she lifted the heavy kettle and poured the scalding water into it without spilling a drop"; at the funeral ceremony "Ottilie brought in a fresh pot of coffee ... and when she spilled some on her own hand, she did not seem to feel it." Even Ottilie's name is unusual, whereas the names of other members of this German family are far more common. Perhaps Miss Porter had in mind the Ottilie Home for Crippled Children in New York (an obvious juxtaposition of *Ottilie* and *crippled*) named after the saint in Alsace, who was born blind but whose sight was restored on baptism.

3. *What important ironies and contrasts are built into the story?*

Among others, there is the immense contrast between Louise's account of life on the Müller farm and the observations of the narrator; "everybody was so healthy," Louise had said, apparently forgetting — like everyone else — the existence of Ottilie. Even the "darling little puppy," Kuno, is seen as "an enormous black dog of the detestable German shepherd breed ... an ugly beast."
The tender care given to the animals (which reaches the ultimate consequence when the mother in effect sacrifices her own life to rescue a calf during the storm) contrasts powerfully with the utter neglect and indifference which Ottilie suffers. This is heavily underscored in the last lines of the story: "There would be plenty of time for Ottilie to have supper ready. They need not even know she had been gone." The irony here is immense and bitter.
The father's dogmatic acceptance of the principles of *Das Kapital* contrasts ironically with the fact that he is the wealthiest man in his community and has renters and share-croppers. He even uses his economic power to get his son-in-law elected sheriff, but has self-protective rationalizations for all his violations of principle.

4. *Why is there no explanation for the troubles that provoked the narrator into fleeing to the Müller farm?*

Because after what she has experienced there — and remember that the story is told in retrospect — they are no longer very important.

5. *Would you describe the tone and style as "hard-boiled" or as "sentimental"?*

Neither. The tone is one of carefully controlled, though highly-charged, emotion. Important statements are made quite straight-forwardly, without an overweighting of unnecessary adjectives and adverbs: "she was no stranger to me and could not be again," "she [Annetje] seemed to have forgotten that Ottilie was her sister," and "her whole body was a mere machine of torture." This style is perfect and in itself serves as an analogue to the resigned compassion that characterizes the author's new-found outlook on life.

J. V. H.

Emmons, Winfred S., *Katherine Anne Porter: The Regional Stories*, Austin 1967, pp. 34—36 — Hartley, Lodwick and Core, eds., *Katherine Anne Porter: A Symposium*, Athens, Georgia, 1969, pp. 149—158; 213 — Hendrick, George, *Katherine Anne Porter*, New York 1965, pp. 108—111.

# JAMES F. POWERS

James Farl Powers was born on July 8, 1917, in Jacksonville, Illinois, and spent his youth in that state. He attended different denominational schools and studied with the Franciscans at Quincy College Academy. After his graduation he was employed in book-stores in Chicago, and published his first stories at that time (1943) in *Accent,* a literary quarterly. His short story "Lions, Harts, Leaping Does" was selected for the *O. Henry Prize Stories of 1944*. With this single story Powers won recognition as a young writer of extraordinary skill and promise. In 1947 a first collection of eleven stories appeared under the title *Prince of Darkness and Other Stories*. In 1948 he was awarded a Guggenheim Fellowship and in the same year received a grant from the National Institute — American Academy of Arts and Letters. Other literary awards followed in the 50's. In 1956 he published a second volume of short stories, *The Presence of Grace,* and in 1962, his first novel, *Morte d'Urban,* which won the National Book Award in 1963. In creating his fictional Order of St. Clement in this novel Powers confirmed Frank O'Connor's judgment that he is "among the greatest living story-tellers."

In his most successful stories he has drawn heavily upon his Catholic background, and his portraits of the life of the Catholic clergy are outstanding for their wry humor and their brilliant perceptions. He is one of the few Catholic writers who can write about the Catholic church without restraint. Seeing it as an institution of divine origin, he feels no necessity to insist on its servants being infallible. They offer him an opportunity to study human nature on the background of the moral demands of their faith.

## The Forks

Text: James F. Powers, *The Forks and The Trouble* pp. 5—20. Schöningh

*Monsignor William Francis Xavier Sweeney and his young curate Father Eudex live together in the rectory of an unnamed community in one of the eastern states. They are of very different dispositions — Father Eudex is of rural origin, contented with a frugal life and always willing to help others, Monsignor is ambitious and pretentious, his friends are rich and he admonishes Father Eudex for his clumsy table manners (he doesn't know how to use the different kinds of forks in a meal). He even suspects him of Communist tendencies. He thinks the prestige of the Church demands that a priest should drive an elegant car and should not disgrace himself by doing rough work. He happily accepts money from the excess-profits of a big firm whereas Father Eudex tears up the check, regarding it as "hush money." When Father Eudex advises a rich woman to give her money to the poor, he finds out that she had come to him for a broker's tip. He wishes to be a real priest, but he finds himself unwanted and even threatened with the prospect of being sent back for another year of study in a seminary.*

"The Forks" is neither a story about "the endless struggle between religious idealism and selfish worldly interests,"[1] nor about "the intense difficulty of being sure of the quality of one's actions."[2] Critics have been misled by the fact that the story has a priest and a monsignor as its central characters and by the fact that its irony is subtler than it seems. Essentially Powers has shaped a social conflict in a religious setting that makes necessary a close association between men of contrasting power and opposing views. The values of *both* Father Eudex and Monsignor Sweeney are class values — proletarian versus capitalistic; religious issues play only an incidental role. Theological or doctrinal questions do not arise, for Powers has rendered the conflict within the church in terms that make it equal to class conflict within any social institution.

However, even though his characters clearly represent diametrically opposed views of what constitutes the social good, they are not mere abstract symbols. This is true in spite of the fact that there isn't a single word describing their physical appearance — height, weight, color of eyes, etc. Concreteness and individuality are achieved by telling nuances of detail in the dialogue (the Monsignor's pompous quoting of Latin clichés: "Damnant quod non intelligunt," contrasted with the priest's charged use of slang: "I guess hush money ... is lousy") and dramatic gestural details ("Monsignor ... gave the rear left fender an amorous chuck and eased into the front seat" versus "Father Eudex [spading up crosses] removed his coat first, then his collar, and finally was down to his undershirt").

The author presents everything from the perspective of Father Eudex, without explicitly taking his part but with obvious sympathy. No judgments are *pronounced*, for Father Eudex "could hear ... others ... giving an account of their stewardship, but could not judge them," but judgments from the point of view of the young priest are strongly implicit in almost every dialogue and segment of the action. Even the idiom of the narrator is that of Father Eudex: "Monsignor's car ... was long and black and new *like a politician's*." In fact, the entire story could easily be converted into an "I-narrative" by substituting the first person pronoun every time Father Eudex is cited as the speaker or meditator (cf. K. A. Porter, "The Jilting of Granny Weatherall"). Since this is so, it is clear that the narrator identifies with the young priest.

The sequence of events is symmetrically arranged in a balanced structure, with Father Eudex's long meditation at the center:

| EUDEX=MSGR DIALOGUE | + | EUDEX=WORKER | + | EUDEX=MSGR DIALOGUE | + | EUDEX=INVESTOR | + | EUDEX=MSGR DIALOGUE |
|---|---|---|---|---|---|---|---|---|
| (with subtle revolt) | | (with open revolt) | | MEDITATION | | | | (with symbolic revolt and defeat) |

---

[1] Current-Garcia and Patrick, *American Short Stories*, NY 1952, p. 619
[2] Heilmann, *Modern Short Stories*, NY 1950, p. 337

The opening dozen lines of the story already embody the basic conflict and the characterizations in swift, sure strokes. We know at once that Father Eudex is a hard-working priest who suffers insult and abuse with patience; he has been to say mass at an orphanage, prepares to say his priestly office, and responds to the monsignor's snide query about the treatment of his car with a calm, "No trouble, Monsignor." The Monsignor, on the other hand, is a pompous ass ("For a moment Monsignor stood framed in the screen door, fumbling his watch fob as for a full-length portrait") whose first remark is neither a polite greeting nor an enquiry about the orphanage, but a concern for his sumptuous new automobile which he significantly refers to as "she."

It soon becomes evident (in the dialogue concerning the model-A Ford that the young priest wants to buy in order to make his sick calls and trips to the orphanage without suffering the noblesse oblige of the Monsignor or "Bumming rides from the parishioners") that their conflict is between the *functional* and *symbolic* values. The Monsignor is primarily concerned with appearances (with what Thorsten Veblen in *The Theory of the Leisure Class* labeled as "conspicuous consumption"), and with the good opinion of such parishioners as Mr. Memmers, president of the First National Bank. Father Eudex assumes that it is not merely pride but futile ambition — to become bishop — that motivates the Monsignor, and he baits the Monsignor by horrifying him with the rumor that the current "crazy" and "socialistic" bishop (obviously a reference to the late Bishop Shiel of Chicago) is to be the next archbishop. This constitutes Father Eudex's subtle rebellion and ends the first phase of the story.

There follows a sharp contrast in the behavior of the two men of the cloth. While the Monsignor drives grandly off through traffic halted by a policeman (until recently the largest proportion of policemen in America's northern cities were Irish and presumably Catholic), the young priest helps the overworked janitor dig up a huge formal garden ordered by the Monsignor. Again, the functional versus the symbolic — the Monsignor proposes, the priest disposes. Father Eudex's shoveling dirt with Joe Whalen expresses his identity with the working classes — *he* can address the janitor as "Joe" in honest camaraderie, but from the mouth of the Monsignor it is presumptuous: "Whalen turned in on himself. 'Joe — is it!'" The young priest resents the Monsignor's command that he not labor any more in the garden ("It's not prudent"), but he submits to authority just as he submitted to his Aunt Hazel when he was a child ("I can't come out and play this afternoon, Joe, on account of my monsignor won't let me").

The middle dialogue between the two men brings the conflict to a crisis and to Father Eudex's open revolt: "the Monsignor . . . had broken wild curates before . . . and he would ride again." He might get rid of the young priest by sending him off to a university but "with your tendencies . . . and with the universities honeycombed with Communists . . . that would never do." In a long meditation Father Eudex recalls all the insults and abuses he had suffered from the Monsignor who thoroughly disapproved of his manners and his social values; "he found Father Eudex reading *The Catholic Worker* one day and had not trusted him since." The crux of their conflict is symbolically focused in "the forks" of the title. Father Eudex simply did not know and did not care to know the table etiquette of high society and had consistently ignored all the silverware except a single knife, spoon and fork. As the discussion came to the disposition of the checks distributed to members of the Church by one of the large corporations (an act which Father Eudex interpreted to mean outright bribery for the Church's support in political-economic matters and a technique for tax-evasion), the curate "placed his knife next to his fork on the plate, adjusted them this way and that until they seemed to work a combination in his mind, to spring a lock which in turn enabled him to speak out." He then announced that he would refuse to accept the money and might even endorse it to the labor union strikers' relief fund. It should be clear at this point that the central conflict of the story is concerned with social values and not with religion or self-doubt. Though his superior remonstrates with him, the priest is adamant and "the Monsignor took leave of Father Eudex with a laugh." That laugh is a sure sign to the priest that the monsignor is confident of ultimate triumph.

While the Monsignor is taking a nap, a widow of the parish comes to consult the church on an important matter and Father Eudex interrupts the reading of his office to talk with her. After revealing her anti-Semitic prejudices by carefully explaining that her name, Klein, is not a "Jew name" (it is significant that the story was written in the 1940's when Hitlerian anti-Semitism was at its height), she makes it clear that she wants advice on how to best invest her excess money for a profitable return. When Father Eudex gives her the classic Christian advice to give it to the poor, she is highly indignant and asks to see his "boss." After telling her to return in the evening when the Monsignor can no doubt give her the kind of information she wants, the priest goes up to his room. He answers his superior's enquiry, "Who was it?" with the bitterly ironic, "A woman seeking good counsel." He tears up the corporation check and flushes it down the toilet, but this act of revolt is heavily charged with a sense of frustration and defeat. "He went to his room and stood looking out the window *at nothing*"; he has nothing to show for his efforts, in his own terms or in the Church's. Though he cannot judge other Church officials for their various compromises and justifications in spending the money for good causes, his own act is implicit condemnation. *Any* use of the "hush money" is a cooperation with capitalistic exploitation of the workers. There is an ironic contrast of his thinking that he "could not judge them" with the Monsignor's earlier warning that he must watch his behavior: "*Damnant quod non intelligunt.*"

It is not true, as Heilman (l. c.) claims, that "'The Forks' does not have a plot in the conventional sense of the word." There is a clear line of movement from conflict to complication to crisis to climax, defeat, and denouement — all quite traditional.

1. *Is the story anti-religious or anti-Catholic?*

    Neither. The religious values of both the central characters are projected in strictly social terms, and although the young priest is defeated his defeat is a personal one. Monsignor Sweeney's point of view is clearly not that of the Church, for above him in the hierarchy is the "crazy bishop," whose social values he despises.

2. *In what various ways is the contrast between Father Eudex's functional values and Monsignor Sweeney's symbolical values manifested?*

    First in their attitude toward automobiles; an old cheap model-A which he could repair himself if necessary would be good enough for Father Eudex, but the Monsignor is primarily concerned with the impression to be made on "the class of people we got here." When the Monsignor wants a magnificent new garden, he draws elaborate plans on embossed paper and hands them to an overworked janitor; Father Eudex takes off his coat and digs. The Monsignor is proud of having studied in Rome where he had learned how to avoid "fair-seeming dilemmas of justice that were best left alone"; Father Eudex is "not the type" for academic study, and his "conception of the priesthood was evangelical in the worst sense." The Monsignor is finicky about the proper arrangements of food and silverware; the priest gives his overshoes to a freezing picket. On a major issue, however, their roles ironically seem to be reversed — the Monsignor can find "a good use" for the cheque sent by the Rival Tractor Company, but the priest destroys his.

3. *What is the effect of the idiomatic language in which the story is cast?*

    It serves to make the characters and their experiences that of ordinary human beings rather than of lofty, rarefied creatures usually found in stories of the church. And it indicates that the point of view is that of Father Eudex.

4. *By what details of symbolism does the author make judgments of the characters?*

    Almost everything in the story functions in this way — the large actions as well as the small details: e. g., when the Monsignor says, "I like green olives, but not in tuttifrutti salad," Father Eudex replies by eating a green olive. The Monsignor's name with three initials, W. F. X., reminds Father Eudex that a chancery wit had observed that "with all those initials the man could pass for a radio station."
    And the Monsignor's last name has powerful negative connotations for readers who know the disgusting protagonist of T. S. Eliot's poems, "Sweeney Erect," "Sweeney Among the Nightingales," and "Sweeney Agonistes." — Father Eudex declines the dessert of strawberry mousse. He enquires of Freda Klein if the "too much" she pays her son is a living wage. Almost any detail chosen at random functions in the same symbolic way. Eudex is also a symbolic name: *eu-* being the Greek prefix meaning "good" or "well", and *-dex* suggesting *dexter* "on the right side" as opposed to *sinister*.

5. *What is the tone of the story?*

    That of slightly astringent, defeatist irony, full of wit but not a happy good humor. "Dear, trusting God forever trying them beyond their feeble powers, ordering terrible tests, fatal trials by nonsense (the crazy bishop). And keeping Monsignor steadily warming up on the side lines, ready to rush in, primed for the day that would perhaps never dawn." "It was evidently inconceivable [to the policeman] that Monsignor should ever venture abroad unless to bear the Holy Viaticum, always racing with death," so he stops the traffic while the Monsignor is "taking her for a little spin."

J. V. H.

Heilman, Robert B., *Modern Short Stories*, New York 1950, pp. 336—337 — Jaffe, Adrian H., and Virgil Scott, *Studies in the Short Story*, rev. ed., New York 1950, pp. 298-299.


# JEROME DAVID SALINGER

Jerome David Salinger was born in 1919 in New York City to a Jewish father and a Christian mother of Scotch-Irish origin. He went to public school, to a Pennsylvania military academy, and to three colleges without taking a degree. He went to Europe (Austria and Poland) in 1937 and again during the War, when, as a staff sergeant in an infantry division, he took part in five combat campaigns in France and Germany in 1944/45. After the war he became a professional writer; since 1953 he has lived in great seclusion in Cornish, New Hampshire. He married in 1955 and was divorced in 1967.

His first short story was published in 1940. Many more followed during the next ten years, among them "Down at the Dinghy" in 1949. His most famous book, a novel *The Catcher in the Rye* (1951), has been called "a modern and urban Huckleberry Finn." Since 1953 he has only published one short story and three short novels including a religiously oriented book, *Franny and Zooey* (1961), but "despite the meagerness of his output, Salinger, at 42, has spoken with more magic, particularly to the young, than any other U. S. writer since World War II" (Jack Skow in *Time*, Sept. 15, 1961).


## Down at the Dinghy

Text: *Five Modern American Short Stories* pp. 19—28. Diesterweg

*Sandra, the maid of the Tannenbaum family of New York, feels dissatisfied during a long summer's vacation in a lake resort. She spitefully comments on her Jewish employer within the hearing of Lionel, his four-year-old son. As he has done several times before, the boy runs away and hides in his father's dinghy. His mother, Boo Boo Tannenbaum, with great love and tenderness manages to gain his confidence and release his tension.*

The mother comforting her child has been a standard image of Western art since the Madonnas and Mariolatry of the Middle Ages. In Salinger's story it receives an unusually compassionate and essentially American treatment, and more effectively than any dozen books on child psychology it reveals how an intelligent modern mother copes with a precociously sensitive four-year-old son. "Down at the Dinghy" is perhaps the gentlest story Salinger has ever told, but his control of tone and of realistic detail keep it from becoming offensively sentimental. The story begins at considerable remove from the mother-child relationship and each of the four sections moves the mother and child closer together until closure is achieved in the final reconciliation — a reconciliation which belies David L. Stevenson's comment that Salinger's characters are "members all of the lonely crowd ... their thin cries for love and understanding go unheard." (*Nation*, March 9, 1957, p. 216). "Down at the Dinghy" shows an immense love and a profound understanding.

"It was a little after four o'clock on an Indian Summer afternoon." With this flat statement of fact Salinger establishes an attitude of strict objectivity which is so consistently sustained that it succeeds in making even passionate avowals seem to be also nothing but flat statements of fact: "she was ... a stunning and final girl." The visual details of the scene and the tone of voice of the speakers are so accurately rendered that there is little need of elaborate adjectival and adverbial labels (though an accumulation of these at the end of the first section slightly mars an otherwise clean narrative style: "she said *malcontentedly*," "Sandra stared *rancorously*," "she gave Mrs. Snell a *hostile* glance"). A careful reader can be perfectly sure of the emotional tone of each situation and speech in all of Salinger's work without such labels.

In the first section a certain amount of suspense is established in the mysterious nervousness of Sandra, the obese maid, who keeps glancing out the lakefront window and keeps repeating "I'm not going to worry about it." Exactly what she is worrying about is revealed in the moment of illumination near the end of the story, but we know that it is something quite serious. Sandra's pseudo-sympathetic friend, the laundress Mrs. Snell, is not very successful at reassuring her: "Either he tells her or he don't. That's all. What good's *worryin'* gonna do?" At this point it is not at all clear who the *he* and the *her* are, or what it is that he might *tell*. From the ensuing dialogue we can assume that he is the shy, quiet four-year-old who "goes pussyfootin' all around the house" and who is apparently able to betray Sandra with serious consequences. In fact Mrs. Snell (whose passion in life appears to be fashionable second-hand clothes) slips into advice-giving "as if it were an ermine coat" and tries to counsel her friend to "look around for another —," "to get" another job.

It is Boo Boo Tannenbaum's interruption that identifies the *her*, for we are told that she is "the lady of the house." Despite her "general unprettiness" she is a "stunning and final girl" because she has a "permanently memorable, immoderately perceptive" face. It is obvious that she is the heroine of the story (as anyone would expect who has read Salinger's idolatrous accounts of the

Glass family in *Franny* and in *Zooey* and who notices that Boo Boo is née Glass), and Salinger succeeds in rendering her without using a single cliché. She is a completely natural, unself-conscious woman; searching in the refrigerator for a pickle to comfort her distressed son, "she whistled, unmelodically, through her teeth, keeping time with a little uninhibited, pendulum action of her rear end." In the dialogue of the second section is embodied the necessary exposition of the story — the past of little Lionel, who is an unusually sensitive boy not at all "babied" by his mother. Since the age of two and a half, he has responded to fears and insults by running away from home; memorable occasions were when a child in the park said, "You stink, kid," and when a little girl "told him she had a worm in her thermos bottle. At least, that's all we could get out of him." Since Lionel is sulking in his father's dinghy, the alert reader can assume that he has once again been frightened or insulted; and since the obese maid is extremely worried about something, we can assume that she bears the guilt.

The third section records the failure of Boo Boo's first attempt to gain the confidence of her son. The failure is foreshadowed in the brilliant description of the setting as Boo Boo approaches the dinghy: "The sun, though not especially hot, was nonetheless so brilliant that it made any fairly distant image — a boy, a boat — seem almost as *wavering and refractional* as a stick in water." The italicized words perfectly describe Lionel's responses to his mother's comic-pathetic blandishments. She offers no threats, no "reasoning" — but a gay plunge into the spirit of play: "Ahoy ... Friend. Pirate. Dirty Dog. ... It is I ... Vice Admiral Tannenbaum. Née Glass. Come to inspect the stermaphors." (That last is a hilarious portmanteau word, garbling together the nautical terms *stern*, and *semaphor* which the city-bred Boo Boo does not perfectly understand; it resembles the "peculiar amalgamation of 'Taps' and 'Reveille'" which she sounds when imitating a bugle call.) These antics serve to arouse Lionel's attention, but they are not sufficient to pierce the mantle of gloom he is wrapped in. He even refuses to divulge his motive for running away in exchange for a repetition of the bugle call.

In the fourth section, Boo Boo, becoming desperate but not losing control, adopts more direct tactics. She appeals to his sense of honor and to his love, maintaining a respect for his person and independence: not "aren't you lonesome for me," but "I'm so lonesome for you." The deeply troubled child flips his uncle's underwater goggles into the lake in an obvious test of his mother's love; if she does not scold him or punish him, then perhaps he can safely repeat to her the dangerous expression he has heard. Boo Boo passes the test. She cannot, of course, condone such behavior; but she appears to understand the anguished motives behind it, and responds with sarcasm: "That's nice. That's constructive." She then mock-threatens to throw his key chain in the water in retaliation, and for the first time he pleads with her: "Throw it [to me]? Please? ... It's mine." Then when he gets his key-chain he flicks it in the water in an apparent gesture of self-punishment and begins to weep. The compassionate mother is with him in a moment, reverting to play-talk:

"Sailors don't cry..." Now completely reassured of his mother's love, Lionel feels he can reveal his troubling secret: "Sandra — told Mrs. Smell — that Daddy's a big — sloppy — kike." The comic mispronunciation of Mrs. Snell's name neutralizes to some degree the powerful charge of the contemptuous anti-Semitic epithet "kike," but even the poised and self-controlled Boo Boo cannot help but flinch. A tremendous tension follows this moment of illumination. Then, to drain the ugly word of its threatening emotional power: "Do you know what a kike is, baby?" Lionel's answer to this question releases the tension in a magnificent burst of comedy, for the boy has understood the fury of Sandra's word without understanding the word: "It's one of those things that go up in the air ... with *string* you hold," a kite! Boo Boo's relief bursts from her in an explosion of plans for a picnic supper in the boat with Daddy, and mother and child race back to the house. Lionel is permitted to win the race, but the mother wins the more important contest against the vague but ugly cruelty that her child is doomed to suffer.

As Eudora Welty says there is no "message" — "he pronounces no judgments, he is simply gifted with *having* them passionately." The basic human decency that informs Salinger's work is as much a factor in his being the literary spokesman of this generation of Americans as his magnificent grasp of the American idiom — and there is no doubt that he is for our time what Hemingway was for the Twenties. And that is cause for rejoicing.

1. *Why did Sandra refer to the father as a "kike"? What is the earliest sign of an ethnic element in the story?*

   Sandra obviously is lonely in the vacation resort away from the city — presumably New York — where she can find company of her own kind. She is not able to establish rapport with the sophisticated Tannenbaum family, and her relations with the pretentious Mrs. Snell are hardly satisfactory: "I'll be gladda get backa the city... I hate this crazy place... It's all right for *you*, you live here all year round. You got your social life here and all." Her frustration finds release in anti-Semitic outbursts to Mrs. Snell. When Mrs. Snell defends the boy ("He's kind of a good-lookin' kid"), Sandra *snorts*, "He's gonna have a nose just like the father." Later when "the lady of the house" is introduced as Boo Boo Tannenbaum, the oddity of the nickname must not distract the reader's awareness of the Jewish surname.

2. *Do you know any other American slang invectives for people of foreign descent?*

   The American Thesaurus of Slang lists hundreds of them. The most familiar (cf. the episode in Evan Hunter, *Blackboard Jungle*, Pocket Book C 183 p. 193) are *limey* for the Englishman, *sandy* for the Scotchman, *mick* for the Irishman, *frog* for the Frenchman, *spic* for a Spaniard, *wop* or *dago* for an Italian, *kraut, fritz, hun* for a German. They are all resented, but perhaps only in the term *nigger* is a contempt expressed as hateful as in *kike*, which derives from the common Jewish name "Isaac" (cf. Erdman B. Palmore, Ethnophaulisms and Ethnocentricity, *American Journal of Sociology* LXVII (January 1962), pp. 442-444).

3. *Why does the boy keep running away?*

He seeks protection in some sheltered place: "he sought refuge under a sink," "he was sitting on the floor of the bandstand," "he was sitting right under the table," he "was sitting in the stern seat of his father's boat." Obviously he senses hostility without understanding it: "At least, that's all we could get out of him." He is sensitive to the prejudices surrounding and threatening him because of his race. So his mother's first word when she finds him is "Friend." Notice that on his shirt he has the picture of an ostrich, which is fabled to bury its head in the sand when hunted. — From his desperate reaction to the hostility he senses, the languid conversation at the beginning of the story between Sandra and Mrs. Snell is unveiled in its cruel irony: "It drives ya loony!" — "Stop worryin' about it ... What good's worryin' gonna do?"

4. *Is there a symbolic value in the two objects Lionel throws overboard?*

He rejects a pair of underwater goggles and a key chain with keys on it, which show how unbalanced his mind is, since these are things he ordinarily loves. But apart from his derangement Gwynn and Blotner suggest that the incident also means that subconsciously he does not want to see and does not want to open the doors to something — a demonstration corresponding closely to his running away and hiding.

5. *What may be implied from the names in the story?*

*Tannenbaum*: is suggestive of the Christmas tree and thus of the fact that Jesus was born a Jew and taught us to love our fellow-creatures;
*Boo Boo*: though a pet name, it is also faintly suggestive of the unpleasant experience of being booed, cat-called, hissed out;
*Lionel*: the boy who "goes pussyfootin' all around the house" will have to grow into a lion able to stand up against a world of prejudice;
*Mrs. Snell*: Lionel calls her Mrs. Smell — her name combines the elements of smell and snail.
All these connotations are not necessarily intended.

6. *Observe how characterization is aided by details of clothing.*

Sandra: "she absently untied and retied her apron strings, taking up what little slack her enormous waistline allowed."
Mrs. Snell: "It was the same interesting, black felt headpiece she had worn, not just all summer, but for the past three summers ... The Hattie Carnegie label was still inside it, faded but ... unbowed." Boo Boo Tannenbaum: "She was dressed in knee-length jeans, a black turtleneck pullover, and socks and loafers."
Lionel: "He was wearing khaki-colored shorts and a clean, white T-shirt with a dye picture, across the chest, of Jerome the Ostrich playing the violin."

7. *What details of dialogue mark it as authentic conversational idiom?*

First, the attempt at indicating colloquial pronunciation: "I hear Lionel's supposeta be runnin' away." "Wuddaya *think?*"

Then the casual, realistic sudden illuminations: "They found him at a quarter past eleven at night, in the middle of — my God, February, I think."
The forgetting of unimportant details: "Naomi somebody."
The repeated reference to the inaudible voice of the despondent child: "Lionel gave a reply, but it didn't carry." "Lionel's answer was complete, but, again, not loud enough."
The stresses of colloquial speech, indicated by italics: "Where's your *fleet*?"
Colloquial idioms: "It's all slightly over my head."
The clipped syntax of the distressed child: "With *string* you hold."
Others can be easily noted.

J. V. H./M. D.

Freese, Peter, Salinger, "Down at the Dinghy," *Amerikanische Erzählungen von Hawthorne bis Salinger*, Neumünster 1968, pp. 271—281 — Hardy, John Edward, Salinger, "Down at the Dinghy," *Commentaries on Five Modern American Short Stories*, Frankfurt 1961, pp. 7—10, 24—25.

# JOHN STEINBECK

John Steinbeck was born on February 27, 1902, at Salinas, Calif. His father was a county treasurer of German descent (the name originally was Großsteinbeck), his mother a teacher of Irish stock. His childhood surroundings were the country of Jody in *The Red Pony* (1937), "the Long Valley" of the Salinas River and the hill country near Monterey, which is also the scene of several novels. He had to support himself by hard work from boyhood, but was graduated from the Salinas High School. For four years he studied science at Stanford University and acquired a thorough knowledge of marine biology. While working on his first novels, which won him little recognition (1929, 1932, 1933), he found various employments, but was very poor for a long time.

His first popular success was *Tortilla Flat* (1935), which showed Steinbeck as a genuine artist of folk comedy and humor. In the following years his work was marked by an increasing sociological awareness. With his most famous novel, *The Grapes of Wrath* (1939), he became one of the most effective protagonists of social justice; it was awarded the Pulitzer Prize, and has been compared in its influence with *Uncle Tom's Cabin*.

During World War II Steinbeck went to Italy as a newspaper correspondent, and afterwards, motivated by his social interests, visited Russia and published a *Russian Journal* (1948). His amazing versatility is further demonstrated by the great contrast in matter and style between the short novel *The Pearl* (1947), a Mexican folk tale in a prose of great purity and beauty, and *East of Eden* (1952), which is based in part on the history of his own family and is his most ambitious treatment of the Salinas country. In his later books, *The Winter* of Our Discontent (1961) and *Travels with Charley* (1962), Steinbeck explored new territories, New England in the former, and the whole continent in the latter, which is subtitled *In Search of America*.

Several of his novels were also successful in dramatized form, both on the stage and on the screen. He died in 1968.

Among the outstanding American novelists Steinbeck is perhaps the most uneven. In his minor works he tends to offer characters without perspective and to obscure moral values in an excess of sentimentality. But he is always a superb story-teller. In 1962 he was awarded the Nobel Prize in Literature, "for his at one and the same time realistic and imaginative writings, distinguished as they are by a sympathetic humor and a social perception."

## The Leader of the People

Text: *Selected American Short Stories* pp. 6—17. Hirschgraben

*The scene of the story is a ranch in the hills of the Coast Range south of San Francisco, within sighting-distance of the town of Salinas. The time seems to be the beginning of this century, there are no automobiles, no electricity ("kerosene lamp"), no telephone. The owner of the ranch, Carl Tiflin, resents the fact that his father-in-law, an old pioneer and frontiersman, who once led a trek across the plains and remembers the dry summers as far back as 1861, is coming to pay a visit. Mr. Tiflin is irritated at the prospect of having to listen to the same tales of "Indians and crossing the plains" which he has already heard "about a thousand times." His wife begs him to be patient with her father. Jody, their little son, looks forward to hearing these exciting tales of adventure, and Billy Buck, the ranch-hand, regards the old man with great respect and sympathy. The first evening passes in an atmosphere of uneasiness, but the next morning Carl Tiflin loses control of his anger. The old man overhears Carl's outbreak and is set to meditating the real values of the "westering" which had been the great experience in his life. His words are directed to Jody, whose mind is deeply stirred by the incident.*

The story was first published in 1938. It is loosely connected with the three-section novelette *The Red Pony* and has in postwar editions been included as a fourth section. These four stories have no plot continuity, but all deal with incidents which shape young Jody Tiflin's character. Although the story is told from Jody's perspective, his grandfather, as the title indicates, is clearly the dominating figure. But his 'message' is carefully prepared for and comes as a striking insight to himself and as a dimly realized lesson to Jody at the climax of the story.

As in the novel *Of Mice and Men*, which Steinbeck wrote about the same time, mice are used here on a symbolic level and they mark significant points in the development of the story. In scene 1 ("On Saturday afternoon"; 6:37—9:40) the boy is described with numerous realistic observations (scuffing his shoes, throwing stones at pigeons, interlacing the wood in the woodbox so carefully that two armloads seemed to fill it to overflowing). He is still "the little boy," but he is obviously adolescent (using "mature profanity" and watching people's reaction to it), which is accompanied by the usual parental snubbing ("He is getting to be a Big-Britches"). The mice on this stage merely appear as appropriate hunting game for this boy.

In scene 2 ("In the lowering sun," 9:41—12:23) grandfather arrives and is met by Jody. The boy's suggestion of a mouse hunt now is seen in a wider sense and sneered at by Grandfather as an idea typical of "the people of this generation."

In scene 3 (evening and night, 12:24—14:37) the tension mounts; Jody's father gives him the permission to kill the mice, but Jody dreams of "the heroic time."

In scene 4 (Sunday morning, 14:38—17:38) crisis, climax and resolution follow. Jody's imagination "twitches away" from hunting out the mice when he sees their fate as symbolic of the fate of all men. So the mice remain "plump, sleepy, arrogant ... smug in their security, overbearing and fat" in their haystack at the end — like the family on the ranch; they have become symbolic of a tame and settled mode of life.

The pathetic figure of the old man thinking and talking continuously about the one "big thing" in his life touches on a theme which was dominant in Steinbeck's work of the 30's. Grandfather realizes at the end that it was not adventure or getting to California which made "westering" heroic, but the fact that "a whole bunch of people [was] made into one big crawling beast ... Every man wanted something for himself, but the big beast that was all of them wanted only westering." In *Dubious Battle* (1936) Steinbeck used the same image for a group of strikers: "It *is* a big animal. It's different from the men in it. And it's stronger than all the men put together." Man finds a full life only as part of a group; modern individualism robs life of its strength and productivity. Only a group can produce a leader: "I was the leader, but if I hadn't been there, someone else would have been the head. The thing had to have a head," says Grandfather.

Steinbeck is a believer in naturalistic communism. His *Sea of Cortez*, a nonfiction study of marine life in the Gulf of California, established clearly the thesis that life functions and survives best when it is organized around a leader as in the schools of fish. Ma Joad was the leader of the Okie family moving west in *The Grapes of Wrath* (1939); those who followed her lead had the best chance of survival. Other stories like "The Raid" and "The Vigilante" develop the group-man theory in modern settings.

The westering movement that "was as big [= creative] as God" is not so much a physical manifestation as an attitude of mind and a spirit. In some way the character of the pioneer as Grandfather sees (and represents) him, corresponds to Frederick Jackson Turner's ideas. In his famous essay *The Significance of the Frontier in American History* (1893) he sees characteristic traits of the frontier in "that coarseness and inquisitiveness; that practical turn of mind, quick to find expedients; that masterful grasp of material things, lacking in the artistic but powerful to effect great ends; that restless, nervous energy; ... that buoyancy and exuberance which comes with freedom." All these could apply to Grandfather's leader, and so might Turner's claim that "the most important effect of the frontier has been in the promotion of democracy," but Turner's idea of democracy is based on another trait of the frontier, "that dominant individualism," and this is where the views of Steinbeck and Turner concerning that creative period of the past clearly differ. The actual problem that each of the persons in "The Leader of the People" faces in a different way and which is impressed most deeply on the boy's mind, is that of the meaning and place which the frontier spirit should have in our time. Various attitudes are illustrated in the five characters in the story, partly expressed in the ranch people's attitudes towards Grandfather.

Carl Tiflin is the settled farmer who succeeded the pioneers. His reaction to the American pioneer past is "That time's done ... Now it's finished. Nobody wants to hear about it over and over." He has to content himself with mastering "anything that was done on the ranch, whether it was important or not" ("You know how he is"), and behind his irritability one is inclined to detect the envious feelings of someone whose life is unheroic. He is not very strong of character, "caught" and "entangled" by his wife's soft voice, and "irritated" by a threat in her voice, and "tearing himself to pieces" in his humiliating apologies, when Grandfather has overheard his angry outbreak.

Mrs. Tiflin's attitude is different. Grandfather's stories of the past are as boring to her as to her husband ("she was not listening at all"), but her love for her father helps her to understand and appreciate him and his obsession: "That was the big thing in my father's life ... when it was finished his life was done ... it's as though he was born to do that, and after he finished it, there wasn't anything more for him to do but think about it and talk about it." She treats him with loyalty and respect and begs her husband to "be patient with him and pretend to listen."

Jody's attitude towards the past is decisively changed by his experiences. At the beginning of the story his mental state is indicated by his parents' reluctance to admit that he is growing up. They keep putting him in his place and looking down at him for his sauciness, he is used to being blamed and punished. But his mother sometimes "relents a little," and Billy Buck at least takes him seriously and is helpful. Of course he finds a boyish delight in Grandfather's stories of "the impossible world [as distant as fairy tales] of Indians and buffaloes" and wishes "he could have been living in the heroic time." But he also realizes that "he was not of heroic timber." His innocent attitude finds satisfaction in "hunting" mice. But talking to Grandfather he realizes, "It wouldn't be much like hunting Indians, I guess." Here he is given his first stirring lesson: Grandfather does not approve of hunting Indians either (11:19—21). Nevertheless, Jody prepares everything for turning the old haystack into a "field of slaughter," but then he is "staggered" by Billy's philosophical remark (15:23). Like Grandfather's disapproval of hunting Indians, Billy's thought is apt to make Jody look at the past in a new way. Grandfather taught him to see the Indian in a new light: as a being that deserves fair dealing and is not just a game for the white man; now Billy shows him that his condition is not different from that of the mice: nobody knows what's going to happen to him. Had Jody before seen himself respectively the white man as a master who conquers nature, he now learns to think of himself as part of nature, subject to laws greater than himself. The past, then, is not merely a story of human enterprise and achievement, but of the powers of nature.

The idea is so "staggering" that Jody's imagination "twitched away from the mouse hunt." And when he finally starts to go down to kill the mice he vainly "tried to whip up his enthusiasm ... he could not go." A dim response to Grandfather's ideas, and pity, and sympathy for him draw him back. Unknowingly he helps Grandfather to discover the real truth in his experience, and for the first time in his life he breaks the shell of his childish self-centeredness. In a way he has gotten the real point of Grandfather's recollections: "I tell these old stories, but they 're not what I want to tell. I only know how I want people to *feel* when I tell them." Jody knows at last that even if one cannot revive such a past, one can respect and honor it — as he does in getting lemonade for Grandfather, and as his mother happily realizes he does when she speaks softly and cooperates in the ritual gesture of honor at the end.

Billy Buck's "reverence" for Grandfather may be partly inherited from his own father who had been acquainted with Grandfather: "A fine man he was." But Billy himself retains much of the self-reliant attitude of the pioneering days ("Grandfather said that Billy was one of the few men of the new generation who had not gone soft") and understands Grandfather better than the others do. His warm feeling is obvious when he enquires after Grandfather in the morning, "He's all right? He isn't sick?", and when Grandfather talked, he "stood politely until the little story was done." His character is well-balanced, more so than any other person's in the story. Not insignificantly the story introduces him in the very first sentence and, though a mere ranch-hand, he gives an impression which makes his philosophical remark plausible.

Grandfather is not merely a symbol of the past, but a full-fledged character as well. In spite of his high age (he remembers the summer of 1861 in California) he is led to a crisis when he realizes that his own attitude towards the past was wrong. He was one in "a line of old men along the shore hating the ocean because it stopped them"; he had not been able to adjust himself to the fact that he could not go on being "the leader of the people" after the Pacific Ocean had been reached. There is a hint of self-complacency and vanity in the way he dwells on "the big thing" in his life, which even finds expression in the great care he takes in dressing. The description of his face and figure and his way of walking (10:40–45) underlines the impression of "a granite dignity, so that every motion seemed an impossible thing." Carl's cruel words penetrate his assuredness and set him thinking, "looking small and thin and black." At first he feels "as though the crossing wasn't worth doing." Then he realizes that he had failed to communicate to the new generation the real spirit and values of "westering." He had degraded himself to telling stories that "only little boys like to hear." If "westering has died out of the people," it died even before in him.

The final meaning of the story is perhaps not quite clearly established, the story is not primarily didactic. How does Grandfather "want people to feel"? Lisca says (p. 107), "Life is always a risk. The call for heroism is heard today as it was yesterday. The need for a leader of the people is still real, for we are all pioneers, forever crossing the dangerous and the unknown."

1. *What purposes do the mice in the story serve?*

   Desired hunting game for a boy — symbol of the weakness of "the new people" — equivalent to Indians hunted by troops — object of demonstration of the law that rules all life — symbol of the sleepy, secure life of modern times; see **above**.

2. *What other realistic details are of symbolic value?*

   The indication of time: Grandfather arrives "in the lowering sun," spins his yarn in the night which reflects it in Jody's dreams, and awakes to a new insight on Sunday morning. The well-fed security of the scene: the ranch is situated in a ranch-cup; the little boy is first seen with a thick piece of buttered bread. Grandfather's belonging to the past: his letter "was mailed day before yesterday." Grandfather's self-complacency: he combs his whiskers and rubs up his shoes and brushes his clothes. Carl's dismissal of the old man's recollections: he breaks and drops the moth which circled the light, unlike the ranch-hand Billy, who still partly belongs to Grandfather's world. Jody's reverence for Grandfather: he offers him a lemonade.

3. *What does Jody find out in the course of Grandfather's visit?*

   Pioneer life was more than his romantic idea of hunting Indians and eating buffalo meat. The real value of "westering" was its capacity to organize groups and create leaders and release vital energy. Killing living beings just for fun is contemptible. Man is not the absolute master of nature, but himself a blind slave to fate. He learns to rate another person's well-being higher than his own pleasure: he doesn't want a lemonade for himself.

4. *In which way had Grandfather failed?*

   He had not been able to teach the new people the great lesson of the past. The real spirit of "westering" had died in him, too, when the coast was reached. He had assumed a "granite dignity."

M. D./W. G. C.

Houghton, Donald, 'Westering' in "Leader of the People," *Western American Literature* IV, 1969, pp. 117—124 — Jaffe and Scott, *Studies in the Short Story*, New York 1949, pp. 172—181 — Lisca, Peter, *The Wide World of John Steinbeck*, New Brunswick, N. J., 1958, pp. 104—107 — Rauter, Herbert, Steinbeck, "The Leader of the People," *Die amerikanische Kurzgeschichte*, eds. Göller/Hoffmann, Düsseldorf 1972, pp. 298—306.

# JAMES THURBER

James Thurber was born on December 8, 1894, at Columbus, Ohio, where his father occupied a position of some political prominence. He attended Ohio State University for three years. Rejected for service in the First World War because he was blind in one eye from a childhood accident, he worked as a code clerk in the State Department and was stationed in Washington and Paris. Later he entered journalism and from 1920 to 1925 was on the Paris staff of various American newspapers and editor of the European edition of the *New York Herald Tribune* until 1929. From then on Thurber worked as a contributing editor for the well-known weekly magazine *The New Yorker*. His first book of prose sketches and caricature (*Is Sex Necessary?*) was published in 1929. In many of his following twenty books his drawings are to be found under one cover with essay and narrative. He was twice married and divorced. In recent years Thurber lived alone in Connecticut, almost blind. He died in 1961.

James Thurber is generally regarded as the greatest American humorist of the 20th century. He has made almost all Americans laugh, but he has also caused many to think, and this establishes his position among genuine humorists. His firm critical perception, always alert for the significant absurdity, has expressed itself with equal force in his humorous essays and in those line drawings in which dogs behave like human beings — and vice versa. T. S. Eliot said that "There is a criticism of life at the bottom of his work ... capable of surviving the immediate environment and time out of which they spring."

## The Secret Life of Walter Mitty

Text:   James Thurber, *Stories and Fables* pp. 31—36. Hueber
*American Short Stories* V pp. 104—109. Schöningh
*British and American Humour* pp. 62—69. Westermann
*Humorous American Short Stories* pp. 74—78. Hueber (Gottschalk)

*Walter Mitty is a middle-aged, hen-pecked husband, who manages to escape the ugly reality of his marriage into reveries of heroism and fame. On his way to town with his wife and while waiting for her return from shopping, he imagines himself to be an admired hydroplane commander in a hurricane, a most successful specialist in a complicated medical case, the greatest pistol shot in the world accused of murder, an imperturbable bomber pilot in the First World War and a man facing stoically the firing squad about to execute him.*

Great humorists are rare creatures, for their skill lies in wit, intelligence, and a delicate sense of timing. They are never merely funny, evoking laughter with pie-in-the-face slapstick. On the contrary, great humor is always meaningful; and frequently there is a tragic sense behind the clown's mask. Thurber's humor is of this kind, and it is almost as difficult to analyze and describe as it is to create a work like "The Secret Life of Walter Mitty." Furthermore, the comic effect is considerably diminished if it comes through a process of ratiocination and analysis, rather than through a spontaneous rhythm of perceptions.

Brooks and Warren have observed that this tale is "very close to a mere character sketch," but it is actually far more complex and embodies a much richer action than such a description implies.

The story was first published in *The New Yorker* in 1939. The title — "The Secret Life of Walter Mitty" — is reminiscent of sensationalist exposures of the private lives of important public figures. Notice the implications of "The Secret Life of Nikita Khrushchev" or "The Secret Life of Konrad Adenauer." However, Walter Mitty is no important public figure (even the name has diminutive overtones — mite, midget, mitigate), and his secret life exists only in his fantasies through which he escapes the drab, ordinary existence of a hen-pecked middle-class husband. Hence, the title is extremely ironic.

The story is constructed of the sequence of five varied fantasy episodes from Mitty's "secret" life interspersed with realistic details of the drive to the shopping-district with his wife, who nags at him, belittles him, scolds him. When she breaks through his first daydream and comments "You're tensed up again ... It's one of your days," she explicitly explains his condition but implicitly reveals why he has that condition. She is responsible for it. The only way that this ineffectual little man (he is nowhere explicitly described as such, but the way the parking lot attendant, the garage repairman, and the woman shopper in the supermarket react to him makes such a characterization likely) can escape her domination is through heroic reveries.

The transition from everyday life to fantasy always involves a linking element common to both worlds. As Mitty drives his car, the sound of the motor leads him to imagine himself as the commander of a hydroplane; as he removes his gloves (in defiance of his wife — after she leaves him alone), he imagines himself a great surgeon removing his gloves on arrival at the hospital; as he is trying to remember what his wife wants him to buy, he imagines a district attorney dramatically stating, "Perhaps this will refresh your memory"; as he reads a magazine article on German air power, he imagines himself as an allied war ace; and finally, as he lights a cigarette while waiting for his wife in the rain, he imagines himself taking a last puff and turning with bravado to face a firing squad.

The heroic fantasies all involve hilarious exaggerations and distortions of the clichés of cheap fiction. Such grandiose absurdity is pathetic and reminiscent of Charlie Chaplin. It is quite amusing that he resorts to such reveries, and it is very sad that he must. In the first little scene, he is flying a plane while incongruously wearing a full-dress uniform with a heavily braided white cap. (The astute reader realizes long before Mrs. Mitty interrupts him that this is not a realistic event!) Each succeeding scene has a similar incongruous feature:

the anaesthetizer is "a huge, complicated machine, connected to the operating table, with many tubes and wires"; the district attorney in his frustration strikes savagely at the girl in Mitty's arms; he tosses off brandies like water in the dugout scene; he smokes a cigarette and disdains the handkerchief blindfold in the firing squad episode. Many details of his fantasies reveal, too, how pathetically little poor Mitty knows about the arenas of masculine power. There is, of course, no such thing as an SN202, eight-engined Navy hydroplane; no such diseases as obstreosis of the ductal tract, streptothricosis, and coreopsis (the latter is, in fact, a common yellow-brown garden flower); no such gun as a Webley-Vickers 50.80; and no such German air group as von Richtman's circus (which is obviously confused with von Richthofen's circus).

But there is much more to the story than a revelation of character through a clever series of contrasts between Mitty's real and his secret life. The order of the fantasy scenes implies a *development* in Mitty's attitude. The careful reader will observe that they move (generally) from the positively and actively heroic with little personal danger actually threatening Mitty (the hydroplane and hospital scene) to self-mutilation — "I'll wear my right arm in a sling" (the courtroom scene), to the threat of imminent death (the dugout scene), to submission to death (the firing squad scene). And this sequence parallels the gradual increase and sharpening of his humiliations from his wife and others. "Things close in," he says to his wife in the midst of her final tirade; Mitty is defeated as in fantasy he faces the firing squad, "erect and motionless, proud and disdainful, Walter Mitty the Undefeated, inscrutable to the last." He is "inscrutable" — his wife's fever thermometer is hardly the appropriate instrument by which his condition can be understood; und it is "the last," for the movement of the story implies that Mitty cannot much longer endure the humdrum pettiness and constant emasculation he suffers at the hands of his overbearing wife. The humorous treatment does not completely conceal the genuine pathos of his situation.

Psychologically, Mitty's case would be diagnosed as schizophrenia. He doesn't merely imagine himself in the various heroic roles that are dramatized in his mind; he really believes himself to be in those situations. Notice that when his wife arouses him from his first reverie, he looks at her "with shocked astonishment. She seemed grossly unfamiliar, like a strange woman who had yelled at him in a crowd." His condition is quite serious, and he really needs the doctor's care that his wife suggests.

1. *From what point of view is the story told?*

> We see Mitty almost completely from the perspective of a detached, noncommittal omniscient observer, who reveals Mitty's real-life and imaginative experiences without analysis or evaluation. Once or twice the narrator betrays his own amusement: "The greatest pistol shot in the world thought a moment." But the details he presents make it possible for the intelligent reader to understand, and they encourage an amused but compassionate attitude.

2. *Robert Heilman (in* Modern Short Stories, *N. Y., 1950, p. 153) says that "Walter Mitty's wife is not especially charming, but her sharpness accompanies a concern for her husband's welfare that seems rooted in a sound understanding of him." Is this a valid observation?*

No. Her first comments — "Not so fast! You're driving too fast!" — are not justified, because driving at 55 mph on a public highway (they are driving toward the city of Waterbury, Connecticut) is not exceeding safe speed limits. Her objection is not based on any concern for his welfare: "You know I don't like to go more than forty." Her insistence that he buy overshoes and wear his gloves may be justified by his age and the weather, but her tone is more domineering than considerate. Any doubts on this point vanish when she meets him in the hotel lobby (and the narrator observes that "she didn't like to get to the hotel first; she would want him to be there waiting for her as usual," which suggests that she had nagged him on that point, too). He is merely sitting in a chair waiting for her, but she accuses him of hiding "in this old chair." And she gives him no chance to answer one question before firing a second at him: "Did you get the what's-its-name? The puppy biscuit? What's in that box?" And she leaves him waiting on a street corner while she shops for something she forgot. It is inconceivable, of course, that he would criticize her for her shortcomings. Far from understanding him, she is certainly a contributory cause of his pathetic condition.

3. *How far must one read before one can be sure that this is not a dramatic tale of real heroism?*

The first sentence is a perfect opening for a better than ordinary adventure story; "his voice was like thin ice breaking" involves a magnificent simile embodying the cold, sharp, brittle, emphatic, tight-lipped tone of command. The second sentence with its reference to the full-dress uniform might make a reader suspicious, but not until the onomatopoetic description of the pounding cylinders — ta-pocketa-pocketa-pocketa-pocketa-pocketa — can he begin to be certain of a satiric quality. Then the accumulation of command clichés begins to seem comic, and finally the reference to an eight-engined Navy hydroplane clinches it. Only the slowest-witted reader must wait until Mrs. Mitty breaks in before he realizes what is going on.

4. *In what specific ways does the fantasy Mitty contrast with the real Mitty?*

Apart from the obvious fact that the fantasy Mitty is a hero, there are details of *speech* (the hero Mitty always speaks in self-assured laconic commands: "Switch on No. 8 auxiliary!", "Get on with the operation!" or brief, exaggerated statements of fact: "I could have killed Gregory Fitzhurst at three hundred feet with my left hand."); *dress* (the hero Mitty is almost always in uniform or wearing a sling or a gun); and *technical skill* (the hero handles all kinds of complicated machinery while the real Mitty cannot take the non-skid chains off.)

5. *Do these contrasts sharpen the humorous effect or are they to be taken seriously as a means of revealing the gravity of Mitty's mental condition?*

Both. They are, of course, very funny and it is natural to laugh; many readers have been observed to laugh so hard that they rolled on the floor or held their sides as tears came to their eyes. But strangely enough, the absurd fantasies of Mitty are true to life — at least true to the life of serious neurotics. The merging of details from both the fantasy and the real worlds is psychologically accurate. Freud himself in producing arguments for the existence of the subconscious mind pointed to exactly such phenomena as Mitty trying to remember what it is that his wife wants him to buy, reverting to a fantasy which culminates in a powerful act of masculine aggression when he hits the district attorney on the jaw with the epithet "You miserable cur!", and the word "cur" reminding him of "puppy biscuits," which is what he must buy. Psychologically, it is perfectly realistic.

J. V. H.

Brooks and Warren, *Understanding Fiction*, 2nd edition, New York 1959, pp. 62-64 — Satterfield, Leon, Thurber's "The Secret Life of Walter Mitty," *The Explicator* XXVIII, 1969, item 57.

## The Macbeth Murder Mystery

Text: *Britain and America*, Oberstufe pp. 80—83. Velhagen und Klasing
*The Thurber Carnival* pp. 46—49. Penguin Book 871

*In a hotel in the English lake country the narrator meets an American lady who is a crime-fiction expert. Having bought a Penguin copy of Shakespeare's Macbeth by mistake one night, she read it like a detective story and suspected Macduff of Duncan's murder. When the narrator now reads Macbeth again he develops an even more extravagant theory and announces his intention to read Hamlet as crime fiction in order to figure it out, too.*

"The Macbeth Murder Mystery" (1942) is one of Thurber's hilariously clever pieces. Although the extravagant and incongruous situation develops with all the spontaneity of reality, this rhythmic evocation of laughter has been carefully made. The typical Thurber story is, primarily, a laugh-making machine, and one should simply submit to it and let it do its joyous work. But after that a careful analysis yields a rich return of fascinating insights.

Like "Catbird Seat," "The Unicorn in the Garden," and "The Secret Life of Walter Mitty," this sketch belongs to a major genre of Thurber's work — The Battle of the Sexes. And, as usual, the conflict is between a powerfully dogmatic, didactic, daytime Philistine woman and a somewhat timid, mousy sort of man who ultimately gets his revenge by letting his imagination run a bit wild, perhaps even going slightly mad. It is impossible to say whether the narrator of this story has actually contracted the disease of trying to interpret Shakespeare's plays as murder mysteries, or whether he cleverly pretends to.

The convention of the I-narrator and the final gag (with its implied wink to the reader) seem to suggest the latter, but in either case the woman is beaten at her own game.

Only the literate and sophisticated reader already familiar with *Macbeth* can enjoy the full, rich, complex humor of this work. Anyone who goes to the text of *Macbeth* to check on the details is automatically disqualified; even as an academic exercise, such a practice is to be discouraged. (The pedant might be forestalled with the information that Macbeth openly announces that he has indeed murdered Duncan: "I have done the deed" II. ii. 15). On one level, "The Macbeth Murder Mystery" is a spoof on literary criticism (see "Here Lies Miss Groby" for another), and much of the wit derives from Thurber's playing off one level of understanding against another. The American woman is, of course, not a fit reader of *Macbeth*, which she considers "a book for high-school students. Like *Ivanhoe*." All set to read crime fiction, she applies the standards of the detective story to Shakespeare's drama: the obvious murderer is never the real one; the first good suspect must be the victim of the second murder; those who flee are never guilty; an innocent person often behaves suspiciously to shield another. Furthermore, the woman's simple-minded realism cannot tolerate Lady Macbeth's carrying a light while sleep-walking or Macduff's spouting poetry upon discovering Duncan's body.

The poor narrator is at first dumb-founded with the woman's arguments and then makes the mistake of trying to confute her with detective story approaches: How about Malcolm and Donalbain? What do you make of the Third Murderer? What about the banquet scene? What about the sleep-walking scene? As soon as he begins this line of attack, he's hooked — and inevitably defeated. He asks to borrow the book because, "I don't feel, somehow, as if I'd really read it"; the joke is, of course, that *as a detective story* he never really had!

The narrator then achieves his revenge by an even more ingenious interpretation which supplies not only a murderer with a motive, but certain "gooseflesh" elements (as George Jean Nathan calls them) — hiding the body and appearing on the scene in disguise. "'Good God!' breathed my companion, softly," amusingly echoes his own "'Good God!' I whispered, softly." The tables are turned. And then the narrator goes one step further by announcing that he will buy a copy of *Hamlet*, which indicates that he has either gone mad or that he is astonishingly adept at the game of one-upmanship.

The story has all the economy and rhythmic development of a good joke, beautifully paced and patterned. America's master humorist has done it again.

1. *Play the detective-story game with Hamlet, applying the principles developed in "The Macbeth Murder Mystery".*

   The real murderer of King Hamlet is Fortinbras, whose motives are revenge for the death of his own father and ambition for the crown of Denmark. He disguises himself as the ghost of King Hamlet to throw suspicion on Claudius, who, in turn, suspects Gertrude and therefore acts guiltily to shield her. Gertrude suspects

Claudius and marries him to shield him. Rosenkrantz and Guildenstern are really agents of Fortinbras, but the master agent of all is Horatio. Further elaborations are easily possible.

**2. How does Thurber quicken the pace of the second part of the story?**

Having no further need to develop the astonishment and involvement of the narrator, he omits the gestures that are interpolated with the dialogue in part one: "I looked at her blankly," "I thought this over while I filled my pipe," "I summoned the waiter," etc. These gestures (especially the ordering of first one, and then a second, brandy) are effectively patterned to reveal the narrator's gradually increasing tension.

**3. Compare "The Macbeth Murder Mystery" with "The Secret Life of Walter Mitty".**

Both have a quite realistic substratum; there is nothing unusual about becoming engaged in utterly unexpected conversations with strangers at a holiday resort or in observing somewhat distracted henpecked husbands with their wives. Both are constructed of a sequence of carefully paced individual comic elements. Both make humor out of serious problems (proper literary criticism, and proper marital relations). And both involve a certain degree of madness, or at least of disorientation from reality. But "Mitty" has far more serious tragic overtones — more quickly loses its humorous quality upon analysis.

J. V. H.

# LIONEL TRILLING

Lionel Trilling was born on July 4, 1905, in New York City. After passing through high school he was graduated from Columbia College in 1925 and took his Master of Arts degree in English literature at Columbia University in the following year. He spent some time at the University of Wisconsin and at Hunter College, New York, but returned to Columbia in 1932, where he passed through the usual academic grades and has been a professor of English since 1948. He loves New York and refuses to accept even visiting professorships elsewhere. His wife is the noted critic, Diana Trilling.

He began writing in 1925; stories, essays, and reviews have appeared since in a variety of literary and academic publications. His first published book, in 1938, was his dissertation on *Matthew Arnold,* which has become the standard critical biography; it was followed by a critical study of *E. M. Forster,* the British novelist, in 1943. In 1947 his first novel appeared, *The Middle of the Journey,* "a book that brings the best critical intelligence now discernible in America into play with an absolutely honest creative talent" (M. D. Zabel).

# The Other Margaret

Text: (no annotated edition yet available)
   first publication in: *Partisan Review XII* (Fall 1945), pp. 481—501
   reprinted in: Ludwig and Poirier (eds.),
      *Stories: British and American*, New York 1953
      West and Stallman, *The Art of Modern Fiction*,
      New York 1949, pp. 374—393

*Soon after World War II Stephen Elwin, a 41-year-old publisher who lives in New York, buys a reproduction of Rouault's "The King." First in the art dealer's shop, on his way home and later with his wife Lucy and his 13-year-old daughter Margaret he experiences a number of disturbing episodes that lead him to a deeper insight into the problem of responsibility and wisdom. At the same time his daughter undergoes a painful process of initiation into adult reality.*

When an eminent literary critic, especially of a moralistic, Arnoldian persuasion, takes a hand at writing fiction, the result is rarely as distinguished an achievement as Lionel Trilling's two short stories: "The Other Margaret" and "Of This Time, Of That Place". And, as is to be expected, his fiction embodies ideas and values which occupy a prominent place in his criticism. The "greatness" of the novel, he has said, "and its practical usefulness lay in its unremitting work of involving the reader himself in the moral life, inviting him to put his own motives under examination, suggesting that reality is not as his conventional education has led him to see it." It may safely be assumed that these are his objectives in "The Other Margaret." More specifically, he is dramatizing the education of a moral realist, i. e., one who has "perception of the dangers of the moral life itself."

"Perhaps at no other time has the enterprise of moral realism ever been so much needed, for at no other time have so many people committed themselves to moral righteousness... We must be aware of the dangers which lie in our most generous wishes... We have the books that point out bad conditions, that praise us for taking progressive attitudes. We have no books that raise questions in our minds not only about conditions but about ourselves, that lead us to refine our motives and ask what might lie behind our good impulses."         ("Manners, Morals, and the Novel," 1947)

"The Other Margaret" is a serious, slow-paced, meditative narrative; the controlling intelligence is that of Stephen Elwin, a 41-year-old publisher of scientific books and an intellectual who cannot observe or act without considering the meaning of every gesture. Hence, the style is neither poetic nor even dramatic, but meditative — à la Henry James; it is not the language, but the events that have symbolic power. Two processes of moral education are delineated — the long, slow build up to an "explosion of light" for Elwin, and at the end the swifter, more dramatic insight of his thirteen-year-old daughter Margaret.

The first part of the story is made up of two public experiences of Stephen Elwin — an examination of a reproduction of Rouault's painting "The King" in the company of an art dealer and a young lieutenant, and a disturbing episode on the bus when a mean-spirited conductor mistreats two little boys. These experiences are then recapitulated and modified in the privacy of the Elwin family. All this serves as an elaborate introduction to the heart of the narrative — the episode involving the other Margaret, the Negro maid.

Neither of the two men who observe the Rouault painting with Elwin really understands it or appreciates it. Mark Jennings, the art dealer, eager to satisfy his friend and customer, pretends to admire it, but is really more concerned with the frame he has made. (Whether this is related with Trilling's concern over the "frame" of his story is difficult to say.) The young lieutenant insincerely comments, "Very nice," but he is himself a considerable contrast with the fierce old warrior depicted in the picture. He hasn't even the courage of his own convictions: "He used to be against anything like that," meaning militarism, "but he was glad to go [into the army] — he said he did not want to miss sharing the experience of his generation." Here is a manifestation of the moral cowardice which is involved in the basic theme of the entire story. Elwin, however, is attracted to the picture because he feels that the old king "had passed beyond ordinary matters of personality and was worthy of the crown he was wearing." The king represents the wisdom and authority of experience and a stern sense of justice, qualities which Elwin himself aspired to. Later when Elwin shows the picture to his daughter, she too rejects it: "It said something to her that was not in her experience or that she did not want in her experience." Youthful sentimentalism and aged authority are incompatible, but at least Margaret was honest enough to admit, "I don't really like it." The bonds of family love do not require the hypocritical politeness; they are strong enough to sustain occasional disagreement and differences in taste.

The second episode involves Elwin's bus ride aboard an ancient vehicle which reminds him of his youth. He has already been thinking about age and death and recalling with poignancy a line from Hazlitt: "No young man believes he shall ever die." Elwin realizes that he is no longer a young man, but if age brings awareness of death it also brings a heightened sense of responsibility which only the wise can bear successfully. As he meditates on these matters he observes two boys waiting for the bus; they seem the kind who "half in awe, half in rowdy levity, troop incessantly through the Egyptian rooms of the Museum, repeatedly entering and emerging from and entering again the narrow slits of the grave vaults." In other words they are too young to be aware of death and, hence, are without responsibility. But the bus conductor, an old man, simply teases them when they ask how much the fare is and he allows the bus to pull away without them. Elwin, observing this incident, lapses into the moral softness of the liberal; i. e., he thinks of reasons for excusing the old conductor's mean behavior: he had outlived his fatherhood and his children "now would have grown and gone and given him the usual causes for bitterness"; he had not the advantage of "the gentle rearing and the good education that made a man like Stephen Elwin answerable for all his actions." Nevertheless, for the first time in his life, Elwin feels both a great anger at the old man—and a sense of wisdom. Hazlitt and Rouault are both at work—the knowledge of death and the age of wisdom.

Upon his arrival home, his daughter serves him the usual evening cocktail, youth's ritual service to age and authority; but she is an independent, modern child and doesn't hesitate to announce her dislike of the picture. A family crisis looms when Lucy Elwin, the mother, begins to express her anger at "the other Margaret," the Negro maid who is a thoroughly unpleasant person and who has broken only the most valuable pieces of China in the household—a fact which suggests deliberate malice. Nevertheless, Margaret, educated in a liberal, progressive school, feels that no Negro can be held responsible for wrong-doing so long as the Negro race is subject to mistreatment and prejudice in the American community. Like father, like daughter—for Elwin, too, until that day, has always looked for mitigating circumstances, excuses, to absolve others from blame and responsibility. He has not yet achieved the fierce sense of justice of Rouault's king. The mother temporarily averts a quarrel by telling about *her* bus incident that day—a conductor had mocked a young woman by pretending that she was Jewish and by speaking to her rudely in a simulated Jewish accent. The delicately balanced and oversensitive Margaret, one of the "morally righteous," misunderstands and is furious with her mother, and makes excuses for the bus conductor—"They are underpaid!" Now Elwin "felt a quick impatience with his daughter's sensitivity." Once again the mother, a forthright, no-nonsense type of woman who takes "no account of finer feelings," averts a crisis by introducing a family joke.

But the repeated drive toward crisis cannot be denied, and when the other Margaret arrives late to serve dinner, matters come to a head. Lucy announces firmly that the Negro maid "is a thoroughly disagreeable person, a nasty, mean person." Young Margaret cannot accept such a judgment as anything but a manifestation of anti-Negro prejudice, and when she insists that "it's not her fault, she's not responsible," Elwin sternly demands, "Why not?" It is for Elwin an "explosion of light . . . an illumination." His day-long meditations on Hazlitt and Rouault finally reach a moment of wisdom in the conscious conviction that "in the aspect of his knowledge of death, all men were equal in their responsibility." Then, as he tries to point out to his anguished daughter that Millie, their former Negro maid, had pride and dignity and a sense of responsibility, a second powerful insight comes to him: "It came suddenly, as no doubt was the way of moments of wisdom, and he perceived what stupidly he had not understood earlier, that it was not the other Margaret but herself that his Margaret was grieving for, that . . . she was defending herself from her own impending responsibility." Here it becomes obvious that Trilling is embodying in complex dramatic form an insight that Gerard Manley Hopkins had expressed in a magnificent poem, "Spring and Fall: To a Young Child":

> Margaret, are you grieving
> Over Goldengrove unleaving?
> Leaves, like the things of man, you
> With your fresh thoughts care for, can you?
> Ah! as the heart grows older
> It will come to such sights colder
> By and by, nor spare a sigh
> Though worlds of wanwood leafmeal lie;
> And yet you will weep and know why.
> Now no matter, child, the name:
> Sorrow's springs are the same.
> Nor mouth had, no nor mind, expressed
> What heart heard of, ghost guessed:
> It is the blight man was born for,
> It is Margaret you mourn for.

And Elwin, "for what reason he did not know, was forcing it on her." The reason is, of course, that he is determined to be wise, forceful, and just — like Rouault's king — even at the expense of mercy. He needn't have done so, for the other Margaret acts in a way that makes any doubt of her culpability, even for the naïve innocent defender of the downtrodden Negro, no longer possible. She announces her resignation and then deliberately smashes a green clay lamb that Margaret had made as a birthday gift for her mother. The daughter wails with grief. The distressed parents drop all efforts at hard justice and truth to try to console the poor girl with reassurance that it must have been an accident, but Margaret had seen the maid in the act: "She meant to do it!" The smashed green lamb is, of course, a symbol of the destruction of Margaret's moral innocence, and the exposed white clay of the fragments a symbol of death. And "she had seen with her own eyes the actual possibility of what she herself might do, the insupportable fact of her own moral life." Elwin suddenly began to wonder "if the king, within his line of vision as he stood there trying to comfort his daughter, would ever return to the old fine, tragic power, for at the moment he seemed only quaint, extravagant and beside the point." His daughter, curled in the foetal position as if to withdraw from adult reality, lies sobbing on the sofa; and he realizes with a pang, too, that no one can possibly console another for the pain of moral insight. We are all ultimately and irrevocably alone in our own skins.

1. *Since the story deals with a sophisticated intellectual family in New York City, several works of art, music, and literature are naturally cited. Examine each to see how it contributes to the over-all meaning of the story.*

    The Rouault painting is a central symbol. Elwin's attraction to it represents his recognition of and longing for the king's wisdom, the sense of stern justice, the aloofness from petty subjective considerations of personality. The weak and the young reject the king, out of some subconscious recognition that they could not survive judgment by such a figure. Elwin himself has always been a man who did not so much "temper" as weaken justice with too much mercy. In this story he moves toward three insights, the first two of which tend to identify him with the king: "in the aspect of his knowledge of death, all men were equal in their responsibility" and "it was not the other Margaret but herself that his Margaret was grieving for... the insupportable fact of her own moral life." But his third and final insight is that at the moment a loved one experiences the anguish of initiation, the fierce visage of justice is no longer relevant — the king seems "quaint, extravagant, and beside the point."

Diametrically opposed to the Rouault is Margaret's green lamb, a "self-portrait" representing youth, tenderness, innocence; its "eyes stared out with a great charming question to the world." Its destruction marks the end of Margaret's innocence, and it too becomes no longer relevant.

The juxtaposition of Picasso and Benton prints on Margaret's wall, "knowing nothing of their antagonism to each other," also reveals Margaret's naïveté.

The books on Margaret's shelf range from *The Little Family*, a children's storybook, to Kipling's *The Light That Failed*; the latter is an interesting title since several "lights" fail in this story and since Trilling had written that Kipling "belongs to our past... firmly fixed deep in childhood feeling." (Nation, 1943)

Margaret playing Mozart on the recorder is a magnificent episode; her progress from the grave concentration of practice to the smiling execution of a swift roulade seems to Elwin a sign of Margaret's growth in conscious life: "Life aware of itself seemed so much more life."

2. *How do memories function in the story?*

There are two "memory scenes" in the story. One occurs in the sequence of public episodes, relating to Elwin's boyhood when he rode on the upper deck of the De Dion buses and "had a boy's certainty that the more he endured, the stronger he would become." The other occurs in the private family scenes when Elwin recalls Margaret playing her first full piece on a *Blockflöte*. Each memory scene serves as a meditative pause before a crisis episode of insight. Such memory is the beginning of wisdom as Elwin realizes when he considers "that this ritual of the drink was Margaret's first traffic with the future... he thought with irony but also with pleasure of his becoming a dim necessary figure in Margaret's story of the past."

3. *What is the moral of Millie's story?*

That justice and good will are complex, paradoxical matters. Millie must be allowed to suffer, sacrifice, and repay her debt to the Elwins, even though the Elwins do not really need or want the money. When Margaret dismisses Millie as a Negro with a "slave-psychology," Elwin feels that his daughter has been corrupted by the pseudo-liberal concepts taught by Miss Hoxie. (Is there a play on "hox" — "hoax" here?) Elwin patiently tries to explain that Millie must be allowed to repay her debt for the sake of her pride and dignity — "She needs to think of herself as a person who pays her debts, as a responsible person." The other Margaret has no such lofty character, and mean-spirited Negroes must not be permitted to hide under the umbrella of fear of anti-Negro prejudice. Every man must be prepared to submit to judgment as an individual human being.

4. *In this story an adolescent's experience is seen from the point of view of an adult. How usual is this in American literature? What are the advantages and disadvantages of this technique?*

> The common pattern is to present such morally-charged situations from the point of a child or adolescent — as in Hawthorne's "My Kinsman, Major Molineux," Anderson's "The Egg," Hemingway's "The Killers," Faulkner's "That Evening Sun," and Warren's "Blackberry Winter." Such a technique is necessarily more "dramatic" and "ironic," presenting bare action and dialogue, avoiding commentary, and putting the burden of meaning on the reader. Trilling's technique makes it possible for him to comment overtly on the moral problems of the story, and makes natural the meditative rather than the dramatic mode. Notice that each episode of the story involves age versus youth, seen from the perspective of age, and that there is practically no irony.

5. *What is achieved by having the girl and the maid both named Margaret?*

> It tends to identify the two characters as one.
> It underlines the fact that the Negro maid's behavior and punishment must be defended by the daughter, because they represent possibilities of her own subconscious self. Black is an appropriate complexion for a Freudian Id-figure. Elwin understood what his daughter felt: "She had been told *she* might go, never to return. She saw the great and frightening world before her. It was after all possible so to offend her parents that this expulsion might follow." ... "She had with her own eyes seen the actual possibility of what she herself might do, the insupportable fact of her own moral life." Or, as Hopkins put it: "Margaret, are you grieving? It is Margaret you mourn for."
>
> J. V. H.

Farrell, James T., *Literature and Morality*, New York 1947, pp. 10-14 — Stanton, Robert, *The Short Story and the Reader*, New York 1960, pp. 256—265.

# MARK TWAIN

Samuel Langhorne Clemens was born on November 30, 1835, on the Missouri frontier, in a straggling log village called Florida. Four years after his birth, the family moved to Hannibal, a larger town with a population of almost five hundred, on the Mississippi River. There he lived the boyhood life described in *The Adventures of Tom Sawyer* (1876) and *Huckleberry Finn* (1884).

When Samuel was twelve years old, his father died, and the boy was apprenticed to the printer of his brother's newspaper in Hannibal. In 1853 he set out to see the world and during the next four years traveled as a journeyman printer to St. Louis, Chicago, Philadelphia and Keokuk, Iowa. On his way to South America in spring 1857, he was fascinated by the Mississippi River and decided to learn to pilot a steamboat. After two years as an apprentice he became a licensed pilot. In *Life on the Mississippi* (1883) he gave a description of these years. His pseudonym Mark Twain is the leadsman's cry to the pilot indicating the minimum depth of safe water (two fathoms = 3.66 meters). With the outbreak of die Civil War all steamboat traffic on the Mississippi was interrupted, and Mark Twain, after serving a few months with a Confederate company, went to Nevada and later to San Francisco as a journalist and unsuccessful speculator. He met Artemus Ward and Bret Harte who encouraged him and taught him to tell a story. In 1865 he made his first success with the story of "The Celebrated Jumping Frog of Calaveras County." A trip to Honolulu in 1866 began his career as a traveling correspondent who would circle the globe and write letters as he went. *Innocents Abroad* (1869) was the hilarious account of his travels in Europe and the Holy Land. He also became immensely popular as a lecturer. During the twenty years between 1875 and 1894 Mark Twain was happiest, and wealthiest, and he wrote his best books. *The Adventures of Huckleberry Finn* (1884) was criticized at its publication, but "except perhaps for Moby Dick, no American book has recently been opened with more tender explicatory care or by critics to whom we are better prepared to listen" (Leary 1960). During the fifteen years which preceded his death in 1910, grief from the deaths of his wife and two of his three children and increasing bitterness darkened his life and his literary work.

Metcalf sums up his importance: "We have at last come to realize that Mark Twain has enduring literary qualities: his style at its best is clear, simple, direct, and sometimes tinged with poetic coloring. As an interpreter of significant phases of American life — the Mississippi Valley region of primitive times and the crude young West — Mark Twain is sure of immortality. As a literary man his fame has steadily grown, and it is evident that he is one of the most original writers in American literature."

## The Celebrated Jumping Frog of Calaveras County

Text:   *American Short Stories* II pp. 19—26. Schöningh

*The narrator visits a decayed mining-camp in California and calls on old Simon Wheeler to enquire after a cherished boyhood companion of a friend — one Leonidas W. Smiley — who later became a minister of the church. Old Simon Wheeler has never heard of Leonidas Smiley, but insists on telling him the story of the enterprising vagabond Jim Smiley, who came to the camp in 1849/50. Smiley was in the habit of betting on anything that turned up: horse-races, dog-fights, cat-fights, chicken-fights and any ridiculous opportunity that presented itself. He was very lucky and usually came out winner. But he was also a genius in teaching a horse or a dog some winning tricks and once he even caught a frog which he taught jumping and catching flies in a way nobody would have thought possible; and he made much money by betting on it with other people. One day, however, he was cheated by a man, who secretly stuffed the frog with small shot so that it could not jump, and lost his bet.*

This famous tall story contains a number of anecdotes of the type that Mark Twain must often have heard during his roving life. The garrulous old man starts by giving the setting of the story (the robust early days of the camp: "I remember the big flume warn't finished") and goes on to give lavish examples of Jim Smiley's enthusiasm for betting. The lively exaggerations are typical of Mark Twain's style of humor. The examples expand into anecdotes, and, after a rather grotesque story about a dog without hind legs, the climax is reached in the tale about the frogs. The manner in which the author succeeds in reproducing the old man's dialect peculiarities and earthy turns of speech without sounding stilted is remarkable in a story first published in 1865, although it should be noticed that expressions that would shock the middle-class reader of the day are avoided as they would not be by a modern author. Not that Mark Twain simply gives us a bowdlerized reproduction of popular speech; his language is injected with qualities of vigor and imagination (note especially the similes) to compensate for the liveliness that is lost through the fact that we cannot hear the actual voice of the speaker, a technique that Steinbeck, among others, has made familiar.

This is a story within a story, and the conventional language of the Easterner in the frame contrasts with the dialect of Simon Wheeler's narrative. There are, in fact, three layers of humor. The reader is amused by the simple fun of the tall story itself and is, at the same time, encouraged to laugh at the old man who tells the story, especially at the seriousness with which he regards the main characters, the bull-pups and frogs. At another level, however, the reader laughs at the unwilling listener, the city slicker who has not sufficient leisure to appreciate Simon Wheeler's tale.

Mark Twain later became more ambitious and did not think very highly of this early story; when "The Jumping Frog" was widely reprinted and made his name known on the East Coast, he felt uneasy and wrote angrily, "To think that, after writing many an article a man might be excused for thinking tolerably good, those New York people should single out a *villainous backwoods sketch* to compliment me on!"

1. *Find examples of Mark Twain's exaggerations.*

   "he would foller that straddle-bug to Mexico"; "always had the asthma, or the distemper, or the consumption"; "They used to give her two or three hundred yards' start"; "so he never done nothing for three months but set in his backyard and learn that frog to jump" etc.

2. *Point out some of the highly imaginative comparisons used to enliven the narrative.*

   The dog's jaw stuck out "like the fo'castle of a steam-boat"; the frog was seen "whirling in the air like a dough-nut"; it came down "flat-footed ... like a cat"; it would "flop down on the floor again as solid as a gob of mud"; Daniel, filled with shot, "give a heave, and hysted up his shoulders — so — like a Frenchman" etc.

*3. What is the purpose of the "story within a story" form?*

The humorous contrast between the two modes of speech, which also underlines the situation of a well-educated, business-like man with friends in the East being buttonholed by a garrulous Westerner. The additional humorous point is obtained by the joke played on the "I" narrator by the friend from the Eastern states in entangling him in this situation. Further simple fun is yielded by the fact that the mythical "Leonidas" about whom inquiries are made is a clergyman, while the adventures described by the old man would be unsuitable for a minister of the Gospel. The story is brought to a neat end by the escape of the unwilling listener who obstinately refuses to be amused.

*4. What stylistic evidence is there that this story was written in the 19th century?*

The simple fun of the tall story with its exuberant exaggerations. A modern author would be more ironic about the boredom of life in a mining camp where bets were made on chicken fights and the possible destination of bugs. The propriety of language.

*5. The reader is told that old Simon Wheeler is boring and garrulous. Why doesn't his story bore the reader?*

The old man's prose style is, in fact, far livelier than that of his listener, who employs worn-out conventional phrases. Simon's simple-mindedness is conveyed by his personification of the bull-pup (named "Andrew Jackson" and "had genius") and of the frog Dan'l ("... scratching the side of his head with his hind foot as indifferent as if he hadn't no idea he'd been doin' any more'n any frog might do"). Thus the reader gathers an *impression* of a long-winded narrative without being inflicted with the thing itself.

*6. Who is the butt of this story, Simon Wheeler or the listener?*

Old Simon (his name suggests the nursery rhyme "Simple Simon") is certainly represented as simple-minded and garrulous. But, in the last resort, the unwilling listener is the butt. He is apparently so wrapped in his own affairs that he cannot appreciate old Simon's remarkable exaggerations and comparisons. This point is underlined by the flat, conventional, business-letter phraseology ("I hereunto append the result") used by the listener. The reader is quite willing to listen to the tale about the cow with the tail "like a bannanner," but old Simon's listener is far too busy and impatient; the typical town-dweller, in fact.

W. G. C.

Branch, Edgar M., *The Literary Apprenticeship of Mark Twain*, Urbana, Ill. 1950, pp. 120—129 — Bungert, Hans, Mark Twain, "The Notorious Jumping Frog of Calaveras County," *Die amerikanische Kurzgeschichte*, eds. Göller/Hoffmann, Düsseldorf 1972, pp. 129—137 — DeVoto, Bernard, *Mark Twain's America*, Boston 1951, pp. 172—178 — Krause, S. J., The Art and Satire of Twain's "Jumping Frog" Story, American Quarterly 16, 1964, pp. 562—576.

# Traveling with a Reformer

Text: *Humorous American Short Stories* pp. 25—37. Hueber (Gottschalk)

*The author relates an experience on his way to the World's Fair at Chicago in 1893. He is traveling together with a major in the army who has "a passion for reforming petty public abuses." He thinks that every citizen of the republic ought to keep watch over the laws and their execution. He does it with much diplomacy and is not afraid of telling lies "for the public good." If necessary he even resorts to force. He is extremely successful but annoys the author by his obstinate lack of humor.*

Rather than a short story, this is a series of entertaining anecdotes illustrating the character of the major as outlined in the first two paragraphs — his serenity and love of peace, his lack of sense of humor and, above all, his public-spiritedness.

After the introduction we slide imperceptibly into the first anecdote that perfectly illustrates the major's methods. The author tells everything in the first person with the happily informal effect of a man entertaining a group of cronies. We receive a slight surprise when another aspect of the major's character, his readiness to deal with an emergency by drastic means is revealed in the incident with the boisterous roughs. When the author attempts to joke with him, the major displays his lack of a sense of humor. Mark Twain's irony is perhaps a little heavy-handed here with its "Now that you mention it, I — yes, I think perhaps you are right" (i. e., I did use force), but the reader smiles at the major's serene unawareness of any incongruity and is swept on to the next anecdote. Mark Twain's habit of laughing at himself is endearing — in fact, as in "The Jumping Frog" there is doubt here as to who is being laughed at. We laugh at the major, but he is, after all, very sensible not to be handicapped by abstract principles in dealing with a concrete situation.

In the course of the anecdotes the major emerges as a public-spirited, independent-minded person. Certainly not a man to be pushed around, but never blustering or threatening in spite of his great physical strength (incident of the card-playing). With his lack of humor and scruples about telling lies (he has apparently argued the whole subject out with himself and decided that he is justified, on practical grounds, in claiming relatives as Presidents of important Boards), his mixture of practical virtue and hard common sense (he knows that brute force is on occasion necessary) he is a worthy descendant of the Puritans and typifies one aspect of the American character. Mark Twain himself has a touch of the Puritan reforming zeal in him, for the major is obviously intended as an example of public-spirited behavior (witness the sincere repentance of the railway company's servants), but he hides this by joking. This slight piece contains touches of telling observation (the station-master is annoyed at the major for insisting on having his state-room, not at the person who had neglected to connect the sleeping-car to the train) and humorous situations. Apart from this, the story gives a glimpse into the America of the late 19th century.

1. *Analyse the humor of this story.*

   Irony — the major's unawareness of incongruity. It is for example strange that a man who renounces force should be an artillery officer. When we see that the major does, in fact, use force when it is required, he seems to be unaware of any discrepancy between declared principles and practice.
   The humor of situation — the newsboy dropping papers into the lap of the sleeping bourgeois; the major, as we last see him, eating chicken from a sense of duty.

2. *What is typically American in this story?*

   Public spirit, independence of mind, unwillingness to accept regulations until they have been proved to be sensible. Pragmatic common sense that recognizes the necessity of departing from principles on occasions. The anxious rivalry for influence in high places (see the incident of the news-boy.) Direct information, e. g. card-playing on Sundays forbidden on trains.

3. *Are these anecdotes convincing?*

   In broad outline, yes. There is realistic good sense in deciding not to be a passive slave of arbitrary rules and regulations. In detail, no. It is impossible for one man, however strong, to remove three roughs from a public conveyance without a great deal of fracas. If the railway company does not provide a sleeping-car, one may be sure that their by-laws provide for this situation. But exaggeration is part of Mark Twain's technique.

4. *Compare this story with "The Jumping Frog."*

   "The Jumping Frog" is a genuine short story where the character of the participants emerges during the course of the story in their words and actions. The doubt as to who is the butt, the teller or the listener, gives the whole story a tension that is lacking here.

   W. G. C.

# ROBERT PENN WARREN

Robert Penn Warren was born on April 24, 1905, in Guthrie, Kentucky. He distinguished himself as a student, being graduated from Vanderbilt University in Nashville, Tennessee, *summa cum laude* in 1925. He received the M. A. degree at the University of California in 1927, pursued further graduate studies at Yale in 1928 and then went to Oxford University as a Rhodes scholar. He is probably the best educated and most scholarly American novelist.

His first book, apart from occasional essays and short stories, was a biography, *John Brown: The Making of a Martyr* (1929). This was followed by several volumes of poetry, which earned him the Shelley Memorial Prize for

Poetry in 1942 and the Pulitzer Prize for Poetry in 1957. He has written seven novels so far, *All the King's Men* (1946) won him the Pulitzer Prize for Fiction in 1947. In that year he also published a collection of 14 short stories written between 1930 and 1946, *The Circus in the Attic and Other Short Stories*.

Since 1931 Warren has been teaching at different universities; in 1950 he accepted a professorship of English at Yale. Together with Cleanth Brooks he founded the influential *Southern Review* in 1935 and wrote two critical introductions into the art of literary appreciation: *Understanding Poetry* (1938) and *Understanding Fiction* (1st edition 1943, 2nd greatly changed edition 1959), with the aim of stimulating the teaching of literature in colleges and universities by means of the analytical approach and the closer reading of texts.

## Blackberry Winter

Text: *American Short Stories* VIII pp. 24—50. Schöningh.

*Blackberry winter is a southern term for a sudden spell of cold weather in summer. At the age of nine, Seth, the son of a farmer in Middle Tennessee, first experiences the threat of violence during a sudden fall of temperature in June 1910. The accompanying storm has ruined several coops of chicks and young turkeys on the farm, and the river bed is filled with a flood that carries driftwood and even a dead cow when Seth goes to watch it. Turning back to their Negro tenants' cabin he finds the garden and yard spoiled and fouled by the drainage water, and old Big Jebb, whom he loves next to his own father and mother, hints darkly at the end of the sinful world. But most disturbing is the appearance of a city-bred stranger who seems to embody the evils of this world.*

Probably the best explanation of Robert Penn Warren's "Blackberry Winter," his finest story (and "presumably the last I shall ever write"), is his own recollection of his intentions and emotions in writing it (cf. Brooks and Warren, l. c.). He tells us it was written in 1945, just after the war, when he had the same feeling Walt Whitman had had about the Civil War — that it revealed "the slimed foundations" of the world. (This idea found imagistic expression in the foul trash washed by the storm into Dellie's pridefully clean yard.) In 1945 Warren had also just completed two important long works, the novel *All the King's Men* and the critical study of Coleridge's *Ancient Mariner*, and he felt that "some sort of watershed of life and experience was being approached." This sense of a "rite of passage" recalled the childhood one that came in June when school was over and boys were permitted to go barefoot — and the "childhood feeling of betrayal when early summer gets turned upside down, and all its promises are revoked by the cold spell." But he wanted to capture more than a mood of nostalgia. "Something has to happen in a story, if there is to be more than a dreary lyric poem posing as a story to promote the cause of universal boredom and deliquescent prose." Hence, the mysterious stranger, the tramp, who is a "creature altogether lost and pitiful, a dim image of what, in one perspective [Warren's], our human condition is." This tramp, who "came up, not merely out of the woods, but out of the darkening grown-up world of time," had to be contrasted with something more innocent — hence the passage of the boy in the woods, the natural innocence of childhood. With this began to emerge "a pattern ... as a series of contrasts" that "would end with a kind of detached summary of the work of time ... with the frightening of the grimmer possibilities of change." Such contrasts include the different reactions to the flood, the father's and son's attitudes to "poor white trash" like Milt Alley, the children's and Old Jebb's responses to Dellie's "woman mizry." Dellie slapping her son's face foreshadows the tramp's threat to cut the boy's throat — a shifting of emphasis "from the lyricism of nostalgia to a concern with the jags and injustices of human relationship." Old Jebb serves as a

> kind of pilot for the feeling I wanted to get; that is, by accepting, in implication at least, something of Jebb's feeling about his own life, we might become aware of our human communion. I wanted the story to give some notion that out of change and loss a human recognition may be redeemed, more precious for being no longer innocent.

Had the boy really stopped or not, when the tramp threatened to cut his throat if he insisted on following him? Warren says, literally yes — "but at another level — no. In so far as later he had really grown up, had really learned something about the meaning of life, in the imaginative recognition, with all the responsibility that such a recognition entails, of this lost, mean, defeated, cowardly, worthless, bitter being as somehow a man." This meaning is embodied in an imaginative reconstruction of varied memories, details, and episodes, but it is not autobiographical.

Warren's commentary on his own story is, of course, extremely valuable; but as he himself suggests "the process was more complicated than that and I shall never know the [whole] truth." There remain many factors of structure, style, detail, and meaning to be elucidated. For example, it may be useful to observe that the story has four main parts and an epilogue: Part I, the arrival of the stranger; part II, the visit to the flood at the bridge; part III, the visit to the Negro cabin; part IV, return to the house and the stranger; and epilogue (beginning "That was thirty-five years ago") which swiftly surveys the passing of those thirty-five years and presents the meaning of the story in the final, puzzling sentence, "But I did follow him, all the years." It is cast in the mode of an autobiographical reminiscence, which makes appropriate the adult vocabulary and the slow, dream-like pace. "Time is not a movement ... but a kind of climate in which things are." There is almost no action at all; therefore, the few dramatic events are rendered powerfully emphatic, as if a figure in a painting were suddenly to move — the flash of the tramp's knife, the dead cow floating on the flood waters, Dellie rising feebly from her sick bed to slap her son, and the tramp turning on the boy at the end. The technique is scenic, but as in a sequence of tapestry tableaux — not as in a drama. For example, note the transition from the boy's careful probing of his mother's precise attitude toward his going barefoot to the entry of the tramp:

"It's June," the voice replied from far away, "but it's blackberry winter." [the betrayal of a boy's expectation of summer]

"I had lifted my head to reply to that, to make one more test of what was in that tone, when I happened to see the man." [Here, the reader naturally asks, "What man?" "Who is he?" etc., but his query is kept in suspense, and the appearance of the man has a mysterious, even sinister effect by the repetition of "I could see the man," and again "I saw the man."]

We are then told that it was strange for a man to be there at all, for the path led into the woods, around a swamp, and ended at the river. And while we speculate about this, the narrator recalls his standing in the wood as a boy and a contrast is evoked between the appropriateness of the boy in the woods and the oddity of a city-bred mysterious stranger in the woods. Six hundred words later, the mystery of it is still under discussion. But two attributes of the meaning of the stranger, whatever it is to be, have already been implicitly suggested: (1) the universality of the experience, when in the fourth paragraph the narrator shifts, almost unobtrusively, from the first person singular to the generalizing second person; and (2) the discovery of a kinship with mysterious strangers, not usually thought of as one's own kind, which is evoked in the allusion to Defoe's *Robinson Crusoe* — "you ... make the perfect mark of your foot in the smooth, creamy, red mud and then muse upon it as though you had suddenly come upon that single mark on the glistening auroral beach of the world. You have never seen a beach, but you have read the book and how the footprint was there." However Crusoe's kinship was a redeeming one; Seth's is to be a kinship with death and evil.

Every suggestion indicates that the stranger is in flight and easily inclines to violence, and as the boy watches him collecting the drowned chicks for burial "his way of looking at me made me so uncomfortable that I left the chickenyard." Before he returns, he is to have experiences in his own familiar and comfortable world that will uncover evil, and violence and death there, too.

At the flooded bridge he observes his mounted father with pride. Here is the image of the old Southern aristocrat — proud, courteous, kind, but aloof from the pains and sorrows of those beneath him:

"Poppa," I said, "do you think Milt Alley has got another cow?"

"You say 'Mr. Alley,'" my father said quietly [insisting that the boy show a formal courtesy to his elders].

"Do you think he has?"

"No telling," my father said [not much concerned with the poverty and loss of the poor white trash].

Other details, too, reinforce the idea (not central, but peripherally important to the story) that it is at one level a condemnation and rejection of the values of the old South. For example, Warren tells us that the boy would see no irony in Old Jebb's name being an echo of J. E. B. Stuart, the Confederate general killed in the Civil War. But he apparently feels that no explanation is necessary, for everyone can see the paradox in an old Negro slave bearing the name of a defender of slavery. But Old Jebb in the story itself is a spokesman of doom, a voice warning of God's withdrawal from sinful mankind: "Lawd say, Yearth, you done yore best, you give 'em cawn and you give 'em taters, and all they think on is they gut, and, Yearth, you kin take a rest." And at the end, old and broken, a survivor in the Waste Land, he says "A man doan know what to pray fer, and him mortal." The Civil War proved the emptiness of the Old South's values, but no new ones took their place. A moral vacuum is revealed — and it is revealed in a context of warm family love, pleasant and amusing banter between son and mother, adoration of son for father. But it is not the father that Seth follows "all the years"; it is the mysterious stranger, who penetrated the idyllic Eden of childhood and showed the boy the brutality of the world. It was a demonstration that recurred again and again.

For example, as the boy sits with his father high up on the mare Nellie Gray, watching the flood, he is as startled by a strange apparition as he was in the house with his mother. "I was sitting there as quiet as I could, feeling the faint stir of my father's chest against my shoulders as it rose and fell with his breath, when I saw the cow." Not *a* cow, but *the* cow — just as it was not *a* man, but *the* man. This dead cow, probably the only one that the "pore white trash squatter," Milt Alley [whose name evokes the place for depositing refuse, unfamiliar to Europeans], owned, floating like a chunk of driftwood, is a powerful and grotesque symbol of death. A hungry boy seeing it speculates aloud whether "anybody ever et drownt cow," and is assured by an old Civil War veteran that under certain circumstances a man will eat anything. (His reference to having eaten foul meat while serving under General Forrest reinforces the concept of the degeneration of the Old South, referred to above.) Thus, the social ritual of gathering at the flood (which may evoke Noah's flood) is also charged with ugly brutality.

It occurs again when young Seth goes up to the Negro cabin where "drainage water had washed up a lot of trash and filth out from under Dellie's house." There Dellie lies in her sick bed, suffering from some malady associated with menopause and muttering "I's sick ... mighty sick." But Seth and young Jebb in the innocence of children begin to play with the Negro boy's toys and become noisier and noisier. The pitifully weak Negro woman summons her son and slaps him. "It was an awful slap, more awful for the kind of weakness which it came from and brought to focus ... It was awful ... I almost ran getting to the door." Once again, in a setting of innocent pleasure the fundamental ills of mankind and the horror of the human situation assert themselves.

Old Jebb, who "was a good man, and I loved him next to my mother and father," tries to explain to Seth: "Hit is the change of life and time." His remark explains more than the condition of Dellie; all men endure the change of life and time. When the boy returns to the farmhouse, he observes his father mocked and insulted by the stranger who with a "twisted sickish grin" spits at his feet. That stranger is almost an allegorical figure of death, sickness, and violence. In the epilogue we learn that while Seth was still a boy, his father had died of lockjaw after being cut by a mowing machine (death during harvest plenty), his mother died within three years "right in middle life," Dellie died, too, many years later, the persecuted young Jebb became a murderer and was sent to prison. But Old Jebb lived to be more than a hundred, a pathetic broken man who felt abandoned by God. Seth did follow the stranger all the years, after his initiation into the dark side of life when he was merely a nine-year-old boy.

This symbolic level of the story is almost lost in the wealth of realistic details, but it is the only level that absorbs and explains everything. The narrator knows the meaning of the events, since he tells of them 35 years later when he is a mature man; therefore, it lacks the sparseness of detail and the skeleton style of, for example, Hemingway's "The Killers," — another story of the initiation of a boy into the evil and horror of life. But it is no more explicit than Hemingway — merely more richly orchestrated, more powerfully suggestive, more evocatively emotional.

1. *Is the presence of the stranger ever explained? What details show him to be out of place in the back country of Middle Tennessee in 1910?*

   No. The mother's suggestion that "he cut across from the Dunbar place" seemed at first to be a perfectly rational explanation, but neither the mother nor anyone else satisfactorily answers the boy's further question: "what would he be doing over at the Dunbar place last night?" He knew nothing about dogs, he wore city clothes rather than blue jeans and he had on low, black, pointed shoes, and his hands did not have the creases and earth-color of the hands of men who work outdoors. In a Hawthorne allegory, such a stranger would probably be the devil; but Warren's technique is much more realistic and his world-view is much more secular. Though the stranger is as much a symbolic figure as Hawthorne's devil, he symbolizes the evils of this world rather than the intrusion of some other world.

2. *Identify the moment of sharpest contrast in each of the four sections.*

   I, when the stranger appears; II, when the dead cow appears; III, when Dellie slaps her son; and IV, when the stranger turns on the boy and threatens to cut his throat. In this sequence, evil becomes more and more directly aimed at the boy.

3. *Three of the four sections embody some passage of explicit commentary — a set piece or essay on some subject relevant to the overall meaning. Identify and discuss them.*

   Most of these set-pieces are signaled by the generalizing "you." In the first section, the principal one is the meditation on Time: "everything is so important and stands big and full and fills up Time and is so solid that you can walk around and around it like a tree and look at it." This paragraph alerts us to the fact that the story is going to be about some BIG MOMENT in Time for Seth. There are in the first section other occasional side comments of this kind; for example, "there is nothing deader than a drowned chick ... the eyes have that bluish membrane over them which makes you think of a very old man who is sick about to die." In Part II, there are two — the discussion of the recurrent floods and the old veteran's talk of hunger. In the first (which goes from "The creek was big here ..." to "Nobody ever came down in winter to see high water") we learn that the flood has occurred so frequently that response to it has taken the form of a ritual ("It was like church or a funeral"). The second begins when the Civil War veteran tries to reassure Cy Dundee's boy and ends with, "Live long enough and a man will settle fer what he kin git." Thus, flood and famine are added to time and death as essay subjects within the story. In the third section, we are treated to old Jebb's apocalyptic prophecy: "Maybe hit is come cold to stay ... I been tellen folks. Sayen, maybe this year, hit is the time. But they doan listen to me, how the yearth is tahrd. Maybe this year they find out." He tells Seth that "everything and everybody" will die. The fourth section is the dramatic culmination of the story; no abstract discussion interrupts the tight coiling of the spring, and none is needed.

In all of Warren's novels and stories these philosophical essays are embedded — usually justified by the fact that the internal narrator is a philosophically inclined man. But they are not strictly necessary. For sensitive readers Warren's dramatic symbolism would be sufficient to carry the burden of meaning without them.

4. *What turns of speech are not standard American English? Does the fact that these are Southernisms add anything to the meaning of the story?*

Such expressions as: "gully-washer," "blackberry winter," the call to an animal — "Here you, Bully!," "down yonder," "poor white trash," "white folks' niggers," "mean and ficey," etc. They establish an authentic Southern setting and suggest the possibility that the death of the old Southern way of life is among the deaths that young Seth becomes aware of in his initiation.

J. V. H.

Beardsley, Monroe, R. Daniel and G. Leggett, *Theme and Form: An Introduction to Literature*, Englewood Cliffs, N. J., 1956, pp. 691-695 — Bradbury, John M., *The Fugitives: A Critical Account*, Chapel Hill 1958, pp. 199-200 — Brooks and Warren, *Understanding Fiction*, 2nd edition, New York 1959, pp. 638—643 — Davison, Richard A., Physical Imagery in R. P. Warren's "Blackberry Winter," *The Georgia Review* XXII, 1968, pp. 482—488 — Male, Roy R., *Types of Short Fiction*, Belmont 1962, pp. 299—307 — Scott, James B., The Theme of Betrayal in Robert Penn Warren's Stories, *Thoth (Syracuse Univ.)*, 1964, pp. 74—77 — Weathers, Winston, "Blackberry Winter" and the Use of Archetypes, *Studies in Short Fiction* I, 1963, pp. 45—51 — West, Ray B., *The Short Story in America: 1900—1950*, Chicago 1952, pp. 77—80.

# EDITH WHARTON

Edith Wharton was born on January 24, 1862, in New York City, daughter of George Frederic Jones. Her parents being wealthy, she was educated by governesses, traveled much abroad, and read widely. In 1895 she married Edward Wharton. Four years later she won her first success by a collection of short stories, *The Greater Inclination,* in which she applied to society life her psychological insight and her sense of artistic form. From 1906 on she lived mostly in France and published several volumes of short stories, long stories and novels, most of them with an American setting. In 1920 and 1924 she was awarded the Pulitzer Prize. She died in France in 1937, after earning more honors than any other American woman writer.

In many ways she resembles her friend Henry James, who, besides George Eliot, influenced her most strongly. She once defined the ideal short story as "a shaft driven straight into the heart of experience." Her idea of realism — as dealing with life selectively and creatively — was opposed to "stream of consciousness" naturalism, an extreme development from which she recoiled.

## Mrs. Manstey's View

Text: *American Short Stories* IV pp. 79—91. Schöningh

Mrs. Manstey's husband died 17 years ago. Her married daughter in California cannot afford to visit her mother, who lives alone in a back room on the third floor of a cheap boarding-house in New York. The only pleasure and interest in Mrs. Manstey's life is afforded by the extensive view from her window. She knows the whole sky-line, every bush and tree, and every bird and cat and housemaid in the windows opposite. Being an aesthete at heart she is sensible of changes of color unnoticed by the average eye. One April day her landlady informs her that the neighboring boarding-house is going to build an extension which will interfere with her view. Mrs. Manstey in vain offers 1,000 dollars to induce the proprietress to refrain from the new building. During the first night after the workmen have begun, Mrs. Manstey sets fire to the neighboring house, but it is soon put out. In the cold of that night the old lady catches pneumonia, and she dies the second morning after the fire — just before the building of the extension is resumed.

"Mrs. Manstey's View" opens with a rather long and garrulous introduction, but once the action begins the story moves in sure, strong movements to its denouement. The narrative point of view is that of an omniscient observer who focuses narrowly on Mrs. Manstey and relates her meditations and experiences with a rather "literary" style (e. g., "earth showed through the snow, like ink spots spreading on a sheet of white blotting paper"). Mrs. Manstey has been widowed for seventeen years and lives alone in a boarding-house in a run-down section of New York. Though she is lonely, she "had never been a sociable woman" and prefers to remain aloof from others; though she is by no means wealthy, she is not poverty-stricken; though she is growing infirm, she is still able to knit "numberless stockings" and to get about when strongly motivated to do so. "The absorbing interest of her life" is the view from her third-floor rear window which looks out upon a varied landscape of gardens, junk yards, and a distant factory. It is not a romantically beautiful view, but full of interest to an innocent voyeur with "a vague tenderness for plants and animals" and the personalities of "the houses and their inmates."

It is a serious fault of the story that nothing significant would be lost if it began with the eighth paragraph; everything of importance preceding that point is implicitly involved in what follows, and the explicit statements of the introduction are not really necessary. Considering the eighth paragraph as sufficient for an introduction, one can analyze the remainder of "Mrs. Manstey's View" into six parts: (1) the threat to her view, the main thing that "shaped her life," when the landlady announces that Mrs. Black (appropriately named) plans to extend the neighboring rooming-house clear to the end of the back yard; (2) Mrs. Manstey's meditation in "the bat-colored dusk" and her feeling that she cannot possibly move away nor live without her view; (3) her attempt to bribe Mrs. Black with an offer of a thousand dollars for not building the extension; (4) the realization that she had been deceived by Mrs. Black — who had considered her insane and had made placating promises — when she observes the workmen carrying bricks and demolishing the neighboring balcony; (5) her desperate and futile resort to arson in the middle of the night; and (6) the denouement in which she dies as a result of pneumonia contracted during the attempt to burn down Mrs. Black's house. On the day of her death "the building of the extension was resumed."

The events are clearly pathetic, but the theme and ultimate meaning of the story are not clear. Is Mrs. Manstey a sympathetic or merely a pitiful character? On the one hand, she is apparently the only one in this drab environment who values the beauties of nature; on the other hand, she is ineffectually eccentric in her attempted bribery and obviously mad in her attempted arson. The opposition between Mrs. Manstey and those around her is both dramatically and symbolically expressed. When, in alluding to "a topic not likely to appeal to her visitors," she points out to her landlady that the magnolia in Mrs. Black's yard is out earlier than usual this year, Mrs. Sampson replies, "Is it, indeed? I didn't know there was a magnolia there." Later, "one of the workmen, a coarse fellow with a bloated face, picked a magnolia blossom and, after smelling it, threw it to the ground; the next man, carrying a load of bricks, trod on the flower in passing." Yet, although the brutality of the practical world is thus repeatedly emphasized, Mrs. Manstey's counter-attack is more heartless than the behavior of her "persecutors." If the apparently intended moral of the story is that the love of beauty cannot survive in a brutal, economically-oriented world, that moral is certainly undermined by at least three factors: the love of beauty is identified with a pathetic and queer, if not mad, old woman; those who do not share it are not necessarily unkind — Mrs.

Sampson visits her regularly and Mrs. Black offers her a room in the new extension; the workmen are not deliberately brutal and cruel — even the "coarse fellow with a bloated face" stops to smell the magnolia blossom. Psychologically, the story superficially delineates a "descent into the utter darkness" of Mrs. Manstey's psyche. Although melodramatic attention to details of violence is avoided, motivation is not realistically complex enough nor sufficiently explored (as it is in, e. g., Henry James and William Faulkner) to make the story valuable on that level. Mrs. Manstey wins a Pyrrhic victory; until the day she dies "the view was undisturbed" and she observes that "the magnolia had unfolded a few more sculptural flowers." But the story, especially the conclusion, remains sentimental pathos, a high-class form of kitsch.

1. *This story was Edith Wharton's first published work (1891). Are there any signs that it was written by a beginner?*

   Learned references — e. g. Quintus Curtius (origin doubtful — probably mistaken), "a coign of vantage" (Shakespeare). A somewhat stilted literary style — "A gust of cold wind smote her"; "The sunset was perfect and a roseate light, transfiguring the distant spire, lingered late in the west." There is some confusion about whether the old woman is presented sympathetically or not — at first we are shown a fairly lonely old lady in fairly poor circumstances in a grasping, hostile world. What are we to think of her after her act of destruction? The old lady's turmoil of mind is not conveyed.

2. *In "The Writing of Fiction", Edith Wharton says, "Every great novel must first of all be based on a profound sense of moral values." Apply this tenet to the short story under review.*

   At the beginning the moral position is clear. Mrs. Manstey with her vaguely aesthetic love of flowers, is confronted with a hard, grasping world that treads flowers underfoot. After Mrs. Manstey's act of incendiarism, our sense of moral values is left in the lurch. Perhaps Edith Wharton wanted to dramatize the idea that one cannot preserve a love of beauty by resorting to the methods of the materialistic world: one merely becomes its victim in so doing.

3. *Edith Wharton also wrote that the writer "must bear in mind at each step that his business is not to ask what the situation would be likely to make of the characters, but what the characters ... would make of the situation." Apply this to the short story under review.*

   Mrs. Manstey is presented to the reader as a gentle, rather colorless person. Even her chief characteristic, her love for plants and animals, is described as "vague." Only in a very unusual state of mind can she be considered capable of committing a dangerous crime, and Edith Wharton does not capture the powerful sense of desperation that led to her incendiary act. Mrs. Manstey's dialogue with the neighbor landlady reveals a woman who has endured disappointment after disappointment and finally determines to preserve the last source of joy in her life.

4. *What is the effect of the exaggeration concerning the state of the pavement at the beginning of the story?*

In some readers at least the feeling is aroused that Mrs. Manstey is not being taken too seriously. The remark is that of a slum visitor, accustomed to more genteel surroundings. In the remainder of the story over-statement is carefully avoided. It is evident that Mrs. Manstey does not suffer the extremes of poverty and loneliness. The statement about the pavement therefore confuses the reader's attitude at the outset.

5. *Why are the extremes of poverty and loneliness avoided in this story?*

The author wants to give the impression of a rather colorless person of fixed habits and sober way of life. Thus the emotional crisis that leads her to her act of incendiarism will appear more startling in contrast.

6. *Are Mrs. Manstey's actions sufficiently motivated?*

The gentle Mrs. Manstey overhears the remark made by one of the workmen about the danger of fire breaking out on the building site. This plants a seed in her mind and impels her to act. Everyone nowadays has at least an inkling of the strange motives for our actions lurking in the subconscious mind. We are willing to accept a motive of this kind as long as the author plays his part by conveying its compelling force and dark origin.

7. *Is there a moral in the last sentence of the story?*

The suggestion is that the world will go on trampling flowers underfoot and that the victim of change — like Mrs. Manstey — can do nothing to stop it. Mrs. Manstey's fire only blackened a few ceilings. There is perhaps a vestige of nineteenth-century romantic melodrama in the final scene — the dying old woman looks out on a "jubilant spring dawn."

J. V. H./W. G. C.

# THORNTON WILDER

Thornton Wilder was born on April 17, 1897, in Madison, Wisconsin, son of a newspaper editor who in 1906 received an appointment as United States Consul-General at Hong Kong and, later, at Shanghai. He began his education in a German missionary school in China and pursued his undergraduate studies at Oberlin College, Ohio. In 1917 he transferred to Yale University, where he graduated Bachelor of Arts in 1920. Having done a year of work at the American Academy of Classical Studies in Rome, he began teaching French at the Lawrenceville Preparatory School in New Jersey, which left him ample time for reading and writing. At that time he made up his mind to write for pleasure and not for profit. His first novel, *The Cabala*, was published in 1925, a year before he received his master's degree from Princeton University; in the same year his first play was produced. In 1927, *The Bridge of San Luis Rey* was an immediate best-seller and was awarded the Pulitzer Prize. After that success he gave up teaching to concentrate on writing. He traveled in Europe, mainly in France, and from 1930 to 1936 served on the faculty of the University of Chicago. During World War II he was an intelligence officer with the army air force in North Africa and Italy.

He wrote three more novels during that time, *The Woman of Andros* (1930), *Heaven's My Destination* (1935) and *The Ides of March* (1948), but his interest centered more on the dramatic field. After a number of experimental one-act and three-minute plays he had great success with *Our Town* (1938) and *The Skin of Our Teeth* (1942), both of which were awarded the Pulitzer Prize for Drama. Two plays received their first performances at the Edinburgh International Festival: *The Matchmaker* (1954) and *A Life in the Sun*, or *The Alcestiad* (1955). Wilder himself transformed two of his plays into opera librettos, *The Long Christmas Dinner* (music by Paul Hindemith) and *The Alcestiad* (music by Louise Talma). In his work on two cycles of short plays, *The Seven Ages of Man* and *The Seven Deadly Sins*, Wilder was discouraged by critics who found that he "repeats, but does not enlarge, his basic credo that life is life, a tautology tinged with profundity" and that "the prevailing sound of the evening is the clink of truism rather than the ring of truth." (*Time*, January 19, 1962)

In 1950/51 Wilder was professor of poetry at Harvard University, in 1952 he led the American delegation to the UNESCO conference in Venice. He has won particular recognition in Europe and, apart from many other honors, was awarded the Peace Prize of the German book trade in 1957 ("dem großen Dichter und Dramatiker, der in wirrer Zeit den Glauben an höhere Mächte aufrechterhalten half").

For his novel *The Eighth Day* (1967) he received the National Book Award. Critics stated that "the basic optimism of his earlier plays, *Our Town* and *The Skin of Our Teeth*, is shaded here with a darker and more bitter irony than before. Life's meanings are less clear." (John K. Sherman) "Everything's hopeless," says one of the characters in this novel, "but we are the slaves of hope."

## Our Town

Text: Thornton Wilder, *Our Town*. Hirschgraben

*The entire play takes place in Grover's Corners, New Hampshire, between 1901 and 1913. In Act I the Stage Manager introduces the audience to the Daily Life in the small town. The interest is focused on the families of Doctor Gibbs and Mr. Webb, the editor of the local newspaper. Act II concerns the Love and Marriage of their children George and Emily, three years later. In a scene-within-scene, George and Emily re-enact the dawning of their Love. Act III takes up the action nine years later, after Emily's Death in childbirth. The scene here is the cemetery at Grover's Corners, and the stage now holds the living and the dead. When Emily begs for one day more on earth she is allowed, in another flashback, to live over her twelfth birthday. But with her awareness of the future she can't bear life among the living and soon returns to the dead. She realizes that human beings are "just blind people" and "don't understand much."*

Our Town is not in any traditional sense a drama at all; it has neither plot nor conflict, neither complication nor climax. By its abandonment of setting and by its use of the Stage Manager as intermediary between the play and its audience, it gives the appearance of belonging to the experimental theater movement; yet, within the experimental theater it is a completely anomalous production. For all its show of technical virtuosity, it aims at a familiar dramatic effect, that of sentimental comedy which is characterized by its attempt to play upon a muted but varied scale of emotions, mingling pathos, nostalgia and humor in a pleasantly innocuous cordial. The popularity of Wilder's play is not difficult to understand when one considers that sentimental comedy continues to dominate the Broadway theater in America and that, from its inception in the 18th century, sentimental comedy has always been popular with a large middle-class audience. Its popularity derives from the fact that it has, at bottom, the effect of complimenting us upon the lives that we lead by assuring us that the surface patterns of our lives are life itself and that, though we do not always appreciate it, ordinary life is, after all, good. It treats life with genteel laughter and death with appropriate tears and, despite a frequent show of profundity, takes neither very seriously.

However, because it disposes of the necessity of a coherently developed story line, Our Town avoids immediate identification with this familiar dramatic category. In itself, it is perhaps best described as a recitation in character of a quasi-philosophical essay, illustrated by selected vignettes from small-town life. The subheadings which the Stage Manager gives the three acts of the play — Daily Life; Love and Marriage; Death — put one in mind of books of popular sociology and philosophy; and the Stage Manager is, himself, a traditional character often known as a "cracker barrel philosopher" or "rural sage." Moreover, the absence of a proscenium curtain and the reduction of setting to a few properties serves to eliminate the normal expectations of a theater audience and to keep complete control in the hands of the Stage Manager, who lectures the audience and arranges brief dramatic sketches for its amusement and edification. Revolutionary as it may seem at first glance, however, Our Town is not quite a reduction to what Molière cited as the minimum essentials of drama — a platform and a passion or two. As George Jean Nathan has pointed out, Mr. Wilder cheats in the use he makes of skeletonized drama:

> While insisting that he abandons all scenery and props, he still compromises with his plan by employing them. He shows us no houses, but he brings out two flower-covered latticed doorways to trick the imagination

into an acceptance of their presence... He uses almost as many lighting tricks as the late Belasco [for] sunsets, dawns, and sunrises. He asks us to... picture a garden or pasture or chicken patch and then pulls a vaudeville act by having someone in the wings moo like a cow or crow like a rooster. He concretely shows us no marriage altar, but he puts his little actress into a white bridal costume and then has the electrician throw a stereopticon slide of a stained-glass window above the spot where he has asked us to visualize it[1].

Nevertheless, the play is not the thing; what matters is the discourse. True to the tradition of the rural sage, the Stage Manager invites the audience to contemplate the superficial patterns of small-town life through the warm glow of his shrewd but benevolent personality. He has no coherently thought out point of view but unself-consciously mixes sentimentalized naturalism with a kind of ambiguous supernaturalism. He is, in fact, not a thinker at all; he is an observer with a certain understanding of the value of the sort of facts that the "rural savant" and Editor Webb are called in to provide, facts which suggest that his way of seeing things is rooted in a concrete awareness of the immensity of time and nature as well as of the here and now. Because he deals with the big, general experiences of mankind — love, marriage, death — what he says carries a gratuitous hint of profundity; yet, he avoids pompousness by a studied pose of simplicity and matter-of-factness, which is a form of anti-intellectualism, and by his gift for detached statements informed by a shrewd, practical wit.

In effect, the Stage Manager attempts to lead the audience to assent to the proposition that the minimal existence of Grover's Corners is an adequate base for encompassing the experiences and finding out the fate of mankind. If the audience takes him seriously, it must accept the assumption that what matters most in human existence is apparent in the limited world which the Stage Manager does, in fact, present. And if this is accepted, the audience may miss the fact that the amused condescension, the shrewdness and the matter-of-factness of the Stage Manager disguise the sentimentality of his viewpoint — "sentimentality" here meaning an unwarrantedly high valuation in moral, emotional and aesthetic terms of the thing presented.

Such sentimentality is the inevitable product of any attempt to make the most commonplace surfaces of life carry the burden of a congenial but amorphous "philosophy," and its presence in Wilder's play is particularly obvious when the play is placed in the context of the rest of 20th century American literature. In these terms, *Our Town* reads as a competently executed but nonetheless sentimental response to the widespread attack upon the stifling ethos and cultural poverty of American small-town life (cf. Sinclair Lewis's *Main Street*). It responds by shifting the focus from those who rebel against the poverty of such a life to those who, superficially regarded, appear contented with it and whose lives remain safely within the middle range of emotion and awareness.

---

[1] George Jean Nathan, *Encyclopedia of the Theatre*, New York 1940, p. 424.

Even Wilder's own view of the play supports such a reading:

> *Our Town* is not offered as a picture of life in a New Hampshire village; or as a speculation about the conditions of life after death (that element I merely took from Dante's *Purgatory*). It is an attempt to find a value beyond all price for the smallest events in our daily life. I have made the claim as preposterous as possible, for I have set the village against the largest dimensions of time and place[1].

These dimensions are referred to most emphatically at the end of act I when Rebecca Gibbs tells her brother about the elaborately addressed letter Jane Crofut received from the minister of her church:

> ... Grover's Corners ... the United States of America; Continent of North America; Western Hemisphere; the Earth; the Solar System; the Universe; the Mind of God.[2]

Though the comments of the Stage Manager imply that through these tepid, unexamined lives we are looking at the core of human experience, no human experience is, as a matter of fact, looked at other than obliquely: birth is a light burning across the tracks; love is finding out that the girl or boy next door has been watching you, and death is a few black umbrellas and tears and a dignified immobility. Whatever hard-fact details he includes are not those of elemental human experience, but of sociology; *Our Town* might well serve as an excellent source of information concerning small-town life in New England before World War I.

Even the "daring" device of the third act, the commentary of the dead, will not bear close examination. Despite the philosophical flourish with which it is introduced — "Everybody knows that there is something eternal" — the play at this point becomes more than usually evasive. The line between life and death is deliberately blurred: the grief and the fearful sense of finality that dwells on this side of the line is evaded, and the profound mystery — even if only the mystery of nothingness — that dwells on the other side is reduced to the non-committal terms of forgetting and waiting. Death, so conceived, provides a viewpoint from which the still living may not be too harshly criticized for failing to look with perpetual, wide-eyed wonder upon the familiar conditions of their daily lives. Actually, this somewhat elaborate device seems designed simply to gain an uncritical assent to Emily's "Oh, earth, you're too wonderful for anybody to realize you," which comes as close as any statement in the play to expressing the theme.

Wilder comes closer than any other modern dramatist to writing non-drama, and he does so deliberately. The maximum of stock response is elicited from the minimum of dramatic action. As Editor Webb says, "Very ordinary town, if you ask me. Little better behaved than most. Probably al lot duller." When Wilder attempts to present the universal in this statistically normal

---

[1] in: "A Passion and a Platform or Two," preface to *Three Plays*, New York 1957.
[2] Wilder borrowed this idea from James Joyce's *Portrait of the Artist as a Young Man* (Penguin Book 1477, pp. 15/16).

particular, he cannot help citing and then deliberately pushing off-stage potential sources of genuine drama. For example, in the very first dialogue of the play, the paper-boy seeing Doc Gibbs returning from a night-call asks, "Somebody been sick, Doc?" "No," says Doc Gibbs, "Just some twins born over in Polish town." In the total context of the play, this has the same effect as Huck Finn's answer to Aunt Sally's question on hearing of an explosion on a steamboat, "Was anybody hurt?" "No. Just a nigger killed." In this smug, middle-class, Anglo-Saxon small town the Goruslawskis hardly rate as human beings. One would think that in a population of 2,640, the birth of twins, even in a Polish family, warrants just a bit more excitement. To a more significant playwright, the impact of Polish immigrants on the Anglo-Saxon population is material for powerful drama — *vide* Tennessee Williams' *Streetcar Named Desire*. But in this play, the Poles and the Catholic church are safely relegated to the other side of the railroad tracks.

At another point in the play, a man in the audience asks Mr. Webb, publisher and editor of The Grover's Corners *Sentinel*, "Is there no one in town aware of social injustice and industrial inequality?" And the facetious answer is, "Oh yes, everybody is, — somethin' terrible. Seems like they spend most of their time talking about who's rich and who's poor." If they do, we hear none of that talk in this play, and out goes the Ibsen-Miller tradition.

Thornton Wilder, like every artist, is faced with a problem in the selection of details; and he has chosen to select only the most ordinary, everyday details of a very small, narrow segment of the American population — a sort of socio-philosophical cross-section of the genus homo Americanus, Anglo-Saxiensis. And he is extra-ordinarily successful in rendering the ordinary. His most crucial flaw in this respect is a revealing one: Emily, dying in childbirth, becomes quite an exception to the statistical norm — an exception perfectly suited to Wilder's sentimental purposes. No doubt *Our Town* will always have a strong appeal to delicately sensitive adolescents; the mature observer will respond as Arthur Miller did, suspecting that its popular appeal lies in "the deep longing of the audience for such stability, a stability which in daylight out on the streets does not exist... the play falls short... because it could not plumb the psychological interior lives of its characters and still keep its present form." (*Atlantic*, April 1956, p. 39)

*Our Town* is fairly representative of Wilder's point of view, his talent and his deficiencies. Because his writings fail to reflect any serious attempt to come to terms with the depth and complexity of human experience, the overt expression in them of a congenial and basically optimistic "philosophy" stands out as an unearned increment. It is for this reason that Wilder has not gained recognition from American literary critics and scholars. Standards seem to be different in Germany if Horst Oppel[1] is right in predicting "with complete certainty that *Our Town* will prove to have had a permanent effect [on play-

---

[1] Horst Oppel, American Literature in Postwar Germany: Impact or Alienation? *Die Neueren Sprachen* 1962, p. 7.

writing] in Germany." So far there is not much evidence of that effect, however, as Oppel himself emphasizes "that among the newer German playwrights there is not a single one who has successfully followed in Wilder's footsteps." — Nevertheless, it is one of the most amazing phenomena of modern literary history that in Germany Wilder continues to be celebrated as a great world author while in his own country he is generally regarded as merely an interesting literary curiosity.

1. *What is the effect of eliminating the proscenium curtain and the usual stage setting?*

In general, this diminishes the normal "aesthetic distance" between the audience and what is presented on the stage and defeats the audience's usual dramatic expectations. To the extent that the device is successful, it undermines the critical assumptions of the audience and renders critical objectivity more difficult. Moreover, the device serves to keep control in the hands of the Stage Manager, allowing him to dominate the entire play.

2. *How does the Stage Manager function in the play? What is his relationship to the audience? Is his relationship to the characters in the play a constant one?*

The Stage Manager, under the pretense of telling us about Grover's Corners, shapes the play as an expression of his understanding and evaluation of human existence. He is something of an amateur philosopher, and what he presents is not so much a commentary on the play as it is a loosely conceived discourse in which the dramatic scenes serve as illustration. In his relationship to the audience, he functions as an informal lecturer and, thereby, gains the authority implicit in the lecturer's position. His relationship to the characters in the play varies from act to act. In the first act, he assumes the role of neighbor and fellow citizen; in the second, he becomes the spiritual and philosophical voice of the community, and in the third, he assumes some of the lesser attributes of God, conceived in the popular image of a non-committal but kindly disposed old man.

3. *From what point of view does the Stage Manager evaluate the human experiences presented in the play?*

His basic assumption, which is stated in his speech before the wedding (Act II), is that nature is an essentially benevolent force and that it is in some way striving for the perfection of man. Each individual participates unconsciously in the striving of nature; this makes life, ipso facto, meaningful, and the individual need only keep himself alert, to *look at* people and things, in order to realize the goodness of it. For, while life may not seem to be interesting and meaningful as most people live it, rightly perceived it is full of wonder and a poignant sweetness. In any event, man cannot lose the future because not only is nature on his side but there is *something* eternal in him which will survive. Unfortunately, there is nothing in the play to suggest that the Stage Manager holds these beliefs for any reason other than that they are comfortable and reassuring.

4. *For what purposes are the "rural savant" and Editor Webb called upon in Act I? What do the hecklers in the audience contribute?*

Prof. Willard and Editor Webb help to establish Grover's Corners as a real place; they do not, however, add anything concrete to our awareness of either the appearance or the atmosphere of this particular town. On the contrary, their citations of facts and statistics simultaneously imply the reality of the town and reduce it to a representative abstraction. This reduction is important in the development of the play, which has to do, after all, not with Grover's Corners but with "Our Town," with the ordinary places in which presumably the majority of men live out their ordinary lives. The Stage Manager might have assumed this function but only at the risk of lessening his rapport with the audience. Introducing the "rural savant" and calling upon Editor Webb spares the Stage Manager both the burden of uncharacteristic pedantry and the necessity of entering into controversy with the hecklers.

The hecklers, themselves, are written in as a kind of controlled audience response. They raise the questions and state the objections that the more critical and sceptical members of the audience might be expected to entertain. Each of the questions represents one of the points of view from which small-town life is frequently attacked. Editor Webb meets each with apparent common sense and humility, and even when he has no direct answer to the implied criticism, his attitude in contrast to the aggressive, uncharitable tones of the hecklers is calculated to win the audience to the defense of the small town. Thus, the hecklers serve to foster the feeling that the usual critique of small-town life is irrelevant, the intellectual plaything of cranks and snobs.

5. *"Our Town" consists of loosely connected dramatic sketches taken from the lives of a few Grover's Corners inhabitants. How, then, does Wilder contrive to give the play continuity?*

There is, of course, the bare hint of a plot in the developing relationship between George Gibbs and Emily Webb. Moreover, though the play spans several years, the fact that it begins at dawn with talk of birth and ends at night with talk of death gives it the appearance of unity and completeness. Most important, however, is the personality and point of view of the Stage Manager. It is immediately established as a convention of the play that the Stage Manager may direct our attention wherever he wishes. He assumes the responsiblity for providing transitions, and it is soon understood that the dramatic elements in the play are subordinate to the elaboration of his point of view.

6. *What is the role of Simon Stimson in the play?*

In a sense, he is the devil's advocate. Unlike the other characters he has been hurt and embittered by life, and, consequently, he dissents from the point of view of the Stage Manager. Thus, the play might be said to have both a thesis and an antithesis; however, no real conflict is allowed to develop. For the nature of Simon's hurt is left vague, and he is not allowed a voice until the last act, in the context of which his dissent is made to appear strictly personal and even pitiable.

A. R. W./J. V. H.

Haas, Rudolf, Thornton Wilder's *Our Town*, Itschert, Hans, ed., *Das amerikanische Drama von den Anfängen bis zur Gegenwart*, Darmstadt 1972, pp. 209—219 — McCarthy, Mary T., *Sights and Spectacles, 1937—1956*, New York 1956, pp. 53—56 — Mennemeier, Franz Norbert, *Das moderne Drama des Auslandes*, Düsseldorf 1961, pp. 111—128 — Szondi, Peter, *Theorie des modernen Dramas*, Frankfurt ⁶1969, pp. 139—145 — Weber, Alfred, *Our Town*, in Hüllen-Rossi-Christopeit, *Zeitgenössische amerikanische Dichtung*, Frankfurt 1960, pp. 180—185.

## TENNESSEE WILLIAMS

Thomas Lanier Williams was born on March 26, 1911, in Columbus, Mississippi, son of a traveling salesman. His father came from pioneer Tennessee stock, his mother descended from Quakers. He started writing poetry as a child, but growing up he rejected what he had written. In 1926 his parents moved north to St. Louis where the discovery of social contrast produced a shock and a rebellion that was to grow into an inherent part of his work. Looking backward on this period he said he was glad that he received this bitter education "for I don't think any writer has much purpose back of him unless he feels bitterly the inequities of the society he lives in." He felt it advisable to add, "I have no acquaintance with political and social dialectics. If you ask what my politics are, I am a Humanitarian."

He entered college during the great American depression and was soon forced to work for his living as a clerk. He began writing short stories at night, until his health broke down and he was sent back South to live with his grandparents in Memphis. After two more years of college he got a B. A. degree at the University of Iowa in 1938. At the university his fraternity brothers nicknamed him "Tennessee" because of his Southern accent and he welcomed the name as his ancestors had fought the Indians for Tennessee "and I had already discovered that the life of a young writer was going to be something similar to the defense of a stockade against a band of savages," as he later said.

In 1940 he received a Rockefeller Foundation Fellowship and wrote his first play, *Battle of Angels*, which was not successful until he rewrote it in 1957 under the title *Orpheus Descending*. Working at various jobs in different parts of the USA during the war, he kept on writing, not with any hope of making a living at it but because to him, this was the only means of expressing things that seemed to demand expression. In 1945 he had the good luck to be employed for six months by one of the film companies in Hollywood, at 250 dollars a week. He was thus able to save enough money to keep him while writing *The Glass Menagerie*, his first great success, which won the New York Drama Critics' Circle Award in 1945. His next play, *A Streetcar Named Desire* (1947), which got its title from the trams of New Orleans, where Williams had made his home, was awarded the Pulitzer Prize for Drama. After another less successful play, *Summer and Smoke* (1948), followed *The Rose Tattoo* (1951), *Camino Real* (1953) and *Cat on a Hot Tin Roof* (1954), which again won him the Pulitzer Prize for Drama and the New York Drama Critics' Circle Award. Repeatedly Williams also turned to the forms of the one-act play, the short story (collections in 1948 and 1954), and the novel (*The Roman Spring of Mrs. Stone*, 1950, *One Day in the Afternoon of the World*, 1964). Many of his long and short plays were successfully transformed into films.

In recent years the number of quickly following plays — *Sweet Bird of Youth* (1956), *Suddenly Last Summer* (1958), a comedy *Period of Adjustment* (1959), *The Night of the Iguana* (1961) and *The Milk Train Doesn't Stop Here Anymore* (1962) — proved his undiminished productivity.

"Every artist," he once said, "has a basic premise pervading his whole life, and that premise can provide the impulse in everything he creates. For me the dominating premise has been the need for understanding and tenderness and fortitude among individuals trapped by circumstance."

## The Glass Menagerie

Text: Tennessee Williams, *The Glass Menagerie.* Hirschgraben
Tennessee Williams, *The Glass Menagerie.* Schöningh

*The action of the play is presented and commented upon by a narrator; "the scene is memory and is therefore nonrealistic." At the time of the Civil War in Spain, Tom Wingfield lives with his mother Amanda and his sister Laura in a dark groundfloor apartment in a narrow side alley of St. Louis. Their father deserted the family sixteen years before. Laura, who is crippled and walks with a slight limp, is too shy and withdrawn to devote herself to a business career and has no contact with other people; her only pleasures are her glass menagerie, a collection of tiny glass animals, and a victrola (i. e. a kind of phonograph), on which she plays records left by her father. As her mother wants her to get married Tom invites a "gentleman caller," who turns out to be the only boy Laura secretly admired at high school six years before. With his warm self-confidence he overcomes Laura's shyness, only to shatter any budding hopes by announcing that he is engaged to be married. Soon afterwards Tom also deserts the family — but cannot forget his sister.*

Since 1945 Tennessee Williams has assumed a position of eminence among serious American dramatists. He and Arthur Miller, in their separate ways, have done more than any other American playwrights to create a new American drama, a drama fully as substantial in what it proposes and far less naive in the means which it has adopted than is the drama of Eugene O'Neill. It is, generally speaking, a drama of subtle technical refinement, of high emotional tension and of symbolic realization. Because it has assimilated thoroughly the modern psychological and sociological critique of man and of society as well as the fruits of the experimental theater of the 1920's and '30's, it has succeeded in probing, as O'Neill wished to do, "the sickness of the modern world." At its best it has done so with an adeptness and acumen that, so to speak, penetrates far beneath and extends far beyond but does not violate or negate the pattern of human action which is the play itself.

*The Glass Menagerie* was the first of Williams' successful dramas; it is not in any sense fully representative of his work. What one has come to expect of Williams is the artistic exploitation of the dynamics of the neurotic personality with its attendant emotional tensions and violence, verging at times on hysteria. Or one expects to find the elemental and the neurotic set in opposition — consider *A Streetcar Named Desire* and *Summer and Smoke* — thesis and antithesis in a bitter struggle that issues in the agony and sometimes fury of uncompromising antagonism. Behind this concern with the neurotic personality is no simple desire for novel dramatic effect; behind it is also the assumption that while the neurotic may be an exaggerated case, he is not a special one. His condition is the human condition, at least as understood by such writers as Williams, but it is the human condition aggravated, magnified, and rendered dramatic. Consequently, the neuroses from which many of Williams' characters suffer are rarely purely personal; they result from or at least reflect the state of the world in which the characters live. Their sickness implies the sickness of their society and of their culture.

*The Glass Menagerie* is, however, atypical, and atypical largely in tone, in its lack of the usual knot of violent exacerbated emotions. It is also unlike other Williams plays in its obvious insistence on the topical, but this difference is of less fundamental importance. If one were to judge by the liability of a play to suffer at the hands of inadequate actors, one might say that the weakness of most of Williams' plays lies in their liability to shrillness and hysteria and that the weakness of *The Glass Menagerie* lies in its liability to flatness and sentimentality. For dealing as it does with dream world within dream world and being, as Williams calls it, "a memory play," *The Glass Menagerie* is subdued and delicate in its characterization. The characters live in a twilight world and delicate — delicate in its theme, delicate in most of its portrayed emotions, between reality and fantasy, and the play itself is shaped within the memory of the narrator who has lived through and beyond the experience of the play.[1] Moreover, at the center of the play is Laura. She is withdrawn and almost

---

[1] Williams calls the narrator "an undisguised convention of the play," and one must recognize that ultimately the advantages of this convention are largely technical. In an early version, Williams wanted the audience to observe the entire action through a transparent curtain hanging from the proscenium arch. The story is not really the narrator's, it is Laura's, and as we are drawn further into the play, the sense of seeing the action at a second remove through memory is quickly dissipated. For example, as the first scene opens, we see Laura and Amanda going through the formalized gestures of eating "without utensils or food," but a few lines later Amanda comes to the table carrying an actual bowl of dessert. However, the convention allows for the expressionistic use of setting and for the free use of lighting and music as thematic and dramatic accents.

inarticulate in her shyness; yet, the climax of the play lies in the tearing away of the protective covering of her secret life, a consummation which is expressed in somewhat tenuous symbols rather than in dramatic action and which is, consequently, in danger of being lost in the anti-climax of the quarrel between Tom and his mother (scene VII).

Laura is a particularly difficult character for dramatic realization. She is essentially passive, driven and shaped inwardly by the circumstances of her life. She is the source of tension and friction between her brother and her mother, and she is the most deeply hurt by the resulting quarrels between them; yet, neither her own words nor her own gestures are adequate to express the felt life within her. Only in the glass menagerie, which is an ulterior image of herself, is she adequately expressed — fragile, odd yet somehow exquisite, and capable of a lucid inner glow that, as it turns out, is not lasting. Her painstaking care of the menagerie expresses her absorption in her own delicate life and her inward brooding upon the anachronistic memories of Jim O'Connor in which her love is hopelessly invested. So close is the identification between Laura and the glass menagerie that what happens to her is largely expressed through what happens to it.

Though she herself remains through most of the play undeveloping and passive, the psychological basis of Laura's character is gradually revealed. Morbidly sensitive about her own slightly crippled condition, she has recoiled from the implicit challenge of the never forgotten charm and popularity of her mother's girlhood. To avoid conflict and challenge has become instinct with her; even in the first scene her few lines interrupt the development precisely at those moments when even the slightest friction seems imminent. When a crisis becomes inevitable, she winds up the victrola and plays old phonograph records left behind by her father. This compulsive action is essentially an attempt to escape back into her childhood, and her childhood is, of course, that time when her apparent lack of interest in men and her lack of connection with practical society did not matter. Even her secretly cherished and hopeless infatuation for Jim O'Connor, a high school hero, is a form of evasion which allows her to live undisturbed in her dream world.

It is, however, only in the final scene that Laura actually assumes the center of the stage. Earlier she is present as the passive catalytic agent of the dramatic action which is realized in the conflict between Tom and Amanda and as a kind of living symbol of the isolation of the whole family.

Amanda, the mother, and Tom, the brother, who carry the burden of actual drama until the seventh scene, are also dwellers in fantasy worlds of their own. They share, however, an urge toward reality, and this renders them active characters. The conflict between them arises because the reality that each seeks, though equally fatuous, is conceived in different and irreconcilable terms.

As the first scene makes clear, Amanda is most vividly alive in the memories of her beau-beleaguered girlhood. Though she has lived for some time in the tenement section of St. Louis, she has retained the southern rhythm and accent of her speech intact, and she has retained, too, a girlish vivacity that in one of her age and circumstances amounts at times to silliness. The world of the Mississippi Delta and the Blue Mountain resorts, to which she repeatedly returns in memory, was a world in which people played at a fatuous gentility and a world in which charm and glamor ruled. Amanda has married charm — the ineluctably smiling but forever absent father — and has been betrayed by it. Yet, she has remained faithful to the very values that have betrayed her, and consequently, she has become in time and through necessity a dealer in shabby and threadbare glamor — *The Home-maker's Companion* which she sells and the rose-silk lamp shade and the vapid genteel chatter of the stereotype southern belle with which she seeks to enchant the only "gentleman" who ever actually calls.

But Amanda has learned, through the experience of her own life, that a world of dreams, however fine and genteel, cannot subsist unless it is rooted somehow in practical reality. Consequently, she is determined to effect some sort of substantial liaison between her daughter, Laura, and the outer world. When her half-hearted attempt to make Laura self-supporting proves a failure (scene II), Amanda is thrown back upon the only means she really believes in; there must be a gentleman, and there must be enough charm and prettiness to ensnare him into marriage. That the first effort was half-hearted is clear enough from the amount of self-conscious theatrics that goes into Amanda's show of disappointment. Nonetheless, given though she is to theatrics, Amanda does have what might be called a second voice, the voice of a desperate and disappointed mother. There is undoubtedly something ludicrous in Laura's comparison of Amanda's look of disappointment with the expression of the suffering Madonna, and there is no doubt a partially ironic intention in the use of the "Ave Maria" in the reconciliation scene between Tom and Amanda (scene IV). Yet, in this comparison there are serious, positive implications as well. Amanda's children are the children of an absent father who, as he beams gallantly throughout the play from a blown-up photograph, is himself little more than the spirit of romance, charm, and unreality, the presiding spirit of the entire household. His desertion has left Amanda stranded in the past, in the fantasy world of memory, and in her effort to realize at least a compromised version of that world for her daughter in the present, Amanda is forced to sacrifice her son.

The son, Tom, is the family's primary link with the workaday world of practical reality; he supports the family by working in a shoe warehouse, and he is, as Amanda knows, the only means by which a "gentleman" may ever be brought to call. Tom is rebelliously resentful of his role, resentful of having to sacrifice his own dreams of poetry and adventure, of having to pay in drudgery for his sister's and mother's isolation from reality. He believes that what he longs for is reality; though, in fact, his vision of reality is merely the adolescent vision of "real" experience, spawned by the romantically irresponsible example of the father, with whom he identifies himself more and more, and fed by the commercially tailored illusions of the movies in which

Hollywood characters are supposed to have all of the adventure for everybody in America, while everybody in America sits in a dark room and watches them have them! (scene VI)

No more realistic and not much less isolated than the rest of the family, Tom nonetheless feels that his personal salvation lies in a break with the family, a break which Amanda in her desperate need to use him must anticipate and oppose. "You've got to look out for your sister; bring home some nice boy for your sister to meet," she demands. And as his last gesture of responsibility toward the family, Tom produces the long awaited "gentleman caller."

Quite by chance Jim O'Connor, the "gentleman caller," is, it at first appears, ideally suited for his role as emissary from the world of practical reality to Laura's delicate fantasy world. For, though he does not suspect it, he has a simultaneous existence in both worlds — in the one, as the high school idol of Laura's secret dreams; in the other, as an order clerk in a shoe warehouse and as an ambitious young man studying public speaking and electro-dynamics. Moreover, though overlain with the crass clichés of popular psychology and with those of an easy faith in the glittering surface of American life with its naive cults of personality and progress, Jim O'Connor's basic nature is warm, sensitive and responsive. In him seems to be united past, present, and future, the breath of reality and the possibility of love.

Confronted by the challenge of Jim O'Connor's actual presence, Laura at first follows her usual pattern of compulsive retreat into the past and then into physical indisposition, but left alone with Jim in scene VII, the climactic scene both of the play and of Laura's life, she is gradually drawn out of her world of private illusions. She is drawn by Jim's warmth and gentleness which have been in turn called out by her delicateness and sensitivity. As they sit in the light of altar candles, Jim convinces Laura of his sympathetic feeling for her, and she puts into his hands that most prized animal in her glass collection.

LAURA: ... Oh, be careful — if you breathe, it breaks!
JIM: I'd better not take it. I'm pretty clumsy with things.
LAURA: Go on, I trust you with him!

That is, she entrusts to his care the fragile totem of her own spirit. Significantly, the glass creature is a unicorn, the freakish beast of medieval fable that could be ensnared only by the attraction of a virgin. As such it expresses Laura, who is completely virginal though, in her relation to Jim, not sterile. The unicorn is placed gently on a table, and a few moments later the couple rise to make a clumsy attempt at a waltz, in the course of which the table is bumped and the unicorn is broken, his horn shattered. Laura accepts the loss — "Maybe it's a blessing in disguise ... The horn was removed to make him feel less — freakish"; she accepts, that is, the violation of her virginal world of private illusions by the emissary from the world of other people's illusions.

The whole scene is, in fact, a disguised fantasy of courtship (the intimate conversation), marriage (the transfer from hand to hand of the unicorn in the light of the altar candles), and consummation (the dance and the breaking of the unicorn's horn). It is as if for the moment the world of things and actions had assumed the quality and shape of Laura's private world. At first the scene appears to foreshadow another more normal consummation, but it turns out to be the beginning and the end in itself. For Jim O'Connor, while he can temporarily bridge the gap between two worlds, is actually committed to the world in which personality and a knowledge of television add up to money and power. For dramatic purposes his practical commitment takes the form of his engagement to Betty, who, so far as the play is concerned, is merely a characterless, ordinary name. In coming to the Wingfield home, Jim has unwittingly stepped back into the past and picked up a strand of his life that he had not known existed, but he is unable and unwilling to follow the strand into the future. And Laura's secret dreams, which have glowed momentarily into a semblance of life, are blotted out. She gives Jim the mutilated unicorn—token both of her violated life and of her tentative approach to the world of normal human experience—and turns to the victrola, preparing to retreat once more into her childhood.

In his final speech as narrator, Tom Wingfield again reminds the audience that *The Glass Menagerie* is a memory play: "... Time is the longest distance between two places." He has traveled that distance, and he has returned, so to speak, to pronounce a final judgment of eternal darkness, oblivion, upon Laura and what she represents: "Blow out your candles, Laura—and so goodbye..." For in following in his father's footsteps, he has failed to find reality. "The cities swept about me like dead leaves, leaves that were brightly colored but torn away from the branches." He has continued to be haunted by Laura both as responsibility and as symbol, for his own flight has been merely an expression in his own peculiar form of that dedication to unreality and to romantic illusion which is characteristic of the whole family. That is, he has been more faithful than he intended, but now in a world of bombardments, of violent and elemental reality—"... nowadays the world is lit by lightning!"—he sees clearly the desperate and irrelevant fantasy that they had all lived.

This fantasy, however, is not an altogether eccentric and private phenomenon of the Wingfield family. Throughout *The Glass Menagerie,* both the convention of the retrospective narrator and the setting of the play itself serve to keep before us the fact that the Wingfields are perhaps more generally representative than they would appear to be. Their isolation may be more obvious and their delusions more colorful and even in some sense more ideal, but they occupy only one cell in the great hive of a tenement apartment, which like all such buildings, Williams tells us, is "always burning with the slow and implacable fires of human desperation." Moreover, Tom, as narrator, repeatedly reminds us that the larger reality from which the Wingfields in their various ways were isolated was itself buoyed up by another order of illusions and compensated by the commercially channeled escapism of the movies, of delicately sublimated stories in ladies magazines, and of "hot swing music and liquor, dance halls, bars and... sex that hung in the gloom like a chandelier and flooded the world with brief, deceptive rainbows." These "deceptive rainbows" are not necessary to a Jim O'Connor, with his dynamic though superficial assumptions; but in the perspective of history, which the narrator also provides, against the unperceived background of events leading toward the Second World War, these assumptions are seen to define a world that is merely more public and more dynamic, not less illusory than the world of the Wingfields.

1. *Why is so much emphasis given in scene I to Amanda's remembrance of the Sunday on which she entertained "seventeen gentlemen callers"?*

Amanda's long reminiscent speech introduces the theme of "the gentleman caller," a theme which increases steadily in importance throughout the play. It also provides a crucial insight into the nature of the Wingfield family's isolation from reality. It does so both by exposing Amanda's own temptation to live in the past or to shape the present in the image of the past and by giving us the first clue to the shy, introspective character of Laura. For, as soon becomes clear in the play, Laura's retreat from reality is to a considerable extent a retreat from the implicit challenge of her mother's girlhood popularity. Morbidly sensitive about her own slightly crippled condition, Laura feels hopelessly inadequate before such a challenge.

2. *What is the significance of the larger-than-life photograph of the father which is prominently displayed throughout the play?*

Tom, as narrator, refers to the father as "a fifth character in the play who doesn't appear." And as a matter of fact, though absent, the father is frequently referred to and, in a sense, even appealed to — by Amanda as the exemplar of charm and gallantry; by Tom as a precedent for the romantic irresponsibility that seems to offer him his only possible escape from the suffocating narrowness of his life. Moreover, the father's desertion has largely created the situation in the play; it has left Amanda stranded in the past with her memories, and it has imposed upon Tom a burden of responsibilities that he is unwilling to bear. But, beyond this, the father — gallantly smiling from his photograph — represents the presiding spirit of the entire family, the spirit of romantic illusion.

3. *What is the significance of the title,* The Glass Menagerie?

Laura Wingfield is the main character in the play; it is in her name, so to speak, that the action of the play is undertaken and it is the abortive climax of her secret life that provides the climax of the play. Being a peculiarly passive character whose secretive inner life finds almost no dramatic expression in the external world, Laura resists dramatic realization. The glass menagerie, however, serves to objectify the essence of Laura's character and situation; in what it is and in what happens to it is reflected what Laura is and what happens to her. Laura is as fragile and as utterly and helplessly exposed as the menagerie itself; in the hands of well-meaning but clumsy people, she is inevitably shattered. The title, then, by pointing to the thing in which Laura is most fully expressed, points to Laura and her situation as central to the play.

4. *What is the main source of the quarrels between Amanda and her son? Why does the first violent exchange between them come immediately after the scene in which Amanda discovers that Laura has not been attending business school?*

Tom resents having to sacrifice his own dreams of poetry and adventure in order to support the worlds of fantasy and shabby gentility inhabited by his mother and sister. He has grown restive under his responsibilities and is, in fact, moving toward rebellion. However, his impulse to rebel is checked by concern for his sister (see the conclusion of scene III), and in his frustration, he turns to the movies as a temporary escape. Amanda, for her part, fears Tom's restlessness, for she realizes that he is the family's only link with practical reality. Though the connection between this general relationship and the violent quarrel in scene III is not developed, it is clearly suggested. Having discovered the failure of her attempt to make Laura self-supporting and having, in consequence, been forced back upon the necessity of finding Laura a husband, Amanda must tighten her control upon her son; he is, after all, the only means by which a "gentleman caller" is ever likely to be brought to the Wingfield home. Naturally enough, the increased pressure aggravates the rebelliousness of Amanda's son, causing the tension between them to give way to open conflict.

5. *At the beginning of scene III and again at the end of scene IV, Amanda is seen and heard on the telephone selling subscriptions to The Home-maker's Companion. What is the purpose of the repetition of this brief scene within a scene?*

The two instances frame the scenes of the quarrel and reconciliation in terms of the deflection and then resumption of Amanda's plans. More than this, however, they suggest what it is that Tom at first attempts to reject but ultimately agrees to accept and to be a party to — that is, the fostering of a shabby, threadbare glamor in the name of helping his sister. For there is an appropriateness in Amanda's selling of this particular magazine; it is of a piece with the whole manner in which she goes about setting the trap for the "gentleman caller." Amanda holds to the qualities she believes in — gentility and charm — though they have betrayed her; she is, however, pathetic and a bit ridiculous in the unavoidable tawdriness of her means.

6. *At the beginning of the play, Tom Wingfield refers to Jim O'Connor as "an emissary from a world of reality." Why doesn't he say the world of reality?*

He doesn't say *the* world of reality because, as becomes clear in the perspective of history which the narrator provides, the world that Jim represents is merely more public and more dynamic, not less illusory than the world of the Wingfields. As his addiction to the clichés of the cults of personality and progress suggests, Jim O'Connor is in harmony with a particular social reality, the normal life of the community. But the society in question is sustained by its own order of illusions in which Jim has implicit faith.

7. *What is implied through the use of the altar candles and of the fragile glass unicorn in scene VII?*

See analysis.

8. *Considering the conclusion of the play, what is the force of Amanda's comment in scene VII, "Very considerate of them to let us get through dinner before they plunged us into everlasting darkness..."?*

The comment is an ironic foreshadowing of the spiritual darkness into which Laura is shortly to be cast and of the sentence of oblivion that Tom, as narrator, will pronounce at the end of the play. Through Tom's last speech, the audience is made aware that, in a sense, Tom has returned in memory to this world of his family with the half-reluctant purpose of exorcising it as irrelevant to the reality which he has finally come to know. There is no place for Laura in such a reality, and, because the play is shaped within his memory, Tom can now grant her the peace of oblivion.

9. *Would it be accurate to call Tom the realistic member of the Wingfield family?*

No, it would not be accurate if we are referring to Tom as the character who participates in the action of the play rather than as the narrator. Tom's vision of reality is simply an adolescent concept of "real" experience such as he finds unsatisfactorily reflected in the movies. In this connection, consider his discussion with Amanda in scene III and his discussion with Jim in scene VI. He is not dissatisfied with the falseness of the reflection provided by Hollywood but with the fact that it is merely a reflection, merely a vicarious form of desirable experience.

10. *What dramatic advantages are there in the use of the narrator in this play?*

It has both technical and thematical advantages. Technically, it allows for a freer, more expressionistic use of setting and staging; thematically, it allows the action of the play to be projected against a background of significant events which are not perceived by those involved in the action. The importance of this last point is elaborated in the analysis of the play.

A. R. W.

Dietrich, Margret, *Das Moderne Drama*, Stuttgart 1961, pp. 259-260 — Kesting, Marianne, *Das epische Theater*, Stuttgart 1959, pp. 117-119 — Luhr, Friedrich Wilhelm, *The Glass Menagerie*, in Hüllen-Rossi-Christopeit, *Zeitgenössische amerikanische Dichtung*, Frankfurt 1960, pp. 147—158 — Mennemeier, Franz Norbert, *Das moderne Drama des Auslandes*, Düsseldorf 1961, pp. 80—90 — Nyskiewicz, Heinz, Drama, Bild und Wort in Tennessee Williams *Glasmenagerie*, Die Pädagogische Provinz XVII, 1963, p. 308 ff. — Tischler, Nancy M. *Tennessee Williams*, New York 1961, pp. 91—116.

# BIOGRAPHY AND GENERAL CRITICISM

### ANDERSON
Anderson, David, *Sherwood Anderson*, New York 1962
Burbank, Rex, *Sherwood Anderson*, New York 1964
Howe, Irving, *Sherwood Anderson*, New York 1951

### BENÉT
Fenton, Charles, *Stephen Vincent Benét*, New Haven 1958
Stroud, Parry E., *Stephen Vincent Benét*, New York 1962

### BIERCE
Fatout, Paul, *Ambrose Bierce: The Devil's Lexicographer*, Norman, Oklahoma, 1951
Fatout, Paul, *Ambrose Bierce and the Black Hills*, Norman, Oklahoma, 1956
O'Connor, Richard, *Ambrose Bierce*, Boston 1967
Woodruff, Stuart C., *The Short Stories of Ambrose Bierce: A Study in Polarity*, Pittsburgh 1964

### CATHER
Bennett, Mildred, *The World of Willa Cather*, Lincoln, Nebraska, 1961
Bloom, Edward A. and Lillian D., *Willa Cather's Gift of Sympathy*, Carbondale 1962
Brown, Edward K., and Leon Edel, *Willa Cather: A Critical Biography*, N. Y. 1953
Daiches, David, *Willa Cather: A Critical Introduction*, Ithaca 1951

### CRANE
Berryman, John, *Stephen Crane*, New York 1950
Cady, Edwin, *Stephen Crane*, New York 1962
Gibson, Donald B., *The Fiction of Stephen Crane*, Carbondale 1968
Stallman, R. W., *Stephen Crane: A Biography*, New York 1968

### FAULKNER
Brooks, Cleanth, *William Faulkner; the Yoknapatawpha Country*, New Haven 1963
Hoffman, Frederick, *William Faulkner*, New York 1961
Hoffman, Frederick, and Olga Vickery, eds., *Three Decades of Faulkner Criticism*, New York 1962
Howe, Irving, *William Faulkner: A Critical Study* (rev. ed.), New York 1962
Longley, John R., *The Tragic Mask: A Study of Faulkner's Heroes*, Chapel Hill 1962
Millgate, Michael, *Faulkner*, London 1961
Nilon, Charles H., *Faulkner and the Negro*, Boulder, Colo., 1962
O'Connor, William van, *The Tangled Fire of William Faulkner*, Minneapolis 1954
Straumann, Heinrich, *Faulkner*, Frankfurt a. M. 1968
Swiggart, Peter, *The Art of Faulkner's Novels*, Austin, Tex., 1962
Thompson, Lawrance R., *William Faulkner: An Introduction and Interpretation*, New York 1963
Vickery, Olga W., *The Novels of William Faulkner: A Critical Interpretation*, Baton Rouge 1959
Waggoner, Hyatt H., *William Faulkner: From Jefferson to the World*, Louisville 1959

## Fitzgerald

Cowley, Malcolm, and Robert Cowley, *Fitzgerald and the Jazz Age*, New York 1966
Eble, Kenneth Eugene, *F. Scott Fitzgerald*, New York 1963
Goldhurst, William, *F. Scott Fitzgerald and His Contemporaries*, Cleveland 1963
Kazin, Alfred, ed., *F. Scott Fitzgerald: The Man and His Work*, Cleveland 1951
Miller, James E., Jr., *The Fictional Technique of Scott Fitzgerald*, den Haag 1957
Mizener, Arthur, *The Far Side of Paradise: A Biography of F. Scott Fitzgerald*, Boston 1951; New York (Vintage Books) 1959
Mizener, Arthur, ed., *F. Scott Fitzgerald: A Collection of Critical Essays*, Englewood Cliffs, N. J., 1963
Piper, Henry Dan, *F. Scott Fitzgerald: A Critical Biography*, New York 1965
Sklar, Robert, *F. Scott Fitzgerald: The Last Laocoon*, New York 1967
Turnbull, Andrew, *Scott Fitzgerald*, New York 1962

## Harte

Stewart, George, *Bret Harte: Argonaut and Exile*, Boston 1931

## Hawthorne

Arvin, Newton, *Hawthorne*, New York 1961
Crews, Frederick, *The Sins of the Fathers: Hawthorne's Psychological Themes*, New York 1966
Fogle, Richard H., *Hawthorne's Fiction: The Light and the Dark*, Norman, Oklahoma, 1952
Levin, Harry, *The Power of Blackness: Hawthorne, Poe, Melville*, New York 1958
Male, Roy R., *Hawthorne's Tragic Vision*, Austin, Texas, 1957
Stewart, Randall, *Nathaniel Hawthorne*, New Haven 1948 (paperb. ed. 1961)
Turner, Arlin, *Nathaniel Hawthorne*, New York 1961
Wagenknecht, Edward, *Hawthorne: Man and Writer*, Oxford 1961
Waggoner, Hyatt H., *Hawthorne: A Critical Study*, Cambridge, Mass., 1955

## Hemingway

Baker, Carlos, *Hemingway: The Writer as Artist*, Princeton 1952; 3rd edition 1963
Baker, Carlos (ed.), *Hemingway and his Critics*, New York 1961
Killinger, John, *Hemingway and the Dead Gods: A Study in Existentialism*, University of Kentucky 1960
Young, Philip, *Ernest Hemingway*, New York and London 1952; Düsseldorf 1954
Young, Philip, *Ernest Hemingway: A Reconsideration*, London 1966

## Irving

Brooks, Van Wyck, *The World of Washington Irving*, Philadelphia 1944
Wagenknecht, Edward, *Washington Irving: Moderation Displayed*, New York 1962

## James

Beach, Joseph W., *The Method of Henry James* (revised ed.), Philadelphia 1954
Cargill, Oscar, *The Novels of Henry James*, New York 1961
Edel, Leon, *Henry James*, 3 vols., London 1953, 1962, 1963
Jefferson, D. W., *Henry James and the Modern Reader*, London 1964
Matthiessen, F. C., *Henry James: The Major Phase*, London and New York 1944
McElderry, Bruce R., *Henry James*, New York 1965
Putt, S. Gorley, *Henry James: A Reader's Guide*, Ithaca 1966

## LARDNER

Elder, Donald, *Ring Lardner*, New York 1954
Patrick, Walton R., *Ring Lardner*, New York 1963

## MELVILLE

Arvin, Newton, *Herman Melville*, New York 1950
Berthoff, Warner, *The Example of Melville*, Princeton 1962
Chase, Richard, *Herman Melville: A Critical Study*, New York 1949
Chase, Richard, ed., *Melville: A Collection of Critical Essays*, Englewood, N. J. 1962
Franklin, H. Bruce, *The Wake of the Gods: Melville's Mythology*, Stanford 1963
Hillway, Tyrus, *Herman Melville*, New York 1963
Miller, James E., *A Reader's Guide to Herman Melville*, New York 1962
Thompson, Lawrance, *Melville's Quarrel with God*, Princeton 1952
Widmer, Kingsley, *The Ways of Nihilism: A Study of Herman Melville's Short Novels*, California State Colleges 1970

## MILLER

Hogan, Robert, *Arthur Miller*, Minneapolis 1964
Nelson, Benjamin, *Arthur Miller: Portrait of a Playwright*, New York 1970
Welland, D., *Arthur Miller*, New York and London 1961

## O'NEILL

Engel, Edwin A., *The Haunted Heroes of Eugene O'Neill*, Cambridge, Mass., 1953
Falk, Doris V., *Eugene O'Neill and the Tragic Tension*, New Brunswick, N. J., 1958
Gelb, Arthur and Barbara, *O'Neill*, New York 1962
Leech, Clifford, *Eugene O'Neill*, New York 1963
Raleigh, John Henry, *The Plays of Eugene O'Neill*, Carbondale 1965

## POE

Bonaparte, Marie, *The Life and Works of Edgar Allan Poe: A Psycho-Analytic Interpretation*, London 1949
Buranelli, Vincent, *Edgar Allan Poe*, New York 1961
Davidson, Edward, *Poe: A Critical Study*, Cambridge, Mass., 1957
Levine, Stuart, *Edgar Poe: Seer and Craftsman*, Deland 1972
Link, Franz H., *Edgar Allan Poe*, Frankfurt-Bonn 1968
Schuhmann, Kuno, *Die erzählende Prosa Edgar Allan Poes*, Heidelberg 1958
Staats, Armin, *Edgar Allan Poes symbolistische Erzählkunst*, Heidelberg 1967
Whitman, Sarah Helen, *Edgar Poe and his Critics*, New Brunswick 1949

## PORTER

Hartley, Lodwick, and G. Core, *Katherine Anne Porter: A Symposium*, Atlanta 1969
Hendrick, George, *Katherine Anne Porter*, New York 1965
Warren, Robert Penn, Irony with a Center: Katherine Anne Porter; in: Warren, *Selected Essays*, New York 1958
West, Ray B., *Katherine Anne Porter*, Minneapolis 1963

## POWERS

Hagopian, John V., *J. F. Powers*, New York 1968

## SALINGER

Belcher, William F., and James Lee, *J. D. Salinger and the Critics*, New York 1962
French, Warren, *J. D. Salinger*, New York 1963
Grunwald, Henry A., *Salinger: A Critical and Personal Portrait*, New York 1962
Gwynn and Blotner, *The Fiction of J. D. Salinger*, Pittsburgh 1958
Laser, Marvin, and Norman Fruman, eds., *Studies in J. D. Salinger*, New York 1963

## STEINBECK

Fontenrose, Joseph, *John Steinbeck*, New York 1962
French, Warren, *John Steinbeck*, New York 1961
Lisca, Peter, *The Wide World of John Steinbeck*, New Brunswick, N. J., 1958
Tedlock, E. W., Jr., and Wicker, ed., *Steinbeck and His Critics: A Record of Twenty-Five Years*, Albuquerque, New Mexico 1957
Watt, Frank W., *John Steinbeck*, New York 1962

## TWAIN

Bellamy, Gladys, *Mark Twain as a Literary Artist*, Norman, Oklahoma, 1950
Budd, Louis J., *Mark Twain, Social Philosopher*, Bloomington, Ind., 1962
Covici, Pascal, *Mark Twain's Humor: The Image of a World*, Dallas 1962
Smith, Henry N., *Mark Twain: The Development of a Writer*, Cambridge, Mass., 1962
Wagenknecht, Edward, *Mark Twain: The Man and His Work*, Norman, Oklahoma, 1967 (3rd ed.)

## WARREN

Bohner, Charles H., *Robert Penn Warren*, New York 1964
Casper, L., *Robert Penn Warren: The Dark and Bloody Ground*, Seattle 1960
Hardy, John E., *Robert Penn Warren*, New York 1962
Poenicke, Klaus, *Robert Penn Warren: Kunstwerk und kritische Theorie*, Heidelberg 1959

## WHARTON

Howe, Irving, ed., *Edith Wharton*, Englewood Cliffs, N. J., 1962
Lubbock, Percy, *Portrait of Edith Wharton*, New York 1947
Lyde, Marilyn J., *Edith Wharton: Convention and Morality in the Work of A Novelist*, Norman, Oklahoma, 1959
Nevins, Blake, *Edith Wharton: A Study of Her Fiction*, Berkeley 1961

## WILDER

Burbank, Rex, *Thornton Wilder*, New York 1961
Häberle, Erwin, *Das szenische Werk Thornton Wilders*, Heidelberg 1967
Papajewski, Helmut, *Thornton Wilder*, Frankfurt/Bonn 1961

## WILLIAMS

Falk, Signi Lenea, *Tennessee Williams*, New York 1961
Nelson, Benjamin, *Tennessee Williams: The Man and His Work*, New York 1961
Tischler, Nancy M., *Tennessee Williams: Rebellious Puritan*, New York 1961